Will Work for Food

The publisher and the University of California Press Foundation gratefully acknowledge the generous support of the Anne G. Lipow Endowment Fund in Social Justice and Human Rights.

Will Work for Food

LABOR ACROSS THE FOOD CHAIN

Laura-Anne Minkoff-Zern
and Teresa M. Mares

UNIVERSITY OF CALIFORNIA PRESS

University of California Press
Oakland, California

Library of Congress Cataloging-in-Publication Data

Names: Minkoff-Zern, Laura-Anne author | Mares, Teresa M., 1978–
    author
Title: Will work for food : labor across the food chain / Laura-Anne
    Minkoff-Zern and Teresa M. Mares.
Description: Oakland, California : University of California Press,
    [2025] | Includes bibliographical references and index.
Identifiers: LCCN 2025013915 (print) | LCCN 2025013916 (ebook) |
    ISBN 9780520391604 cloth | ISBN 9780520391611 paperback |
    ISBN 9780520391628 ebook
Subjects: LCSH: Food industry and trade—United States—Employees
Classification: LCC HD8039.F72 U66 2025 (print) | LCC HD8039.
    F72 (ebook) | DDC 338.4/733819—dc23/eng/20250606
LC record available at https://lccn.loc.gov/2025013915
LC ebook record available at https://lccn.loc.gov/2025013916

GPSR Authorized Representative: Easy Access System Europe, Mustamäe tee
50, 10621 Tallinn, Estonia, gpsr.requests@easproject.com

34   33   32   31   30   29   28   27   26   25
10   9   8   7   6   5   4   3   2   1

This book is dedicated to all the workers across the food chain.

CONTENTS

List of Illustrations ix

List of Abbreviations xi

Introduction: A New Opening for Worker Justice in
the Food System 1

1 · Industrialization and Racialized Dispossession on the Farm 20

2 · Deskilling in the Assembly Line and on the Factory Floor 48

3 · Precarity and Deregulation in the Warehouse and on the Road 69

4 · Consolidation and Vulnerability from the Corner Store
to the Superstore 97

5 · Intersectionality and the Fight for a Fair Wage in Food Service 127

6 · Reproductive Labor, Gender, and Food Work in the Home 153

7 · Value, Work, and Food Waste at the End of the Line 173

Conclusion: Working toward a Just Food Future 199

Acknowledgments 209

Appendix 213

Glossary of Terms 227

Notes 231

Bibliography 253

Index 293

ILLUSTRATIONS

FIGURES

1. Percentage of frontline food workers employed by sector of the food chain, 2023 *13*

2. Number of frontline food workers employed in the food chain, 2023 *14*

3. Cotton sharecroppers, Greene County, Georgia, 1937 *26*

4. Mexican girl, carrot worker, Edinberg, Texas, 1939 *31*

5. Tomato pickers and allies of the Coalition of Immokalee Workers urge Wendy's to join their award-winning farmworker-led human rights initiative, the Fair Food Program, Sarasota, Florida, 2018 *44*

6. Female workers prepare Brite stackers shrink wrapping cans for shipping at NEFCO-Fidalgo packing plants in Ketchikan, Alaska, 1975 *54*

7. Migrant workers process green peppers on Uesugi Farms, Gilroy, California, 2013 *57*

8. Pork processing worker at Triumph Foods, St. Joseph, Missouri, 2017 *62*

9. Packard trucks transporting California Sunkist oranges and lemons from Los Angeles to London *73*

10. Warehouse Workers United protest, Mira Loma, California, 2012 *91*

11. Deliveristas protest, New York, New York, 2021 *94*

12. Vazquez grocery store, Bronx, New York, 1977–78 *105*

13. Walmart protest, Washington, DC, 2014 *111*

14. Supermarket meat department employee wearing a mandatory mask *113*

15. Striking workers at Stouffer's Restaurant, Detroit, Michigan, 1937 *133*

16. Fast-food workers on strike, St. Paul, Minnesota, 2016 *145*

17. Starbucks employees react to union election, Buffalo, New York, 2021 *149*

18. Woman prepares food in a kitchen, 1910–30 *157*

19. Domestic servant, Atlanta, Georgia, 1939 *163*

20. Heather Hernandez cares for children during the COVID-19 pandemic, Denver, Colorado, 2021 *169*

21. US Environmental Protection Agency Wasted Food Scale, 2023 *180*

22. Huerta del Valle employee Nicolas Reza picks up organic waste for composting, Ontario, California, 2018 *182*

23. Rose Thackeray rescues food from supermarket compost bins, Burlington, Vermont, 2017 *196*

TABLES

1.   Employment Numbers and Wages across Food Systems Sectors, 2023 *15*

A.1. Industries and Sectors Included in Employment Data *214*

A.2. Frontline Workers in Production *215*

A.3. Frontline Workers in Processing *217*

A.4. Frontline Workers in Distribution *219*

A.5. Frontline Workers in Retail *220*

A.6. Frontline Workers in Service *221*

A.7. Frontline Workers in Waste *222*

A.8. Industries and Sectors Analyzed for Unionization Data *223*

A.9. Percentage of Total Employment in Food Chain Sectors, BIPOC Workers and Female Workers, 2022 *225*

ABBREVIATIONS

ACS	American Community Survey
AFL-CIO	American Federation of Labor and Congress of Industrial Organizations
AI	artificial intelligence
BLS	US Bureau of Labor Statistics
CALRA	California Agricultural Labor Relations Act of 1975
CATA	El Comité de Apoyo a los Trabajadores Agrícolas / Farm Workers Support Committee
CIW	Coalition of Immokalee Workers
EPA	Environmental Protection Agency
FCWA	Food Chain Workers Alliance
FLP	Farm Labor Program, Puerto Rico
FLSA	Fair Labor Standards Act
FLOC	Farm Labor Organizing Committee
FNB	Food Not Bombs
FNS	Food and Nutrition Service
FRESH	Food Retail Expansion to Support Health
FRN	Food Recovery Network
FWMA	Farm Workforce Modernization Act
ICE	Immigration and Customs Enforcement
IRCA	Immigration Reform and Control Act of 1986
MD	Milk with Dignity
MSPA	Migrant and Seasonal Agricultural Workers Protection Act
NAWS	National Agricultural Workers Survey
NLRA	National Labor Relations Act

NLRB	National Labor Relations Board
NSLP	National School Lunch Program
OEWS	Occupational Employment and Wage Survey
OSHA	Occupational Safety and Health Administration
PCUN	Pineros y Campesinos Unidos del Noroeste
PPE	personal protective equipment
QCEW	Quarterly Census of Employment and Wages, US Department of Labor
RCIA	Retail Clerks International Association
RCRA	Resource Conservation and Recovery Act
ROC-United	Restaurant Opportunities Center United
RWDSU	Retail, Wholesale and Department Store Union
SNAP	Supplemental Nutrition Assistance Program
SPLC	Southern Poverty Law Center
UFCW	United Food and Commercial Workers
UFW	United Farm Workers
USDA	US Department of Agriculture
WSR	Worker-Driven Social Responsibility
WWJ	Warehouse Workers for Justice
WWRC	Warehouse Workers Resource Center
WWU	Warehouse Workers United

Introduction

The food industry is one of the most underpaid jobs in the country, and it's also the most undervalued. I know that with the pandemic the narrative has sort of changed but it didn't translate materially into much. What would make these jobs better? Dignified workplaces, dignified wages, safe working conditions, safe and dignified living conditions for those working in agriculture (because the housing is combined with the work), protections, not just from abuses from the employers, but also protections from things like pandemics or extreme temperatures. Like the heat, the cold, the quality of air from the forest fires. And I think that at the core of all of that is the right to organize, for everybody to have protections . . . for all food workers. And that way, folks can fight for better wages, better housing, safe working conditions, job security.

When you see folks across the food chain coming together, that's so powerful, that's so powerful, right?! Because you hear folks working in their restaurants, in New York City, and in Oregon, and in Massachusetts, and they all are sharing the same problems. And that's very powerful in itself. Farm workers across the country are also dealing with stolen wages, and everybody is sharing their problems, and they're very similar in some ways with the other industries. And then you see the possibilities of what folks can achieve by coming together, not just by sector, but across industries. How powerful to hear these folks in this restaurant, their tips are being stolen, they're serving up produce that is also handled in these particular warehouses, and that is produced on these particular farms and everybody's here, right? So the possibilities for solidarity that creates, it's very powerful.

FABIOLA, *Director of Organizing, Food Chain
Workers Alliance*

LAUNCHED IN 2009, the Food Chain Workers Alliance (FCWA) is a coalition of thirty-three member organizations across the United States and Canada that represents more than 375,000 frontline food workers. As Fabiola emphasizes, the power of the FCWA approach is the solidarity that the organization builds across food sectors that have been divided historically. Frontline food work, meaning the labor directly involved in growing, processing, packaging, shipping, preparing, and serving food and in food waste, is often underpaid, undervalued, and unsafe. Because of this, organizing across food sectors is necessary for realizing a food system that is sustainable, just, and fair. In an age of increasing worker precarity amid rapid gains in corporate profits, it is crucial to understand the conditions under which some of the most vulnerable workers labor.

This book is an inquiry into the conditions and organizing strategies of frontline workers in the food system, workers who provide the sustenance on which all our lives depend. *Food systems* are the complex web of institutions, resources, and processes that bring food from the farm to the table and into the waste stream. A food systems approach provides an important bridge across academic discourses and research, social movements and activism, policy making, and civil society. Concerted attention to the work of maintaining the food system is more necessary now than ever before, given the interconnected crises of worker exploitation, climate change, criminalized migration, and racial inequities confronting us. With the surge of worker organizing in response to declining wages and deteriorating protections, it is time for the food movement to address labor head-on and for the labor movement to take the food system seriously.

Over the past few decades, there have been strategic consumer-based advocacy efforts and legislative initiatives to reform—and transform—the food system. Today broadly defined "good food" movements focus largely on environmental and health-related goals, such as supporting farmers' markets, increasing fruits and vegetables in school lunches, and expanding access to organic products. Yet scholars and activists have long argued that good food movements prioritize ecological sustainability over social and economic sustainability and justice.[1] Food justice activists and scholars criticize mainstream good food movements for being predominantly white and elitist and reflecting the biases that come with racial, social, and economic privilege.[2] Further, they tend to exclude labor justice from their projects, as labor activism can be seen as too controversial or as secondary to ecological goals.[3]

This book is a call to scholars, educators, consumers, and food and labor advocates to engage a food systems approach in addressing labor injustice and move beyond focusing on food sectors in isolation. We argue that improving labor standards and creating opportunities for solidarity among frontline workers across sectors is necessary for building a more just food system. Workers active in food-based labor coalitions like the FCWA have built linkages and strength in numbers, making successful demands of the most powerful actors in the corporate food chain, from business owners to legislators. The *food chain* comprises the sequential steps through which food is produced, processed, transported, sold, served, consumed, and put to waste or recycled. Labor organizers who connect across these steps can build solidarity between supporters, political actors, and consumers and workers who currently do not see themselves as part of the same struggle. We draw on workers' stories, government statistics, and social and economic histories to allow readers to imagine a food movement that prioritizes justice for those who work across food sectors. By addressing the question of labor head-on, food systems activists and scholars are in a better position to challenge the social ills and injustices that our food system has wrought in terms of income disparities, racial discrimination, gendered inequalities and violence, and ecological destruction.

In the following chapters, we aim to temper realism with optimism, spilling as much ink to celebrate labor achievements as we devote to unpacking the structural inequalities and historical processes of violence that engender exploitation. We are fully aware that this is a difficult balance to strike, and we do not want to give the illusion that change will come quickly or easily. It is very different work to unionize farmworkers than it is to organize those engaging in unpaid reproductive labor, and justice for meatpackers requires a distinct set of policy reforms from those needed for restaurant workers. It is also true that there has been uneven progress for labor activists and advocates across the different sectors of the food system, with some sectors benefiting from activism and broader policy reforms more than others. There is no one-size-fits-all solution. However, we are firm in our belief that sustained, effective change will only be possible through an approach that acknowledges that mobilizations, strategies, and policies must be attuned to the workers themselves and their visions of what just food looks like.

The energy that has been built by good food movements using a food systems lens has motivated people to fight for a more accessible and ecologically sustainable food system. We contend that this momentum has the potential to be leveraged by labor activists and advocates more broadly. Over the past few decades, there has been a transformation in worker identity at the grassroots level and related social movement organizing after a period of stagnant unionization and antiunion legislation nationwide. Much of this labor organizing success has been in the food system, from the growth of unions at Amazon (transportation and distribution) to Trader Joe's (retail) to Starbucks (service). A *union* is a group of workers formed to make decisions and protect their rights and interests in the workplace and is a common model of worker organizing. Other worker collectives and movements such as Restaurant Opportunities Center United (ROC-United), the Coalition of Immokalee Workers (CIW), and the Fight for $15 have built innovative strategies outside of the union model.

While there are many professions that keep the food system running (including those in the management and research fields), this book focuses on frontline and *essential workers* who do the direct labor to keep us all fed. These workers, whose jobs are necessarily in person and crucial to the functioning of businesses and services, were brought to the forefront of our collective envisioning of the food system during the COVID-19 pandemic. They are field workers and meat processors, warehouse packers and long-haul truckers, bakers and grocery store cashiers, dishwashers and fine dining servers, and homemakers and food waste workers. We examine the historical, legal, social, and political contexts that make labor conditions so precarious for food workers, as well as the social struggles led by food system workers.

Many jobs in the food system have been devalued, gendered, and racialized over time, as workplaces have become increasingly occupied by economically vulnerable and marginalized people.[4] For example, according to our analysis of the 2022 American Community Survey Data, BIPOC workers make up 44% of essential workers in the food and agricultural sectors, despite comprising only 38% of the US population. It is important to note that these numbers do not account for undocumented workers or gig workers. Further, a study from 2020 shows that these racial dynamics intersect with class signifiers, as 86% of frontline food and agricultural workers do not have a college degree.[5] Taking these multiple forms of social difference into account, we engage an intersectional analysis to interrogate the ways that systemic racism, classism, and sexism are inextricable from labor in the food system.[6]

Scholars in many disciplines have been at the forefront of drawing attention to labor inequality and labor-related social movements within the food system.[7] However, much of this research examines specific food sectors in isolation. For example, research that looks specifically at farm labor does not typically connect apple pickers to people bagging apples in the grocery store or trash collectors hauling away apple cores. Our goal in this book is to bring different sectors together, and this includes paid work outside the home and unpaid work inside the home. This broadens our collective understanding of what labor in the food system entails, building on decades of feminist scholarship that highlights the unequal burden that women shoulder in feeding their families.[8] This labor, like that of paid food service workers in restaurants and schools, is essential to feeding dependent children, the elderly, and others who are unable or unwilling to feed themselves. Despite the gains that women have made in the wage labor economy, they still perform the majority of food-related reproductive labor in the home. *Reproductive labor* is work performed for the reproduction of society and is usually done in the private space of the home, while *productive labor* is thought of as work that contributes to the capitalist or exchange-driven economy occurring largely in the public sphere. The absence of domestic labor from food systems analyses, in which food labor is largely studied as distinct from productive and reproductive labor, means that researchers have missed the opportunity to draw important connections in support of social change across the food system.

Moreover, we engage key concepts from the field of political economy and critical analyses of racial capitalism to explore the complexity of labor across seven sectors of the food system: farming, processing, transportation and distribution, retail, service, home, and waste. *Political economy* is an interdisciplinary academic field that incorporates a critical and comprehensive analysis of economic systems and their relationship to society, including the influence of political and social institutions, morality, and ideology.[9] As scholars have demonstrated, the histories and contemporary realities of the food chain provide fertile ground for a better understanding of capitalism, which is indispensable for analyzing our food system.[10] Moving the critiques of political economy beyond those focused primarily on class relations, *racial capitalism*, as defined by the Black studies scholar and political scientist Cedric Robinson, argues that capitalist processes are historically rooted in the extraction of wealth and labor from racialized populations.[11] Although we primarily ground our examples and conceptual framework in the US political economic context, we underscore the ways that the US food system is inextricable from migration patterns and labor policies that span the globe.

We hope this analysis provides a deeper knowledge of food labor and a fuller understanding of how this labor shapes and is shaped by a capitalist system.

WHAT'S WRONG WITH THE FOOD SYSTEM?

Through the supposed miracle of the global industrial food system, tomatoes picked by undocumented farmworkers can be transported by precariously employed logistics workers, sliced by underpaid kitchen staff, rung up by food insecure superstore cashiers, and fed to children by uncompensated domestic caregivers. Our food system is embedded in complex transnational commodity chains that depend on the exploitation of human labor to provide cheap food to global consumers on demand.

Exploitative food chains are maintained by international, national, and state-level policies that enable corporate control of our food. Since the end of the 1970s, our food system has been shaped by the twin pressures of globalization and neoliberalism. *Globalization* is the increasing interdependence of global political economies and cultures resulting from the expansion of trade, technology, and transnational investment. *Neoliberalism* refers to a philosophy that promotes economic integration and deregulation of business.[12] In this context, agriculture and food companies have consolidated both vertically and horizontally, creating the mega food companies we all know today. From production (Bayer and Purdue) to consumption (Kroger and McDonald's), there have been intensifying efforts by multinational corporations to keep wages low and workers in deskilled and replaceable positions. The vast majority of money in the food system goes to large-scale agricultural input companies, food processors, and grocery retailers, all of which have profited from deregulation and the stagnation of wages and unionization.

Corporate consolidation and the weakening of labor regulations have increased inequality between average workers and the highest earners in the United States. Moreover, this gaping disparity between corporate profits and worker livelihoods exists at both national and international scales. While the inequalities between the shareholders of multinational food corporations and vulnerable global consumers have been thoroughly studied and globally protested, what is often missed by activists and scholars alike is the fact that food workers are also food consumers. This complicates matters as underpaid workers are stuck in a cycle of relying on inexpensive food, which is made cheap partly by their own exploitation. Following social movement organizers, we believe in the radical notion that rather than claim food must remain cheap because people cannot afford to pay more, we must demand that workers be paid living wages so they can afford food produced under humane conditions.[13]

Food system reformers often focus on greening or localizing food, but exploitative working conditions are not merely a question of scale or size. Labor exploitation can be found on small-scale organic farms, at high-end restaurants, or in well-intentioned household labor arrangements. Alternative and localized food systems are certainly not free from abusive working conditions and in some cases foster insidious forms of paternalism and exploitation.[14] However, small-scale farms, neighborhood bakeries, and family-run restaurants are all struggling to stay afloat against increasingly global competition. Labor-centric arguments to raise wages and improve working conditions can come at a significant cost for small-scale businesses, many of which are central to regional approaches to creating an ecologically diverse and sustainable food system.

It might seem that calls for workers' rights will necessarily mean further consolidation of the food industry, toward more megafarms and fast-food chains, which can absorb higher input costs that smaller-scale businesses cannot. Strengthening labor regulations and standards along with a focused effort to break up agrifood monopolies must be a necessary goal for all advocates for a just and sustainable food system. In the short term, we acknowledge that worker-centric policies cannot be a uniform or singular solution and that some smaller-scale businesses will need more time and flexibility to make up for the cost of increasing workers' wages and standardizing positions as they adjust to higher labor standards. We understand these solutions are ambitious and reflect the complexity of the food system itself. However, as scholars and advocates, we cannot ignore these issues. As long as people are suffering to get food to our plates, we need to center food workers in any vision for a just food system.

FROM *THE JUNGLE* TO THE FRONTLINE WORKER

There is a long history of workers across the food and agriculture sectors being denied basic safety protections and rights while simultaneously being exposed to intersectional violence, hazardous conditions, abysmal pay, and few opportunities for advancement. The immediate concerns of low pay are often more visible than the long-term impacts of not having adequate benefits, the gradual wear on the body, and the inability to save for retirement or emergencies. At periodic moments in this history, the plight of food system workers has garnered national attention, at times galvanizing improvements in legal and political protections and at other times shifting consumer knowledge and purchasing behaviors. Prompted by these worker struggles, both popular media and applied research have drawn attention to the working conditions and the contributions of food workers.

The publication of *The Jungle* by Upton Sinclair stands out as a key moment in highlighting workers' struggles and the unsafe working conditions that persist in the US food system. Based on his undercover journalistic research, Sinclair explored the harsh labor environments immigrant workers faced in meatpacking plants in the Midwest. First published in 1905 as a serial in the socialist newspaper *Appeal to Reason*, *The Jungle* was intended to rally public support for workers who labored in terrible conditions. And yet it was more successful at generating public disgust because of its graphic descriptions of filthy processing plants. Readers were more outraged by the conditions of the facilities where their food was produced than the human costs of terrible working conditions. Public outrage brought about reforms, including the Federal Meat Inspection Act of 1906, which was intended to improve sanitation for public health and had little to do with working conditions. Sinclair famously lamented, "I aimed at the public's heart and by accident I hit it in the stomach."[15]

More than half a century later, Edward R. Murrow provided an up-close look at the lives of migrant workers in *Harvest of Shame*, a documentary broadcast on CBS on the Friday after Thanksgiving in 1960. Viewers recoiled in horror at the stark black-and-white footage of impoverished Black and white farmworkers living in rat-infested quarters. One farmer brutally observed, "We used to own our slaves, now we just rent them." While the impacts of *Harvest of Shame* are profound and brought broad public attention to the daily struggles of farmworkers, this piece of investigative journalism prompted attempts by members of Congress and the farm lobby to discredit Murrow. Despite this, many believe the film paved the way for a new wave of farmworker organizing and successful movements like the Delano Grape Strike Boycotts, led by Larry Itliong and other Filipino members of the Agricultural Workers Organizing Committee. Gaining the support of Cesar Chavez, Dolores Huerta, and Latinx workers in the National Farmworkers Association, the grape boycott would go on to become one of the most visible manifestations of worker organizing in the food system. Importantly, this campaign underscored the links between consumption and production and the potential of mass consumer action to create change.

In 2020, the COVID-19 pandemic introduced a new term to our shared lexicon: *essential worker*. Today more than 20% of essential workers—nearly 11.4 million people in the United States—labor in the food system, and this work is marked by deep inequities linked to race, class, gender, and citizenship status.[16] It goes without saying that frontline workers in the food system were essential long before the onset of the pandemic. For these workers, even a global pandemic did not translate into a day off but instead exposed them to more danger and discomfort. Across the food system, workers covered by unions fared significantly better during the worst times of the pandemic, with workers having more access to paid sick days and processes for demanding better personal protective equipment (PPE) and safer work conditions.[17]

Meanwhile, domestic food labor—the unpaid work of the food system—increased, leading to the exhaustion of parents and other caregivers. The pandemic laid bare that essential workers are indispensable to our collective well-being, even though they are very rarely recognized or compensated fairly for putting their bodies and lives on the line. The pandemic also drew attention to what some have called a labor shortage, but those critical of capitalist labor exploitation would argue it is really a wage shortage. Despite the ways that the COVID-19 pandemic brought greater attention to the contributions of essential and frontline food workers, as we discuss throughout this book, this attention did not result in enduring improvements in their daily lives or a more just food system.

These historical moments have captured popular attention in meaningful but often fleeting ways. Applied researchers have engaged in diverse research strategies to support sustained and profound social change on the ground. As two social scientists who have studied both the good food movement and labor in the food system, we are inspired by the activists and organizers who have shaped our collective understanding of the challenges faced by food workers and their role in our economy. Advocacy organizations and coalitions such as the FCWA and the Applied Research Center (now Race Forward) are leaders in applied research, publishing policy reports and recorded narratives of food workers' experiences. The Food Policy Network, housed at Johns Hopkins University Center for a Livable Future, has collected case studies of Food Policy Councils across the United States, looking at how these regional grassroots organizations have supported food chain workers through campaigns, working groups, resolutions, and procurement policies.[18] These organizations have used surveys, interviews, and case studies to collect data and have shared those data in accessible reports for the purpose of creating solidarity among food chain workers.[19] We see tremendous value in this kind of action research and use their reports and policy papers in our teaching and research—and in this book.

THE LABOR BEHIND THIS BOOK

Our academic careers in research and teaching have been rooted in and influenced by our time as workers in the food system. This includes our years working in farming, retail, and service, as well as our experiences as mothers and caregivers—from part-time jobs as teenagers to our present-day roles as scholar-activists and university professors. For Laura-Anne, who grew up in the suburbs of Washington, DC, a lifelong interest in preserving environmental resources guided her first to study sustainable agriculture as a college student and then to an internship in organic farming. It was in California that she started working on a fruit and vegetable farm alongside dozens of immigrant farmworkers from Mexico, whose deep agricultural skills and knowledge made a lasting impression that guides her research to the present day. For Teresa, who grew up in Colorado where her parents owned a franchised ice cream store, food service was the first entry point into paid employment and remained central to her income for nearly two decades. She followed this path through various stints in fast-food restaurants and high-end catering and as a barista during graduate school in Seattle. Through our lived experience, we gained an early and genuine appreciation of those who keep food on our tables.

Inspired by our scholarly interests, political commitments, and firsthand participation in food systems labor, we started making connections between food sectors and the people who do the work to link the points of production to those of consumption. In that journey, we both paid close attention to activists and organizers like those at the FCWA, who were taking a food systems perspective to addressing food labor inequality and harnessing consumer and political interest in sustainable and good food movements. Together, we share a commitment to learning from social movements and bringing them into the classroom through the materials we teach our students.

In addition, this book is influenced by our own research focus on farm laborers in the present. As scholars studying farmworkers' structural and racialized working conditions, as well as their organizing strategies, we have spent hours walking through fields, traveling to worksites, and sitting at workers' kitchen tables in deep conversation. We have spoken with farmworkers about their daily lives, access to resources, and efforts to create new spaces for opportunity and advancement. Our overlapping interests and research on farmworker livelihoods and foodways brought us into discussion with others in the food system, from processing workers who pack produce boxes to service workers who clear tables and clean dishes. To better understand the conditions and forms of resilience we saw in farmworkers, we started looking across the food chain to all workers who were organizing for fair wages and benefits in the workplace and improved lives overall.

Our analysis of food chain labor is also influenced by conversations with our students and the ways they introduce us to new perspectives and critiques. In the courses we teach, we commonly see students approach the food system as concerned environmentalists, aspiring foodie tastemakers, conscious nutrition and health consumers, and budding anticorporate activists. Their self-identified roles as critical actors in the food system are rooted in an attention to environmental and human health but rarely labor injustice. Other professors of food, environmental, and community studies courses have struggled with this as well and have documented and analyzed such limitations through the lens of the neoliberal politics of choice.[20]

However, many of our students have worked as food laborers, as servers and bussers, food delivery drivers, and summer farmhands. While working with food is a common experience, few see themselves as food workers and even fewer understand the connection between their labor and that of other workers in the food system. While students from more working-class and low-income backgrounds may be more likely to make such connections, many US consumers working in the food system do not identify as food workers. In some ways, this makes sense, because for many of these students this work is either temporary or part-time, whereas many long-term and full-time food workers are reliant on this work because of racialized and economic inequalities. It usually takes a particularly focused moment in the classroom to help students recognize their own positionality in relation to the broader food system and start to identify and think in solidarity with food systems workers.

For students, and so many other food movement advocates, issues like personal health and environmental concerns are often more tangible than those related to worker justice. This limited framing and involvement with the food movement often reproduces a neoliberal politics of individual choice and impact. It is our hope that this book helps readers look beyond these individualized perspectives on social change to instead see their lives as inextricable from those of food workers. By identifying more closely with food workers and mobilizing our energy to change the food system through the lens of labor, a broader politics of deep sustainable food systems change can emerge.

Throughout the following chapters, we integrate our own qualitative and field-based research experience with findings from other scholars, policy work by labor advocates and activists, and data from original analyses of publicly available labor statistics. In doing so, we offer a unique interdisciplinary and mixed-methods analysis of food system labor, which we hope changes the way that food activists, scholars, and policy makers think about labor and social justice movements across food system sectors. This book builds on historical, spatial, cultural, political, and sociological analyses to untangle the production of unequal and unjust conditions of labor across the food system.[21]

In addition to integrating existing scholarly and activist research and popular media sources, we add our own analysis of US Bureau of Labor Statistics (BLS) data and the US Census Bureau surveys. We draw specifically on the Occupational Employment and Wage Survey (OEWS) and the Current Population Survey (CPS).[22] To understand who does the frontline labor within the complex categories of workers and occupations collected in these survey data, we asked ourselves, "Who touches our food?" and "Who is an essential food worker in times of emergency?" With the excellent support of our research assistants, Quinn DiFalco and Esi Oppong, we closely examined the size and scope of each sector in the food system, the median hourly and annual wage, and the degree to which each sector is unionized. The statistics we share throughout the book are organized in line with our chapters focusing on the production, processing, distribution, retail, service, and waste collection sectors. While other organizations have drawn on these data to understand labor across the food chain, such as the FCWA and Race Forward, we build on this analysis to include food waste workers in our study. We share these data with three important caveats. First, the data do not include independent contractors or gig workers, as they are categorized as self-employed, an issue that we problematize in chapter 3. Second, data are not available for food-related reproductive labor that takes place in the home, given that it is unpaid and occurs in the private sphere. And third, undocumented workers and those working in the informal sector are undercounted or miscounted due to lack of official paperwork. Despite these gaps, these

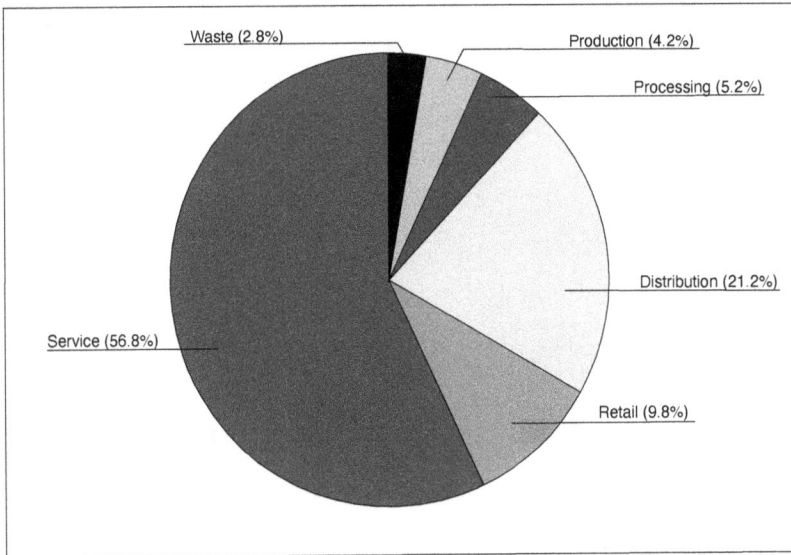

FIGURE 1. Percentage of Frontline Food Workers Employed by Sector of the Food Chain 2023. *Data source*: Occupational Employment and Wage Survey (OEWS), US Bureau of Labor Statistics.

data are useful for understanding the sheer numbers of paid workers in the food system, where they are concentrated, and how they are compensated and organized.

What the data tell us is that in 2023 there were 17,003,169 paid frontline workers in the food system overall. This accounts for about 10% of the total US workforce, or one in ten US workers. As can be seen in figures 1 and 2, the highest employment sector is in food service, nearly 57% of food workers, with the lowest number of workers, only 2.8%, in food waste.[23] In each chapter, with the exception of chapter 6 on home labor, we highlight sector-level data to give a broad picture of this workforce and related wages and unionization rate.

With respect to wages, workers in distribution and waste management had the highest incomes, although almost all workers were earning below a reasonable wage for a decent standard of living in the United States today. In many industries, such as farm labor, most workers earn a *poverty wage*, meaning they do not make enough money to meet the standards of living in their own community. This contrasts with a *living wage*, or the wage required for a full-time worker to meet their basic needs and the needs of their family

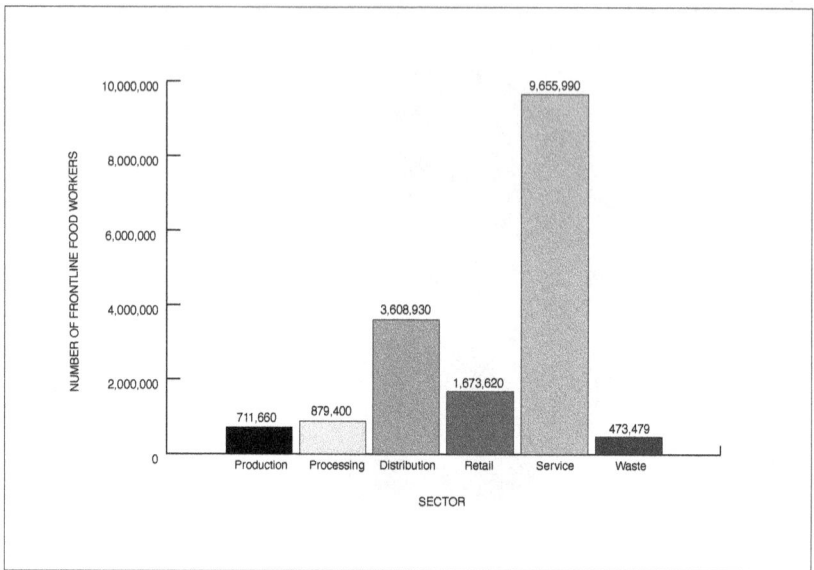

FIGURE 2. Number of Frontline Food Workers Employed in the Food Chain, 2023. *Data source*: Occupational Employment and Wage Survey (OEWS), US Bureau of Labor Statistics.

where they live. The *minimum wage* determined by federal and state governments, the lowest amount that can legally be paid by an employer, leaves workers in many parts of the United States below the poverty level when supporting a family, even if they are employed forty hours a week. In some sectors, *wage theft*, or not being paid the legal minimum wage or the wage one is contracted for, is rampant. As we discuss in the following chapters, a combination of policies and practices, such as the tipped wage system, subcontracted labor, and piece rate work, leaves workers vulnerable to such violations.[24]

LINKING THE FOOD CHAIN

We offer a robust and systems-informed perspective on food labor, using political economy as a guiding framework. When looking at food systems labor through this broad lens, we see frontline workers struggling within a powerful system that is fundamentally designed to maximize the profits of business owners and shareholders at the expense of workers' wages and conditions. A political economic framing helps us connect the sectors of the food

TABLE 1 Employment Numbers and Wages across Food Systems Sectors, 2023

Sector	Employment	Hourly Mean Wage	Annual Mean Wage
Production	711,660	$19.34	$40,225.91
Processing	879,490	$18.59	$38,666.67
Distribution	3,608,930	$20.32	$42,271.33
Retail	1,673,620	$15.66	$32,573.33
Service	9,655,990	$16.24	$33,772.50
Waste	473,479	$22.05	$45,862.11

DATA SOURCE: Occupational Employment and Wage Survey, US Bureau of Labor Statistics

system and see all workers as linked in this larger struggle to improve their status within a global capitalist system. Key terms and concepts are in italics and defined in the text, as well as collected in a glossary at the back of the book to facilitate understanding of complex and often-connected political economic processes.

In the chapters that follow, we provide an in-depth examination of labor across the food chain using a systems-based approach to analyze the sectors within a relevant political economy framework. We look at historical and contemporary conditions, contexts, and forms of resistance that workers experience in food sector jobs, from farm to compost pile. As we devote attention to both the work that takes place in public spaces and the labor that keeps families fed in the private sphere, we navigate the interconnected webs of both paid and unpaid food work. Each chapter is centered on a core political economic concept, from industrialization and corporate consolidation to reproductive labor and exchange value versus use value. While these concepts cut across each sector, we anchor each chapter with a particular focus. We add to existing analyses by not only discussing the conditions of workers but also contributing action-oriented approaches that tie together workers from different ends of the food system, including those working in noncommercial and nonpublic spaces, such as the home and food waste and recovery. In each chapter, we also interrogate the ways that systemic racism, classism, and sexism are inextricable from these structural inequalities.

In chapter 1, we discuss workers in the spaces of food production, including plant-based and animal-based farms. Field work can vary from apple picking on vast monocropped orchards to milking cows on small family-managed dairies. We frame farm labor conditions within the ongoing processes of racialized dispossession and related exclusions at the policy level. In the most literal of ways, the US food system is founded on slavery's legacy, as well as the enclosure of Native land and the forced removal of Indigenous peoples. Without slavery and the brutal labor systems that followed, plantation agriculture and the normalization of both the exploitation of farmworkers and industrial agriculture as we know it today would not exist. The afterlife of the plantation is ongoing, as most farmworkers come from outside the United States, primarily from Mexico and Central America. Race, ethnicity, and immigration status are constant themes in farmworker exploitation and in their advocacy and activism. This chapter covers the range of work done in the field and on the farm, including the complex issues of labor migration and guest worker programs and the history and present-day status of unionization and other state-level organizing movements, as well as climate change–induced and other health risks.

Almost all food needs to be processed or transported in some way to get to the end consumer. In chapter 2, we discuss how raw goods are processed into foods destined for the kitchen table. From industrial tomato canning to boutique cheese making, products from the farm and field must be made into the final products for the store and market. We frame this chapter by looking at the creation and persistence of Fordist approaches to food processing and the impacts of this kind of scientific management on worker skill, health, and well-being. We offer an extended case study of meat and poultry processing and describe how worker exploitation is intertwined with racism, sexism, classism, and vulnerabilities linked to citizenship. We conclude the chapter with a focus on the continued importance of labor organizing and unionization and new forms of worker power that are on the horizon in this sector of the food system.

Further, across the food system, we have seen a move away from traditional full-time work with stable schedules and full benefits to part-time and erratic employment, as well as outsourced and subcontracted labor. On highways and in stockrooms, we have seen a shift to online food provisioning and its effect on transport and logistics workers. This move, combined with an increase in temporary labor, outsourcing, and subcontracting by third-party agencies, has led to an increasingly precarious work environment. Chapter 3 therefore focuses on the concept of precarity, discussing the ways that these jobs have become progressively insecure as food chains have become increasingly globalized. The chapter looks at the conditions of warehouse, transportation, and distribution workers, who might pack pallets all night, drive thousands of solitary miles in a tractor trailer each week, or weave through high-speed traffic on motorbikes to make meal deliveries as commanded by app-based food services. In food delivery in particular, we have seen the encroachment of the gig economy, where workers are categorized as independent contractors and denied the rights of a minimum wage and days off. This sector of the chain is extremely diverse in terms of the identity and wages of workers, and it is also one of the most hidden from the sight of consumers.

Corporate consolidation is a concern throughout the food chain but is particularly striking in the food retail sector. Large-scale retailers have benefited from national policies that have shifted to allow both the unprecedented mergers of corporate-scale companies by reducing the enforcement of antitrust laws and the reclassification of big box supercenters, which now lead the nation in retail food supply. While food retail workers may serve customers in corner grocery marts, member-owned food cooperatives, traditional grocery outlets, or supercenters, they are increasingly being squeezed by competitive pressure to reduce both the hours and the number of workers present in stores. In chapter 4, we cover the issues affecting these retail food workers, including the historic shifts from mom-and-pop neighborhood groceries to the current consolidation of grocery store chains and supercenters, as well as the continuing push for automation and online procurement, retail worker vulnerabilities during the pandemic, and related antiunionization efforts of food retailers.

Chapter 5 highlights intersectionality as an organizing feature of capitalism, with a particular focus on the gendered and racialized ways that food service labor is structured. The food service industry accounts for the largest proportion of workers in the food system and is made up of front and back of the house workers who labor in privately owned full-service restaurants, fast-food chains, bars, catering companies, and cafés, as well as public institutions such as schools and hospitals. Franchises have become widespread in this sector and serve to distance corporate leadership from the everyday laborers handling our food. We look at issues related to gender and racial discrimination and harassment in the service industry, with a focus on restaurants and school cafeterias. Despite the difficulties of organizing food service workers, this chapter highlights how these workers are challenging the inequalities in this sector—from organizing public campaigns and unions to improve working conditions to opting out of this work altogether.

Continuing with a focus on intersectional identities, we also recognize that for all workers in the food system, gendered dynamics play into nearly every dimension of their lives, both in and outside the workplace. In chapter

6, we discuss in detail the concept of reproductive labor and changing gendered expectations over time. Food labor in the home is part of care work, the labor that sustains families and communities. This work is essential to society's functioning and is performed disproportionately by women but is chronically undervalued and taken for granted. In this chapter, we look at home-based food labor done by hired workers and the relationship of this work to race and slavery in the United States. We also examine food work performed by family and household members, motherhood guilt and the pressure to feed families more "natural" and less processed food, and how the dominance of heteronormativity and binary gender norms confine the social expectations of private lives and spaces. Reproductive work is often not categorized with other food work, as it is done in private settings and is part of the home-based labor of society. In structuring this chapter through the lens of reproductive labor, we challenge scholars of food labor and labor more broadly to take seriously the ways in which care work is food work.

In the penultimate chapter, we examine one of the more understudied areas of food systems labor, the work that is involved in disposing, rescuing, and recycling food waste. We frame this chapter with questions regarding exchange value versus use value of food labor, highlighting social movements and mutual aid networks that challenge capitalist structuring and valuations of work. Especially in the Global North, food waste is a mounting concern and reflects social standards about what is and isn't acceptable to eat. The majority of the work to contain and dispose of food waste is done through traditional waste collection, a highly underappreciated workforce that is exposed to health and safety hazards and social stigma on a daily basis. Other food waste workers labor in less traditional channels, both as paid laborers and unpaid volunteers, managing emergency and food recovery programs and composting, gleaning, and dumpster diving to transition wasted food into a valued resource, all while being undervalued as workers themselves. This line of work is often an afterthought in food systems discussions, as the environmental impact of waste and the recipients of emergency food are the focus of most research and advocacy work looking at the end of the food chain. This chapter, while difficult to research given the lack of scholarship on food waste workers, contributes a new perspective on who is included in food chain conversations and why their work is (de)valued as it is, despite its essential role.

In the conclusion, we look more closely at advocacy work within the various food sectors while making the comprehensive argument that to create the most effective and lasting structural change for workers across the food chain, a food systems approach must be taken. We hope that these points provide a foundation for other scholars, activists, and organizers to engage a systems framework, bringing together the currently disparate arguments and movements for food workers' rights and a deeper movement for social sustainability across the food chain. Food workers are the largest combined labor sector in the US economy, and as organizers have noted, the sheer number of workers involved in food systems labor is evidence of the potential for large-scale social change. This can happen if those workers have the support they need to build solidarity across the food chain. To create a truly "sustainable" food system, which recognizes social and economic sustainability, along with ecological goals, workers must be at its heart.

ONE

Industrialization and Racialized Dispossession on the Farm

For women, to be able to work with dignity and respect is huge, because before the program the women were sexually harassed, but now that the program exists there is zero tolerance for sexual harassment and woman can report sexual harassment anonymously, because that did not happen before. Therefore, now women are working and our human rights are being respected, which is very important, especially because as women there are many things that we face and this alleviates one of our worries to be able to work as a woman free and with respect.

One of the programs that is helping the workers is the bonus that the participating corporations are offering. They are increasing one cent per pound, which means a big increase for the workers because now they are getting between $50 and $100 [per week]. This may not be a lot of money for people who have a lot of money, but for the workers it is a big amount because to earn this, it takes a lot of work. Furthermore, now corporations have a program to eliminate poverty by paying a little bit more per pound.

LUPE, *tomato picker and Coalition of Immokalee Workers organizer*

FARMWORKERS LIKE LUPE ARE CENTRAL to food production in the United States, from New England's dairy farms to vineyards on the West Coast to tomato fields in the Southeast. Yet across these regions workers labor under grueling physical conditions and in one of the lowest paid and least regulated industries in the country. In the small agricultural town of Immokalee, Florida, farmworkers have organized a powerful campaign, affecting how their labor is valued from the grassroots level to the very top of the corporate food chain. The Coalition of Immokalee Workers is a worker-based organization focused on protecting the human rights of farmworkers. They have coordinated one of the most forward thinking and strategic programs to address labor abuses and sexual violence against farmworkers in the United States today, called the Fair Food Program.[1] In developing this program, the CIW has articulated a strong analysis of the power dynamics within the industrialized food system and has found creative ways for their demands to fit within its confines. Moreover, they recognize farm labor as part of a food system, where power and profits remain at the top, in the service and retail sectors, and outside of the direct relations between agricultural workers and their farm-level employers. Their role in creating the broader framework and network of the *Worker-Driven Social Responsibility* (WSR) model is profound and engages a different set of organizing principles from that of more traditional forms of worker activism. The WSR model is a worker-led approach to monitor labor standards and fight labor abuses, which can include mechanisms for handling complaints and worker trainings. Organizations engaging in WSR models, such as the CIW, exemplify a food chain perspective. The CIW successfully looks up the food chain to the highest-profiting companies in retail and service and puts pressure on them to absorb the cost of higher worker wages at the farm level. Because of their successes, thousands of farmworkers like Lupe have benefited from better pay and working conditions. The organizing work of the CIW and others challenges the structural inequalities embedded in the industrial mode of producing food today.

Agricultural work in the United States—and globally—has historically been a poorly paid and undervalued profession, with deeply rooted racial inequalities. Since the middle of the twentieth century, agriculture has become increasingly industrialized, as seen in intensified mechanization, reduced agricultural diversity, larger-scale farming operations, and the reliance on off-farm chemical inputs. However, as we argue in this chapter, we must understand the growth of industrial agriculture as a product of both scientific and technological development and also as stemming from the deliberate exploitation and control of agricultural workers. Despite the skilled nature of the job, the ongoing demand for regionally and domestically produced food, and high profits made up the food chain in processing, retail, and food service, farmworkers have been systematically excluded from the rights to fair wages and work-related benefits and protections to organize afforded to other US workers. These exclusions are tied to the historical and continued construction of agricultural workers as a racialized and immigrant workforce.

Workers in the farm production sector, according to 2023 BLS data, include those in crop and animal production, forestry, fishing, hunting, and

FRONTLINE WORKERS IN FOOD PRODUCTION, 2023

Total Employment:

711,660 workers

Union Density:

2.93% coverage, 2.44% membership

Mean Hourly Wage:

$19.34

Mean Annual Wage:

$40,225.91

Data Source: Occupational Employment and Wage Survey (OEWS), US Bureau of Labor Statistics

trapping and make up 711,660 frontline workers.[2] This is roughly 4.2% of paid workers in the food system who work outside the home. However, we emphasize that this number is a severe undercount given the number of undocumented and subcontracted farmworkers. While the BLS reports that farm production workers make an annual median wage of $40,225 and an hourly median wage of $19.34, practitioners and researchers in the field know that even those low numbers are overestimates of the true wages of farm laborers.[3] Union representation in this sector is minimal, at 2.93%, due in no small part to legislation which does not protect farmworkers who collectively bargain.[4] According to 2018–20 data from the National Agricultural Workers Survey (NAWS), 70% of farmworkers are foreign born, and roughly 41% worked without authorization (as undocumented workers).[5] These numbers are also likely a significant undercount given that much agricultural work happens off the books. Also, these figures only reflect crop workers, not farmworkers in industries such as dairy. Moreover, research shows that workers who lack legal authorization receive significantly lower wages than authorized (documented) workers.[6]

Today one of the most dangerous and insidious challenges to farmworkers stems from the human-induced changes to the global climate. Climate change is causing record extreme heat, catastrophic fires, increased droughts and dust storms, and even disease related to soil-borne fungus.[7] These increased risks build on already tenuous farm labor conditions, where workers lack even the most minimal protections. For example, farmworkers die of heat-related causes twenty times more often than those in all other professions.[8] Because of their exclusion from federal labor regulations, farmworkers often work eleven- and twelve-hour days, five to six days a week, and in some regions hours at a time in 100-plus-degree heat. States across the South, with some of the warmest and most humid conditions, have no regulations to protect workers from extreme heat, even though temperatures have been rising steadily since the 1980s. While workers do what they can as individuals, including carrying water and wearing appropriate clothing, what they are asking for is far from unreasonable: more regular breaks with pay when they need to cool down, access to more water, and shady spaces for sun protection.[9] With increased climate disruption due to human-induced environmental change, it is highly likely that these risks will only increase.

This chapter begins by examining the historical and contemporary processes and policies that have enabled the often-brutal control of farmworkers in the United States, underscoring how industrial agriculture is predicated on racialized dispossession and exceptionalism from labor protections. *Dispossession*, the process of taking away property or rights by legal or illegal means, is deeply affected by structural and interpersonal racism in society. *Racialized dispossession* points to the specific patterns and impacts that people of color have experienced as they have lost rights and property due to their racialized identities. In the United States, this originated in *settler colonialism*, the systematic genocide of Indigenous communities by people who established a settled community in their place and the enslavement of Africans, and it has continued with the exploitation of immigrant workers today. Thus, the development of an industrial agricultural system in the United States has only been possible by unleashing physical, symbolic, and structural violence against immigrants and people of color. After tracing the violence of the early formation of our food system, we explore how history shapes the current inequalities and challenges that farmworkers face today, including gendered forms of violence and patterns of segregation, or what the anthropologist Seth Holmes calls an "ethnicity-citizenship hierarchy."[10] Further, we discuss the ways that artificial intelligence, mechanization, heightened border politicization, and *guest worker programs*, which are government programs giving foreign workers permission to work in another country, are influencing the current landscape for worker mobilizations. Finally, we highlight the various forms of organizing taking place that challenge these structural conditions, from farm-level mobilizations to organizing up the food chain.

PLANTATION AGRICULTURE AND THE
DISPOSSESSION OF LIFE, LIBERTY, AND LAND

The conditions farmworkers experience today are rooted in the plantation economies that fueled the agricultural boom of the US colonial period. During this period, intensive production of cash crops for domestic and transatlantic trade replaced the diverse subsistence production and grazing practices of Indigenous peoples in the Americas. Colonizers struggled to coerce Indigenous communities and nations into an exploitative agrarian labor system, as many had a shared governance system of land use and were not accustomed to working for a wage for others.[11] While untold numbers of Indigenous peoples were forced into servitude, Europeans found it more cruelly productive to expel them from their lands through violence and starvation, encroaching on and decimating their territories and natural resources.[12]

As Indigenous peoples were dispossessed of prime agricultural lands, colonizers started cultivating crops on a scale beyond what could be supported by the family unit. Tobacco and cotton, two of the most profitable cash crops, were extremely labor-intensive. As these crops required many bodies to perform difficult work, colonists turned to the violent enslavement of African people to labor in their fields.[13] It is estimated that anywhere between 350,000 and 500,000 people were brought directly to the United States through the transatlantic and intra-American slave trade, and a total of 10 to 12 million individuals were forcibly trafficked to the western hemisphere, not accounting for the horrific numbers who perished along the journey.[14] Some Southern plantation owners also employed white immigrant indentured servants. However, indentured white servants were guaranteed freedom after a set time and had the possibility of legal redress for abuse and contractual fraud. In contrast to enslaved Black workers, white indentured servants could join colonial society after forced employment, and many achieved middle- and upper-middle-class status.[15]

The economic profits from plantation slavery became the foundation of wealth for white colonists and settlers. Historians have noted that the American colonies that profited from slave labor were the wealthiest in the region, due to higher levels of agricultural production and trade.[16] Rice cultivation along the coastal areas of what is now South Carolina transformed the region's geography and cultural histories, making Charleston one of the richest cities in the world.[17] In the Caribbean, sugar cultivation generated immense affluence for both plantation owners and colonial nations, forever changing consumption patterns by making this former luxury into an everyday ingredient.[18] In cultivating these crops (and others), the development of extractive monocropping systems was seeded, simultaneously brutalizing workers and the land.

The labor, skills, and knowledge gleaned from racialized agricultural workers are foundational to the development of the US food system. Like immigrant farmworkers today, enslaved Africans brought both agricultural knowledge and technical skills with them across regional and political borders, contributing to the vast amounts of wealth generated on plantations. As food scholars like Judith Carney and Michael Twitty have argued, many if not most enslaved Africans were kidnapped and brought to the western hemisphere specifically because of their deep knowledge of growing, harvesting, and preparing particular crops.[19] While the most profitable cash crops included rice, cotton, indigo, sugarcane, and coffee, other crops with less market value such as ground nuts, oil palm, watermelon, cowpeas/black-eyed peas, rooibos, okra, millet, yams, sorghum, and some leafy greens also followed Africans westward.[20] In addition, a number of cultivars that were not native to Africa were diversified and naturalized by African gardeners and became common in agricultural systems and plantation economies in the Americas. These included different varieties of plantains, bananas, taro, mangoes, peanuts, chilis, sweet potatoes, and tomatoes.[21] Without violently appropriating these deep forms of knowledge, the generation of wealth in the colonies would not have been possible.

The tensions over slavery between the North and the South came to a head with the US Civil War. At its core, this war was fought over the issue of slavery, although states' rights and expansion westward (and whether slavery would be permitted in those newly colonized areas) were interrelated sources of division. However, the Civil War was also about the future of agriculture and the food system. For the Southern states that seceded to form the Confederacy, maintaining the plantation system of agriculture, with large plots of land and masses of enslaved workers, was seen as essential to continued economic expansion. In contrast, in the North, where smaller-scale farms were typically maintained by family labor, urban *industrialization*, or the process of a regional transition from a primarily agriculturally based economy to one focused on manufacturing, was a primary driver of economic growth. While factory owners benefited from widespread worker exploitation and labor conditions in Northern cities that were notoriously horrendous, for the most part this labor was not forced through systems of slavery but rather

FIGURE 3. Cotton Sharecroppers, Greene County, Georgia, 1937. Dorothea Lange, photographer. Library of Congress, Prints & Photographs Division, Farm Security Administration/ Office of War Information Black-and-White Negatives.

driven by the crushing poverty that drove many workers onto the factory floor.[22]

After the Civil War ended in 1865, the Reconstruction era saw the growth of sharecropping across the US South, reconfiguring agricultural economies and labor patterns. For white plantation owners, sharecropping served to reestablish a labor force when slavery was outlawed, allowing for the continued cultivation of crops like cotton, rice, and tobacco on an immense scale. In the sharecropping system, farmers did not own the means of production (land, seeds, and necessary equipment) but instead rented them from the landowner to produce crops, a share of which was due to the landowner. This often resulted in cyclical debts to landowners, leaving sharecroppers effectively bound to the land, yet without land rights.

While most sharecroppers were white (based on raw numbers), formerly enslaved people had few employment opportunities in the South other than sharecropping.[23] For formerly enslaved African Americans who could not legally own land, sharecropping provided some means of subsistence and a way to avoid imprisonment for vagrancy after legislators in former Confederate states instituted the Black Codes. These "codes" were restrictive laws designed to limit the freedom of African Americans, which ensured their availability as a source of underpaid and exploited labor after slavery was abolished. While sharecroppers had some autonomy, racialized inequality within sharecropping arrangements ran nearly as deeply as under slavery.[24] Throughout the South, most productive agricultural lands stayed in white hands, while Black farmers rarely had the opportunity to escape the worker-owner relation inherent to these land arrangements.

From emancipation to the second half of the twentieth century, US agriculture moved toward increasingly highly industrialized food production, culminating in the formal endorsement of Earl Butz's "get big or get out" approach by the US Department of Agriculture (USDA). This further marginalized farmers of color, especially Black farmers, who were disproportionately underresourced and farming on smaller plots and less likely to receive government aid and support.[25] Eventually, a mass exodus of Black families migrated North to urban centers, largely leaving their agrarian past behind, and white landowners started recruiting workers from immigrant communities. Extending this history of exploiting both enslaved and free Black farmworkers, newly arrived groups of immigrant workers were treated differently from other laborers in the United States, as we discuss below.

AGRICULTURAL EXCEPTIONALISM AND FEDERAL POLICY

Despite advances in broad labor protections in the United States in the first half of the twentieth century, farmworkers were excluded from most federal labor policies. In addition, at key moments in history, federal labor law has intersected with immigration policy to determine who can legally enter the United States to work in agriculture. These exceptions and policy maneuvers are the foundation of what scholars now call agricultural or agrarian exceptionalism, where agriculture is regulated differently from other industries.[26] Agrarian exceptionalism derives from the Lockean notion that when one mixes their labor with the soil, they become entitled to the land as private property. It sets agriculture apart as somehow a higher moral venture than other economic pursuits, despite the modern-day development of agriculture into an industrial venture.

These exemptions to labor laws were justified in part by the idyllic image of a small-scale and wholesome operation where typically white farm families work together to support their family business.[27] As the geographer Don Mitchell has written, this imaginary erases the experiences of racialized workers in service of romantic visions of agrarian livelihoods, free of what is perceived as contaminated or "dirty" workers.[28] Within our current food system, small-scale farms maintained by family labor alone are rare given the difficulties of competing with large-scale operations that require more workers. Moreover, the legal exceptionalism bolstered by agrarian imaginaries supports the dominance of industrialized agriculture and the exploitation of agricultural workers.

Following the Civil War, from roughly the mid-1860s through the 1930s, large-scale growers (many of which were heavily backed by capitalist financiers) pursued farming on an immense scale.[29] While sharecroppers were actively working on large-scale holdings in the South, the number of large-scale farming operations along the West Coast grew as well. Given that there was not the same availability of African American laborers, white farm owners increasingly sought out workers beyond their family units. Beginning in 1863, US railroad executives worked with labor contractors to recruit Chinese immigrants to build the transcontinental railroad. When this project was complete, farmers saw them as available laborers who would tolerate lower wages than white workers. White workers started to blame Chinese workers for depressed wages, creating tension between racialized groups. Eventually, in 1882, the US Congress passed the Chinese Exclusion Act, prohibiting the immigration of all Chinese workers for ten years and declaring Chinese immigrants ineligible for naturalization. This was the first law prohibiting immigration to the United States, which quickly led to a severe agricultural labor shortage. Soon after, Japanese workers were recruited to fill the gap, following their immigration to the US mainland after Hawaii's annexation by the United States in 1898.[30] The racialized blame game whereby immigrant workers are seen as the cause of low wages suffered by white workers, only to be replaced by new groups of immigrant workers, continues to the present day.

In the following decades, new legislation was enacted to explicitly exclude an Asian immigrant workforce from the United States, many of whom were engaged in agricultural labor. These included xenophobic and violent laws to prohibit immigration as well as laws that barred Asians from landownership, such as the Immigration Act of 1924, the Alien Laws of 1913–27, and the Japanese Internment Act of 1942. Through the creation of these laws, Asian immigrants were legally categorized and defined as a racialized group, which facilitated their exploitation as workers moving forward.[31] Ultimately, these exclusions made it difficult for the Asian immigrant and Asian American population to become landowners and farm operators, either by explicit legal prohibition or because they could not amass enough capital to become part of the agricultural owner class.[32] The experiences of Asian immigrant farmworkers, as described above, and those of Laotian, Sikh, Japanese, and Filipino workers, help us understand the conditions for today's exploited agricultural workforce in the United States. While they come from different world regions, they struggle in similar ways, pigeonholed into low-paying jobs due to their race and immigration status and prevented from pursuing economic upward mobility.[33]

In addition to exclusionary laws like these, federal policies, including the New Deal, have contributed to the exceptional legal treatment of farmworkers. The New Deal era encompassed a broad set of US federal programs and reforms enacted from 1933 to 1939. This sweeping array of legislation included labor reforms that established the basis for most labor laws today. Specifically, the National Labor Relations Act (NLRA) of 1935 established the right to collectively bargain (organize a union), and the Fair Labor Standards Act (FLSA) of 1938 set a federal minimum wage, created the standard for a forty-hour workweek with overtime pay, and prohibited child labor. These laws applied broadly to almost every category of worker. Only two kinds of workers were exempt, domestic workers and agricultural workers.[34] In defending this exclusion, which has been maintained at the federal level even as some states have made reforms, agricultural industries have long claimed that farming is different from or exceptional compared to other modes of production, as agriculture is seasonal in nature and traditionally drew on a family-based labor structure.[35] At the time these laws were passed, most agricultural and domestic workers in the US South were African Americans, and it is commonly agreed that the exclusion of these workers from these protections was a bargaining chip to get southern politicians heavily invested in maintaining the dominant racial order and Jim Crow laws to support the broader New Deal efforts. As the legal scholar Juan F. Perea argues, "Specifically, southern congressmen wanted to exclude black employees from the New Deal to preserve the quasi-plantation style of agriculture that pervaded the still-segregated Jim Crow South."[36]

As many Black workers transitioned out of agriculture to more urban and northern locations, white farmers, including those who did and did not own their land, faced increasingly intense economic and environmental pressures such as the Dust Bowl to abandon farming. Many of these former tenants and sharecroppers moved west to look for work on others' farms. Eventually these workers also fled to more urban positions, and farmers who had not already done so started looking to more actively recruit newly arrived immigrant workers as well those still living abroad.

During World War II, labor dynamics in agriculture came to a head, as the rural workforce was drawn into overseas and domestic wartime positions and there was a legitimate need for more farm laborers. The first and still most well-known agricultural guest worker program in the United States, the Bracero Program (*bracero* literally means "arms" in Spanish), began after the Mexican Farm Labor Agreement was signed in 1942. As a temporary worker agreement between the United States and Mexico, the Bracero Program was designed to bring in Mexican farmworkers on an "emergency" basis. Yet in the years that followed the war, the Bracero Program was extended with the support of intense lobbying by farm interests despite the return of US-born workers.[37] Over the next two decades, over four million men were brought to the United States on short-term labor contracts to work in agriculture and building US railroads. Workers were subjected to dehumanizing physical examination to apply and enter the program and on entering, deplorable living conditions.[38] Historians, including Mireya Loza, have shown how braceros sought to resist and defy these forms of abuse and exploitation, carving out spaces of mobilization and intimacy in the most unlikely conditions.[39] While the program was finally terminated in 1964, it left a legacy of cross-border migration streams from agricultural regions in Mexico to the United States.[40] The Bracero Program also set the standard for other guest worker programs today, wherein workers may not change employers, creating a dangerously captive and highly vulnerable workforce.[41]

In addition to the Bracero Program, which recruited Mexican workers, the British West Indies Temporary Worker Program of 1942–64 was available for farmers to utilize throughout the country. While it is less well known than the Bracero Program, it created the relationships that formed the basis of today's agricultural guest worker program, the H-2A Temporary Visa Program, which initially recruited Jamaican workers to labor on East Coast apple farms.[42] Following the development of the Bracero and West Indies Programs, Puerto Rico's Farm Labor Program (FLP) brought thousands of Puerto Rican farmworkers to the US mainland between 1947, when the program was established, and its end in 1993. As Ismael García-Colón argues, the

FIGURE 4. Mexican Girl, Carrot Worker, Edinberg, Texas, 1939. Russell Lee, photographer. Library of Congress, Prints & Photographs Division, Farm Security Administration/ Office of War Information Black-and-White Negatives.

arrangement of the FLP was distinct from other guest worker programs as it represented a form of colonial control, where the workers already had US citizenship but continued to experience racism and other forms of discrimination when working on mainland farms as colonial subjects.[43]

Despite farmworkers' exclusion from the most comprehensive labor laws in US history and their essential role in national and global food production, there have been few federal laws passed specifically to address agricultural labor. Laws addressing these exclusions have been largely passed at the state level in recent years, as discussed below. The 1983 Migrant and Seasonal Agricultural Workers Protection Act (MSPA) is the primary federal law that protects farmworkers in the United States today. It standardizes the process for migrant labor recruitment and contract arrangements, which are historically exploitative of migrant workers. Yet this law is in no way comprehensive of all farmwork and only touches on some of the problems with the agricultural industry.[44] This law, and many others regarding farm labor that have been passed at the national and state levels, includes a "small business exemption." Like the FLSA, it does not apply to many smaller farms that do not hire year-round laborers.[45] Unfortunately, smaller-scale farmers are not guaranteed to be better employers, despite their often-perceived more wholesome image.[46]

One of the more encompassing pieces of federal legislation that has affected farmworkers is the Immigration Reform and Control Act of 1986 (IRCA), signed into law by President Ronald Reagan, which made it illegal to hire someone who is in the United States without legal authorization. At the same time, over two and a half million people without authorization were given amnesty. The IRCA included a special provision for anyone who had worked in US agriculture for at least ninety days between 1985 and 1986, with over one million undocumented farmworkers receiving amnesty through the act.[47] Despite this group of workers and their employers benefiting from this provision, it was temporary, and undocumented workers entering the United States from that point on were subjected to other aspects of the law, including increased patrols at the US-Mexico border and violent crackdowns on undocumented migrants. Whereas in the past migrants came across the border to work seasonally and returned home with little overt resistance from the state, the border became increasingly dangerous to cross.[48] In addition, this policy politicized the notion of the "good/legal Mexican" worker in contrast to the "illegal" worker, which functions economically to keep immigrant workers deportable and exploitable by employers.[49] These constructed vulnerabilities largely have been taken advantage of by industrial farm owners and operators, who have continually expected a simultaneously available and disposable farm labor force.

The federal policies we discuss in this section have reinforced a highly segregated workforce and an unequal distribution of power that persist to this date. With the intensification of industrial agriculture, exclusions from comprehensive rights to labor protections and the related rights of citizenship have deepened for agricultural workers. Given that the racial demographics of agricultural work (and domestic work) have changed dramatically in the past ninety years, exclusion from the full protections associated with the NLRA and FLSA now disproportionately affects immigrant laborers, particularly undocumented workers who are understandably hesitant to speak up when their basic rights are violated. These forms of exceptionalism, enabled by federal labor and immigration policy, underscore how processes of dispossession and *racialization*, or the social processes that designate racial identities and meaning in the context of hierarchical power relations, work in tandem with inequalities related to gender, ethnicity, and citizenship status. We now turn to the contemporary realities of agricultural workers in the United States, showing how industrialization and the policies that support it have fundamentally reshaped labor patterns in agriculture, including how workers are compensated, treated, and recruited to work across borders.

INDUSTRIALIZATION, WORKER VULNERABILITY, AND THE MYTH OF LABOR SHORTAGES

As we discuss above, federal labor and immigration policy in the United States has long affected the agricultural workforce and continues to shape the demographics and the treatment of farmworkers today. Agricultural workers are still exempt from federally required overtime pay for work over forty hours. In addition, farms that do not hire workers for more than a combined five hundred days in a calendar quarter are exempt from federal minimum wage requirements. Anyone who works primarily with livestock, works for a piece rate for fewer than thirteen weeks a year, or is a minor under the age of sixteen working on a piece rate may be paid below the federal minimum wage.[50] *Piece rate* means that a worker is paid per unit that they produce or tasks that they complete or, as may be the case for agricultural workers, per pallet or pound of produce they pick. These structural and political inequalities have intensified the exploitation of women, children, and foreign-born workers (many of whom are women and children).

In the absence of comprehensive federal policies on agricultural labor and farm positions, farmers frequently claim that there is a national farmworker labor shortage. Yet what is commonly called a labor shortage today is better understood as a product of a long and often-violent history of structural racism and devaluation of farmwork in the United States. Most farmers, when faced with so-called labor shortages in traditional or formal labor markets, look to new groups of vulnerable workers, including undocumented workers and/or legal guest workers, instead of increasing wages. According to most agricultural economists, labor shortages stem from an uneven relationship between the demand for and the supply of workers, mediated by compensation. Compensation should theoretically rise if there is more demand than supply, moving toward an equilibrium where employers have a sufficient supply of suitable workers. If farm owners cannot afford to pay higher wages, they should substitute capital or management for labor.[51]

Critical scholars in fields such as geography, sociology, and history have problematized this neat supply-demand equation to examine how these relationships are shaped by the construction of vulnerable immigrant workers, racialization, and capitalist exploitation. However, many researchers have noted that, apart from absolute labor shortages during wartime, the underlying issue causing so-called shortages is the fact that it is hard to fill such positions because they involve grueling work for low wages and few benefits.[52] Following the racialization of agricultural work during slavery and the postbellum period, US labor policy has consistently denied farmworkers the same rights and opportunities as other workers, maintaining farmwork's low social and economic status.

The limited availability of experienced laborers to do skilled farmwork in the United States stems from a confluence of many factors: global and national urbanization, tighter borders and stricter immigration policies, and increased labor demands in Mexico's food system.[53] The industrialization of US agriculture and patterns of urbanization have contributed to the steady movement since the early 1900s of rural populations away from farming and toward urban professions, a form of internal migration that has accelerated over the past several decades.[54] In comparison to agricultural work, most off-farm jobs are higher paid, operate year-round, and are not subject to fluctuations in weather. During this period, the limited rural population gains have often been due to increasing numbers of immigrant workers, including those working in agriculture.[55] Persistent low wages, combined with the strenuous and skilled nature of agriculture work, undergird these demographic and employment trends.[56]

Another factor contributing to the lack of willing US-born farmworkers is that farmwork is a skill developed from one's early years in rural areas. Most farmworkers have done this labor their entire lives and are experienced and skilled agriculturalists, despite the policy narrative that farm labor is not skilled work. In fact, many farmworkers in the United States come from backgrounds of managing their own farms in their home countries and bring that set of skills and knowledge to the fields when they immigrate, a point we have both observed in our fieldwork.[57]

Over time, more women have migrated from Latin America to the United States in search of work. Among those without legal authorization, undocumented women earn even less than their male counterparts. In their analysis of NAWS data from the period 2005–9, Bowers and Chand found that farmworker women earned close to $4,700 a year less than men.[58] Moreover, migrant women farmworkers and their children are more likely to work off the record, with their male partners being the ones who are officially enrolled by employers. As Monica Ramirez, advocate and founder of Justice for Migrant

Women, observes, "This is beneficial to the employer because they pay fewer taxes and benefits, but for the women it's really terrible. . . . They of course should be entitled to their own wages, but this also makes it incredibly difficult for them to leave an abusive relationship or prove to immigration authorities that they work."[59]

High rates of intimate partner violence in the home have been found among women farmworkers, which is compounded by the violence that many experience in the workplace.[60] In a groundbreaking report, the Southern Poverty Law Center (SPLC) highlighted both the contributions of undocumented Latina immigrant women and the injustices they confront while working in the US food system.[61] With particular attention to women farmworkers, the SPLC drew on extensive interview data to reveal stories of exploitation and suffering that are remarkably similar and illustrative of the brutalities of industrial food production. The SPLC report cites a previous study that found that 80% of Mexican women surveyed working in the Central Valley of California as farmworkers had experienced sexual harassment on the job.[62] Given the heightened risk of sexual abuse, undocumented women are especially hesitant to report these crimes out of fear of being detained, deported, and possibly separated from their families. These forms of violence stem from a toxic combination of racism, classism, and sexism that often flourishes on industrialized farms with little oversight and accountability.

Not surprisingly, women farmworkers are often mothers and have no choice but to bring their children to the fields, either because of a lack of available and trusted childcare or for economic reasons, such as helping pay off steep immigration debts. An estimated 30,000 to 79,325 children between the ages of ten and seventeen work in agriculture in the United States today, many in dangerous work environments and earning below the minimum wage.[63] Most of the children's parents are migrant and immigrant farm laborers, and they labor as hired workers alongside their parents to support their family's meager income. Many of the children migrate seasonally and struggle to keep up with their peers in school if they attend school at all.[64] According to federal regulation, at age fourteen, child workers can start working outside of regular school hours. At the age of sixteen, children can legally work in agriculture full-time, with no hourly limitations, including during school hours. In some states, there is no minimum age for farmworkers if they have parental consent, whereas other states specify the age for work on certain crops; for example, Oregon has a minimum age of nine for berry pickers. According to the US Department of Labor, no documentation needs to be provided to show minimum age.[65] The intersectional forms of violence these children face highlight a particularly egregious dimension of agrarian exceptionalism that is tied to industrial agriculture.

LOOKING FOR ALTERNATIVES TO
UNDOCUMENTED WORKERS

The US agricultural industry's increasing reliance on an undocumented workforce has come with heightened vulnerability to international political and economic policies. The combination of a progressively militarized border with Mexico after the September 11, 2001, attacks and the historical racialization of a largely industrial farm labor force has led to a decreasing number of workers who can legally enter and labor in the United States.[66] Many of these workers traditionally traveled across the US-Mexico border and returned to their home communities between growing seasons. However, the border has become more dangerous and costly to cross, and throughout the United States undocumented people feel increasingly frightened by the threat and reality of immigration raids and deportations.[67] These combined factors have led farmers to look for alternatives to an undocumented labor force, ranging from legal pathways to hire foreign workers to mechanization and other technological solutions.

Given the difficulties of relying on undocumented workers, an increasing number of farmers are turning to agricultural guest workers, hired through the H-2A visa program. Low-end estimates state that H-2A guest workers make up about 10% of the workforce on US farms.[68] The H-2A program was initiated in 1953, overlapping with the Bracero Program.[69] Both programs are a result of strong political organizing by growers who claimed that they could not find willing domestic farmworkers. While it has existed for over half a century, the H-2A program has expanded exponentially over the past fifteen years in response to tighter border restrictions and increased immigration raids and therefore more demand from farmers.[70]

Today the H-2A program draws in workers from Jamaica, Haiti, and Mexico, as well as other countries throughout Latin America and the world, to labor in temporary agricultural positions for up to ten months at a time. Without this visa program, such workers would not be legally eligible for employment on US farms.[71] Workers who are enrolled in the program must return home after the season each year and may reenter the United States only if invited by their boss. This process prevents workers from establishing strong family ties in the United States, which ensures their availability to work long hours without other obligations or distractions. Further, under their visa conditions, workers are only allowed to labor for the employer who recruited them and may not change jobs. This policy leaves workers vulnerable to mistreatment, as any complaint can lead to a loss of employment and deportation.[72]

With the growth of the H-2A program, there has been an increase in documented abuses by farmers using it, from overworking employees, threats of deportation, and dangerous housing conditions to outright human trafficking.[73] Due to high bureaucratic and management costs, the H-2A program has been more beneficial to larger-scale farms with more employees and higher profit margins.[74] The H-2A program, which is expected to grow, has the potential to contribute to the further industrialization of the agricultural workforce.[75]

Larger-scale farmers are also more likely to pursue options like mechanization and artificial intelligence (AI). In the current world of increasingly sophisticated AI technology, the familiar refrain of replacing human workers with robots has been reignited. Yet as the food systems scholars Patrick Baur and Alastair Iles aptly point out in their historical analysis of the attempt to mechanize California agriculture during the twentieth century, developers of such technology "never perfectly replaced human work, and [the technology] often led to degradation in quality, effectiveness, and efficiency of cultivation and harvest that caused a variety of new agronomic, environmental, and supply chain problems. Human workers have intelligence, physical dexterity, and experiential know-how that engineers have long tried to replicate."[76] As they note, agriculture is technical labor, and farmworkers are difficult to replace with even the most well-researched and heavily invested technology.

While we recognize that agricultural technology and robotics are becoming more advanced over time and the incentive to develop these technologies is motivated by the perceived "shortages" of underpaid and easily controlled labor, we do not see a near future where human farmworkers are made completely obsolete. Such technology takes time and money to develop, and the up-front cost of purchasing the necessary tools is beyond most farmers' financial capabilities and is therefore limited to only the largest food producers. For example, robotic milkers that allow dairy farmers to reduce labor cost $150,000 to $200,000 per robot. These machines can milk fifty to seventy cows each and require one computer operator. This equates to two eighty-hour-a-week employees who would work directly with cows at the same scale of operation. Research has shown that this technology is still not as profitable as low-wage human labor because of the up-front cost.[77] While dairy is the one of the industries most motivated to develop and support technology, as it does not currently have access to seasonal guest workers, a full switch to robotic milking is still not a feasible option for most farmers.

Further, research has shown the ways that AI and other agricultural technologies have only deepened economic divides between farmers, allowing for increased consolidation among agricultural producers who can afford such technological shifts. Since the development of mechanized lettuce pickers in the 1970s, when the United Farm Worker (UFW) union organizer Cesar Chavez famously argued that mechanization of agriculture should benefit the workers, not just the growers, we have seen that agricultural technology development, while not an inherently negative development for workers, has failed to benefit them.[78] Instead, sustained efforts to improve workers' lives are best attributed to worker organizing, from structural policy reform to grassroots activism.

WORKER ORGANIZING AT THE FARM LEVEL

Despite the structural inequalities underpinning the national struggle for farmworker justice, there is a significant history of farmworker organizing in the United States. This organizing has resulted in important policy changes for worker protections at the state level, shaping the conditions at individual farms. In the absence of comprehensive federal reform, this state-level progress, while slow, continues to this day. Perhaps the most well-known are the accomplishments in California, instigated by the organizing work of the United Farm Workers Organizing Committee. In 1965, Filipino grape workers, led by Larry Itliong and members of the Agricultural Workers Organizing Committee in Delano, California, which was affiliated with the American Federation of Labor and Congress of Industrial Organizations (AFL-CIO), started striking against low wages and dreadful working and living conditions. They soon asked a newly formed, predominantly Latinx union, the National Farm Workers Association (NFWA), to join them, and together they became the United Farm Workers.

To gain national attention and support the strike, Cesar Chavez, Dolores Huerta, Itliong, and other organizers orchestrated a march on Sacramento, California's capital. Over the next four years, the UFW and its collaborators organized the largest food boycott in US history. By 1970, all table grape workers were under union contract, and by 1977, the UFW had secured over a hundred union contracts, including a 40% wage increase. These contracts guaranteed improved wages, benefits, and working conditions for farm labor.[79] The tactics, successes, and failures of the UFW have been addressed in painstaking detail by scholars, as has the complicated leadership of Chavez himself.[80]

In response to the widespread national grape boycotts and labor strikes organized by workers and advocates, California passed the California Agricultural Labor Relations Act (CALRA) of 1975. This was the first state-level labor law establishing the right of farmworkers to collective bargaining and thereby to form a union. In the following years, the UFW was crucial to getting specific legislation passed to protect farmworker rights at the state level, playing a large role in helping pass CALRA and establishing California's Agricultural Relations Board in 1975.[81] There is a wealth of research and literature on the history of the UFW, including important critiques about leadership's sidelining of Filipino, undocumented, and Indigenous workers.[82]

The UFW remained a powerful force in farmworker organizing over subsequent decades, inspiring other farmworker groups from the 1980s through the early 2000s. These unions and other groups included El Comité de Apoyo a los Trabajadores Agrícolas / Farm Workers Support Committee (CATA) in the mid-Atlantic region; the Farm Labor Organizing Committee (FLOC) in the Midwest, South, and Mexico; Pineros y Campesinos Unidos del Noroeste (PCUN) in Oregon; and the Farmworker Association of Florida.[83] Collectively, these groups organized around issues as diverse as pesticide exposure, minimum wage violations, workplace safety, improved worker housing, the rights of guestworkers, and federal immigration policy.

In the years leading up to this book's publication, several new laws protecting farmworker rights have been passed, perhaps evidence of a new wave of attention to labor injustices in the food system. In 2019, after years of organizing and advocacy by the Workers' Center of Central New York, Rural Migrant Ministries, the New York State AFL-CIO, the New York Civil Liberties Union, and the Hispanic Federation, the New York state legislature passed the Farm Laborers Fair Labor Practices Act, which now awards farmworkers overtime pay when they work more than fifty-six hours a week (notably not more than forty hours a week, like most other US workers). This bill also included the right to collectively bargain in New York, which was also won in a lawsuit filed by the New York Civil Liberties Union on behalf of a farmworker, Crispin Hernandez, the Workers' Center of Central New York, and the Worker Justice Center of New York, in a state supreme court case just before the bill's passage.

Following legislative changes in New York, in 2021, two more states signed farmworker labor bills in law. Washington State passed State Bill (SB) 5172, which creates overtime protections for agricultural workers specifically. In Colorado, a more comprehensive bill, SB 21-087, was passed that removes long-standing regulations exempting farm laborers from state minimum wage laws, the right to unionize, and overtime pay. The law also bans the use of a short-handled hoe, which is known to cause debilitating back problems; California, Arizona, New Mexico, and Texas had previously banned the tool. In 2022, California approved additional farmworker legislation, making it easier for farmworkers to vote in a union election, after a decline in farmworker unionizing since they had gained the right in California in 1975.[84]

As the threat from extreme and dangerous temperatures due to climate change is growing, state legislation regarding heat exposure has been increasingly prioritized by organizers and politicians in recent years. There are many known risks of heat exposure, including dehydration, chronic kidney disease, poor pregnancy health and increased risk of miscarriage and stillbirths, and death. Tragically, there is currently no enforceable federal heat safety standard, despite advocates calling for federal reforms and regulations for the past decade.[85] The consumer protection organization Public Citizen petitioned the Occupational Safety and Health Administration (OSHA) and released public statements to the Biden administration as part of its campaign to call on the federal government to protect workers from extreme heat. As noted in its report, "Extreme Heat and Unprotected Workers," increasing temperatures from climate change will put hundreds of thousands of workers at risk: "By 2050, more than 600,000 agriculture and construction workers will work at least one-fourth of the year in dangerous heat conditions."[86] More recently, in March 2021, the Asunción Valdivia Heat Illness and Fatality Prevention Act was introduced in Congress by House and Senate Democrats, named in honor of Asunción Valdivia, a California farmworker who died of heatstroke in 2004. As we write this, the bill is yet to be voted on.

While workers are still waiting on federal regulation, some states have taken decisive action to mitigate exposure to increasing heat and smoke for farmworkers and other outdoor laborers. In 2006, two years after Asunción Valdivia's death, California passed the nation's first heat standard to protect outdoor workers, the California Heat Illness Prevention Standard. Under this law, when temperatures rise above 80 degrees, employers are required to provide training, water, and shade for workers who are outdoors. Following another worker's death from heat in 2021, during an especially dangerous summer of extreme heat and exposure to wildfire smoke, both Oregon and Washington passed emergency heat regulations for farms, including temporary measures for training, water, and cooling breaks. In Oregon, state regulators have adopted two distinct laws, one to address exposure to wildfire smoke while working and the other related to high heat in farmworker housing.[87]

Another timely issue for farmworkers is the mobilization to both expand and regulate the H-2A agricultural guest worker program. Currently, the program is only available to seasonal operators. Yet the farm lobby, especially industrial dairy producers, have been pushing for new legislation that would allow more farmers to take part in the program. A proposed expansion to include year-round workers was central to the Farm Workforce Modernization Act (FWMA) introduced in 2021, which garnered bipartisan support in the House of Representatives. This act was defeated in the Senate in 2022, after being folded into the Affordable and Secure Food Act. While some farm labor groups like the UFW were in strong support of the FWMA, other groups, including the Food Chain Workers Alliance, Familias Unidas por la Justicia, Community to Community, and Migrant Justice, were staunchly opposed to expanding a program they viewed as exploitative and a superficial solution to a much deeper problem and where promises of a "path to citizenship" were largely hollow.[88]

While the FWMA ultimately failed, expanding and reforming agricultural guest worker programs has been debated by US legislators for years. There have been ongoing attempts to reform the H-2A program on the federal level, but these efforts have been focused mostly on growing the program via bipartisan legislation in response to industry requests.[89] Organizers have had some success in improving protections for workers, yet again, these have been largely at the state level. For example, in Washington State, the advocacy group Community to Community worked tirelessly to pass SB 5438, which funded an office to monitor the labor, housing, and safety requirements for farms engaged in the H-2A program, the first of its kind to create independent oversight of the program.[90] State-level initiatives like this one may be the best short-term approach to protecting agricultural guest workers if nationwide reform remains elusive.

There are additional ongoing efforts to pass legislation challenging the federal exemptions for farmworkers, which we can only hope will continue to succeed. In Massachusetts, a bill called the Fairness for Farmworkers Act was introduced in both state houses in 2021, raising the regular state minimum wage from its current rate of $8 per hour and providing overtime pay after fifty-five hours of work and one day of rest a week, neither of which is currently required.[91] At the time of writing, it has not been passed. A federal bill with the same name was introduced in Congress in 2021 and reintroduced in 2023 by Senator Alex Padilla (D-CA) and Representative Raúl Grijalva (D-AZ) that also repeals the exemption from overtime pay for farmworkers and any remaining minimum wage exceptions nationally.[92] It has never been voted on.

Many farmworkers are socially isolated even from their local communities in the United States, making it harder for them to communicate, organize, and even know their legal rights. Given that such a large proportion of the agricultural workforce is undocumented, there is fear among this population of speaking up or organizing when laws are violated or practices do not meet basic regulations. As we have seen in the history of the UFW and the evolving views of Chavez, the divisions between US-born and naturalized farmworkers, guest workers, and undocumented farmworkers have been barriers to deep forms of solidarity and collective action.[93]

Currently the unionization rates for farmworkers, even in states with legal protection, remain extremely low. Sadly, there have been attempts to limit the power of unions in states where collective bargaining is legal. A key provision of CALRA that allowed union organizers to enter places of work to organize farmworkers was struck down by the US Supreme Court in 2021. This allowance was included in California law precisely because it was the only practical way to organize farmworkers, who are a difficult to reach and often migratory population.[94]

In all these cases, farmworkers, advocates, and community organizers have spent years mobilizing, protesting, and rallying to bring attention to the unequal system of farmworker labor laws and the historical lack of worker protections in the agricultural industry. Local and national community-based groups such as the Workers' Center of Central New York, Community to Community in Washington State, and the Colorado Farmworkers' Rights Coalition, among others, have worked to bring farmworkers' rights to the attention of both the broader population and policy makers. The examples of mobilizations and legislation we describe in this section largely address farmworker conditions by addressing power at the farm level, by organizing and lobbying for policies directed at farmers. While these efforts are necessary, as we discuss throughout this book, profits and power in the food system are concentrated at the top, not at the farm level, and there are limits to how much farmers can adjust their practices and pay structures given their own financial insecurity. In the next section, we look at approaches that organize up the food chain, through WSR programs and more broadly based food system campaigns.

WORKER ORGANIZING UP THE FOOD CHAIN

Traditional models for improving the working and living conditions of farm-workers, including unions and policy making, have been successful in many respects, but unions can only organize in the states where they are legally allowed, and the law is only as strong as its enforcement. Without the funding and political will to enforce such standards, the power of these traditional models remains limited, and other models have developed alongside them or in their stead. *Worker centers* are nonprofit, community-based organizations that provide support and advocacy for low wage workers who are not already part of a formal union, whereas *third-party certification* is a process whereby an independent organization certifies the stated quality and standards of a product, such as labor standards. Worker centers and third-party certification programs are filling the gap where federal reform has fallen short and the traditional union model is not the best or most appropriate model for organizing.

We opened this chapter with a discussion of the success of the CIW Campaign for Fair Food, whose worker-organizers have catalyzed a growing network of labor organizations committed to the WSR model. The CIW was formed in 1993, when a small group of workers began weekly meetings in response to rampant labor abuses and violations in Florida's tomato fields. Using organizing tactics of widespread work stoppage, a well-publicized hunger strike, and a 234-mile march across Florida, these workers followed in the footsteps of many farmworkers before them, attempting to structurally address low wages and abusive conditions. However, unlike other farm-worker movements in US history that have largely focused their efforts on unionization, the CIW pinpoints who holds the most money and power in our industrialized food system. Rather than follow the dollar only to the farm level, farmworkers and organizers in the CIW recognized that large-scale retailers and restaurants are making much more of the food dollar than the farmers who directly employ them.

FIGURE 5. Tomato Pickers and Allies of the Coalition of Immokalee Workers Urge Wendy's to Join Their Award-Winning Farmworker-Led Human Rights Initiative, the Fair Food Program. Sarasota, Florida, 2018. Vera Chang, photographer.

For the past few decades, farmworker organizers at the CIW have worked with students and other food movement activists to pressure multibillion-dollar food retail and restaurant corporations to sign on to the Fair Food agreement, a hallmark of the WSR approach. These forms of solidarity are beautifully illustrated in the 2014 documentary *Food Chains* and more recently in the 2023 documentary *Food, Inc. 2*. To date, fourteen corporations have signed on to the Fair Food agreement, including Walmart, McDonald's, Burger King, Subway, Sodexo, and Whole Foods, with three additional consumer packaged goods (CPG) companies signing on. These companies promise to purchase produce only from growers that are engaged in the Fair Food Program, which entails oversight by a third party to ensure humane treatment of workers, including monitoring of sexual harassment violations, proper human resources communications, regular and predictable hours, and basic rights such as water and work breaks. The program also guarantees a price premium paid to workers, which comes from the profits of the chain retailers and restaurants rather than the farmers. This WSR model centers the priorities and needs of workers and diverges from corporate social responsibility, which are typically designed by corporate executives rather than workers on the front line.

The CIW's success depends in part on the mobilization of consumers, college students in particular, and protesting and boycotting chain restaurants and retailers that refuse to sign on to the Fair Food agreement. In doing so, the organization has drawn on the strategies but not necessarily the organizational structure of previous farmworker organizing groups, such as the UFW on the West Coast and the FLOC of the AFL-CIO in the Southeast and Midwest. Despite their differing structures and organizing tactics, these farmworker-led organizations have partnered with nonworker activists, mobilizing people to act beyond their consumer choices.

Despite the often-grim realities confronting farmworkers, there are reasons for optimism thanks to this activism and the effective organizing within the farmworker justice movement. In a *Civil Eats* piece examining the influence of the #MeToo movement on farmworker organizing, Vera Chang shows how one of the most important accomplishments of the CIW has been to tackle sexual violence in the field head-on.[95] With a combination of education, monitoring, and enforcement, the Fair Food Program and the CIW have provided fertile ground for both preventing and addressing sexual violence in the workplace. In addition, according to the CIW, as of 2024, the program has provided more than 1,200 worker-to-worker educational sessions, has fielded more than 3,900 complaints to the Fair Food Hotline, and has distributed more than $44 million of premiums paid by participating buyers.[96] As of a 2021 report, they have recovered nearly $500,000 in stolen wages.[97]

As the CIW has expanded its influence, the development of the WSR network is an inspiring example of worker solidarity across sectors as the network includes both food and farmworkers and those in other industries, such as garment production. One member of the WSR network, Migrant Justice, has benefited from a close collaborative relationship with the CIW as it has drawn heavily on the Fair Food Program and its principles to develop the Milk with Dignity (MD) program with dairy farms in the northeastern United States. In October 2017, Ben and Jerry's signed on to the MD program after years of worker organizing. As of 2024, sixty-five farms in Vermont and New York supplying Ben and Jerry's with milk are abiding by a farmworker-authored code of conduct. More recently, Migrant Justice has expanded its organizing to the retail sector, calling for the supermarket chain Hannaford to join the MD program as well. In designing the MD program with farmworkers at the center, Migrant Justice has regularly visited Immokalee and hosted worker organizers from the CIW in Vermont, and there is little doubt that the successful campaign bringing Ben and Jerry's (which is owned by Unilever) into the MD program was due in part to the solidarity between the two organizations.

These contemporary initiatives that address fair labor standards in the United States also include consumer-based domestic labor certification schemes such as the Agricultural Justice Project and the Domestic Fair Trade Working Group. They allow consumers to purchase their way into a supposedly more ethical food system. Yet, as the labor scholars Sandy Brown and Christy Getz argue, in these initiatives laborers become another standard to be consumed rather than being regarded as participants in achieving justice.[98] Broader farmworker movements and unionization efforts are not incorporated in these schemes, and therefore third-party certification, no matter how well meaning, can thwart efforts to create structural changes to the social relations of production.[99]

CONCLUSION: ENDING AGRICULTURAL LABOR EXCEPTIONALISM

In this chapter, we examined the policies and processes that have perpetuated the exploitation of farmworkers in the United States from the nation's founding to the present day. By analyzing how these processes and policies are both shaped by and serve to extend agricultural exceptionalism, we showed how structural violence against farmworkers is anything but accidental. Ultimately, these dynamics benefit industrial agriculture at the expense of the well-being and the lives of vulnerable workers. While significant, laws protecting farmworker rights have been passed in a piecemeal manner, with variations in agricultural labor regulations by state. Also notable is that these laws merely bring farmworkers up to the same basic level of rights and protections as those of nearly all other workers in the United States. In some cases, like overtime pay, new legislation still does not match standards for other workers. Though there are wins for workers, millions of farmworkers across the country still do not have certain basic rights. Despite state-level progress, federal legislation is still needed for comprehensive national protections of agricultural workers.

The exclusion of farmworkers from protected unionization has led to a long-standing absence of agricultural interests in traditional food labor organizing. In addition, given the racialized history of farm labor, especially in the South and the West, some labor unions were averse to including work-ers based on racial difference. Although there were early efforts to coordinate unionizing efforts across food sectors, such as field work and processing in canneries, ultimately farmworkers were left behind in unionization efforts.[100] As we argue throughout this book, if coordinated change is going to be made throughout the food system, farmworkers must be seen as colleagues and comrades with workers in other sectors, and labor organizers must find ways to incorporate farmworkers in their strategies and campaigns.

For meaningful and lasting transformations for workers in the fields, structural change is necessary. As the final section of this chapter emphasizes, there is tremendous potential in looking up the food chain. This approach enables stronger alliances of food worker organizations that embrace and include farmworkers with other food laborers, such as more traditional unions and other public facing organizations. This also means coming to terms with the violent histories of racism, classism, and sexism in agriculture and pushing for an emancipatory future of farming where all who produce our food are recognized for their skills, knowledge, and contributions to our food system.

TWO

Deskilling in the Assembly Line and on the Factory Floor

I've been in the meat industry since I was fifteen years old. First as a meat cutter, and I went into meat inspection for thirty-two years, and I'm back in the meat industry now operating a facility in Ferrisburgh, Vermont. It's a slaughter and processing facility, where we process animals for the owners' own use, or many of them now are selling it. I tell people that I got a high school credit for skipping school because I was cutting meat and my homeroom teacher took the day off and he came in and saw me cutting and told me to come to his office the next day, and I did and I was able to get a high school credit for the cutting after he had watched what it was I could do. So that's what got me started, and I enjoyed it very much. That gave me the opportunity to get into meat inspection. I had some challenges lifting, so as an inspector, those challenges went away. I was able to stay with the meat industry, and where I am now, I have employees to do all of that, and we've gotten new equipment to make the least amount of lifting possible. So that's kind of where I get started and where I am.

When COVID hit and the big plants were being shut down, because of the congestion—all of the people. We had a small plant, but they were so congested that they infected the vast majority of the people that were working in those plants. So our business grew during that time because people didn't want to be buying product that was weeks away or something that had been started a couple of weeks before. The people who were providing the service, the retail service part of what we do, they did quite well during that time. So by us modernizing and getting the equipment that we need, and to get the people in here means that we can keep a lot of these animals right here, and people can consume them, whether it be people who live here or people that visit here. There's some real value in that.

STEVEN, *owner-operator,*
small-scale livestock processing facility

THE SIZE OF THE PROCESSING facility that Steven manages in a rural Vermont town is tiny in comparison to the plants that have come to dominate the US meat and poultry industry. As he describes, plants run by corporate giants like Tyson, Smithfield, Perdue, and ConAgra faced unprecedented challenges during the early days of the COVID-19 pandemic, but shutdowns were only temporary. In a 2020 blog post titled, *Feeding the Nation and Keeping Our Team Members Healthy*, then board chairman of Tyson Foods, John Tyson, declared, "We have a responsibility to feed our country. It is as essential as healthcare. This is a challenge that should not be ignored. Our plants must remain operational so that we can supply food to our families in America."[1] Just days later, President Donald Trump signed Executive Order 13917, which forced meatpacking plants to remain open despite growing concerns about the increased risks of their employees contracting COVID, the very same risks that Steven describes above. Using authority under the Defense Production Act, this order situated meat and poultry processing facilities among the nation's "critical infrastructure," categorizing their workers as essential as those working in nuclear facilities, emergency services, and healthcare. Most of the critical infrastructure of meat and poultry processing in the United States takes place at enormous scales, far larger than the small facility that Steven operates in rural Vermont. In industrialized countries like the United States, the supply chain links that are particularly vulnerable in times of crisis are those that are heavily labor dependent, like meat processing.[2]

This chapter traces the history and legacies of scientific management in food processing and examines the consequences of the assembly line on worker skill, health, and well-being, with a focus on the meat and poultry industry. We argue that scientific management principles and Fordist models of production have enabled the purposeful *deskilling* of workers, the process by which employers reduce the necessary skilled or technical work within an industry. This pattern has produced a vulnerable workforce in food processing. Henry Ford, founder of Ford Motor Company, found inspiration for his assembly line in the "disassembly lines" of midwestern meat processing facilities and then replicated that system for the purpose of automobile manufacturing. In an assembly line, each worker has a specific and monotonous production task that is performed as components of the final product move along a mechanized conveyor belt. These tasks are simplified and easy to learn, but the workers completing them are often viewed as both replaceable and disposable. Yet without their labor our food system comes to a grinding halt.

Deskilling is the core ingredient in Fordist models of production and results from the hyperspecialization of tasks in industrialized labor systems wherein workers perform one primary task repeatedly, typically while remaining stationary and often while engaging with some kind of machinery. It also refers to the broader political, economic, and social shifts from artisan or craft production to an overall increase in the number of workers performing "unskilled" jobs in any given economy. We focus on the ways that deskilling relates to decreasing actual wages and deepening constraints on worker skill and labor power. In this chapter and others, we take care to problematize the terms "skilled" and "unskilled" as these categories typically do not reflect the actual skills of the worker but rather the valuing of the work that is being performed and the tasks that are assigned by management. As Philip Howard, a rural sociologist specializing in food systems, observes, "Deskilling increases control for capitalists but makes us more dependent upon them by eroding our knowledge and abilities."[3]

According to BLS data, in 2023, 879,490 frontline workers were employed in food processing in the United States, roughly 5.2% of paid workers in the food system who work outside the home.[4] These frontline processing workers earn a mere $18.59 an hour, or a median annual wage of $38,667.[5] Approximately 11.7% of processing workers are covered by a union contract. For some of the most dangerous work in the food system, this compensation is abysmal and typically has few if any benefits like comprehensive health insurance, paid time off, or retirement.

The labor that occurs within food processing is diverse, ranging from slaughtering animals to pasteurization, fermentation, chopping, grinding, grating, and parboiling. Food processing is typically divided into three stages: primary, secondary, and tertiary. Primary processing is the step of taking raw agricultural products and transforming them into something that can eventually be eaten. In the case of plant-based foods, this includes drying, threshing, winnowing/shelling, and milling. For poultry, meat, and fish, this includes stunning and slaughter, deboning, evisceration, and butchering. Secondary food processing is the step of taking the resulting ingredients from primary processing and transforming them into food and drink that is ready to consume, something as straightforward as baking a loaf of bread, culturing cheese, or fermenting beer. Tertiary processing is typically understood as the commercialized and industrialized phase of processing, responsible for foods as complex and far from nature as Flamin' Hot Doritos, Hot Pockets, and microwavable TV dinners. The Fordist model of production has

FRONTLINE WORKERS IN FOOD PROCESSING, 2023

Total Employment:
879,490 workers

Union Density:
11.7% coverage, 10.27% membership

Mean Hourly Wage:
$18.59

Mean Annual Wage:
$38,666.67

Data Source: Occupational Employment and Wage Survey (OEWS), US Bureau of Labor Statistics

influenced each of these stages, and Ford himself would likely marvel at the speed and efficiency that now dominate industrial food factories.

Tertiary processing is also the stage where ultraprocessed foods are created, which should be distinguished from other, more minimally processed foods. Ultraprocessed foods often contain ingredients like high fructose corn syrup and hydrogenated oils and, as Howard notes, "are nearly impossible to make in your own kitchen."[6] These ingredients, and the foods that contain them, are widely considered detrimental to human health, whereas foods that are processed using primary and secondary means are typically seen as having fewer negative health consequences. Processed foods often get a bad rap for being inherently unhealthy, but it is important to distinguish between the different forms of processing. Further, food processing is a necessary step in making food edible, and the labor it demands must happen somewhere, whether in the local bakery, a Wonder Bread factory, or a family's kitchen. The production of highly processed foods has created specialized technical professions often filled by people with advanced scientific degrees and laboratory experience, but these positions are far from the frontline workers who are the subject of this book.

We begin by discussing the histories of scientific management and how this approach laid the groundwork for the assembly line model and the associated deskilling of the workforce. Next, we turn to the specific ways that deskilling produces a vulnerable workforce, a vulnerability that builds on intersectional inequalities that are pervasive across the food system. We then analyze how vulnerability and exploitation in this sector interacts with racism, sexism, and classism and how such vulnerabilities exacerbated the extreme dangers of the COVID-19 pandemic for this group of frontline workers. While there are countless areas of food processing to examine, we focus on meat and poultry processing given the scope and depth of research on this part of the food system and the extreme vulnerabilities that exist for modern-day workers in these industries. We conclude the chapter by highlighting the continued importance of labor organizing and unionization within food processing and new forms of worker power that are on the horizon in this sector of the food system.

THE LEGACY OF TAYLORISM AND FORDISM IN FOOD PROCESSING

It is difficult to imagine the mass production of food in our contemporary food system without the assembly line. The development of the assembly line model that has come to dominate factory production was strongly influenced by Frederick Taylor's theories of scientific management, called *Taylorism* by scholars of commodity production. A mechanical engineer by training, Taylor developed scientific methods of studying workplace efficiency, including the use of time and motion studies that placed heavy emphasis on developing strong management and compliant workers. Born into a family of considerable means, his disdain for the working class was clear, as evident in his declaration, "Hardly a competent workman can be found who does not devote a considerable amount of time to studying just how slowly he can work and still convince his employer that he is going at a good pace."[7]

The widening gulf of power and reinforced hierarchies that developed between supervisor and worker on the factory floor was a natural outgrowth of Taylor's beliefs that some workers are better suited for management because of their intellect and others are better suited for manual labor because of their less mentally intensive capabilities and motivations. His views on worker compensation are important in this regard: he believed that pay is the ultimate motivator for manual laborers and that "a fair day's pay for a fair day's work" should be the overriding practice for allocating wages. Of course, the determination of what is fair is decided not by the worker but by capitalism's push for profitability at all costs. Drawing on a critical reading of both Taylor and Karl Marx, the agroecologist and sociologist Devon Peña observes:

Taylorism is not so much a system of technological innovations as it is a series of engineering methods critical in establishing managerial monopoly over the knowledge base. Workers are effectively stripped of responsibility for mental tasks. The intent is that workers follow the pace and content of unskilled manual labor as defined and designed a priori by management. The principle of absolute managerial control over the knowledge base corresponds with the separation of mental and manual labor that Marx criticized some sixty years before Taylor outlined his plan for the further deskilling of labor.[8]

The separation of mental from manual labor and the different ways society values each kind of work undergird a false dichotomy of unskilled versus skilled labor and divert attention from the intentional management decisions that result in a precarious and replaceable workforce. We see this distinction, and the inequities that result from it, across the food system, but they are particularly visible in the slaughterhouse, as we discuss below.

Henry Ford was influenced by Taylor's scientific management work and by the Chicago meatpacking plants he visited early in his career. While Ford was not the first to realize the potential of the assembly line, his name has become synonymous with this approach to production. *Fordism*, a term coined by the Italian political philosopher and theorist Antonio Gramsci, describes the manufacturing technology of the assembly line model and an ideology motivating advanced capitalism and the drive toward efficiency and standardization. Whether the final product is a Model T or a boneless skinless chicken breast, the approach to labor is the same: shuttle the component parts along a belt or some kind of pulley system while stationary workers complete the same tasks repeatedly, at a pace not set by themselves but by the machine.

The perfected assembly line model would go on to revolutionize the production of countless goods, edible and otherwise.[9] The mass production enabled by the assembly line was crucial to military efforts, and by the end of World War I, assembly lines were becoming a dominant mode of production. Fordism and the assembly line model have been adopted not only in food processing, but across the broader food system, in the service industry in particular. The adoption of the assembly line and the ideals of efficiency and standardization in spaces such as fast-food kitchens has been called the *McDonaldization* of food preparation and service (see below).[10] While recent years have seen an increase in automation in the preparation of fast food, the widespread adoption of the assembly line and principles of standardization is a key factor in the explosion of fast-food chains like McDonald's in the second half of the twentieth century.

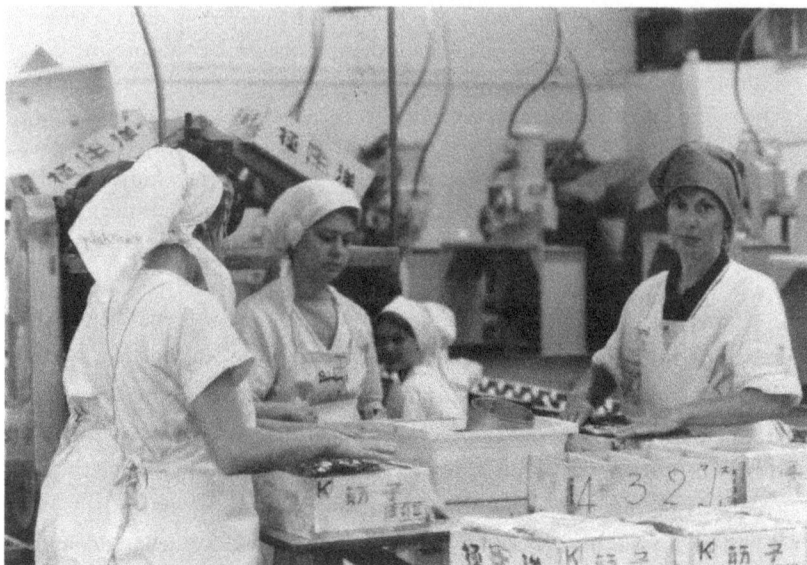

FIGURE 6. Female workers preparing Brite stackers shrink wrapping cans for shipping at NEFCO-Fidalgo packing plants in Ketchikan, Alaska, 1975. Photographer unknown. University of Washington Libraries, Special Collections, PH Coll 1044.151.

The assembly line is arguably one of the most influential technologies that has pushed human societies toward mass production and thereby mass consumption. Some scholars claim that we would not be able to feed the current world population without the assembly line and the industrial food system it supports. And yet the social, embodied, and ecological consequences of both the technology and the ideology are substantial. Henry Ford's desire for his employees to also be loyal consumers was one motivation for the relatively higher wages he paid. In 1914, he raised hourly wages at his Detroit plant to $5 an hour, roughly double what other automobile manufacturers were paying at the time. Simultaneously, he reduced the workday from nine to eight hours.[11] Unfortunately, the consequences of contemporary assembly line production are far more brutal than Ford might have imagined.

Although much has been said about Ford's supposed benevolence and his sense of social responsibility, his decisions were calculated moves to retain employees in an increasingly competitive industry and a response to the human limits of engaging in such monotonous and alienating work for so many hours at a time. At the same time, the speed of the line itself has remained a critical point of power and control, with owners and managers often pushing for the line to speed up and workers exerting the little control they typically have by slowing it down or walking out altogether. The wildcat strikes that occurred during Ford's lifetime at numerous factories underscore the considerable unrest that prevailed among Ford workers.[12] The adoption of the Ford model, including the purposeful manipulation of both skill and the rate of production, has resulted in a socially and economically vulnerable workforce in the food system.

DESKILLING THE ASSEMBLY LINE AND THE PRODUCTION OF VULNERABILITY

The term "deskilling" has come to mean many things when referring to the changes in worker capacities and the types of labor in the food system. While food processing takes place both inside and outside the home, here we discuss the work that occurs outside the home. In the food processing sector, deskilling makes workers more replaceable because of the ease with which they are trained to take on specialized tasks. If a worker is sick or quits, management can treat them as disposable or replaceable, like a cog in a wheel. Workers designated "unskilled" earn lower wages, receive fewer benefits, and are less likely to benefit from union protections. Further, deskilling can lead to an ever-shifting workforce, which can make it even more difficult to organize around poor working conditions. The vulnerabilities that food processing workers experience today are a result of decades of deskilling. The COVID-19 pandemic has been a critical moment where this vulnerability has become evident to the mainstream consumer.

In tracing some of the main theoretical approaches to understanding skill, the sociologist Paul Attewell notes the importance of connecting the categories of skill with questions of worker control and autonomy: "For Marx and Braverman, a craft worker decides how to accomplish a particular piece of work, chooses the appropriate tools and procedures, and is self-directed in the work. This contrasts, with, say a machine operator, who is told what to do, is given instructions, tools, or procedures on how to do it, and is overseen by management."[13] There has been a renewal of artisanal and craft production in the US food system, but the result has often been high-end and costly products like artisan cheese, craft beer, and other value-added products that are not widely accessible to the average consumer.[14] These craft products, while revered by many consumers with money to spend, have not displaced their more processed counterparts, and most food processing still happens at the industrial level, where there are rigid divisions between workers and management. It is also important to acknowledge that even in the processing of "craft" products, the raw materials used are often still grown on farms where agricultural labor remains devalued and exploited.[15]

In a particularly poignant example of deskilling in meat processing, the political scientist Timothy Pachirat details an extensive list of tasks, 121 to be exact, that are completed as a cow is processed on the kill floor.[16] Based on ethnographic research conducted in a slaughterhouse in Omaha, Nebraska, during which Pachirat started as a liver hanger and ended up in quality control, his work offers deep insight into the tasks that are necessary to transform a live cow into packages of specific cuts and whole organs. These tasks, from the cattle driver to the tail ripper to the pizzle remover to the kidney dropper, cut across the boundary of the "clean side" and the "dirty side" of the kill floor. As Pachirat notes, the need to prevent cross-contamination results in the segregation of workers, whereby "dirty men" have their own spaces to shower, use the restroom, and eat lunch, separate from those of the "clean men." Notably absent are spaces for the women working in this slaughterhouse.

Deskilling is a necessary ingredient in assembly line production and increasing the speed at which goods are produced. The speed of the line has significant implications for both the rate of production and the risk of injury and exhaustion for workers, in addition to disease exposure, as described above. This hyperspecialization and emphasis on speed results in dangerous workplaces, and the impacts of the assembly line on worker well-being include both physical and emotional or mental health concerns. As the disability scholars Kelly Somers and Karen Soldatic critique in their analysis of disability and disabling processes among both people and animals involved in food work, the push toward productivity linked to neoliberalist capitalism creates expendable "nonproductive" bodies as a result of injury and death.[17]

Food processing workers commonly experience temporary and permanent disabilities caused by repetitive stress injuries, lacerations and burns, strains and sprains, overexertion, dismemberment and amputations, sexual violence and harassment, emotional trauma and numbing connected to witnessing and participating in animal deaths, exposure to allergens and dangerous chemicals, and exposure to infectious diseases. Performing forceful tasks with the hands, wrists, and arms can result in carpal tunnel syndrome, tendonitis, and tears in ligaments and tendons. According to BLS data from 2021, the total

FIGURE 7. Migrant Workers Process Green Peppers on Uesugi Farms, Gilroy, California, 2013. Bob Nichols, photographer. United States Department of Agriculture.

recordable cases of nonfatal injuries and illnesses across all industries was 2.9 per 100 full-time workers and the average rate of incidence for all food manufacturing workers was 4.8. For workers in animal slaughtering, the rate was more than double (5.9) the overall average, and for seafood preparation and packaging, it was even higher (6.5). That same year, of the total 5,190 workplace fatalities recorded, 57 were in food manufacturing.[18]

For Latinx poultry processing workers, the prevalence of carpal tunnel syndrome can be as high as 2.5 times the rate experienced by other manual laborers.[19] Repetitive stress injuries are also common among seafood processing workers.[20] Standing for long periods and bending repeatedly can cause bursitis and muscle pain. Lifting and moving heavy objects can result in hernias and back problems. While ergonomic interventions and better workplace safety training are both helpful in mitigating some of these problems, they cannot eliminate them. Some employers have turned to Pre-Employment Physical Ability testing, which requires potential employees to demonstrate their abilities to do the work required of them, often in an off-site location like a doctor's office. However, many have charged that these tests disproportionately affect the likelihood of women being hired for jobs that are physically demanding.[21] In a 2022 *Civil Eats* exposé, the growing use of on-site care systems in Tyson Foods plants is linked to efforts to downplay the rates of injuries that might alert OSHA interventions and reports of violations. As the authors note, "The model is emblematic of others in the meatpacking and poultry industries, designed to streamline efficiency, cut costs, and reduce liability, practices that are being emulated by animal feeding operations farther down the supply chain. Crucially, the on-site nursing model also reduces hospital trips and doctor visits that would otherwise trigger mandatory reporting to OSHA."[22]

Less visible than the embodied injuries experienced by processing workers but just as detrimental to health are the psychosocial impacts of assembly line work on worker well-being. The very process of deskilling is detrimental to worker mental and emotional health and is likely to worsen with increased automation and reliance on robotic technologies in the future.[23] Being an active witness and participant in industrial animal slaughter at such an intense scale has also been linked to significant psychological impacts for workers. In a systematic review of fourteen studies addressing the psychological impacts of slaughterhouse labor, Jessica Slade and Emma Alleyne show that slaughterhouse workers have lower levels of psychological well-being compared to control groups. Researchers documented that slaughterhouse workers face increased rates of depression (up to five times the rates of the general population), anxiety, and varying levels of trauma, shock, guilt, and shame.[24] Slaughterhouse workers also commonly demonstrate increased anger and hostility, and one study notably demonstrated higher aggression scores among female employees than males. While it is impossible to trace the direct cases, it seems likely that these mental health issues stem both from doing the work of killing and the terrible working conditions in which the work takes place.

The unsafe pace of work also raises important questions about how workers physically and mentally keep up with the speed required of them. Beyond the legal but addictive substances like caffeine and sugar, some scholars have claimed that slaughterhouse workers resort to using methamphetamine, an illicit substance that is a highly addictive and dangerous stimulant.[25] While this may of course be true for individual workers or common in individual plants, the generalization of slaughterhouse workers as a group of cranked-up addicts is not only inaccurate, but potentially stigmatizing. Based on their analysis of eleven years of hospital admission data and information from annual livestock reports, Joshua A. Hendrix and Cindy Brooks Dollar show that the "meatpacking methamphetamine hypothesis" is only modestly supported and that as "the level of total livestock slaughter increases within a given state, so do hospital admissions for methamphetamines; likewise, states that produce more meat also tend to have more methamphetamine-related hospital admissions."[26] However, as the authors note, given that their study was based on state-level data, there is no way to confirm that this higher rate of drug use was found in the general public or among meatpacking workers. While substance abuse is of important concern for all workers, it is essential that we look at the systemic causes for addiction linked to occupation rather than stigmatize and criminalize those workers who resort to drugs to cope with crushing work demands.

The issue of line speeds and worker safety has been an ongoing point of contention between meat processors, unions, lawmakers, and federal offices like the US Department of Agriculture (USDA). In 2019, under the Trump administration, the USDA eliminated limits on line speeds for pork processing as part of a rule connected to the "New Swine Inspection Service." Critics, including the UFCW International union and the nonprofit consumer rights organization Public Citizen, charged that this change was made without considering the impacts it would have on worker safety and with outright disregard of the public comments posted for the proposed change. With the massive outbreaks of COVID-19 in food processing facilities the following year, the speed of the assembly line and the close quarters in which factory workers labor became even more dangerous.

It is also notable that US meatpacking workers were disproportionately exposed and affected by the COVID-19 pandemic as compared to other global regions. Most meatpacking facilities in the United States are immense. In June 2020, there were nine times more reported cases in US meatpacking plants than in European ones, even though the United States employs only a third more workers. European meatpacking plants are generally smaller and not as heavily consolidated, which allowed some plants to shut down while others continued in production without risking as large an effect on the food supply, thereby better protecting workers' health and safety. In addition, in comparison to the United States, where the average pork processing worker handles one thousand pigs per hour, in Europe workers process about four hundred an hour. Faster line speed and more jam-packed factory floors mean increased injury for workers and in the case of COVID-19, higher rates of infection and death.[27]

According to a report by the US House of Representatives Select Subcommittee on the Coronavirus Crisis, at least 59,000 cases of COVID-19 and 269 deaths in the first year of the pandemic could be traced to plants owned by five major meatpacking companies.[28] Others tracking these outbreaks estimated that these numbers could be as high as 86,000 cases, with 423 deaths.[29] An analysis of emails and other documents by investigative journalists revealed that top officials in the meat industry had long ignored warnings about the potential dangers of a global pandemic and tried to overrule health officials in handling worker safety conditions. In one particularly egregious case, it was alleged that a plant manager for Tyson Foods in Iowa organized a betting pool with other supervisors, wagering how many employees would contract COVID-19.[30] It was this kind of neglect and outright disregard for worker safety that prompted unlawful death lawsuits by the families of workers who contracted the virus and ultimately died.[31] This case shows the ease with which deskilling can result in the dehumanization of workers.

In April 2020 alone, the USDA approved fifteen new regulatory waivers to allow poultry plants to increase the maximum line speed. The National Employment Law Project found that all plants who received the waivers had a record of "severe injuries, OSHA citations and/or had experienced recent COVID outbreaks."[32] As the COVID-19 pandemic was intensifying, this disregard for essential workers was particularly reprehensible, as noted in a 2021 report by the Food Chain Workers Alliance: "The meat processing industry consistently pushes for increased line speeds, which subsequently increase the risk of injury and, during a pandemic, the risk of infection." In 2021, the removal of limits on line speed in pork processing was determined to be unlawful in a federal district court ruling under the Biden administration, and the USDA reverted to the previous maximum line speed.[33] The impossibility of socially distancing became a new source of danger. The assembly model means workers are packed into tight spaces on factory floors and when not at work, in trucks transporting them to and from the fields and in housing where they can only afford to live with other families due to their low wages.

However, the pandemic is just the most recent manifestation of the vulnerability to illness and injury that has long existed in meat and poultry processing. Punitive measures ensuring that meatpacking workers did not take sick days were common before the pandemic; it then follows that reports show that when workers started showing symptoms they were not excused from work unless they had a positive COVID-19 test. It seems sadly predictable then that a disproportionate number of COVID-19 mortalities in the

United States were tied to meat and poultry plants.[34] These deaths are a tragic reminder of the structural violence that pervades food labor, raising questions about whose lives matter and who is expendable. Moreover, the violence that food processing workers experienced during the pandemic is not new but rather an extension of decades of abuse and exploitation.[35]

Tragically, the dehumanizing impacts of deskilling are not only experienced by adult workers in the food system. In an extended 2023 exposé of child labor in the United States, the *New York Times* found an increasing trend of migrant children from Latin America working in food processing: packing cereals like Lucky Charms, tending ovens to make granola bars, and even in very dangerous worksites like Perdue chicken processing facilities. These children from Mexico and Central America, some as young as twelve, crossed the border alone and are living with sponsors who cannot afford to raise them. They are finding their way into twelve-hour factory shifts to survive, sacrificing their education and their well-being.[36] The fact that children are being allowed to work in these plants is a direct extension of the deskilling of food processing labor, where an untrained worker can enter the workforce and become both exploitable and disposable. As the journalists Hannah Dreier and Meridith Kohut report, young children are suffering from severe illness and often life-threatening injuries in these facilities and are working under falsified documents that conceal their true ages. This is another horrific example of the decreasing enforcement of labor safety and violation oversight more broadly.[37] Even more troubling, several state bills were introduced in 2023 and 2024 to lower the minimum working age in hazardous industries, including those in the food system. At the time of writing, most of these bills have not been approved, but in Iowa, new legislation allows children as young as fourteen to engage in "light assembly work," in violation of federal law.[38]

INTERSECTIONAL VIOLENCE IN MEAT AND POULTRY PROCESSING

The dangers of meat and poultry processing are not shared equally among all workers. While official statistics on injuries and illnesses demonstrate the severity of these dangers, it is necessary to dig deeper to understand how workers of color, women, and immigrants disproportionately experience them. Moreover, it is crucial to unpack the broader shifts in consumption

FIGURE 8. Pork Processing Worker at Triumph Foods, St. Joseph, Missouri, 2017. Preston Keres, photographer. United States Department of Agriculture.

that have led to a demand for cheap meat at the expense of food processing workers.

The anthropologist and public scholar Angela Steusse offers a nuanced intersectional analysis of the changing racial histories of the Deep South, focusing on the unprecedented in-migration of workers from Latin America to states like Mississippi.[39] Steusse shows how desegregation efforts linked to the civil rights movement brought growing numbers of African American workers into poultry processing plants in the mid- to late 1960s, replacing jobs in cotton fields and as cooks, domestic workers, and nannies. The refusal of northern consumers to buy chicken from segregated plants, "in combination with the poultry industry's expansion, the deskilling and intensification of its labor, the increasing availability of new manufacturing jobs to white workers, the waning opportunities for small Black farmers, and mounting political pressure, likely contributed to the widespread integration of Black workers into Mississippi poultry."[40] As Steusse notes, Black women made up a majority of these workers in the 1960s. However, over the past fifty years there have been seismic shifts in the demographics of workers in meat and poultry processing.

The voracious American appetite for chicken and processed chicken products like boneless skinless breasts and chicken nuggets since the 1980s has propelled the explosive growth of chicken processing in areas of the US South, fundamentally changing the racial demographics and the agricultural economies of this region. Based on his embedded ethnographic research at a chicken processing facility, the anthropologist Steve Striffler details the interethnic dynamics of the workers processing this exceptionally versatile animal. At this facility, the vast majority of workers were undocumented immigrants from Latin America (mostly Mexico and El Salvador), with Southeast Asians and Marshallese workers making up the remainder. Striffler, recalling an encounter between workers in the lunchroom (where, ironically, they were eating fried chicken purchased by a floor manager who had been pushing the line speed to unbearable limits), writes that a Mexican worker exclaimed, "Look we're all Mexicans here. Screwed-over Mexicans."[41] Despite the presence of Laotians, Salvadorans, Hondurans, Vietnamese, and Marshallese and Striffler (who is white), "Mexicans," as a category, collapses all of the ethnic differences among workers into one oppressed group. Despite this shared identification observed by Striffler, it remains crucial to understand the nuances of the racialized and gendered violence that is normalized in these kinds of facilities.

The need for better data on all meat and poultry workers, and the conditions in which they work, is particularly acute as undocumented workers, most of whom are incentivized and systematically recruited by labor contractors from their countries of origin, are targeted by Immigration and Customs Enforcement (ICE) raids.[42] In the case of a 2008 raid of a meatpacking plant in Postville, Iowa, nearly 400 workers from Mexico and Guatemala were detained and deported. Following this raid, the shocking and dangerous conditions in which these vulnerable workers toiled were made more visible, including fifteen-hour workdays, mental and physical abuse and intimidation, and dangerous equipment.[43]

In 2019, 700 workers were detained in raids at seven Mississippi chicken plants, the largest single-state immigration crackdown in US history. As Steusse observes, these raids create panic in the communities where they occur, though the social and economic effects extend far beyond the lives of the workers who are detained.[44] Rather than have any impact on immigration trends, they keep immigrant workers from raising concerns about working conditions and depress the wages and working conditions for US-born workers. ICE raids, which instill great fear in workers and communities, are a particularly visible manifestation of the intersectional violence that persists in food processing. They also underscore that demands for the rights of workers are inextricable from movements for immigrant rights, civil rights, and women's rights. As the labor scholar Carrie Freshour argues, during intensified crackdowns on undocumented workers, corporate giants in the poultry industry have often returned to employing US-born Black women. These women are vulnerable to the threat of a switch back to undocumented workers if and when anti-immigrant politics subside or to the offshoring of processing facilities altogether.[45]

Based on a close and critical reading of data from the US Department of Labor's Quarterly Census of Employment and Wages (QCEW) and the American Community Survey (ACS), Stuesse and Nathan T. Dollar, a sociologist and demographer, offer one of the most comprehensive and recent demographic portraits of laborers in meat and poultry processing.[46] Their report, which was written in response to the rampant spread of COVID-19 in meat and poultry processing facilities at the outset of the pandemic, is useful for understanding how the demographic trends stem from broader patterns of racialization that are shaped heavily by geography, migration of both people and industry, and the distinctive agricultural histories of various US regions.

While workers in both meat and poultry processing share a number of common concerns (dangerous work, substandard pay and benefits, and repetitive stress injuries, to name a few), there are notable differences in the demographic trends between workers in meat versus poultry: more women work in chicken processing (40.1%) than meat processing (32.2%), more workers in chicken processing are Black (37.2%) versus Latinx (26.5%), and more workers in meat processing (including beef and pork) are Latinx (47.7%) versus Black (12%). Stuesse and Dollar argue:

> These distinctions in the present moment build upon a past in which the historically more urban meatpacking industry has relied heavily on immigrant men of diverse backgrounds for over a century, a trend that continued as the industry shifted production to more rural areas. Meanwhile, in much of the rural South, poultry processing operated predominantly on the backs of local African American women and men (and poor white women) until the industry's more recent turn to immigrant labor.[47]

According to this report, as of 2018, there were nearly 500,000 workers in US meat and poultry processing, with the top five meatpacking states being Nebraska, Iowa, Texas, Kansas, and Illinois and the top five poultry processing states all located in the South: Georgia, Arkansas, North Carolina,

Alabama, and Mississippi. The majority of meat and poultry workers combined are male (64%) and people of color (65%), and most are not US citizens (70%). Roughly 37% (more than double the national rate for all workers) are immigrants and refugees—with Mexico being the most common country of origin for foreign-born meat and poultry processors. While the QCEW and ACS data are the best available, Stuesse and Dollar express their concern regarding the estimates for undocumented Latinx poultry workers, which they believe are seriously underestimated. In closing, they call for a more comprehensive, and potentially more accurate, survey of poultry and meat workers, similar to the National Agricultural Workers Survey (NAWS).

A 2022 *Civil Eats* story shares the experiences of "María," a Guatemalan worker whose job on the assembly line was to remove chicken wings, as many as thirty-four per minute.[48] After this work became debilitating, causing extreme pain in her hands, María repeatedly visited the on-site nurse, who reportedly had her ice her hands briefly and then asked her to return to work. These so-called first aid visits do not require OSHA reporting, and if employees seek medical care on their own, it is at their own cost. For immigrant workers, seeking care outside of what is provided by employers is extremely difficult given language barriers and lack of knowledge of available resources. It is also reported that nurses are often pressured to downplay the extent of injuries by plant managers. María's requests for a doctor referral were repeatedly denied, and it was only eight months after the initial complaint that Tyson approved the surgery finally recommended by a company doctor. Despite the doctor's orders to rest for several weeks after the surgery, María's supervisor asked her to return after just three days.

The experiences of María are not unique, and it is important to connect this kind of violence that plays out at the individual level with a broader understanding of the racialized, gendered, and class-based changes that have unfolded in the animal processing sector. As is the case in all sectors of our food system, women workers in meat and poultry processing face different challenges and opportunities than their male counterparts. Women make up just 36% of the meat industry workforce and are typically found working in the lowest-paying jobs with little opportunity for advancement. In this industry, women hold only 14% of board-level director roles and 5% of chief executive roles.[49] Immigrant women like María are extremely unlikely to advance into managerial or supervisory positions. As we discuss in the next section, despite the complex and intersectional forms of inequality and violence in meat and poultry processing, there is a long history of worker organizing that challenges the exploitative assembly line model that persists today.

THE CONTINUED IMPORTANCE OF WORKER ORGANIZING IN FOOD PROCESSING

In food processing and manufacturing, unions and worker-led organizations have been crucial in fighting for worker protections, documenting the racialized and gendered impacts of the pandemic on workers, and, tragically, prosecuting the wrongful deaths that have occurred because of managerial greed and negligence. Their organizing strategies have included actions like the deliberate slowing of assembly lines, walkouts, and strikes to challenge managerial control and secure better working conditions. As the historian Vicki Ruiz demonstrated in *Cannery Women, Cannery Lives*, unionization has historically provided a foundational strategy for women in the food processing sector. Through their organizing, women working in canneries in the early to mid-1900s successfully organized for benefits like maternity leave and daycare, important wins even if they were temporary.[50] Drawing on these kinds of histories, unions and other worker organizations utilized various approaches during the pandemic, from staging walkouts to filing lawsuits to organizing high-profile media campaigns and petitions.

In many of the southern antiunion states that endorse right-to-work policies, workers' centers are becoming a more common alternative to traditional unions. Because workers' centers are not unions, they do not function under the conditions (or protections) outlined in the National Labor Relations Act. They are therefore able to engage in tactics prohibited for unions, like business boycotts. An example of such an organization is Venceremos, a women-led worker organization in northwestern Arkansas that formed in 2019. Following the same WSR approach as the Coalition of Immokalee Workers and Migrant Justice, discussed in the previous chapter, Venceremos focuses on educating poultry workers at companies like Tyson and George's about their rights. Although Venceremos is a new organization, during the height of the pandemic, it fought for access to PPE, social distancing, and the right to quarantine and basic medical leave, as well as transparency about increasing line speeds and a living wage. It is partnering with the FCWA as part of the broader movement to address labor violations across the food chain.[51]

Food processing workers' centers are not limited to right-to-work states. One of the most successful food processing worker organizations today, the Brandworkers, is based in Queens, New York, and has organized food manufacturing workers, from bakers to cheese makers, throughout the New York City region since 2007. It regularly partners with food service and other workers' unions to build broader worker power in the food system, organizing strikes and rallies and community fund-raisers, as well as conducting research on the state of food workers in New York City. Through policy work and organizing, the Brandworkers emphasizes the need for good jobs as part of local food movements, intentionally drawing on the good food narrative and growing consumer interest in locally and regionally produced and processed food.[52]

Finally, another example of workers taking the lead in reforming the food processing sector is the creation of worker-owned cooperatives, which have a long history in the seafood industry.[53] In this sector of the food system, there is a unique combination of harvesting and processing tasks that happen on fishing vessels, and cooperatives allow fisherpeople to pool resources and engage in more collective forms of marine resource management. It is also an industry in which serious issues like forced labor persist, particularly in international waters.[54] Some of the strongest seafood cooperatives have expanded their operations to direct-to-consumer marketing and sales, cutting out middlemen to ensure that a greater percentage of the profit goes directly to the frontline seafood worker.

CONCLUSION: TAKING THE LONG VIEW

In this chapter, we provided an overview of the histories and expansion of scientific management and the assembly line model of food processing, showing how deskilling has created a replaceable workforce vulnerable to health and safety issues and poor wages and working conditions. Meat and poultry processing represents one of the most dangerous and exploitative areas of the food processing sector and therefore demands immediate and comprehensive reform. The exploitative conditions in food processing are intertwined with inequalities related to race, class, citizenship, and gender and perpetuate intersectional forms of violence against socially marginalized frontline workers. Moreover, these forms of violence cannot be separated from histories of racial capitalism, migration (both domestic and international) and dispossession that have an impact on all food sectors, albeit in uneven ways. For instance, the demographic shifts that have influenced labor patterns in chicken processing facilities in the US South must be understood in the context of slavery and sharecropping discussed in chapter 1.

More recently, the COVID-19 pandemic revealed both the vulnerabilities in our food supply chains and the essential contributions of workers to the food system. As we discussed in this chapter, the designation of food workers as essential often meant that they faced a disproportionate risk of contracting the disease, exacerbating decades of other injuries to worker safety and well-being. While the pandemic created an important opening for renewed attention to the need for worker organizing across the food system as a means of ensuring safe and productive workplaces, serious issues of worker abuse persist in the food processing sector.

If we take the long view and think about other moments when food processing workers have made headlines, we must acknowledge that these openings for worker justice are often short-lived and that public concern over the working conditions of those who process our food is typically fleeting. The organizers and activists currently calling for change in food processing build on a long history of labor resistance in this sector. New approaches that draw on food chain worker alliances and unions as well as nonunion organizing strategies will be key to ensuring that food processing workers are safe, well paid, and respected for the work they contribute to our increasingly interconnected food system.

THREE

Precarity and Deregulation
in the Warehouse and on
the Road

I work for Coca-Cola distribution and I've been working with
Coca-Cola for two and a half, three years. It's very interesting
work, I'm able to see a lot of grocery stores and understand the
diversity of how each one works. And it's an interesting job, especially with Coca-Cola, I'm able to transfer places that I never
thought a job could take me.... I took advantage of that situa-
tion and actually moved to Hawaii from Vermont and have been
living here for a few months now and the difference between
the two places is very interesting. Obviously, it's more expensive,
the food here, but there's not many big grocery stores. It's a lot
more small grocery stores. The distribution networks here are
very interesting too. There's not a lot of tractor trailers, it's more
cargo shipping containers, on the backs of trucks getting pulled
into grocery stores. And it's a very interesting environment, to
think that all the food, if not like 90% of the food, gets shipped
here.

The best thing about my work would be being able to be
outside and be in a fresher, open environment when it comes
to traveling between stores. Also not necessarily having somebody on your back the whole time you're working. It's like you
by yourself, when you get it done is when you go home. And
that's very rewarding to be your own boss in that sense. And
one thing I wish that would change ... walking into stores,
and not necessarily having that deep of a relationship with managers, because you're only in there like, once or twice every few
months, depending on if somebody calls out. So walking in,
you're essentially a stranger most of the time, unless you go there
a lot. And that's the nature of my position, specifically where I
run around and flex to different routes and such. So it's very solo
in the job, and you're by yourself a lot of times. There's pros and
cons to that.

ETHAN,
delivery driver for Coca-Cola

WAREHOUSE, TRANSPORTATION, AND DISTRIBUTION WORKERS are among the most often overlooked laborers in the food system, yet they are as central to the nation's food supply as any other sector. This part of the food chain involves the people who take finished food products from the point of processing to the point of sale in retail or service. Workers in this sector may be warehouse workers, truck drivers, or delivery people. Together, they maintain complex systems of logistics, coordination, and organization that ensure the continued movement of goods. They are the people who get food from place to place, who connect the various stages of the food supply chain. As we see in Ethan's story above, these supply chains that connect consumers with their food—and drinks—are often maintained by workers divided by considerable distances. Transportation workers frequently labor alone; the image of a (typically male) solo trucker like Ethan is both familiar and stereotypical. In other spaces, such as warehouses, hundreds if not thousands of workers of all races and genders labor side by side. These workers are often at the whim of giant corporations like Amazon and Walmart, which have reshaped how food moves around the country and the globe. Regardless of where and how distribution labor happens, the stability of the food system is dependent on the health and well-being of these workers.

In this chapter, we look at workers employed in the distribution and logistics sectors of the food chain, covering the shift in warehouse and distribution labor patterns to temporary contracts, the takeover of retail by logistics in the case of e-commerce, the deregulation of the trucking industry, and, finally, the increase in gig work in the food delivery sector. *Logistics* refers to the general management of product flow from the point of production to the point of consumption—in other words, the workers who connect the links of the chain.[1] *Deregulation*, meaning the removal of legal regulations or restrictions, has a strong pattern throughout this industry, affecting the legal bounds of how transportation and logistics workers can be treated. In looking at these various sectors, we explore the historical shift from a "traditional" labor force, with workers tied to a specific company or brand as employer, to a highly disjointed industry, dependent on third-party employers, temporary hiring agencies, and independent contract work. *Temporary hiring agencies* are businesses that connect workers to employers for temporary positions. We argue that this sector has been largely influenced by the global push toward neoliberal governance, which allows for deregulated and highly competitive workplaces, with disregard for workers' rights, wages, benefits, health, and safety. This contributes to a precarious workforce, one in which the traditional lines of employer and employee are becoming increasingly blurred. This *precarity*, where workers live in a state of persistent economic insecurity, makes worker organizing challenging and in some instances impossible.

The work involved in logistics and transportation is diverse, and just as the type of work in this sector varies, so do the working conditions. In addition to transportation, logistics work includes wholesale and warehouse workers in grocery, raw farm products, and beverages, as well as food storage and refrigeration. Some workers, such as truck owner-operators, are relatively highly paid compared to other food chain workers, although they work very long and challenging hours away from home. Others, including hand packagers in warehouses, labor in temporary and low-wage positions. According to data from the BLS, the transportation and warehousing of food products is performed by 3,608,930 frontline workers, or 21.2% of all paid food workers. The median hourly wage for frontline distribution and transportation workers in 2023 was $20.32, with a median annual wage of $42,271.[2] Of those workers, 6.98% had a union membership and 7.89% were covered by a union contract, regardless of membership. These figures do not include gig workers, who do most personal food delivery in today's economy and are typically considered *independent contractors*, working on a per assignment contract or freelance basis rather than as regular employees.

The neoliberal transition and related deregulation of corporations globally has been a part of the blurring of traditional employer-employee relationships. Over the past several decades, and most intensively since the 1980s, workers in transportation and logistics have been increasingly hired into temporary or contract work by third-party hiring agencies rather than the more traditional relationship between a company and a directly hired employee. Hiring employees by a third-party or contract agency allows companies to externalize the costs and responsibilities of labor, including following labor laws and meeting obligations to employees transporting their products to the point of sale. *Temporary workers*, who are paid for a specific period or a time-limited task, are employed workers like truck drivers, as well as workers hired through a third-party labor contractor. These workers are experiencing the effects of the deregulatory processes of neoliberalism in the food transportation and distribution industries whereby employers are not held directly accountable for compensating their workers as full-time employees. In addition, these workers are usually hired for a limited period in accordance with a particular task or job responsibility, as compared to the more long-term employment arrangements that workers in such industries have historically expected and benefited from. Another dimension of precarity in this sector involves gig workers, who are increasingly the dominant workforce in direct-to-consumer food delivery and access work via companies such as DoorDash and Uber Eats. They are considered independent contractors rather than employees of the food delivery app companies. This means they pay for their own transportation, are accountable if injured on the job, and are not entitled to benefits or protections such as sick leave, health insurance, or even minimum wage requirements.

We begin this chapter with a discussion of how the processes and policies of neoliberalism have reconfigured the food logistics sector. With increasing deregulation and workplace fissuring, neoliberalization has led to a precarious logistics workforce over the past four decades. *Fissuring*, the specific process of employers shedding direct responsibility for their employees, has been enabled by corporate deregulation and the weakening of protective labor laws in the United States over time.[3] While we focus on frontline workers in the United States, we note the ways that neoliberalism has occurred in tandem with broader changes spurred by globalization. After this theoretical and historical framing, we turn to an examination of the histories, working conditions, and forms of worker precarity in three areas of food logistics, warehouse, transportation, and the *gig economy*. Although the worker histories in these areas overlap, we have organized them by subsectors rather than a single timeline to follow the food as it moves from processing into retail. In each of these areas, technological changes such as AI and surveillance are rapidly affecting worker demographics, labor patterns, and the relationships between

FIGURE 9. Packard Trucks Transporting California "Sunkist" Oranges and Lemons from Los Angeles to London. Photographer unknown. Courtesy of the National Automotive History Collection, Detroit Public Library.

workers and management. Finally, we focus on organizing efforts and related policy changes that precarious logistics workers are mobilizing around, from unionization at warehouses and among truck drivers to the collectivization of gig workers who challenge their designation as independent contractors. As we demonstrate, logistics workers play an essential role in connecting the food chain. As workers increasingly form connections throughout this sector, they build a foundation for solidarity across the entire food system.

NEOLIBERALISM AND PRECARIOUS WORK IN THE LOGISTICS SECTOR

Political economists and labor scholars draw on the notion of neoliberalism to describe the international shift toward a market-led approach to social relations, which has had profound impacts on international food supply chains. This process began in earnest in the 1980s, when the United States and the United Kingdom, under Ronald Reagan and Margaret Thatcher, respectively, led a worldwide push to "roll back" state-led investments and regulations, including labor laws, environmental protections, and social service provisioning. In tandem, there was a "rolling out" of private forms of governance and *corporate consolidation*, or the merger of smaller companies into a larger one, increasing scales of operation. These patterns, which took global form through international trade agreements and lending institutions, led to an increase in worker precarity and insecurity on a transnational scale.[4]

Neoliberalization in our food system is linked to a growing push for efficiency that means higher profits for companies as they produce and sell more goods to consumers. The more a company can externalize the labor costs of production, the more they can profit from such sales. The externalization of costs generally means worse working conditions, more precarious work arrangements, and reduced compensation for workers.[5] While neoliberalization affects food system workers across all sectors, we apply this analytic lens specifically to our discussion of transportation and logistics workers in this chapter, as this is the sector where we perceive the most aggressive change in workplace structure. In such cases, companies have been relieved of responsibility for stable worker wages and well-being and workers have become increasingly responsible for their own labor conditions and affiliated risks.[6]

Despite the many configurations of labor in this sector, all workers in warehouse, transportation, and distribution are vulnerable to the global pressures of deregulation, shrinking worker protections, and the related growth of labor outsourcing and subcontracting, also called workplace fissuring.[7] *Outsourcing*, or hiring a worker from outside a company to perform a specific job, task, or project, can be done locally by hiring a contract worker or moving a job to a region or country with lower wages or fewer labor regulations. *Subcontracting* similarly refers to when a person or firm is contracted outside of the lead company. The consequences of workplace fissuring include a slew of precarious conditions. When workers are not directly employed by the company responsible for the product or labor process but rather by a firm contracted simply to manage labor, there is an associated increase in labor squeezes through lower wages and reduced benefits. These changes also lead to shrinking worker protections via weaker labor law enforcement. As workplaces become harder to monitor legally, they become more unstable and unsafe.

Further, when workers are not hired directly, it is more difficult for them to build solidarity, organize unions, or demand better conditions and wages.

The fissuring process, including the global outsourcing of labor, is connected to the broader corporate goal of weakening unionized labor.[8] As the non-profit workers' center Warehouse Workers for Justice (WWJ) has shown in its research, employees who work in a warehouse moving products to be sold at a mega-scale company such as Walmart may be employed by as many as ten different subcontracted companies in one warehouse location. These workers are hired by third-party logistics firms or temporary hiring agencies that get competitive contracts with Walmart by offering the lowest costs for labor, putting downward pressure on wages over time.[9]

In the context of growing corporate and global consolidation of food industries, the economic risk of hiring employees and maintaining worker well-being is shifted to smaller employers and individual workers themselves. Finally, the surplus profit created by the process of transporting and housing goods en route to sale is shifted from workers to company investors, as the companies save on costs such as increased wages and benefits paid to workers. This shift to an increasingly fissured supply chain, through approaches such as utilizing third-party contractors and gig work, creates vulnerabilities for workers throughout the transportation and logistics sector of the food supply chain. Further, these workers are experiencing increasing levels of surveillance through AI and other technological means, so while they are losing workplace stability and negotiating power, they are being exposed to intensifying oversight and disciplining measures, which often can mean increased vulnerability to punishment and firing based on their algorithmically determined productivity.

With increased globalization of the food system, there is a growing distance between production and consumption. The volume of people and the distances involved in this work have both grown in relation to the development of the global agrifood supply chain, as coordinated global corporatization has increased what some call "food miles," both the literal and the figurative distance between producer and consumer.[10] Workers in food transportation and distribution are the ones connecting those food miles, and as that distance has increased in relation to the industrialization of the food system, they have become more disconnected not only from consumers but also from their direct employers through the fissuring process. With the growing influence of the broader good food movement, direct-to-consumer food options, such as community supported agriculture weekly produce boxes, farmers' markets, and meat shares from local farms have become more widespread. While these options do provide an alternative to the long and largely opaque food supply chain, they are often expensive and unavailable to most consumers.

As the distances between transportation, warehouse, and other logistics workers and food consumers have grown, these workers have become more hidden in terms of food system visibility. In comparison to service or even production workers, transportation and warehouse workers are often invisible as their work takes place in more liminal spaces, and they are increasingly hired by contractors and temporary hiring agencies rather than identified with a known food brand or corporation. When you purchase a carton of milk or a bag of chips at a recognizable chain grocery store with its own in-house brand, such as Walmart, Wegmans, or Safeway, it may seem that this product has been produced, packaged, and transported by employees of this chain, but this is not usually the case. In fact, grocery chains regularly contract with producing, processing, warehouse, and transportation companies, which in turn contract with third-party hiring agencies, which hire the workers. In the case of the retail chain Trader Joe's, a company that boasts that over 80% of its products are branded with its private label, many of those items are manufactured by third-party processors such as PepsiCo and ConAgra.[11] These items may have passed through multiple warehouses, handled by people hired by various employment agencies, even at one worksite. In the next section, we describe in more detail what warehouse and distribution work looks like and how its workers are treated.

PRECARITY IN THE WAREHOUSE

Like workers in other industries and sectors involved in the global supply chain of goods, warehouse and distribution workers have been negatively affected by the neoliberal shift to more flexible or *just-in-time* labor schemes, where workers are hired only as needed for a particular order, task, or job. This approach to the production and movement of goods, combined with the shift to more temporary and third-party employment, has made it increasingly difficult to organize or unionize workers in warehouse and distribution. In addition, workers in this sector are mostly immigrants, people of color, and undocumented workers, who can be intimidated from taking part in organizing efforts.[12] In what follows, we discuss the increasing patterns of subcontracted labor and the e-commerce takeover and expansion of warehouse work. In both these prevailing trends, workers are seeing less enforcement of labor regulations and increased surveillance of their day-to-day work.

Most workers in the warehouse and distribution sector are "picker-packers." Picking involves locating, scanning, and sending an item, often on a conveyor belt, to the packer, who prepares it to leave the warehouse center. These workers also move materials and, therefore, engage in a wide range of physical activities, from moving products through a line for inspection to lifting boxes and packages either by hand or with a forklift. Shifts can last from eight to twelve hours and entail repetitive tasks, often with personal productivity monitored by devices either worn by workers or embedded in their product scanning devices. Constant surveillance leads workers to move more quickly and with less awareness of their own physical needs and limitations, which has been shown to lead to an increased rate of injury and exhaustion.[13]

While warehouse and delivery facilities might be owned and managed by a producer or large retailer, the day-to-day functions and labor in such facilities frequently are outsourced to a third-party logistics company. That firm, in turn, contracts for labor services with temporary hiring agencies, which are for-profit labor market intermediaries. The number of these firms grew rapidly beginning in the 1970s, as more companies started to outsource labor across sectors. Labor flexibilization, the externalization of cost, and unionization resistance are all accomplished through these staffing companies.[14] Employment in this sector has doubled in recent years, particularly in relation to the pandemic.[15]

The Chicago-based workers' center, Warehouse Workers for Justice, conducted an eight-month study of warehouse workers in Will County, Illinois, a hub for the Chicago logistics industry. The study sampled over three hundred workers at 165 different warehouse and delivery centers and found that 81% of initial hires and 63% of all workers were temporary hires, with a median hourly wage of $9.00. Temporary workers were paid on average $3.48 less than direct employees, and only 4% of temporary workers had health insurance. Temporary workers were much less likely to receive sick days, vacation time, or health insurance benefits. Only 5% of temps received sick days and 8% received vacation time. Of all the workers, 25% relied on public assistance, 37% worked a second job, and 20% had been injured on the job.[16] This trend toward temporary hiring, and the related lack of accountability, wages, and benefits, has only increased with the growth in e-commerce in food and rising customer expectations for nearly immediate delivery upon ordering.

Over the past decade, we have seen a dramatic growth in the relationship between logistics and what has traditionally been retail work—the end process of selling the product to the consumer.[17] The consumer grocery industry has become increasingly competitive since the early 2000s, with an influx of e-commerce (online shopping) options, produce delivery boxes, and meal kits. As these options emphasize rapid response times to meet shifting customer demand, the role of warehouse and distribution workers has become more important. The shift to increased online retail purchasing through Amazon and other large-scale retail operations has meant an even stronger push for faster and leaner operations in warehouse work as the more visible work of retail grocery shifts to behind-the-scenes warehouse labor. These companies tend to adopt more technological and experimental approaches not only to sales, but their entire operational structure. As e-commerce quickly becomes the leading driver of new job development in the warehouse and distribution sector, including for food purchases, more companies are experimenting with new technologies that are meant to reduce labor costs. These include automatic picking and packing and other technologies to speed up, streamline, oversee, and control human workers, further deskilling and potentially displacing the traditional workforce.[18] These trends in e-commerce and e-groceries follow the neoliberal move toward deregulated corporate consolidation. Amazon, for example, has moved into what was formally a more diverse food retail environment, with fewer labor protections and a downward push on unionized workforces.

The trend toward online food and other home goods purchasing intensified on a global scale with the onset of the COVID-19 pandemic as consumers preferred to reduce trips to the store and public spaces in general. This has included companies with a full line of groceries like AmazonFresh and smaller-scale companies focusing on specific products, such as produce in the case of Hello Fresh. While most people resumed in-person shopping as the pandemic waned, there is much to be learned about this new dynamic and the ways labor in the food system has been affected.[19]

While some more regionally based online grocery companies have a focus on more sustainable products and "disrupting" the corporate agrifood supply chain in the spirit of facilitating more direct consumer purchases, most of these companies are established large-scale product distributors that have simply expanded their logistics branches to incorporate more food products. The largest and most well-known case is that of AmazonFresh. Amazon, an e-commerce behemoth, entered the grocery business in 2017 with the goal of expanding Amazon's online reach beyond books, electronics, and other goods and further into food and fresh products. This was the same year that Amazon purchased the US-based high-end food grocery chain, Whole Foods. This buyout allowed Amazon to offer a wider selection of organic and similarly priced specialty foods and expand their delivery and in-store pickup options to a wider range of customers. While AmazonFresh is mostly available in larger metropolitan areas as of 2024, it has an international reach, with operations in the United Kingdom and Germany as well as the United States.[20]

The move to online grocery purchasing increases the number of workers in the warehouse and logistics sector and decreases the number of workers in traditional retail, intensifying some of the labor and hiring practices and patterns discussed above. This push for an increased level of intensity from traditional just-in-time production in the context of online ordering has real-life consequences for workers picking and packing those goods. In an analysis of data submitted by Amazon to OSHA, the worker injury rate at Amazon warehouse facilities increased 20% from 2020 to 2021. In that same year, Amazon workers sustained 49% of total warehouse injuries nationwide, despite employing only one-third of warehouse workers. Amazon warehouse workers were seriously injured at twice the rate of other warehouse employees.[21] These rates of injury commonly result in worker disability.

As part of this shift, we are seeing a move to increased mechanization to replace workers, as well as to dehumanize labor still done by people through surveillance and monitoring of speed and efficiency. In particular, Amazon conducts electronic monitoring using handheld scanners that can tell supervisors which employees are meeting productivity goals based on their individual tasks, who is making errors, or who is taking too much time away from their given tasks. When they do not meet their goals or are off task, employees may be warned or terminated.[22] While Amazon is certainly not the first company to approach food delivery through a techno-fix, it is the first to succeed at reaching consumers on such a wide scale and with such a large workforce and therefore has affected the food economy in unprecedented ways. Amazon is well known for its approach to high-speed delivery, which includes a highly efficient and streamlined warehouse and transportation system. What scholars, activists, and investigative journalists have found is that this efficiency and productivity comes at a cost to worker health and well-being. With the heavy emphasis on technology to manage human behavior in the workplace, there has been little flexibility to adjust to the very human realities of illness, stress, and injury, along with mental health and workplace culture.[23] With chronic high turnover rates due to workplace unrest and injury, the company has received strong backlash and criticism from former workers, organizers, politicians, and media outlets.[24]

As one employee explained in an interview with *The Guardian* after Amazon purchased the Whole Foods grocery store chain, "They want us to become robots. That's where they are going, they want to set it up so they don't have to pay someone $15 an hour who knows all about the food, they can pay someone $10 an hour to do these small tasks and timed duties."[25] This shift to dehumanized labor in food distribution, both literally and metaphorically, reflects today's neoliberal treatment of workers on a global scale and builds on historically exploitative food system labor practices rooted in plantation economies and industrial-scale food manufacturing. In this process, workers are increasingly perceived by employers, and even policy makers and politicians, as collateral damage in the economic expansion of industry and technology.

Amazon has taken surveillance of workers to an extreme level, pushing the boundaries of employees' civil and human rights. Reports show that warehouse workers must clear themselves of all personal belongings on entry to work, except for a water bottle and a plastic bag of cash. Throughout their workday they are monitored with sophisticated AI technology, tracking their every move and productivity levels. When leaving work, they are screened to ensure that they did not steal any company items. These screenings can take from twenty-five minutes to an hour and are not paid time. Delivery workers are also tracked, using navigation software, to ensure that they are on the route prescribed by Amazon. Like warehouse workers, drivers work under a strict productivity minimum. In drivers' cases, they must deliver 999 out of every 1,000 packages on time or face the possibility of being fired. The mental and emotional strain on workers is astounding. One report showed that among 46 Amazon warehouses in 17 states, 189 calls for emergency services were made between 2013 and 2018 for a variety of mental health incidents, including suicide attempts and suicidal thoughts.[26]

Online grocery and food e-commerce means an increase in the fissured model of employment already embraced by large-scale warehouse-based companies such as Amazon and Walmart. While, of course, many people still prefer to shop in person for groceries, to ensure freshness and particularity, and it is not predicted that all food shopping will convert to e-commerce, it is significant to note how this shift has affected labor across the supply chain.

With increased vertical consolidation from warehouse to transportation to retail, there is an opening to increase their scale of business, which as history tells us unfortunately means a loss of workers' rights and voices in the food chain.

PRECARITY ON THE ROAD

The final steps of moving goods to their service, retail, or consumer endpoint are reliant on transportation workers. This section covers traditional food transportation, such as *drayage* and trucking, showing how the move to independent contracting in commercial trucking has replaced more traditional employer-employee relations. While this is not a new process and is rooted in the transition to industrial agriculture going back to the 1920s, the neoliberal push for workers to take on all economic precarity and safety risks of food transportation has intensified in recent decades.

Drayage and trucking are two key tasks performed by workers in the food chain transportation sector. Drayage involves the transportation of goods over short distances, such as from a shipping port to a warehouse, whereas trucking entails hauling containers on trailer chassis by diesel-powered truck cabs, usually for long distances. Workers involved in drayage and trucking are essential links in the movement of goods from the docking or shipping terminal to warehouses and/or rail transport.[27] As noted at the beginning of this chapter, truck drivers are better compensated than most other workers in the food chain. Trucking is particularly well paid considering that it does not require formal education: 75% of truckers have a high school degree equivalent or less, and only 7% hold bachelor's degrees, versus 35% for all workers.[28] On average, truck drivers earn about $43,252 annually, lower than the median for all full-time workers ($47,016), yet more than other workers in other blue-collar jobs. They are also on average older (median age of forty-six compared to 41 for all workers) and more likely than other workers to be veterans (at least one in ten are veterans, double the rate of other occupations).[29]

Reflective of other higher-paying jobs considered "blue-collar" work, as opposed to low wage or entry level jobs, trucking is dominated by men, white men in particular, especially in contrast to other food occupations discussed in this book. A report by the US Census Bureau shows that of 3.5 million people who work as truck drivers, over 90% identify as men, with younger demographics including more women and BIPOC workers.[30] Based on a study of 20 million driver inspections, along with US Social Security Administration data, researchers found that women truck drivers made up only 3.2% of drivers who had undergone inspections nationally, yet their representation grew 23.1% from 2010 to 2019. While the number of women employed in trucking is increasing, they still occupy less desired positions with lower pay and less control over their schedules.[31] As we discuss below, trucking involves long hours away from home, with decreasing benefits from employers and increasing precarity over the past several decades.

The food transportation industry is characterized by small logistics and trucking firms that compete for contracts with shippers. In trucking business ownership, about 75% of all trucking firms are white-owned, about double that of Black-owned or Asian-owned firms. While women-owned trucking firms make up less than 10% of the industry, they have an average higher revenue than those owned by men: $460,000 versus about $349,000 per firm on average.[32]

Much of the work in the transportation sector is done by long haul truckers. Long haul truckers are drivers who complete more than two hundred fifty miles per trip; they can drive thousands of miles in a single job, crossing state lines and even international borders. These drivers work and live out of their trucks when on the road and are regularly away from home for almost two weeks at a time. If one considers all their time on the road as part of their working hours, they work the equivalent of two full-time jobs and make less than minimum wage.[33] Like farmworkers, truckers are not fully protected by the Fair Labor Standards Act (FLSA) and are not entitled to overtime pay.[34]

Drivers may be employees of a large company, but more commonly they are self-employed as owner-operators. Trucking firms—which do not own trucks or hire employees—contract with drivers who own or lease their vehicles. Contracting with owner-operators frees trucking companies from any obligations they would incur as employers, including social security taxes, unemployment compensation, workers' compensation, health benefits, pensions, and compliance with occupational health and safety and nondiscrimination statutes. As owner-operators, the drivers are not provided with health insurance by their employer and thus may lack access to health care. Owner-operators are prohibited from joining with other owner-operators to act collectively to improve wages and working conditions through a union or a business association.[35]

In *Trucking Country*, Shane Hamilton, a scholar of food and agribusiness, takes a historical look at trucking in the United States, in particular, hauling food across the country from rural farm towns to superstores.[36] He connects sectors of the food system through the lived realities of workers, linking the rise of industrial agriculture and consolidation of small-scale farms with the increase in independently minded truckers looking for flexible lives and control over their own livelihoods. Many of these drivers entered the trucking industry as a direct result of farm closures. As Hamilton writes:

> Independent truckers, encouraged by agribusiness and farm policymakers, challenged the regulatory structures and labor policies of the New Deal political economy from the outset. A new breed of trucker was born out of the 1920s and 1930s, as industrialized agriculture forced many farmers off the land and onto the roads to seek a living. These rural truckers developed a culture of fierce independence, encouraged by farm-friendly policies that shielded them from federal regulations and discouraged unionization.[37]

Ironically, the same flexibility desired by drivers benefited industrial agricultural production. When freed from railroad shipping, large-scale agricultural industry moved processing away from the city and closer to the farm and low-wage nonunionized workforces. "Flexible" independent truckers could adjust to the unpredictability of farming, helping solve the logistical challenges of industrial-scale farm and food processing consolidation.[38] Hamilton continues:

> By the 1960s, these "wildcat" rural truckers had upended the nation's railroad based farm economy. Agribusiness and factory farmers relied on nonunion rural truckers to deliver cheap food to suburban supermarket shoppers, enabling the affluence of post-war consumerism while fostering a broad transformation of U.S. economic culture and politics. Throughout the 1930s and 1940s, urban workers and consumers had called upon labor unions and the federal government to contest the power of industrial agriculture in the food marketplace. By the late 1960s, however, working- and middle-class consumers accepted agribusiness's ability to decimate organized labor and defy government regulation in the countryside in exchange for low food prices.[39]

As Hamilton's work makes clear, there is a long history of food system industrialization connecting workers across various sectors through increasingly precarious labor conditions.

In a more recent multiyear ethnographic study of truck drivers, the sociologist Steve Viscelli found that there is little difference between the wages and working conditions of truck owner-operators and trucking company employees.[40] Yet owner-operator status is the professional goal for most truckers given the common perception that it will allow more control over their schedules and incomes. His findings show that instead they become beholden to labor contracts with trucking firms, which have the upper hand in determining wages and terms of labor. Rather than gain independence and achieving the "American dream" of business ownership, truck owner-operators experience structural exploitation by trucking companies that hold sway over their loads or shipment schedules, including increased or decreased (unpaid) waiting times, mileage, and paperwork. As with other laborers in the fissured economy, such as the warehouse workers discussed above, these truckers take on risk factors outside of their control such as the cost of gas and vehicle maintenance as well as work gaps due to supply chain issues. This contrasts with a traditional employer-employee relationship, where companies take on such risks.[41]

Congress first established rules and regulations for the trucking industry in 1935, under the original Motor Carriers Act. It was in this law that uniform freight rates as well as certifications and standards for entry were established to both increase safety for drivers and ensure an economically stable transportation industry. At that time, truck drivers earned significantly more than other blue-collar workers and unionization rates were high, as truckers played a significant role in the national Teamsters Union.[42] Yet truckers hauling agricultural commodities were exempt from the Motor Carriers Act from the start, based on the notion that some farmers would be bringing their own goods to market and did not need to be overburdened with unnecessary regulation.[43]

The Motor Carrier Act was modified in 1980 in a series of legislative acts that removed regulatory restrictions on transportation industries in the United States. This bill, signed by President Jimmy Carter, was designed to deregulate the trucking industry specifically and had the goal of increasing competition and reducing consumer costs, paving the way for more comprehensive neoliberal policy in the next decade. This deregulation process also led to the increase in trucking owner-operators, building on the model in agricultural shipping where truckers are instead independent contractors and therefore take on the risks and costs of moving goods. We have seen that over time, truckers' wages and benefits have decreased related to these shifts while their productivity (and profit making for industry) has increased.[44] As Hamilton's work shows, truckers themselves were a leading voice in this deregulatory move, which was directly related to the fact that many truckers in the food and farming industries had never experienced the same regulations as other truckers. Hamilton explains, "Many of the independent truckers who took part in the protests of 1979 earned their living hauling the nation's food and farm products—which meant they already worked in an economic environment that had been deregulated since the mid-1930s."[45]

In a study of the relationship between deregulation of the transportation industry and truckers' wages, Dave Belman and Kristin Monaco found that truck drivers' wages fell 21% between 1973 and 1995. It was during this time that the transportation industry experienced the most dramatic forms of deregulation, accounting for one-third of the decline in drivers' wages. Further, there was a larger negative effect on nonunion workers during this time, with union members earning 18% to 21% more than their nonunion counterparts at the time of the study.[46] While the Teamsters Union retained some bargaining power with truckers after the deregulatory period of the 1970s and 1980s, the move toward an increased owner-operator model has left only a small portion of truck drivers unionized and therefore more vulnerable to shifts in wages and costs of the trade.[47] The Teamsters Union itself has an infamous and long history of disfunction and corruption, which had an impact on the decline of transportation organizing as well.[48] This deregulatory process, of course, is linked to the broader phenomenon of neoliberalization during this period and the competitive degradation of global labor standards.

In her book *Tangled Routes*, which focuses on the people who work within the transnational "tomato trail," from Mexico to Canada, the sociologist and food systems scholar Deborah Barndt analyzes the working conditions of truckers who travel across international borders to deliver seasonally fresh produce.[49] She frames this work in the context of the North American Free Trade Agreement (NAFTA), an international accord signed by the United States, Mexico, and Canada that took effect in 1994 as part of the broader push to increase neoliberal globalization by reducing restrictions on trade, labor, and environmental protections. This agreement increased the exchange of goods across borders, such as agricultural products, by eliminating tariffs (taxes on international imports and exports) and other barriers to international economic exchanges. Increased trade between the signatory countries led to increased wait times and unpredictability at the borders, adding to the stress of the job. With respect to food specifically, Barndt discusses the timeliness of the driving and delivery work of tomato truck drivers and contrasts the ease with which delivery workers crossed international borders (and most importantly, the ease with which their goods crossed) with the struggles of tomato pickers crossing and returning home from Mexico to Canada. She also explores the gendered aspect of the trucking profession and the ways that men in both Mexico and the United States are socialized into the career, often from one generation to the next.[50] Food transportation is truly a transnational industry, and although not all drivers cross borders, food is constantly moving and engulfing workers from diverse cultural and political environments to arrive on our plates.

Notably, trucking companies are apt to take advantage of drivers through the requirement of driver training programs. As Benjamin Lorr explains in his book, *The Secret Life of Groceries*, carrier companies make huge profits from student drivers.[51] Student drivers are paid below a standard driving wage, but because they are training, they drive with someone else. Because there are two drivers, they do not need to take legally mandated breaks on their routes. While there is a high level of turnover at this level of training, it is productive for the companies and essentially underwrites the training system. In addition, drivers in training are subject to sexual harassment and abuse due to the nature of long hours alone in a truck with one other person.

Women composed under 5% of the 1.37 million truck drivers in the United States in 2021. This training system, and the companies' desire to avoid sexual harassment claims, has led to discrimination against women drivers broadly. Instead of providing hotels for the trainees to stay in during the training period or increase sexual harassment trainings, companies have simply denied women drivers the opportunity to train for the job, even after they complete the certifications. This is despite the fact that in 2014 a federal court ruled that required same-sex training was unlawful. In 2023, the National Women's Law Center filed a class action discrimination charge against Stevens Transport with the Equal Employment Opportunity Commission, which is still in process in 2024.[52]

As the physical spaces and structures that have long served drivers and other workers continue to disappear, we see a loss of rural communities and a push for a transition to automated driving. Over the past several decades, drivers have lost the physical support system of truck stops. Truckers have historically been dependent on small towns and specialized retail and service providers for basic amenities such as showers, laundry, and hot meals. As rural towns and regions have been on the economic decline in recent years, related to broader shifts in consolidated agricultural economies, truckers are increasingly losing these spaces of respite as well.[53]

In another significant structural change to the industry, there is the potential for automated driving systems that would be organized and advanced enough to affect trucking on a wide scale and would have massive effects on the US economy overall, including employment in the transportation industry. Yet these changes are still a long time coming. The US Department of Transportation conducted a macroeconomic survey that predicts that the faster this transition occurs, the higher the impact will be on direct employment, while a longer-term adaptation will mean a more natural occupational turnover to other forms of employment.[54] Labor scholars have broken down the trucking sector to look at the predicted effects on short versus long haul trucking and assessed that long haul trucking will be easier to automate. While such technology is in development, it will not lead to a comprehensive shift away from human drivers. What is of relevance to our analysis here is that truck drivers do not simply drive; they engage in a multitude of tasks, and this work is not as easy to displace as some accounts are predicting.[55] We argue that the challenges of automating trucking, along with other food system–related work, reflect the skills necessary to keep the food chain operating. While technology is certainly making a daily impact, especially regarding monitoring labor and standardizing workplaces, human workers are still essential and most likely always will be.

Ultimately, the past several decades have shown a large shift from a higher wage and often unionized trucking workforce to a more precarious self-employed industry. While trucking is still dominated by US-born men, white men in particular, who are among the highest-paid workers in the food chain, the profession may soon be at a crossroads. Automation has the potential to shift roles and responsibilities and therefore push trucking to a deskilled and lower-paid work category if there is not some form of organized resistance.

PRECARITY IN DELIVERY WORK AND THE GIG ECONOMY

Like truckers and warehouse workers, delivery app workers, such as those that labor for companies delivering food from restaurants to consumers, including DoorDash, Grubhub, and Uber Eats, are not directly employed by the companies that profit from their labor. As gig workers, they are employed as independent contractors, as opposed to full-time employees. The structure of the gig economy is based on flexible, temporary, or freelance jobs and often involves connecting with clients or customers through an online platform.

Some workers, and certainly industry proponents, are quick to note the perceived benefits of the gig worker structure. Workers can choose their hours and easily pick up a side job in addition to a typical 9 to 5 job, and gig work is adaptable to the demand for flexible lifestyles. Consumers benefit from the convenience of to-order task requests, including having their food delivered nearly anywhere at any time. At the same time, the gig economy has downsides due to the erosion of traditional economic relationships between workers, businesses, and clients.[56]

Many gig workers are immigrants and people of color, who are already vulnerable to workplace discrimination and experience barriers to seeking better pay and working conditions.[57] According to a Pew Research Center Study, 16% of all Americans had participated in doing some kind of gig economy labor. Self-identified Hispanic adults labored as gig workers at a much higher percentage (30%), compared to 20% of Black adults, 19% of Asian adults, and 12% of white adults. They also found that about one in five gig workers say they have experienced unwanted sexual advances while completing jobs, and those who do not identify as white are more likely than white workers to say they have felt unsafe or experienced an unwanted sexual advance on the job.[58]

Gig work is a relatively nascent mode of food transportation and based on more direct consumer relations via digital platforms, or apps. Gig-based food delivery workers are a new formulation of the food labor market, as the logic for just-in-time inventory is extended to labor services. Compared to the traditional labor economy, where workers are hired for jobs, gig economy workers are hired to do tasks and are subject to quantitative ratings and reviews from customers, which are highly subjective. Similar to Amazon workers, gig workers are increasingly being surveilled through nonhuman technology: algorithms embedded in app-based labor captures data from workers' personal smartphones, including their geographic locations and efficiency, allowing the parent company to determine the allocation of jobs and payment and even the penalization and firing of workers from the platforms.[59] Finally, as independent contractors, they must rely on their own equipment for transportation and pay for any other operating costs, such as accounting and taxes, as well as personal insurance, when they can afford it. Like other independent contractors in trucking and warehouses, they are not entitled to sick days, worker compensation, minimum wage coverage, social security, unemployment insurance, or coverage under the NLRA.[60]

The 2021 report on delivery workers in New York City, "Essential but Unprotected," written by the Workers' Justice Project and the Worker

Institute at Cornell University, included a survey of five hundred app-based couriers making deliveries.[61] The report found that their hourly net pay, with tips included, was around $12.21, well below the region's minimum wage and certainly below a living wage for New York City. About two-thirds of survey respondents reported that they regularly work at least six days per week, and 85% said delivery work was their only form of employment. Delivery workers complained that the apps' algorithms, which are based on customer reviews as well as acceptance rate of orders, unfairly affected their pay and their ability to get work. Forty-nine percent of respondents in the survey said they had been in an accident or crash while making a delivery; of these workers, 75% said they paid for their medical care out of their personal funds.[62]

A separate report published by the New York Office of Consumer and Worker Protection found that food delivery drivers who did not have a car had the highest rate of work-related deaths (36 deaths per 100,000 workers) over the period from January 2021 to June 2022, even higher than the rate for construction workers.[63] These delivery workers, the vast majority of whom are recent immigrants, typically move through major city traffic on bicycles, and the cost of any safety protections like lights or helmets comes out of their own pockets. Food delivery worker deaths are so common in New York City that there is a Facebook group that regularly organizes vigils and funerals to commemorate their colleagues; it is called "El Diario de Los Deliveryboys en La Gran Manzana" (The Journal of the Deliveryboys in the Big Apple).[64] Such safety hazards are a clear indication of both the precarious working conditions experienced by delivery workers and the need for worker organizing.

LOGISTICS WORKERS RESISTING THE RACE TO THE BOTTOM

Despite the many challenges facing logistics workers across the warehouse, distribution, and transportation sectors, there has been significant progress in organizing through the innovative strategies of unions, worker centers, and other advocacy groups that are supporting workers in standing up for their rights on the job and passing new legislation that promotes better labor conditions. Warehouse workers and delivery workers have made new inroads in the past few years, from a successful unionization campaign at Amazon to a food delivery workers' movement for new city and statewide legislation protecting their rights.

Warehouse organizing has taken many forms in recent years, given the organizing challenges of temporary hiring as well having a large portion of new immigrant workers who come from various language backgrounds and may fear threats of deportation. WWJ was founded in 2008, with the goal of supporting workers in Illinois's logistics and distribution industry. In addition to the research discussed above, WWJ helps individuals recover unpaid or stolen wages and organizes workshops and training sessions to make warehouse workers aware of their legal rights. Cognizant of how subcontracted and temporary labor challenges traditional organizing, they have orchestrated large-scale protests and rallies to raise consumer awareness, in addition to strikes, petitions, and community delegations. In this work, they fight for basic rights such as raises, paid sick days and holidays, and better safety conditions, as well as a larger role in workplace decision making.

On the West Coast, Warehouse Workers United (WWU) and Warehouse Workers Resource Center (WWRC) in Southern California also take a nontraditional approach to organizing warehouse workers. As the geographer Juan De Lara and colleagues note, these organizations use "hybrid" organizing strategies in response to the temporary, subcontracted, and largely undocumented immigrant workforce, which, as a constantly shifting group without one consistent employer, is difficult to organize using traditional labor union tactics.[65] Unlike unions, which are focused on recruiting workers to fight for union contracts with their employers, they recruit workers to their campaigns in their own communities, not at their workplace. To recruit from immigrant communities, they focus first on the immediate needs of workers, offering English-language classes and know your rights trainings, to build their movement and work toward challenging labor law violations in the industry. Specifically, WWU has been successful at ensuring better enforcement of existing labor laws, forcing employers to pay back wages to workers who experienced wage theft, and ensuring statewide heat and safety standards for workplaces.[66] Worker organizations such as these were particularly important in ensuring safe working conditions and making sure vaccines were available to warehouse workers during the height of the COVID-19 pandemic.[67]

These organizations have taken a supply chain approach to raising awareness of warehouse workers. While WWU is not a union, it has financial support from unions, such as the United Food and Commercial Workers

FIGURE 10. Warehouse Workers United protest, Mira Loma, California, 2012. Joshua Sbicca, photographer.

Union (UFCW), which organizes workers in Walmart retail stores and saw organizing workers along Walmart's supply chain as key to successes in that sector.[68] The UFCW has also taken legal action, targeting retail chains for labor abuses and violations, and have forced big box stores such as Walmart to monitor and improve worker treatment by third-party hiring agencies.[69] Further, they work closely in coalition with national labor groups, including the UCLA Labor Occupational Safety and Health Program, the Council on Occupational Health and Safety, the Staffing Workers Alliance, and the Food Chain Workers Alliance.

As today's most powerful presence in the warehousing sector, Amazon has been notoriously effective at squashing unionization campaigns since its inception, taking advantage of the weakened political and regulatory environment for union organizing in the United States as part of the neoliberal roll-back of workers' rights. Armed with unlimited funds to combat union drives, Amazon successfully fought an aggressive unionization effort by the Retail, Wholesale and Department Store Union (RWDSU) at a plant in Bessemer, Alabama, in 2021, receiving extended media attention and ultimately discouraging large unions from attempting to organize workers at the company.

Amazon spent $4.3 million on antiunion consultants in that one year. Then, in 2022, in a shocking turn of events, workers themselves created a new union, called the Amazon Labor Union, on Staten Island, New York, surprising the media and labor advocates alike with a 2,654 to 2,131 vote in favor of the union. The union president, Chris Smalls, gained nationwide recognition and was invited to the White House by President Joe Biden. Throughout their efforts, the refrain, "We are not robots!," was a key sentiment and chant, reflecting the push to automate worker management at the company.[70] Despite this big win, continued progress has been slow, as other locations in the Northeast have failed union votes and the Staten Island union has yet to secure a contract as of early 2024.[71] Certainly, the union push is not over. The Teamsters Union, which has successfully organized other warehouse workers as well as truck drivers, has an active campaign to unionize Amazon.

As noted above, truck drivers, despite having a strong history with the Teamsters Union, are largely unorganized today. This is related to deregulatory moves in the 1970s and 1980s that led to the increase in the independent contractor model. This draws on the long-standing independent leanings of many truckers, who prefer working alone and do not see themselves as workers but as owners. Yet the Teamsters are still succeeding in unionizing some drivers today who are directly employed by transportation and logistics firms as part of their Freight Division, where they support drivers to bargain for union contracts, including increased wages, benefits, and fair grievance procedures, as well as increased regulation and standardization of protections for drivers. The Teamsters have a strong history of organizing workers across sectors and building broad support between workers in disparate fields. For example, most Teamster contracts include language that protects Teamster members who refuse to cross active picket lines of other striking unions.[72] This strategy has been used to build solidarity across unions throughout the labor movement. As we discuss throughout this book, coalition building throughout the food chain, such as when unionized workers in one sector stop work to support other workers on strike, is an example of solidarity that can be leveraged to build a broader food chain workers movement.

As seen in the trucking industry, working as an independent contractor can be a draw for some logistics workers. However, for gig workers, this classification has been a central point of contention given how it limits their wages, rights, and protections. The ongoing challenge of organizing gig workers stems from the fact that workers are not directly affiliated with one employer and therefore cannot easily be mobilized as a cohesive group.

Despite these challenges, there have been important attempts at policy reform and organizing gig workers at the local and state levels. In September 2019, California Assembly Bill 5 (AB5), also known as the gig worker bill, was passed with the intent to address the misclassification of gig workers, such as delivery drivers, as independent contractors and ensure their protections as employees. Under this law, gig workers would gain access to the basic labor and employment protections and benefits that are denied to independent contractors. These include minimum wage and overtime protections, paid sick days, workers' compensation benefits, and unemployment insurance benefits.[73] AB5 went into effect in January 2020, but in November 2020, voters passed Proposition 22, which legally designates drivers for app-based delivery services independent contractors (albeit with some benefits) and overrides AB5. Tech companies, including Uber, Lyft, Instacart, DoorDash, and Postmates, invested a record-breaking $200 million in promoting the proposition.[74] In a continuing and highly publicized saga, in August 2021, a county court ruled that Proposition 22 was unconstitutional. DoorDash, Uber, and Lyft appealed the ruling, and after years-long legal strife, in 2024, the California supreme court upheld the law, which was seen as a huge loss by labor organizers.[75]

One of the first groups to organize gig workers is the Gig Workers Collective (GWC), which was originally formed to help Instacart shoppers organize for fair compensation in 2016.[76] Initially organized through a Facebook group of Instacart shoppers, the GWC was composed of eleven women around the United States who organized strikes and protests between 2016 and 2019, gaining additional traction during the early days of the pandemic.

For gig workers across the United States, the COVID-19 pandemic was a turning point for organizing, as app-based delivery workers were considered essential workers but left out of protections provided by more traditional employers.[77] At the beginning of the pandemic, delivery workers started organizing more intensively. During this period, when many white-collar workers stayed home and ordered in, delivery app usage rose sharply, and companies started seeing an increase in growth and profit.[78] Yet delivery workers continued to be exposed to the virus while their wages stayed stagnant (often below the minimum wage), and no systematic projections were offered. In response, a new movement was formed that included advocacy groups such as Los Deliveristas Unidos, Workers Justice, Justice for App Workers, International Alliance of Delivery Workers, and others, to address issues like transparency in payment and tipping, health and safety protections, and general industry accountability.[79]

FIGURE 11. Deliveristas protest, New York, New York, 2021. Gerardo Romo, photographer.

In 2021, DoorDash workers organized a nationwide strike, New York City delivery workers took part in a march through Times Square, and other rallies were held throughout the country.[80] In response to these protests, in September 2021, the New York City Council enacted a set of new protections (which went into effect in 2022) for the city's sixty thousand delivery workers who transport food via third-party apps. This set of regulations includes transparency in tipping and pay, written agreements with restaurants ensuring delivery workers access to bathrooms, allowing delivery workers to set the distances and routes they are willing to travel, and other protections.[81] In 2023, the city government took these regulations a step further, by requiring app-based delivery companies to ensure an hourly wage of $17.96, the first law of its kind in the country. This was a controversial step in the world of gig work, which is grounded in the notion that workers benefit from a flexible schedule. Yet worker activists and organizers argue that a guaranteed hourly wage such as the one instituted in New York would ensure that delivery workers are not dependent on tips and have a reliable income.[82]

In 2022, companies, including Lyft and Uber (the parent company of the food delivery service Uber Eats), spent a combined $17.8 million in support of a ballot measure in Massachusetts to classify gig drivers as independent contractors. This measure was thrown out by a state court, ruling that the measure violated the state constitution.[83] We have seen in the examples above that one of the primary goals of shifting to independent contractor labor is to reduce risks for companies and offload those risks on workers. While this measure has been rejected by the judicial system for now, there is a concentrated and well-funded effort and strategic pattern behind the shift to contractor and contingent labor across the food system, particularly in the transportation sector. As of this writing, these companies are pushing for a statewide ballot measure to classify gig workers as independent contractors in Massachusetts.

As can be seen in the ongoing fight to regulate delivery and other gig work in New York, California, and Massachusetts, increasing protections for contingent food transportation and other gig workers is a highly charged battle, with app-based companies heavily invested in the outcomes. There is some hope that these more localized efforts will culminate in federal policies that will enable gig worker organizing or at the very least make it more difficult for companies that are reaping immense profits from gig workers to manipulate the classifications of independent contractors. In 2019, under the Trump administration, the National Labor Relations Board (NLRB) decided on a ruling that made it easier for companies to classify workers as contractors, as opposed to employees, which denies such workers the protections to unionize. In 2023, under President Biden, the NLRB threw out the previous ruling, reverting to the independent contractor test under the Obama administration, which takes into account factors such as the degree of control that companies have over workers and the degree to which workers are dependent on a single company for their livelihoods.[84] This version of the independent contractor test makes it more likely that gig workers are classified as employees rather than independent contractors. It is unclear whether this return to a more worker-friendly test will enable gig workers to organize more effectively.

CONCLUSION: CONNECTING THE LINKS
IN THE CHAIN

In this chapter, we described how the interrelated trends toward corporate deregulation and fissuring have had an impact on the transportation and distribution sectors of the food chain. Such shifts have been mediated by the global process of neoliberalization, whereas local, state, and national governments have pulled back on standards for international labor, to the benefit of transnational corporations, trade, and commerce. As a result, corporate powers in the food system have perpetuated a "race to the bottom" for workers' rights, pay, and safety precautions. While these trends affect all sectors of the global food chain, logistics workers, warehouse, distribution, and transportation workers in particular, have seen a massive loss in power in relation to their employers. Large-scale retail operations have not only consolidated their supply chains vertically, increasing their ownership over the warehouse and transportation sectors, but they have simultaneously increased their use of subcontracting and third-party employers from the top down. And while neoliberalism is generally sold under the guise of increased freedom for individuals to negotiate their own labor conditions, these sectors instead show increasing violations of individual freedom as companies constantly surveil and evaluate worker behaviors.

While warehouse, transportation, and delivery workers are often overlooked as food workers, they are essential to the food system. Given this, it is still uncommon to see connections being made between worker organizing in logistics and broader worker movements across the food chain. We can look to successes in unionization among Amazon workers and legislation to protect gig and delivery workers as examples of growing and connected labor movements in this sector. This notion of a food chain workers movement can build on the strategies that unions such as the Teamsters have integrated to support other workers in the food chain. By incorporating transportation workers in these organizing efforts, logistics workers could emerge as a powerfully organized group of food system laborers. While neoliberalism has led to worker precarity in countless and often unexpected ways, the worker organizing described in this chapter shows that there is reason for optimism that workers can successfully fight for and win much-needed rights and protections.

FOUR

Consolidation and Vulnerability from the Corner Store to the Superstore

Everyone, except for the managers, can sign a union card and have it in effect after ninety days. My first year I wasn't really involved very much because I was doing all this other stuff. Then, the first time contract negotiations came around, I got involved in that and then I was hooked! I've done the past four or five contract negotiations. I was involved in the first two and then I've kind of been the leader of the last two. . . . And then because we're a union shop, we as workers get to have a say. We get to have an effect on how the shape of the coop will be. Before I worked here, my dad was a teacher and did a bunch of union work and I sort of saw it from a distance. I knew about unions but until very recently they were in the tank for popularity, so I didn't really know much about them. But then I just sort of got hooked on it! I'll be honest, I really like the place. I've been there for ten years, and I think it does a lot of really good stuff in the community. I think it strives to be a pillar and a place that is stable for people. I say this all the time when I do our new employee orientations. You know, this isn't the 1920s and City Market isn't a steel mill, so there isn't a huge animosity, but there are still disconnects and there's still misunderstandings.

JOHN, *union local president, food cooperative employee*

IN THE CURRENT LANDSCAPE of grocery stores, unionized food cooperatives are certainly more the exception than the norm. For those who shop at coops, the distinctive smell of the bulk aisle, an ample selection of Fair Trade coffee, and rows of organic and local products are a (typically expensive) draw. And while food cooperatives offer certain benefits to their employees that are unique relative to big box food retailers, such as kombucha on tap and the kind of community leadership that John mentions above, the fact remains that grocery retail work is much more similar than it is different.

Food retail workers are among the most visible laborers in the food chain. They serve customers in supercenter chain stores, convenience markets, and traditional grocery outlets, in addition to alternative food outlets such as food cooperatives and farmers' markets. Workers in this sector are all those who perform their jobs at retail locations, including in-house cooks and bakers, as well as appliance and maintenance workers. In this chapter, we look at the labor conditions of workers in grocery and other retail establishments that sell food products, examining in detail the increase in horizontal and vertical corporate consolidation of grocery store chains and supercenters over the past several decades. We argue that this consolidation, from mom-and-pop grocery stores of the early twentieth century to the dominance of dollar store chains today, has led to an intentional decrease in workers' wages, benefits, and full-time employment, which has mirrored a drop in unionization in the sector. Despite these trends, recent shifts in the industry have brought worker resistance to the forefront, and we are in a moment with renewed potential for retail labor organizing.

Food retail has changed dramatically over the past several centuries, and unfortunately these changes have not benefited the worker. Workers have become casualties of a highly concentrated industry, with less control over their schedules and work conditions and virtually no access to those in power to challenge these conditions. According to our analysis of 2023 BLS data, the average wage for frontline food retail workers is $15.66 per hour and around $32,573 a year (including stores selling food and beverages specifically and not including superstores). They average only 27.9 hours of work per week, less than full-time, which keeps their weekly and annual wages below a living wage.[1] Workers in this sector make up 9.8% of food systems workers outside the home, with a total of 1,673,620 frontline workers.[2] Just over 11% of these workers are covered by a union contract.

The material and mental consequences of low-wage work in food retail were highlighted in a 2022 study by the Economic Roundtable, a nonprofit research organization. This study was the largest independent survey of grocery workers in the United States. It was conducted in response to a request by the United Food and Commercial Workers Union and focused on Kroger's, the second largest purveyor of US groceries. Its survey of workers in Colorado, Washington State, and Southern California found that the living and working conditions of Kroger workers have declined markedly over the past twenty years. Specifically, it found that over three-quarters of Kroger workers are food insecure and that workers reported high rates of

FRONTLINE WORKERS IN FOOD RETAIL, 2023

Total Employment:

1,673,620 workers

Union Density:

11.27% coverage, 10.6% membership

Mean Hourly Wage:

$15.66

Mean Annual Wage:

$32,573.33

Data Source: Occupational Employment and Wage Survey (OEWS), US Bureau of Labor Statistics

depression and anxiety resulting from their unsafe and insecure working conditions. It also reported that since 1990, the most experienced Kroger food clerks' wages declined from 11% to 22% (adjusted for inflation) and that across the entire grocery industry, 29% of the labor force is below or near the federal poverty threshold. Fourteen percent of Kroger workers are homeless now or have been homeless during the past year, which the report attributed to the company's emphasis on part-time and just-in-time work schedules.[3] While the study focused on just one retail chain, these conditions parallel those in other national chains.

Historically, high rates of unionization compared to other sectors have meant better jobs for food retail workers. Union representation is a bit higher in the retail sector than other food sectors, with about 7.3% of workers covered by a union contract.[4] From the 1950s through the 1980s, stable full-time jobs, seniority rights and promotion systems, procedures for grievances, protection against arbitrary firings, and higher wages all resulted from union organizing in the sector. Part-time work and erratic scheduling were regulated and restricted, and organized grocery workers had good pension plans and affordable health and dental coverage.[5] However, there has been a decrease in union power in the grocery sector over the past several decades. We discuss how corporations moved workers from full-time to part-time positions, the related vulnerabilities that come with this shift, and some of the causes of lower rates of unionization.

In the following sections, we look closely at the progression of corporate consolidation and the twin processes of government deregulation and corporate maneuvering that has resulted in such highly concentrated grocery retail today. We then explore the historical trajectory of grocers in the United States, discussing how largely family-operated and neighborhood-centered grocers were outcompeted by more standardized self-serve grocery stores to eventually pave the way for the chain superstores, dollar stores, and increasingly amalgamated grocery retailers of today. After examining the consequences of this consolidation on food retail workers, from wages and benefits to outcomes like rampant worker food insecurity, we look at alternative models of grocery retail such as cooperatives and farmers' markets, drawing out the differences and commonalities among workers. Finally, we discuss labor organizing in this sector, from traditional unions to localized worker centers, highlighting important forms of worker power that are on the horizon.

CORPORATE CONSOLIDATION IN FOOD RETAIL

As we see throughout the food system, consolidation in food retail has been enabled by both governmental deregulation and corporate tactics that often act in synergistic ways to concentrate power in large firms. The neoliberal transition to an increasingly deregulated and industrial-scale food system, where companies encounter less resistance from the state in terms of corporate concentration and labor standards, has created the backdrop for the economic precarity experienced among food retail workers. The retail grocery sector has steadily experienced mergers and consolidations since the mid- to late 1990s. This shift followed a national movement of corporate consolidation, enabled when President Reagan directed regulatory agencies to reduce their enforcement of antitrust laws. These laws were meant to prevent corporate mergers that would discourage competition among firms.[6]

Another federal approach to reducing enforcement of antitrust laws in retail food industries came from the Federal Trade Commission, with the introduction of the Standard Industry Codes. These codes designated what class of retail an establishment falls under, determining its access to suppliers and allowing different categories of businesses to source different products. Superstores, such as Walmart, Kmart, and Target, were classified differently from independent and chain grocery stores, such as Albertsons and Safeway. This differentiation effectively allowed supplier discrimination against different categories of retail stores, furthering the precarity of independent and chain grocers as compared to superstores.[7]

The rapid proliferation of mergers, spurred by deregulation and increased competition from trade reclassification, was further propelled by new competition from superstores in the retail food market, with Walmart at the helm.[8] Before Walmart recognized the enormous profit potential of selling food and entered the grocery scene in 1988, there was a greater diversity of large grocers in the United States. Yet once Walmart gained a national presence, other grocery chains were compelled to compete by also expanding into new regions.[9] Walmart is now the largest retail provider of grocery products in the United States and the largest corporation in the world. From 2018 to 2022, Walmart saw a gross income increase from $126,513,000,000 to $142,754,000,000, with a gross profit margin of 25.1%.[10] After Walmart, the other national chains that round out the top four as measured by grocery sales are Kroger, Costco, and Albertsons. Kroger, the largest traditional grocery outlet (although it does operate some department stores as well), has based its business model on merging with other chain stores. In 1999, Kroger bought out Smith's, Ralphs, Food 4 Less, and QFC (all previously owned by Meyer's Inc.), as well JayC, Owens Market, and Pay Less. It then merged with Baker's in 2001, followed by buyouts of Harris Teeter in 2014 and Roundy's, Pick 'n Save, Metro Markets, and Mariano's in 2015, expanding into new regions with each merger.[11]

As noted in research conducted by the US Department of Agriculture (USDA) Economic Research Service (ERS), supermarkets experienced major consolidation and structural change through mergers, acquisitions, divestitures, and internal growth over the past several decades. Specifically, two large mergers—the acquisition of Safeway by Albertsons in January 2015 and the acquisition of Delhaize by Ahold in June 2015—have had a significant impact on the overall makeup of food retail ownership. The share of food sales by the top four retailers has risen exponentially since the mid-1990s.[12] In 2019 alone, there were over three hundred food retail industry mergers and acquisitions.[13] This trend continues today in the proposed buyout of Albertsons by the Kroger supermarket chain. This $25 billion buyout would expand its market share to 13.5%, just behind Walmart's 15.5%.[14] Albertsons and Kroger anticipated this merger would be finalized in 2024 if approved by the Federal Trade Commission. Yet as of early 2024, they are facing opposition from US lawmakers and politicians, who are understandably concerned that further consolidation of the grocery sector will lead to fewer shopping options and higher food prices.[15]

Consolidation is supported by various corporate tactics, including vertical integration and building economies of scale. *Vertical integration* is the process by which companies attempt to streamline the production process by purchasing various stages of production. For example, a retail grocery chain may own vehicles for transporting products and its own warehouse facilities. Consolidation of the food sales business and vertical integration of the supply chain has helped grocery retailers obtain immense financial gains, even though profit margins in the food business have historically been quite thin. By vertically integrating their supply chain and bypassing the wholesale and transport sectors, grocery chains profit from an artificially cheap government-subsidized food supply, particularly grains and meats.[16] By taking advantage of purchasing these products directly at low prices, grocery chains have gained and retained a large percentage of the food market share.

Some grocery stores manufacture and produce some of their own branded products as well. This business model allows for the combination of transportation, distribution, and retail under one company's ownership and purchasing inputs in larger quantities to save on costs. Since their input costs to operate their business are reduced as they scale up, they can offer products to customers at lower prices. This process of vertical integration and the growth of such *economies of scale*, or the ability to outcompete established grocery stores due to cost savings throughout the production chain, create tougher competition for smaller companies. When vertically integrated stores, especially superstores such as Walmart with its own Great Value brand, come into a region, they often undercut family-owned and/or locally owned nonchain grocery stores and even other grocery chains.

Although vertically integrated employers may not hire all the workers in these facilities directly, they can still save on labor costs by having a centralized human resources process and streamlined policies on hiring and benefits. As we know from other food sectors, leadership at large-scale corporations is more than willing to pay workers the lowest possible wages and save on labor costs as well. While smaller and locally owned establishments are not always better places to work, they typically hire upper-level managerial staff from the local community. With superstores and large-scale chains, the better-paid white-collar jobs are usually located in corporate headquarters, far from where most employees at individual stores live and work. In this way, people in decision-making roles, such as those setting policies for labor and working conditions, are detached from those working in the retail environment. Store managers, whether in a supercenter like Walmart or a traditional chain grocer like Kroger or Safeway, are also disconnected from decision-making powers and beholden to policies that come down from a depersonalized and centralized upper management division. Decisions that affect workers' day-to-day experiences such as scheduling of shifts, sick day policies, the timing of breaks, what they can wear to work, and even how to style their hair are made by people they will never meet and enforced by people with little control over these policies.

This process of grocery retail consolidation has pronounced effects on the cost of food. As consumers have fewer options for grocery shopping, retailers with larger market shares have systematically raised prices, with dramatic increases after the pandemic, higher than the overall rate of inflation. In 2022, the consumer price index for home food purchases increased by 11.8%, almost five times its twenty-year historical average of 2.4% increases. The most noticeable effects have been felt in low-income households, which have reduced or changed their food purchasing practices as a result.[17]

THE HISTORY OF US FOOD RETAIL: FROM MOM-AND-POP MARKETS TO MEGASTORES

Before 1900, consumers in the United States largely bought their food in small-scale specialty shops, from butchers and bakers to vegetable stands, that were owned by sole proprietors and accessible on foot.[18] In the early twentieth century, grocery stores offering a larger selection of basic food items became a common family profession. With meager savings, a family could become business owners and, often, pillars of their local community. Compared to the available jobs at the time in unregulated industries such as farming, iron, coal, and textiles, the labor involved in running a grocery store was safer and less strenuous.

Small grocers were mostly mom-and-pop owned and operated, with a male owner of record and his unpaid wife partnering in the management and labor. It was a relatively accessible career to enter without much training or experience. The kinds of gendered family labor seen in these early grocers are common throughout the food system, as women customarily do work that is not seen in the public sphere and not rewarded with a wage or financial control. This is customary in other family-owned businesses like farming, where women's labor is part of a business's foundation but the company or land is typically passed along male family lines.[19] Most family-owned stores also offered delivery service, which was staffed by the children of store owners after school or part-time teenage boys who worked for tips and were not recorded on the payroll. While the hours were often long, starting at 4 o'clock in the morning to travel to the whole produce markets and closing after dark, food retail was considered secure and respected work.[20]

While one part of the grocery clerk's or store owner's job was to maintain a wealth of information regarding the products being offered, another part of the job was to offer an intimate level of customer service. While this meant that they could offer lower-income customers lines of credit and even discounts on a personal level, they could also choose how to price items in the moment, based on race and immigration status, as well as income. Such a power dynamic between clerk and customer could be used to help someone in need, as well as to discriminate and cultivate more desired customers.[21] Because of this, many grocery stores in the early 1900s were immigrant owned and specifically tailored to the needs of their own communities, whether Irish, Czech, Jewish, or Mexican, who encountered discrimination in other retail operations. While meager English-language skills might have been limiting in other professions, owning and operating a small grocery in one's own neighborhood could serve as a lucrative way out of low-wage jobs. If successful in the grocery business, a family could build their enterprise and move out of the working class.[22] However, African Americans owned only one in fifty food stores in the early twentieth century, and racialized grocery ownership continues to the present day.[23]

Self-serve grocers, where customers browse the store and choose items as they like, was not an option until 1916, when a local retailer opened the first King Piggly Wiggly grocery store in Memphis, Tennessee. The founder of the chain, Clarence Sanders, started as a grocery store worker himself and eventually launched the Piggly Wiggly as the first self-serve grocery that divorced the relationship between the clerk and the customer and created a streamlined experience for the consumer. For the first time, customers could enter a store and take their time looking at a variety of items without having to ask for each item from a person behind the counter. While the primary purpose of this new design was to increase the diversity and quantity of items a customer could purchase, it also achieved the goal of reducing labor costs, as customers retrieved their own items and employees simply checked them out instead of personally assisting them with each item on their list. This new model for grocery shopping stuck: the Piggly Wiggly chain grew to over twelve hundred stores in just eight years. Other grocery chains followed suit, including the grocery behemoth A&P.[24]

As Raj Patel, a prolific food systems scholar and journalist, points out, the removal of the grocery clerk owner or employee from the experience of food

FIGURE 12. Vazquez Grocery Store, Bronx, New York, 1977–78. Joe Conzo Jr., photographer.

shopping served to dehumanize the process of food decision making, distancing the consumer from the origins of their food, as grocery clerks were no longer expected to retain knowledge concerning the quality or origins of food products.[25] Yet, as noted above, interactions in locally run stores were often dependent on the relationships between the individual shopkeeper and the shopper, which could be stacked against shoppers of color. Because of this, some scholars argue that self-serve supermarkets appealed particularly to Black shoppers who could avoid lengthy interactions with store owners and other clerks.[26] In locally owned and operated stores, quality and price were not evenly distributed, as the grocery clerk had control over each item and how it was sold. A certain level of suspicion of grocery clerks was also weaponized by manufacturers of packaged products. These manufacturers argued that consumers want consistency and reliability, both from the products and from the stores and workers where they shop.[27]

While the Piggly Wiggly did eventually attempt to remove the grocery clerk altogether, an effort that failed at the time, this was the first step in the automation of grocery store labor. What followed quickly, though, was the specialization of grocery work, similar to Fordism discussed in chapter 3, where employees were given repetitive piecemeal tasks to increase efficiency among the grocery workforce. This is in sharp contrast to the over-the-counter worker who took the time to work directly with each consumer and had to amass a wealth of food-related knowledge to properly do their job. Patel aptly describes this transition for workers:

> Their job description was downgraded from the almost artisanal knowledge of customers, of providers of consumer credit, and conduits of information, to a job that primarily involved stacking shelves and pointing customers through a maze. Under the reign of supermarket logistics, every other function that the shopworkers performed prior to the invention of the self-service store has been dismantled and redistributed.[28]

This deskilling of labor parallels many other changes across the food system and is linked to scientific management techniques that emphasize efficiency and profit over worker well-being.

The first grocery retail chain to attain national prominence, the Atlantic and Pacific Tea Company (better known as A&P), changed both the way the grocery industry operated and the way labor was managed. A&P started as an import and shipping company, with retail tea and coffee shops in New York City by 1859 and a mail order food business. Over the next several decades, the store expanded to include dry goods, dairy, meat, and produce while also growing its own food manufacturing arm. By 1912, A&P had 400 retail grocery stores, and by 1915, the chain operated 1,600 stores. From 1915 to 1975, A&P was the largest grocery retailer in the United States (and, until 1965, the largest US retailer of any kind).[29]

This chain-led expansion also began the standardization of labor in grocery stores as A&P developed its food and grocery business as a heavily top-down and streamlined retail operation. Unlike the small mom-and-pop grocers of the past, headquarters decided everything, from how managers, bookkeepers, and clerks should use their time; how products were selected; how to arrange products; and how to create window displays. Inspectors were sent from headquarters regularly to ensure that each store and its employees followed established rules and regulations.[30]

A heightened scale of integration and subcontracting came later in the grocery store game. A&P was the first vertically integrated supply chain in US grocery sales, owning its own factories, warehouses, and trucks.[31] Yet even in these early stages of grocery chain development, there was backlash from mom-and-pop food stores as well as wholesalers and producers. The ability to buy larger quantities of product for lower prices (economies of scale) allowed chains such as A&P to undercut smaller family-owned operations, most of which employed entire families and the occasional nonfamily worker. Chain grocery stores could buy directly from wholesalers and producers in large quantities, while family-owned and family-operated stores had to pay higher prices to go through a middleperson or a smaller and more limited wholesale operation.[32]

While chain grocery stores were quick to grow nationally, an anti–chain store movement began in the 1920s and gained in popularity during the Great Depression. At the same time, the owners of A&P, the Hartford brothers, emphasized loyalty between the worker and the company and made employee retention a cornerstone of their company philosophy. In one effort to retain workers, they offered subsidized stock shares to any employee who had worked for at least five years, at a time when there were no public stock options in the store. Despite this brand of employee loyalty, A&P and other chain grocers were charged with gutting local economies as regional stores offered minimal employment options and no high-level or executive salaried positions, compared to locally owned stores. While independent retailers and wholesalers tried to forge a legal battle against chain stores by claiming unfair competition, they eventually lost; the chain operations and their ability to offer lower prices to customers prevailed.[33] As we discuss in the next section, purchasing larger quantities for lower prices and integrating multiple links in the supply chain are the primary methods national grocery chains and supercenters utilize to undersell locally owned competition.

The shift to chain grocers reflected a consumer desire for more consistent products and shopping experiences and resulted in the import of the Fordist assembly line model to grocery stores, reducing labor costs by cutting back on staff and setting the stage for the emergence of a workforce that mostly filled shelves and performed other repetitive tasks. Eventually, this model, including low-wage labor but expanding to a larger selection of groceries, was picked up by Kroger and then others. Over the decades that followed, straightforward advances in technology and design, such as the individual costumer shopping cart and expanded store aisles, allowed for increased purchasing without grocery clerk assistance. By the mid-1960s, the US self-serve supermarket had become a staple in every town.[34]

The building of the Trader Joe's empire deserves special mention in the history of food retail labor. Originally called Proto Markets, Trader Joe's was started by Joe Coulombe in Southern California in the 1950s. Coulombe decided to pay his employees the median family income at the time, in contrast to the standard at convenience stores like 7-Eleven. Further, he valued product knowledge and sophistication among employees. By offering higher wages, and as a store designed to cater to a more informed clientele, Trader Joe's drew an educated employee base with low turnover compared to other grocers. In addition, it consciously hired women and people of color in leadership positions, in contrast to other chains even twenty years ago.[35] Some of these early commitments to worker agency have shifted over the past two decades, a point we examine in detail when discussing current unionization efforts. And despite attempts to brand itself as a unique shopping experience, Trader Joe's has benefited from the same technical advances that have streamlined the grocery industry.

An important ingredient in the streamlining of retail operations came in the 1970s when grocers introduced the Universal Product Code, which allows managers and workers to look up items and see their price. Combined with the development of the supermarket checkout scanner, cashiers could now send data to management and warehouses to track inventory and purchases. Also during the 1970s, a new grocery store warehouse model was introduced: it dispensed with aesthetically pleasing displays and engaged customer service in exchange for offering deeply discounted high volume groceries. At warehouse stores like Thriftimart, Penn Fruit, Acme, and Pantry Pride, customers could buy products in bulk and supposedly save money. These warehouse chains also got rid of sacking clerks, employees whose sole job was to bag and carry groceries to the customer's car. This was an effort to streamline the grocery industry in response to a period of economic recession, saving money on labor and giving consumers the impression of a bare bones cost-saving option.[36]

Warehouse stores paved the way for the membership-based wholesale stores such as Costco and Sam's Club, as well as other supercenters. As noted above, the advent of supercenters such as Walmart and others in the 1980s, followed by the federal deregulation and reclassification of food retail in the 1990s, led to the further intensified consolidation of the industry. These wide-scale shifts in the food retail sector provide the backdrop for the kinds of company mergers and labor practices we see today.

THE CONSEQUENCES OF CONSOLIDATED GROCERY
GIANTS FOR RETAIL WORKERS

Grocery retail has long served as one of the few sectors where people without a college degree can earn a living wage, receive a range of benefits, and work in a relatively safe environment. However, working in this sector also comes with a host of challenges, which have worsened since the 1980s as a result of the combined effects of government deregulation, corporate consolidation, and union decline. Whether working at Walmart, Safeway, or Trader Joe's, grocery clerks today must simultaneously work efficiently, create an aesthetically appealing and seemingly pristine sanitary environment, and charm the customer. Efficiency is emphasized in all chain food retail stores, with workers heavily monitored by management while performing tasks such as stocking and store opening. Grocery retail is also intense work as the product is not just valuable but often perishable. Making sure that the most highly perishable and valuable product sells without spoiling and that it remains fresh and appealing is no small organizational feat. While managers and owners may oversee product placement and strategy, the clerks and stockers are responsible for making this happen.

As they juggle multiple tasks, food retail workers also confront the stressors of erratic and part-time scheduling. Workers' economic vulnerability is made worse as the scheduling of retail shifts has fallen prey to the dark side of just-in-time production. At most large chain operations, workers are not given regular or predictable schedules. Schedules can change depending on projected demand at the store, and employees can expect to have shifts changed or rearranged at a moment's notice. This shift has not only occurred in food retail, but across the labor spectrum, part and parcel of the shift to temporary and flexible labor.[37] The emphasis on just-in-time retail schedules creates constant stress for workers but saves companies money on wages and benefits, increasing their bottom line.

One of the primary reasons that food retail work has become so precarious is the increasing power of superstores like Walmart and corporate giants like Amazon (both as a delivery company and as parent company for Whole Foods) and the mergers of large chain grocers like Kroger and Albertsons, which attempt to maintain profitability amid increased competition. Since the 1990s, Walmart has made significant inroads into the retail grocery industry, and this expansion has been a significant factor in the restructuring of grocery employment and the US labor market overall. As of 2024, Walmart is still the single largest private employer in the United States (although Amazon is fast approaching), with 1.7 million employees, 94% of whom are hourly workers. Walmart is also the largest retail grocer and currently makes up over a quarter of US grocery sales overall, larger than the combined total of its next two competitors, Kroger and Costco. A little over half of its sales come from groceries, health, and beauty.[38] Walmart is not only dominating the retail and food markets in the United States; it is the world's largest retailer, expanding its brand of just-in-time supply chains, low wages, and documented worker exploitation globally.[39]

When Walmart moves into a regional market, it first offers lower prices than other local food providers to outbid the competition. Once other grocery stores get priced out and close, it raises its prices, with consumers taking the hit.[40] There is also evidence that when Walmart enters a region, it not only means low wages for its direct employees but also functions to lower the prevalent wage in the area, as its dominance in the retail market drives down overall wages and other industry standards.[41] Walmart's atrocious reputation for employee treatment is not due to financial limitations, which may be the case for smaller locally owned businesses. In 2017–22 alone, Walmart had over 120 recorded legal violations, ranging from wage and hour violations (their number one offense) to employment discrimination and environmental offenses. The company was charged $2,076,780,239 in penalties from 2000 to 2022, a tiny percentage of its overall profits.[42] Of course, these are just the violations that have been pursued and recorded, which many precarious workers are reluctant to do.

Yet perhaps the starkest contrast between Walmart's employment practices and that of grocery stores of the past is its focus on part-time work. As noted above, grocery work has historically been a full-time job that has included benefits and a living wage for employees. While for most, it is not an upwardly mobile position, it allowed middle-class workers a dignified opportunity, with few barriers to enter the position. At Walmart, the barriers to entry may still be low, but so are the rewards. In 2013, the economic vulnerability of Walmart employees made national headlines when it was reported that a store in Ohio held an annual food drive for its own employees, many of whom were part-time workers.[43] In a 2018 survey of 7,098 current and former Walmart associates, researchers found that the chain has been reducing the number of full-time workers and increasing part-time employment, with an estimated 50% of employees hired part-time. Most part-time workers

FIGURE 13. Walmart protest, Washington, DC, 2014. Drew Angerer, photographer. Courtesy of Redux Pictures/New York Times.

preferred full-time work, and people of color were more likely to be involuntarily part-time.[44]

Another huge shift in the retail food labor landscape has been the entry of the e-commerce giant Amazon, as discussed in the previous chapter. The transition to the larger role of logistics and warehouse in traditional retail has emphasized the mechanization of these tasks, not just in terms of actual robots or computers doing the work, but the mechanical management of human workers themselves in creating work schedules, assigning tasks, and measuring and monitoring workers' efficiency. Amazon Fresh, the subsidiary of Amazon that sells food directly to customers online, employs workers in the warehouse, distribution, and transportation sectors, yet these workers have been taking on labor that was previously done in retail. In 2017, Whole Foods was purchased by Amazon and has been at the heart of the expansion of grocery delivery, combining online ordering sites for both outlets. While not all of their workers are in the physical retail location interacting with customers, they are still part of the world of food sales.

Despite this push, wide-scale automation has yet to fully succeed in grocery retail. Technological changes such as barcode scanners and self-checkouts have not given way to a fully automated system. In fact, as such technologies were developed to reduce labor input, other changes in the industry occurred, including the availability of more prepared foods and other specialty items such as cut flowers, increasing the need for more diversified and skilled labor. These increased offerings helped secure the power of unions in the sector, despite some growth in automation of the industry. Human labor is still essential to grocery stores' functioning.[45] This is also linked in part to consumer pushback on automated checkouts, or a "self-checkout reversal," and the concerted effort by store owners to replace human workers with computers in food retail.[46]

This concentration of power in firms like Walmart and Amazon and the mergers of grocery giants that are attempting to compete with them has coincided with a concerted attempt to undermine the power of unions, which had established solid footing in the grocery industry throughout the twentieth century.[47] This transition from unionized grocery stores to low-wage employment supercenters is part of a long and continuing history of US food retail workers getting further squeezed in the name of efficiency and expansion. One reason for this is the historical power of unions to expand and maintain union density in these businesses, even as their traditional stronghold of manufacturing declined.[48] The UFCW, which primarily represents grocery retail workers, is the second largest private sector union in the United States. Yet, as we have noted, the entry of Walmart into grocery retailing has forced major supermarket chains in low-income areas to reduce both prices and employment to compete and sometimes leads these stores to leave the area. Most of these grocery chains have historically been unionized.[49] Consequently, the entry of Walmart has decreased retail employment levels and reduced overall wages and benefits in the industry as unionized grocery workers have been replaced with more part-time and vulnerable labor.[50] Unionized supermarket workers made on average 30% more in wages and benefits when Walmart started in the late 1980s. By the 1990s, when Walmart had gained a foothold in the grocery sector more broadly, its influence meant it could negotiate for major wage cuts and other concessions, even with its unionized workers in the food chain. A broader effect was that other supermarket chains then argued for their own concessions, particularly with the UFCW, which had been forced to negotiate for a worse deal with Walmart. Other superstores such as Kmart and Target, though they have a smaller footprint, have similar antiunion stances.[51]

The vulnerability of food retail workers was made abundantly clear during the COVID-19 pandemic and in its aftermath. In a study conducted in

FIGURE 14. Supermarket Meat Department Employee Wearing a Mandatory Mask. Gilbert Mercier, photographer. Creative Commons.

Boston in June 2020, researchers found that grocery store workers in public-facing positions were five times more likely to contract the virus.[52] In addition to the physical health risks from exposure to the virus, grocery workers experienced high levels of distress. Lacking options for social distancing, basic safety training, and consistent enforcement of consumer behavior, grocery workers tried to navigate their own risk in relation to their need for income.[53] Large food retail chains had more instances of sick workers attending work and larger rates of virus spreading in the workplace. Workers who were already living below the poverty line were more likely to continue to work while sick.[54]

There was a short period when some workers received "hero" or "hazard" pay, a temporary wage bump to compensate for the risk they were taking to ensure consumer food access. However, these efforts were not enough to rectify the risks that these workers endured or the lack of protections from their employers. In one study of US food retail workers conducted from July to October 2020, researchers found over 40% of workers nationally felt poorly protected by COVID-19 safety protocols in the workplace.[55] Not surprisingly, workers in grocery stores with active employee unions fared better than those without. Unions were active in negotiating access to proper protective equipment such as masks and sanitizer for workers, paid sick leave, and enforcing customer mask usage.[56] Employers without strong unions and generally lacking in worker benefits and protections before the pandemic were of course the most vulnerable to high levels of virus outbreaks, employee illness, and death. Unsurprisingly, the pandemic brought to light frustrations many grocery and other retail workers were already feeling about the jobs, and turnover in the industry has remained high as the risk of severe illness has decreased and other sectors have recovered, despite pay raises overall.[57]

Amid global inflation, which has caused many to go hungry and struggle to buy basic necessities in the post-pandemic period, grocery chains have increasingly profited. In 2020 alone, Kroger earned a whopping $1.64 billion in net income and a 2.27% increase in gross income. The following year, in 2021, Kroger saw an 8.35% increase in sales, $2.56 billion in net income, and a 15.66% increase in gross income.[58] The compensation for Kroger's CEO, Rodney McMullen, increased 296% from 2012 to 2022, 909 times greater than the median pay for company employees, representing one of the largest CEO-worker pay gaps of any major American company.[59] McMullen made the news in 2020 when his take-home pay equaled $22 million, just as he decided to cut hazard or hero pay for his workers.[60] This hazard pay was cut only two months after the pandemic began, even as the pandemic continued to affect grocery workers for years to come. Further, the company actively closed stores in jurisdictions that put policies into effect mandating hazard pay, apparently to avoid the costs.[61]

Kroger is not alone in these unprecedented financial gains. Albertsons, currently the fourth largest grocery chain, reports similar profits. In 2020, Albertsons had a 3.7% sales increase, $466 million in net income (a shocking 255.76% increase), and a 4.14% increase in gross income. In 2021, the company saw an 11.58% sales increase, $850 million in net income, and an 8.26% increase in gross income.[62] With regard to Albertsons' skyrocketing profits in 2020, this increase in profitability was due to fewer people eating outside the home and continued exploitation of essential workers, whose wages were not increased commensurately with the increase in sales and profits. Yet these profits have not translated into better working conditions or compensation for employees. The disparities in compensation between frontline workers and management are one more reminder about the devastating impacts of corporate consolidation for food system workers.

Like national chain grocery stores and supercenters, convenience and dollar stores have crowded out locally owned and even smaller chain grocers in recent years. Convenience and dollar stores typically carry a variety of products, including a limited number of food items. While many corner stores are locally owned and operated with few nonfamily employees, we refer here to national chains of convenience stores, which have also displaced many locally owned corner stores. Utilizing the *franchise* model in convenience stores and a reduced service model in dollar stores, these retailers are expanding their hold on the grocery market and consequently pushing wages and benefits for grocery workers even lower, all while decreasing available healthy and affordable food for consumers. In a franchise arrangement, the lead corporation provides permission for a local owner to use the company's name, brand image, and products. This approach allows for brand growth at the corporate level while leaving local owners vulnerable to market shifts, health, safety, and labor issues.

The convenience store was born in the early twentieth century, just as larger full-service grocers were taking hold. The first known convenience store opened in 1927 when a Dallas ice vendor named John Jefferson Green, who kept his small dockside stand open from the hours of 7 a.m. to 11 p.m., started carrying a small selection of grocery items such as eggs, bread, and milk. Green went into business with a larger ice company called Southland, which eventually grew the idea into a chain operation. Inspired by Green's original business model, Southland was renamed 7-Eleven, and by 1951, it was the largest retailer of beverages, milk, and bread in Texas.[63] Today convenience stores like 7-Eleven can be found around the world at busy street corners and neighborhood intersections. They offer a greater variety of food products, including those essential fresh products the concept was built around, a small variety of fresh fruits and vegetables, and meats. However, the selection of food products sold at convenience stores today is typically dominated by sweetened beverages, candy, salty snack foods, and sweet frozen treats.[64]

Like many retail, fast-food, and convenience chains, 7-Eleven operates as a series of franchise establishments and is consistently ranked as one of the top ten nationally grossing franchises in North America, with 81,887 locations in 2022.[65] While the 7-Eleven parent company holds all branding rights, the individual franchise owners take on most of the financial and legal risks as independent contractors.[66] 7-Eleven obligates all franchises to operate twenty-four hours a day, according to its franchise contract. During the recent pandemic labor shortages, franchise owners struggled to fill these positions and were forced to fill the undesirable overnight shifts themselves, which they have argued has been "bad for their health."[67]

The franchise structure not only puts local management in a precarious position but also leads to a lack of accountability for workers in the context of a larger corporate structure. In one instance of egregious worker abuse in 2013, US immigration officials found fourteen 7-Eleven operations in Virginia and New York committing labor violations and exploiting undocumented immigrants; this was one of the largest criminal immigrant employment investigations by the Department of Justice and the Department of Homeland Security at that time. Franchise owners were found to be furnishing workers with fake identification, forcing them to work more than one hundred hours a week for a fraction of their hourly rates, and housing them in unregulated boardinghouses, in what officials called a "modern-day plantation" ring. 7-Eleven corporate headquarters effectively distanced itself from individual franchise holders and placed all the blame on them, abdicating responsibility for the workers abused under its brand name.[68] Unfortunately, there seems to be an international trend of abuse among 7-Eleven franchises. In Australia from 2011 to 2016, there was a widespread series of wage violations involving foreign workers holding temporary work visas at 7-Eleven franchises across the country.[69]

Like convenience stores, the dollar store model includes several national chains, all of which advertise items at or around a dollar. These stores sell a variety of convenience items, including food, mostly canned and/or processed, with little fresh meat, fruits, or vegetables. Despite their meager food offerings, in areas with limited food access, dollar stores are often the only food retail available. This business model has grown at such a rapid rate in the past decade that dollar stores have started to crowd out full-service grocery stores, saturating the grocery market with lower prices yet fewer food options and exacerbating food insecurity in poor regions. There are currently more dollar stores than Walmart and McDonald's locations combined. Sadly, some grocery stores that survived the influx of Walmart are now falling to the competition of dollar stores, leaving many communities with limited food options, especially in rural areas.[70]

The biggest dollar store chains, Dollar Tree and Dollar General, utilize a lean employment model, with only eight to nine employees per store, according to their own reports. This is in comparison to small independent grocers, which hire on average fourteen employees.[71] During the pandemic, the number of Dollar General stores ballooned, with expansion into new products, including fresh food and with an eye to capture new, younger, and wealthier customers. After an aggressive rollout of self-checkout in 2022 in order to reduce labor costs, they have in fact reversed course as part of a suite of retailers that has reassigned check-out workers after finding that they lost money due to theft and consumer error.[72]

As is the case with other large-scale chain retail employers, the increase in automated scheduling of shifts, with the goal of maximizing profit and minimizing labor cost, leads to employees and their direct managers having little control over their work hours. In an ethnographic study of the Dollar General chain, the sociologist Tracy Vargas revealed that automated scheduling in the dollar store setting led to decreased equality among workers as well as chronic understaffing.[73] Moreover, these scheduling systems were not well understood even by frontline managers given that last-minute scheduling decisions were centralized in upper management. In addition, her study makes the connection between poor labor practices and structural inequality at the consumer level. In stores where workers are not paid or treated well, especially in geographic areas with limited employment options, the extended community feels the struggle.

Dollar stores, and stores like Walmart and other large-scale retail chains that utilize these unfair labor practices, are increasingly consolidating the retail grocery market by opening stores where food is not their primary product, thereby underpricing stores with broader and healthier options. This has significant implications for the health and food security of low-income and geographically isolated customers in rural and urban areas where people have limited access to transportation to shop for food. While the root causes of poverty or hunger are connected to broader histories of racialized economic redlining in urban areas and disinvestment in rural areas over many decades, these stores accentuate these inequalities and take advantage of already vulnerable local economies, worsening healthy food access in their communities. While the power of consolidated grocery stores, megastores, and dollar stores is clear, there are alternative retail structures that must be acknowledged as well. In the next section, we discuss the labor context of alternative food retailers and why, despite being outside the corporate food retail structure, such alternatives often replicate the same unequal labor dynamics as the more consolidated grocery chains discussed above.

In contrast to superstore and chain retailers that have grown in power because of corporate consolidation, many alternative retail options exist for purchasing food. These retailers, such as corner stores or small-scale grocers, often bill themselves as more supportive of local businesses and economies. These include food cooperatives, farmers' markets and stands, and family-owned corner stores. Yet, as in other sectors of the food system that are seen as alternative to the conventional or mainstream, there is little attention paid to the labor required to keep alternative retailers functioning. Consumers often assume that the scale or aesthetics of a food product or space implies better labor practices, whether or not that is the case.[74] In this section, we look at these retailers, which serve as an alternative to more highly consolidated grocery models and discuss the pressures they face to conform to a global food retail market and a downward pressure on workers.

Direct from producer models, such as farmers' markets and farm stands, reduce the distance between the eater and the producer, yet someone typically needs to be employed to sell the food in the marketplace. As discussed above, the transition to chain operations with consistent and less personalized consumer interactions was a way for many communities of color, particularly in the US South, to escape these historical race relations between food consumer and retailer. However, scholarship on farmers' markets has highlighted the ways in which these alternative spaces reinforce normative whiteness and exclusivity based on class and race.[75] In particular, farms that sell directly to the public often use the image of the white heteronormative family in their appeal to wholesomeness in the marketing of products. While it has been noted that this imagery obscures the labor on the farm, which is usually performed by immigrants of color even on family owned and operated farms, it can also obscure the labor off the farm, such as at farm stands and farmers' markets.[76]

Farmers selling in direct-to-consumer spaces such as these are aware of the value of their personal presence; what consumers are looking for is to "know your farmer," as the bumper sticker goes. The pressure to present a white "traditional" farm family is strong, and white farmers have an advantage over farmers of color in their ability to showcase this family structure in marketing.[77] Farmers' personal labor is valuable, and the time it takes to pack a truck, drive to the market, and work at a stand can mean a financial loss given their very real need to run farm operations, especially when it is a small-scale venture. In these cases, farmers hire family or nonfamily labor to take on the retail tasks of farm-to-consumer sales.

More research is needed on the labor dynamics within alternative food retail spaces, including the factors that influence farmers' hiring preferences and practices such as race, class, and gender. In one of the few studies concerning labor on "ecologically oriented and organic farms," the geographer Michael Ekers and colleagues show how dependent such farms are on unpaid apprenticeships and volunteer workers, which is ultimately an unsustainable economic model.[78] In our own personal experiences working on alternative farms and at farmers' markets in Seattle and the California Bay Area, we have seen how racial segregation is reinforced by the workers who represent farms at the market. On farms that are mostly staffed by immigrant labor, it is often white high school or college students and farm interns who take on the job of selling at markets and farm stands and representing the farm to the public. We also observed that when college-educated white apprentices with little farming background are employed, they are quickly promoted to less strenuous tasks such as market sales, while immigrant workers are not usually offered such opportunities.

This is not to say that farm stand labor is easy or even preferable. Working a farm stand or farmers' market can require waking at 4 a.m., driving from one to six hours, loading and unloading a truck, standing outside for up to eight hours in all kinds of weather, often with little access to bathroom or meal breaks, and then driving back to the farm, only to have to unload again. As farm stands and markets are typically assumed to be staffed by the owner operator or their family members, they are not regulated by OSHA, which has an exception for any farm with ten or fewer nonfamily employees.[79] Yet the labor of direct farm-to-consumer sales is difficult work, and when nonfamily labor is hired, it is usually at the same low wage rates as farmworkers. While there is no clear research or data on farm stand and farmers' market employees, related research discussed here can lead to some primary assumptions: this work is segregated by race and class and is not well compensated or regulated.

Cooperative grocery stores are frequently likened to farmers' markets, in that consumers can find more locally sourced as well as organically or ecologically produced food products. Yet unlike farmers' markets, whose main purpose is to support small-scale producers, cooperative buying models were originally developed in the United States by workers as a response to blacklisting for striking in response to poor labor conditions and have historically had a strong tie to union organizing.[80] In the 1970s, consumer- and worker-operated food cooperatives were part of broader social and environmental movements where food was seen as key to community engagement. While intentional food consumption was at the heart of the food cooperative movement of the time, broader social activism was also central. Members were expected to be active participants and coops were prime space for consumers to align with other worker movements, such as the UFW grape boycotts. Retail food cooperatives were part of a larger movement to restructure the food system from the ground up, based on community networks.[81]

Despite the more labor-centered ethics of food purchasing that were common in the early days of US food cooperatives, today's cooperative grocery stores are more structured around consumer needs and preferences. There has been a shift away from worker-owned cooperatives and toward member-owned ones, and most do not require members to work regular shifts in the store but instead offer discounts and voting rights in exchange for a paid membership. Food cooperatives are mostly staffed by hourly (rather than salaried) employees, much like other retail grocery workers. Although food cooperatives often have better health care coverage and offer higher wages than conventional grocery employers, most are not unionized and cooperative employees experience many of the same challenges as other retail food employees in terms of working conditions and access to decision making, particularly regarding part-time employment and scheduling shifts.[82] Unfortunately, and perhaps not surprisingly, research has shown that food cooperatives often fall short when exercising shared responsibility and striving for social justice given the need to compete in a capitalist food system.[83] Of course, there are exceptions to this struggle: cooperatives that put labor at the core of their mission with leadership that supports unionization. Yet these organizations must do so by actively resisting the pressure of retail market structures.[84]

Finally, corner stores, which we define as locally and often family-owned outlets, are distinct from convenience stores, which are large-scale chains. Although both provide similar products—a selection of limited food items such as beverages, snacks, and essential groceries—corner stores are usually staffed by owners and their families. Owners may also hire some nonfamily workers, who typically labor for minimum wage. As the anthropologist Ashanté Reese notes, corner stores often serve an important community function and facilitate neighborhood social cohesion.[85] While there is extensive research on the impact of corner stores on the nutritional health of consumers and the potential for healthy product interventions, little is understood about the employment context of such locations. In a study of corner store owners and workers in Baltimore in 2016, researchers found that participants noted numerous workplace safety and work-related stress hazards. They found significant reports of corner store owners and workers contending with violent crime and related worker injury. They also experienced ergonomic hazards, such as back pain and numbness, from working in small spaces, moving stock, and performing repetitive tasks.[86]

Alternative food retail spaces offer opportunities to rethink how we might structure consumer access to food products in ways that offer good-paying and respectable jobs to the people who do this essential labor. However, all alternative food spaces must also contend with the current globalized capitalist food system and struggle to achieve the goals of providing truly just options to business as usual. Next, we examine successful examples of food retail organizing and resistance, where workers attempt to center labor justice in the retail sector.

ORGANIZING WORKERS IN THE GROCERY INDUSTRY

Despite the negative consequences of increasing consolidation and precarity, there is a long history of unionization in the grocery industry for today's workers to draw on. What had once been a highly unionized sector is now more reflective of the rest of American retail, with lower levels of unionization than in the past and increasingly precarious employment.[87] However, the past few years of increased unionization in retail and other food sectors show the tide may be changing.

The original mom-and-pop grocery stores that preceded today's large-scale chains were allied with unions, as they were typically worked by the family alone. In the early 1900s, when there was a push for longer operating hours in the grocery industry, family-operated stores fought back along with unions as they operated their stores themselves and, like hired labor, wanted to maintain their nonwork time. Specialty food trade unions, such as the Amalgamated Meat Cutters Union, bakery unions, and other retail unions, also saw their professions being swallowed by the grocery industry as it beat out small specialty food shops such as butchers and supported the grocery union struggles. Not surprisingly, large chain operations resisted unionization, both with carrots (higher wages and pension plans) and sticks (threatening to fire employees and closing unionized stores and warehouses). As there were no legal protections for workers to unionize until the National Labor Relations Act was passed in 1935, only a few grocery chains were unionized before this time.[88]

While large chains such as A&P initially fought the advent of unions in their stores, the American Federation of Labor (which later became the AFL-CIO) and others eventually won this struggle after an explosive battle, and by the 1960s, grocery retail became one of the most highly unionized sectors in the country, with about 40% of all retail food workers organized (compared to 12% of all retail workers). At that time, all the large supermarket chains were highly unionized, mostly by the Retail Clerks International Association (RCIA), as well as three other major unions: the Meat Cutters, the Teamsters, and the RWDSU. These unions supported each other by refusing to cross picket lines across the food chain, as they represented food workers in other sectors, such as trucking and warehouse work. This kind of cross-sector support was crucial to successful food retail organizing.[89]

In the 1980s, rates of unionization across the country were generally taking a downturn, grocery workers included. The expansion of Walmart as a global retailer of food and other products played no small part in that decline for the grocery sector, as its antiunion tactics, including closing a unionized store, drove down labor standards for the industry.[90] Other grocery retailers followed Walmart's lead. In 2003, Safeway workers staged the longest grocery strike in US history. For nineteen weeks, workers stayed off the job fighting cuts to wages and benefits. Safeway's so-called competitors, Albertsons and Kroger, agreed to also lock out their union workers, conspiring with Safeway, and the companies shared their losses and revenues to weather the strike. Ultimately, the grocery chains won, arguably signifying a shift in the industry from middle-class employment to low-wage jobs.[91]

Nevertheless, the grocery sector today still has a relatively high proportion of unionized labor compared to other private industries in the United States. In 2023, only 6% of the private sector was unionized, whereas just over 11.27% of food retail workers were unionized. While this is a low number compared to unions' height in the 1960s, it is still significant and is potentially growing as part of the post-pandemic labor movement.[92] Grocery unions have survived relative to other retail due to the place-bound nature of the industry, which is not easily moved abroad. Across the food supply chain, retail is arguably the most place-bound, especially regarding perishable goods that consumers often prefer to choose in stores themselves.[93]

The sociologists Justin Myers and Josh Sbicca tell the story of a successful union coalition movement to resist Walmart entering the food retail market in New York City in 2012. Activists came together with the union, UFCW, and Jobs with Justice to launch the "Good Food, Good Jobs" campaign.[94] They successfully campaigned for the mayor, the city council speaker, the Department of City Planning, and a coalition of community groups to create the Food Retail Expansion to Support Health (FRESH) initiative, which provides financing and zoning incentives to expand grocery stores and supermarkets in underserved communities. Rather than the planned arrival of Walmart, a unionized ShopRite supermarket was successfully brought in to anchor a large suburban-style shopping mall in New York City, a defeat for the notorious antiunion chain.

Workers at the growing retail chain Dollar General are also being inspired by a growing labor movement. Despite the downward pressure on employment and wages when these stores enter a region or market, some dollar store employees are looking at their minimum wage jobs and starting to ask for more. Many have been inspired by workers organizing unions and asking for better working conditions at national food-related chains such as Starbucks and Amazon, as well as the Fight for $15 movement at fast-food chains. In 2022, in Tennessee and Louisiana, employees at Dollar General, Dollar Tree, and Family Dollar started drawing attention to low pay, unsafe work conditions, and pest infestations, which were all being ignored as the companies focused on growing their store locations. These workers have been organizing without forming a formal union, and some have been partnering with local worker centers, which they see as a more efficient and locally focused approach.[95] In addition, there has been a large-scale movement at the consumer level to block the entry of new dollar stores in specific communities.[96]

Even at Trader Joe's, with its worker-friendly beginnings, there has been a push for better worker pay and higher standards. Trader Joe's is now owned by the same German company that owns Aldi supermarkets, and despite retaining some worker-friendly policies, such as a relatively high wage and ratio of employees to customers compared to other grocery stores, it has consistently fought unionization efforts by employees.[97] Despite its success at suppressing unionization over the years, the company began facing successful nationwide unionization efforts in 2022, with workers asking for benefit increases and appropriate pay rates as the retail industry tries to recover from the global pandemic.

When employees made gains in unionization efforts at Trader Joe's in some stores in summer 2022, forming Trader Joe's United, an independent union, the chain immediately increased compensation and benefits nationwide. This created tensions between workers who were organizing and those with newfound loyalty to the store because of the raises and better benefits. However, the company did not extend the same benefits to the stores that had unionized, citing the need to bargain first. Simultaneously, workers who had been attempting to unionize at a Trader Joe's in Boulder, Colorado, filed an unfair labor practice charge against the chain after the store took back increases in pay and benefits it offered during the pandemic, claiming it had illegally made changes to compete with their efforts. Further, the UFCW filed charges alleging that Trader Joe's closed a wine shop in New York City just days before workers had planned to file for a union election on August 2022.[98] While increasing wages and benefits may be generally positive for employees, it is illegal when stores do so in direct competition with labor organizing.

Despite the corporate control over policies like uniforms and schedules, workers in retail positions often find camaraderie and solidarity in their workplaces. While most see the jobs as temporary due to the lack of professional development opportunities and chronically low wages and are therefore less likely to be invested in workplace organizing and improvement, they still form relationships with other workers from similar cultural and ethnic backgrounds and with those from the same neighborhoods. In his research on resistance among chain retail workers, including Target supercenters that sell groceries, the sociologist Peter Ikeler found that the corporate bureaucratic structure results in retail workers generally having low levels of job identity, opposition, and union support but higher levels of worker solidarity. Limited structural power combined with deskilled labor leads to workers lacking identity within their workplace, which leads to muted interest in labor organizing. While these patterns do not preclude unionizing and other forms of labor resistance and workers do indeed identify with one another on a personal level, the corporate structure of workplace management creates increased barriers to reclaiming worker agency in retail settings.[99]

As discussed in this chapter's opening, unionization and labor organizing among retail and other workers are increasing. After decades of being "in the tank for popularity," the past few years have seen an impressive growth in unionization and other organizing across food sectors. This push for collective bargaining rights across companies that have historically led the retail and service sectors in wages and benefits is indicative of the ways that food retail and food service workers have struggled throughout the pandemic and the increasing precarity of their positions.[100] The pandemic, which has increased the visibility of frontline workers' vulnerability, and the related economic downturn, has led to increasing political support of unions more broadly in the United States.[101] What this means in the longer term for grocery unionization is still unknown, but organizers are thus far succeeding in taking advantage of this moment. As we argue throughout this book, a more cohesive and intersectional food chain framework could help this movement.

CONCLUSION: FOOD RETAIL WORKERS ARE CONSUMERS TOO

The shifts that accompany consolidation in the food retail industry have had the cumulative effect of eroding the power of workers and unions across the board, leaving food retail laborers in increasingly precarious positions. This precarity has broader impacts that ripple across society, affecting other workers and consumers alike. A 2020 study by the nonpartisan Government Accountability Office, which reports to the Budget Committee of the US Senate, found that Walmart, McDonald's, Amazon, Kroger, and Dollar General were among the top employers with employees receiving federal aid such as Medicaid and the Supplemental Nutrition Assistance Program (SNAP), otherwise known as food stamps.[102] While the rate of reported food insecurity overall in the United States is 12%, it is a shocking 55% among Walmart workers.[103] And although Walmart might be the most infamous, it is not just happening there. A recent study of Kroger workers nationwide found that *three-quarters* of all the company's workers are food insecure, and among single parents who work at the store, *85% are food insecure.*[104] These statistics tell us a lot about the need for new policies and social movements that can directly address these structural inequalities throughout the food system.

Moreover, the consolidation of the grocery retail industry has pushed out locally owned and operated grocery stores, which has direct effects on the social fabric of a community and the economic well-being and physical health of people who live and work in locations vulnerable to predatory expansion of consolidated firms. Food justice activists, media sources, and scholars alike comment regularly on the lack of food access in relation to food deserts or food apartheid. Research has focused on the effects of supercenter stores on consumer health in terms of increasing packaged and ultraprocessed food and reduced nutritional quality.[105] Yet not many scholars or even journalists discuss the direct impact of chain retailers and superstore groceries on the buying power of these stores' employees and the relationship between community-level food insecurity and the introduction of retail grocery low-wage jobs.

As with all other sectors of the food system, food retail employment does not inherently have to equal bad or undesirable jobs. Grocery stores started out in the United States as community and neighborhood based, offering families stable incomes and respectable roles in their diverse communities. Many forms of resistance as well as alternatives have been persistent in attempting to reform food retail as we know it today—from fighting back against superstores like Walmart to creating worker-owned cooperative groceries. We must keep looking to these models as we search for solutions to the many problems created by corporate consolidation and connect the dots between the well-being of food retail workers and the well-being of society as a whole.

FIVE

Intersectionality and the Fight for a Fair Wage in Food Service

I really like being on my feet and I like interacting with people and I like that it's fast paced. One of my bosses who I worked with always described it like a dance. If you're doing it well, if you're paying attention, you can see the way that people are sort of dancing through the room and there's a rhythm to it. There is a weird camaraderie, a family feeling that happens fairly quickly and there's a strange trust and mutual bond that happens. I know some people have had issues where there's a big gender difference between the front of house and back of house just because front of house tends to be typically more dominated by women and experiencing harassment from back of house. I've been lucky to work in places where that's not the case at all. . . .

I think what a lot of people struggle with is health insurance and working hours that are disruptive to their family lives and being able to participate with other parts of the world that operate on a completely different time schedule. That's something I know I've struggled with when I have to be somewhere at 8 a.m. but my shift ended at midnight. All of those things are trade-offs. Also, retirement funds, most places don't offer any kind of employer-sponsored 401K, definitely no match. Most of the people I worked with were without health insurance or were young enough that they were still under twenty-six. This is where I could see a shift happening in the pay structure where people just charge more for their food and people pay their workers a higher wage, and also offer comprehensive benefits.

QUINN, *food service worker for 9 years*

IN FEBRUARY 2014, restaurant workers and activists, most of them women, gathered outside New York's City Hall, telling stories of sexual harassment and abuse, from catcalling to overt threats to their livelihoods. "I am not on the menu!" became the rallying cry. This local protest, part of the national One Fair Wage Campaign, organized by the Restaurant Opportunities

Center United (ROC-United), was connected to a range of events across the country. The shared goal was to draw attention to the connection between the tipped wage and structural and chronic harassment of servers and other food service workers whose income is based on voluntary customer tips. As research from ROC-United reports, four in five female restaurant workers have experienced some form of sexual harassment from their customers. Workers who receive a *tipped wage*, which is a legally lower base wage paid to a worker who receives a substantial portion of their wage in customer tips, may earn as little as $2.13 an hour (the federal tipped wage) from their employer and are assumed to make up the rest of their income in tips from customers. If their tips do not reach the minimum wage, the employer is supposed to make up the rest, but there is little oversight of this process, and most tipped workers depend on their customers' benevolence to make ends meet. As Quinn shares in the story above, in addition to fair wages, food service workers desperately need access to comprehensive benefits if these jobs are to be considered good jobs.

While restaurants and other food service outlets are often sites of joy, celebration, and social connection, they are also simultaneously sites of worker dissatisfaction at best and worker abuse at worst. Having gained traction since the turn of the century, labor activists are challenging the poverty-level wages that are endemic to food service and have highlighted serious and persistent problems of discrimination and harassment in the industry. Various movements, including the Fight for $15, are working to bring powerful abusers to justice and eliminate the tipped wage. In this chapter, we take inspiration from these efforts and engage an intersectional approach to argue that inequalities related to race, class, gender, and other markers of difference and identity are deployed as mechanisms of capitalist growth and profiteering within food service. Amid a broader movement for livable wages across the United States, there has been a noticeable growth in food service workers organizing for better pay and better working conditions.

The food service industry has the largest proportion of workers in the food system and is an incredibly diverse sector—in terms of the kinds of work being done and who is doing it. Food service workers come from all walks of life. More than half of frontline workers in the food system who work outside the home do so in food service, which includes full-service restaurants, fast-food chains, bars, cafés, and catering companies, as well as institutions such as schools, prisons, and hospitals.[1] Also included in this sector are the thousands of people who feed workers in the lunchrooms of corporate giants like

Total Employment:	*Union Density:*
9,655,990 workers	1.81% coverage, 1.52% membership
Mean Hourly Wage:	*Mean Annual Wage:*
$16.24	$33,772.50

Data Source: Occupational Employment and Wage Survey (OEWS), US Bureau of Labor Statistics

Google, Meta/Facebook, Apple, and Morgan Stanley. While there are important differences in who eats at these places, who owns these places, and how they operate, their purpose is the same: to feed and serve people when they are away from home.

According to BLS data, 9,655,990 people worked in food service in the United States in 2023, which is 56.8% of frontline food workers.[2] Though food service is the largest sector of food systems work, it is poorly paid, with workers earning an annual median wage of $33,773 and a median hourly wage of $16.24.[3] These median wages are due in part to the federal tipped minimum wage, which as of 2024 remains the same rate ($2.13 per hour) as it was in 1991. Only 1.81% of workers in this sector are covered by union contracts. The work in this sector is highly gendered: more than 70% of the restaurant workforce are women, and an estimated 94% of school cafeteria workers are women.[4]

Organizing restaurant workers through the union model has historically been difficult, whereas unions among food service workers in hotels, airports, schools, and hospitals have found a bit more traction. Since 2020, however, it appears that unions are finding more inroads in the food service sector. This may be due in part to improving public perceptions of labor unions, which in 2022 was at the highest point since 1965, with 71% of respondents to a Gallup poll approving of unions.[5]

We begin this chapter by providing a conceptual overview of how intersectional differences related to workers' identities become a tool of capitalist profit in the service sector. As feminist scholars and activists have observed, the extraction and exploitation of the labor of women and BIPOC workers produces deep inequalities. We then turn to an examination of how such inequalities play out in two primary sites, restaurants and K–12 schools, where there are important differences in the forms of labor and the volume of people who are fed. In the restaurant section, we discuss both untipped and tipped work, drawing out important observations about how tipping exacerbates inequalities related to race, class, and gender. Next, we discuss organizing work in food service, including both the influential public campaigns like the Fight for $15 and the unions that are seeking to improve working conditions in this sector. We conclude by reflecting on the several years that have passed since the pandemic as people have been leaving low-wage and erratic service labor—what has been called the Great Resignation—and what this means for the future of food service.

INTERSECTIONALITY AS AN ORGANIZING FEATURE OF CAPITALISM

An intersectional approach that engages with a critique of capitalism is essential for understanding how race, class, gender, ability, and other elements of identity play out in food service and who profits from these arrangements. *Intersectionality*, an analytic approach first proposed by the legal scholar Kimberlé Crenshaw, has influenced scholarship in diverse disciplines and social movement activism. However, many studies of labor, particularly food labor, do not take an intersectional approach.[6] In their argument for its importance, Psyche Williams-Forson, a food studies scholar, and Abby Wilkerson, a scholar of disability studies, offer a powerful synthesis: "Intersectional analysis resists essentializing or prioritizing any category of difference and does not seek simply to add categories to one another (e.g. first gender, then race, class, age or sexuality). Instead, this methodological and theoretical approach strives to understand what is experienced at the intersection of two or more axes of oppression at different historical moments and in different contexts."[7] We believe that intersectionality is essential for understanding the experiences of workers across the food system, particularly service workers given that their earnings are often determined by the identities they hold.

Critical treatments of capitalism and feminism often unfold on parallel paths, with Marxist feminists offering a critique of how capitalism is only possible through the exploitation of women and their labor and intersectional feminists asserting that different elements of one's identity, including race, class, and gender, combine to enable both privilege and oppression in highly contextual and socially specific ways. Capitalism, at its core, is based on the squeezing of labor power from workers to the direct benefit of owners. Yet the way in which workers experience capitalist production, and their own exploitation, is through intersectional identities of race, gender, sexuality, ability, and citizenship, and is related to historical processes.[8]

In the restaurant industry, unlivable wages persist as the federal tipped wage and related sexual harassment are the norm rather than the exception. Further, racial segregation underlies the hierarchies built into the service industry, with Latinx and other immigrant workers typically in the position of dishwasher and white and often male workers making up a higher percentage of fine dining servers.[9] Similarly, for school food workers, dynamics of gender, race, and class are constantly at play. Part-time care-based positions are filled primarily by women. As schools are pressured to lower the cost of providing meals, labor costs are often where cost-cutting happens first and most severely. Food service is also a common occupation for workers with intellectual disabilities; the National Restaurant Association makes a special point to note that disabled workers can fill labor gaps.[10] Capitalist profits in the service sector are driven by and benefit from these intersectional inequalities, as the most economically vulnerable workers, including young women, single mothers, and undocumented immigrants, make up a large portion of these low-paid and insecure positions.

Despite the immense size and reach of the food service sector, it is important to note that the dependence on food prepared outside the home is a relatively recent social shift. In her book *Making Modern Meals*, the anthropologist Amy Trubek traces the changes in cooking over time, underscoring how US households have transitioned over the past century from eating food mostly prepared at home to spending a majority of the food budget outside of the home.[11] Of course, these shifts have affected different workers and eaters in different ways, shaped by their social identities and work demands. As Trubek notes, when the USDA started tracking food expenditures in 1929, only 15% was spent on food eaten away from home. This rate has steadily increased since that time, and as of the time of writing, food spending away from home has rebounded even higher than it was before the pandemic. In 2021, spending on food away from home accounted for 55% of total food expenditures in the United States, for a total of $1.17 trillion.[12] This was due in part to inflation and increased overall food costs but also to fundamental shifts in how US households feed themselves.[13] By looking at the service sector through the lens of intersectionality, we pay close attention to the fact that the American tradition of being waited on has been subsidized by the exploitation of a low-wage workforce, one largely composed of women.

FROM DRIVE-THROUGHS TO FINE DINING: INTERSECTIONAL INEQUALITIES IN THE RESTAURANT INDUSTRY

Restaurants have existed since ancient times, but the dramatic proliferation of restaurants in their contemporary form began in earnest with the Industrial Revolution and urbanization. From inns and taverns where weary travelers were served basic fare at shared tables to hypermodern minimalist restaurants where diners spend hundreds of dollars for deconstructed entrees and an extensive wine list, restaurants have long been places where social hierarchies are particularly visible and often detrimental to the lives of workers. In these spaces, meals are a commodity to be bought and sold, and the preparation and service of the meals is paid work. The cultural significance of eating out in contemporary culture is evident not only in restaurants themselves but also in popular representations of dining and restaurant work.

From the pioneering home chef Julia Child to Pioneer Woman Ree Drummond, popular media provides countless examples of books, television shows, and movies that both romanticize and masculinize restaurant culture and reinforce that the place of women is in the home kitchen.[14] In shows featuring chefs like Bobby Flay and Gordon Ramsay and more recently *The Bear*, viewers live vicariously through aggressively competitive portrayals of restaurant workers. Unfortunately, these portrayals often downplay or outright ignore the labor of women and immigrants and other workers of color in food service (*The Bear* is the exception) and the particular forms of violence and exploitation they endure. They also focus on upscale dining rather than fast food or even the fast casual options that are more common for most consumers. While fine dining can offer at least the possibility of making a living wage, or enough to meet basic daily needs, in fast-food and fast-casual restaurants poverty-level wages are the norm.

While the monetary value of meals and work varies widely across restaurants, it is inherently a different position to be the waiter and the person who is being waited on. Ask anyone who has waited tables for a living, and you will hear countless tales of being stiffed on tips and drunken rowdiness but also heartwarming stories of marriage proposals and birthday celebrations.

FIGURE 15. Striking Restaurant Workers at Stouffer's Restaurant, Detroit, Michigan, 1937. Photographer unknown. Walter P. Reuther Library, Archives of Labor and Urban Affairs, Wayne State University.

Regardless of the type of restaurant, you are also likely to hear stories of sexual harassment, perpetrated by customers and coworkers alike. For workers of color, accounts of racist attitudes and behavior are just as common, stemming both from the patterns of segregation that exist in food service establishments and from interactions with clientele. Due to these factors, the costs of working in this sector of the food system are much more than just financial. We extend and apply an intersectional analysis to look at the experiences of restaurant workers in two main subgroups: fast-food workers who rarely receive tips as part of their compensation and workers in casual and fine dining for whom tips are a significant if not *the* most significant part of their income.

FROM THE GOLDEN ARCHES TO STARBUCKS: UNTIPPED RESTAURANT WORK

Fast food was at first a distinctly US phenomenon, and its expansion unfolded in parallel to other massive social transformations of the twentieth century.

The exponential growth of fast-food restaurants across the United States in the mid-1900s was intertwined with more women working outside the home, suburban growth, "car culture," and new social values glorifying speed and efficiency. While it may not have been the first fast-food restaurant (A&W is often credited with this distinction), McDonald's was the first to take the assembly line model of production and the principles of scientific management and adapt them to creating a meal through the 'Speedee Service System." This assembly line model was an important factor in the successful early expansion of the McDonald's franchise under Ray Kroc into a company that now has 38,000 locations in a hundred countries. The McDonald's model of speed, efficiency, uniformity, and predictability has reached far beyond the fast-food counter. The term "McDonaldization," coined by the sociologist George Ritzer, describes "the process by which the principles of the fast-food restaurant are coming to dominate more and more sectors of American society as well as the rest of the world."[15] This model, and an emphasis on consistency, is as true for the workers as it is for the food.

In what is perhaps the most widely read exposé on fast food, Eric Schlosser's *Fast Food Nation*, which was made into a feature-length Hollywood film, examines both the immense power of the fast-food industry and the ways that fast food has harmed our health and environment and expanded in imperialistic fashion outside of the United States. In examining the power of this industry, he points to the ways that fast-food giants have targeted specific workers to maintain control and a competitive edge by keeping labor costs low.[16] While Schlosser notes that for some time, teenagers made up the main group of fast-food workers, as baby boomers aged out of entry-level work, new groups of workers, including the elderly, the disabled, and recent immigrants, have started filling this role.

Efforts to improve the pay of fast-food workers have often been met by the argument that because they are largely teenagers who are working for pocket money rather than supporting families, salary increases are not necessary. The extension of this argument is that if wages increase, teen employment would be reduced. There are two problems with this argument. First, it is not true that most fast-food workers are teenagers; in fact, it is estimated that half of all fast-food workers are over the age of twenty-three, and only 30% of fast-food workers are teenagers.[17] Second, as studies have shown, many teenagers are in fact providing income to support their families today, and in some families, they are the primary earners.[18]

Despite the fact that fast food is available in nearly every corner of the globe, as the historian Ken Albala notes, its glory has faded over recent decades, partly because of the well-known negative health consequences of fast food but also because of "the way in which it transforms the nature of basic food work, requiring little or no skills and therefore making labor largely expendable."[19] This transformation of work is inextricable from the development of automation technologies designed to produce uniform and predictable products, from the McDonald's French fry to the Taco Bell crunch wrap, filled with perfectly diced tomatoes and rehydrated ground taco meat. As Robin Leidner notes in *Fast-Food, Fast Talk*, the standardization of food preparation is extended to service work itself, as workers' speech, behavior, attitudes, and appearance are forced to conform to corporate expectations of speed and uniformity.[20] The question designed to upsell, "Do you want fries with that?," has come to signify many things in contemporary US society, but at its core it is a reminder of the degree to which customer-employee encounters are scripted by executive management.

The pressure on workers to labor quickly or be replaced has had a negative impact on the wages and well-being of frontline fast-food workers. Fast-food work is widely understood to be low-paid, and the pay disparities between counter workers and top executives are especially pronounced. According to BLS data, in 2021, there were 3,095,120 fast-food and counter workers in the United States, representing just over 30% of all food service workers. These workers earned a mean hourly wage of $12.53 and a mean annual wage of just $26,060, which fall short of the overall averages for all food service workers outlined in the opening to this chapter.[21] The same year, McDonald's CEO, Chris Kempczinski, raked in over $20 million, with about $14 million dollars of that compensation in stocks and options.[22] The year before, Brian Nichol, CEO of Chipotle, earned over $38 million, including stocks and options. These gross disparities in pay have been called out by politicians like Senators Bernie Sanders and Elizabeth Warren who have called for raising taxes for companies where the top executives earn more than fifty times the pay of the median worker. As with other food work, these inequalities ripple out to other parts of the economy, as seen in higher usage rates of food entitlement programs and other forms of welfare. Along with food retail, fast-food companies like Taco Bell, Wendy's, Pizza Hut, Burger King, Subway, and McDonald's are among the top employers of people using SNAP.[23]

In addition to low wages, the health and safety risks of frontline fast-food work are significant and include burns, lacerations, injuries from slipping and falling, stress and workload hazards, and sexual harassment and violence. These increased risks are compounded by the fact that historically few fast-food workers have received health insurance from their employers or have access to paid sick days. As might be expected, the COVID-19 pandemic had a particularly pronounced impact on frontline fast-food workers. A study published by the UCLA Labor Center in 2022 reported that among the estimated 150,000 fast-food workers in Los Angeles, "nearly a quarter . . . contracted COVID in the last eighteen months, and less than half were notified by their employers after they had been exposed to COVID."[24] Many workers surveyed reported that employers did not respond to concerns about their exposure risks, and some even faced retaliation after raising their concerns. Even more disturbing is their finding that nearly two-thirds of workers experienced wage theft during the pandemic, when workers were quite literally putting their lives on the line for work.

We must recognize how service work in fast food is racialized and gendered. According to BLS data, when comparing the proportion of fast-food workers to all workers, there is a greater proportion of women (64.2% vs. 46.8%), Hispanics (21.4% vs. 18.5%), and Asians (7.7% vs. 6.7%). For African American workers, the proportion is much closer (12.7% vs. 12.6%). This concentration of women and racialized groups in fast-food work means that the poverty-level wages that are paid in this sector disproportionately affect groups that are already forced to navigate other intersecting social inequalities. As we discuss when we turn to the Fight for $15, these are also the same groups that have been successfully mobilizing for change in the fast-food industry.

FROM DENNY'S TO THE FRENCH LAUNDRY: TIPPED RESTAURANT WORK

For those who work in restaurants where tipping is the norm, interactions with customers take on heightened meaning as the vast majority are not guaranteed a livable hourly wage and are therefore dependent on the whims of diners for their livelihoods. However, even as tipping has become normalized in US society, there remains a significant gray area where both customer and employee are confused about what is expected. For example, it is unclear whether you should tip when picking up take-out and when you order at a counter and bus your own table or if you should tip more for excellent service and less for poor service. Ultimately, that gray area does not work to the benefit of food service workers.

As of early 2024, only seven states require restaurant employers to pay tipped employees the state minimum wage before tips are factored in. In the remaining forty-three states, restaurant owners can choose to pay their employees who receive tips a tipped wage, which, at the federal level, is set as $2.13 per hour, a rate that has not increased since 1991. Of these forty-three states, twenty-eight (plus the District of Columbia) require employers to pay tipped employees a minimum cash wage above the federal rate of $2.13, with a significant amount of variation in that difference. The remaining fifteen states allow employers to only pay the federal rate.[25] Importantly, some cities like New York and Portland, Maine, have set their own minimum wages higher than the states in which they are located. In 2023, the One Fair Wage campaign had a major victory in Chicago, home of the National Restaurant Association, an organization representing more than 380,000 restaurant locations that has lobbied for years against minimum wage increases. As result of a hard-fought campaign that supported the election of progressive candidates in key political positions, One Fair Wage reached a compromise with the Illinois Restaurant Association whereby the tipped wage will be phased out over five years and replaced with a minimum wage of $15.80.[26]

The first legal guidelines for employers to pay a tipped wage (in contrast to a federal or state minimum wage) began with amendments to the Fair Labor Standards Act in 1966, in what is known as the "tip credit" provision. This provision allowed income from tips to count toward half of the minimum wage guaranteed under the FLSA, with the tipped wage making up the other half. In a report for the Economic Policy Institute, Sylvia Allegretto and David Cooper argue that this provision fundamentally changed restaurant work and who is actually paying the wages of tipped workers: "Whereas tips had once been simply a token of gratitude from the served to the server, they became, at least in part, a subsidy from consumers to the employers of tipped workers. In other words, part of the employer wage bill is now paid by customers via their tips."[27] This dependence on the customer results in a host of issues, from tolerating sexual harassment and being forced to flirt with customers to instances of racial discrimination against diners of color, who are assumed by some to be bad tippers.

Many argue that the practice of tipping and its intersectional impacts in the United States can be traced much farther back to a legacy of slavery.[28] The civil rights activist Michelle Alexander notes:

> After the Civil War, white business owners, still eager to find ways to steal Black labor, created the idea that tips would replace wages. Tipping had originated in Europe as "noblesse oblige," a practice among aristocrats to show favor to servants. But when the idea came to the United States, restaurant corporations mutated the idea of tips from being bonuses provided by aristocrats to their inferiors to becoming the only source of income for Black workers they did not want to pay.[29]

However, as the journalist Nina Martyris observes, the history of tipping in the United States is a complicated one, and as the practice spread after the Civil War, many characterized it as "offensively un-American," given its roots in the master-serf relationship of the Middle Ages in Europe.[30] In fact, six states outlawed tipping between 1915 and 1926. Over time these laws were repealed as the culture of tipping became more firmly grounded in US service occupations.

For others in the early 1900s, tipping was acceptable only if the tips were being paid to Black workers given the entrenched racial hierarchies that persisted after Emancipation. The racialized history of tipping bleeds into current disparities in tip earnings, with white men working in the front of the house earning an average of $4.79 more per hour than Black women working in the front of the house. This disparity is also linked to the fact that women and workers of color are more likely to find work in casual dining instead of fine dining, where meal prices and therefore tips are lower. When they are employed in fine dining, women are concentrated in jobs that receive lower tips, such as bussing instead of serving or bartending.[31]

The gendered consequences of tipped work are significant, as women make up roughly two-thirds of tipped workers.[32] More claims of sexual harassment are filed in food service than in any other industry, with more than 70% of men and 90% of women experiencing sexual harassment on the job.[33] The pervasiveness of sexual harassment stems in part from the dominance of men in managerial positions and other highly paid roles in food service, where, in contrast, most frontline servers and hostesses are young and female. The power dynamics that result from these differences can create a setting where sexual harassment is tolerated, ignored, or normalized. In particular, because of these gendered differences, workers do not feel comfortable reporting customer conduct to their manager or boss.[34]

In some workplaces, poor treatment from customers creates an environment of harassment, where managers and employers feel emboldened to disrespect service workers as well, withholding good shifts and making them tolerate verbal abuse if they complain. Workers report that they usually do not speak up, as tips still make up most of their income, especially in states where the tipped wage is $2.13 an hour. The common belief that "the customer is always right" compounds the situation. Having to depend on tips for a large part of one's income forces many food service workers to flirt with customers, downplay their experiences of being harassed, or dress in provocative ways to increase the tips they receive. During the COVID-19 pandemic, there were documented cases of servers being asked to remove their protective masks so that customers could decide how much to tip based on their appearance.[35]

Of course, there are significant differences in the experiences of front and back of the house employees, differences that are heavily influenced by the kind of establishment and the demographic and cultural dynamics surrounding the establishment. Front of the house employees work directly with customers as hosts, servers, baristas, bartenders, and bussers, while back of the house workers manage inventory, prepare food, cook, and wash dishes. There is much variation in the practices of sharing tips between the front of the house and the back. In pooled tipping, tips are collected from all tipped workers and distributed by the employer or manager. This practice can encourage a "we are all in this together" mentality, although it can also lead to resentment and a toxic environment between workers when there is a perception that not all workers have labored equally.

In contrast, the practice of "tipping out" is a voluntary and relatively informal practice where servers count tips at the end of the night and share small amounts with workers of their choice, often including hostesses, runners, bartenders, dishwashers, cooks, and bussers. Key changes to the FLSA made in early 2018 (as part of a budget spending bill) changed two important elements of tipping. First, it was prohibited for employers or supervisors to collect or retain any tips from their employees. Second, in restaurants paying the full minimum wage to all workers (with no workers making the tipped wage), it was now permitted for servers to share tips with nontipped employees. These changes were in response to a new set of standards established by the Department of Labor in 2011, whereby servers had been disallowed from sharing tips with non-tip-earning staff, such as cooks and dishwashers behind the kitchen doors. Responses to these changes (re)allowing tipping for the back of the house were mixed, with some arguing that these jobs would become more desirable as workers could now receive tips on top of their regular (presumably minimum) wage, thus eliminating some labor shortages and equalizing the pay imbalance between the back and front of the house. On the other hand, others argued that the increased wages for back of the house employees should be paid by the employer rather than subsidized by customers.[36]

In addition to differences in pay, the line dividing the front and back of the house is the most obvious form of racial segregation in the hospitality sector due to racial discrimination in hiring and promotions. Relatedly, this segregation is linked to differences in citizenship, a point explored in depth by the sociologist Eli Wilson in his research on high-end restaurants in Los Angeles.[37] Wilson follows other ethnographers who have been employed at their field sites, in this case working at three high-end restaurants. Wilson shows how he, a white, educated man, was quickly promoted to higher-status and better-paid jobs over his Latinx immigrant coworkers. The segregation that persisted in the restaurant extended outward to social spaces where front of the house workers would often drink together after work while the kitchen staff would stay behind to clean up. Racial preference in promotions is also well documented in the stories of various workers in Jayaraman's book, *Behind the Kitchen Door*.[38]

As we saw in chapter 3 with reference to food delivery workers, the gig economy has also made inroads into shaping the contemporary labor structures of restaurants located in US cities, as app-based platforms like Pared, Instawork, and Poached Shifts become more established.[39] Most recently, gig work has spread to service positions like waiting tables, bartending, and even dishwashing. Through these platforms, restaurants facing labor shortages or particularly busy periods advertise positions, and the app helps place chefs, cooks, and service staff in restaurants on a shift-by-shift basis. As a *New York Times* piece reports, the benefits and costs of these digital tools are a mixed bag, given that workers taking these shifts do so as independent contractors. While the hourly earnings for these gig workers might be higher than those of a regular restaurant position, like most restaurant workers, they do not have access to collective bargaining or receive benefits like health care, unemployment insurance, or paid time off.[40]

While fast-food restaurants often receive much of the public criticism for unfair labor practices, the toxic work cultures of fine dining, including those looked to as models of sustainable practices, have recently been exposed by investigative journalism. In an in-depth look at the venerated restaurant Blue Hill at Stone Barns, Meghan McCarron reveals that behind the imaginary of farm-to-table perfection, ongoing cases of abusive behavior, wage theft, sexual assault, and abysmal wages were reported in the kitchen of the "philosopher chef" Dan Barber.[41] Like other restaurants receiving Michelin stars and a place on the 50 Best Restaurants List, this exposé reported that Blue Hill at Stone Barns relied on unpaid externs from top culinary schools like the Culinary Institute of America to staff its kitchen.[42] As these students simultaneously worked more than full-time hours for free and paid for their academic credits, they experienced double exploitation, supposedly in exchange for a shot at a lucrative career in fine dining. The persistence of these problems raises the question of whether there is any hope of ensuring fair and socially just workplaces in food service if worker exploitation persists even in these supposed beacons of "sustainable" dining.

SERVING MORE THAN SLOPPY JOES: THE IMPORTANCE OF SCHOOL FOOD WORKERS

School lunch has been available to children in public schools since the 1910s, although at the outset programs were operated largely by a volunteer staff of mothers who came in to prepare simple hot foods during the school day. While school meals provided an important source of sustenance for children during the Great Depression, they were not standardized until 1946, when Congress authorized the National School Lunch Act, expanding school lunch across the nation. School breakfast was not widely available until the 1960s, when the Black Panthers, a comprehensive social movement for Black liberation, started feeding children free breakfast in Oakland, California, as part of their social welfare efforts to get Black children out of poverty. This program was run by movement volunteers who solicited food donations and prepared the food for children each morning. While the federal government started a pilot free breakfast program simultaneously, it was not until the success of the Black Panthers program spread across the country (and was subsequently dismantled by the FBI) that the government program took off.[43] Today the National School Lunch Program (NSLP) is administered by the USDA's Food and Nutrition Service (FNS) and operates in nearly 100,000 schools and childcare institutions across the United States. As of 2021, an estimated 127,350 people worked in elementary and secondary school cafeterias, earning a mean hourly wage of $13.87. The NSLP provided 3.2 billion meals in 2019, including both meals served during the school year and those provided through the Seamless Summer Option (SSO).[44]

In contrast to the numerous studies that have been conducted on restaurant work, few have examined the lives of workers in institutional food service, including those working in schools, hospitals, and prisons. An important exception to this is the school food scholar Jennifer Gaddis's book, *The Labor of Lunch*, which provides an in-depth examination of the workers who maintain school cafeterias and contribute to what some feminist scholars call "community mothering."[45] As Gaddis notes, school meals have served as an anchor for many efforts connected to the contemporary food movement, and well-known figures like Michelle Obama, Jamie Oliver, and Alice Waters have centered school meals as a necessary leverage point for improving the health and nutrition of children. However, guaranteeing dignified working conditions and fair compensation for cafeteria workers caring for these children has rarely been a priority for those seeking to improve institutional food. As is the case in so many of the caring professions where women make up the majority of the workforce, the contributions of these frontline workers in the food system, including the emotional labor that is involved in caring for and feeding children, are not adequately valued or recognized.

In her book, Gaddis discusses the "negative cultural baggage" that accompanies the term "lunch lady," and while some gender-neutral terms like "food service employee" and "cafeteria worker" have caught on, "lunch lady" persists as a common term used to describe this kind of work, including by the workers themselves. While identifying as female is not a formal requirement for this work—Teresa's own father did a short stint in an elementary school cafeteria after his retirement from the construction industry—as many as 94% of school cafeteria workers are women. The school meal workforce is also older than the general workforce (average age of 50 vs. 42) and has higher percentages of Black workers (18% vs. 12%) and Hispanic workers (21% vs. 17%). More than half of school food workers have a high school education, with 22% having some college experience.[46] The feminization of this kind of work and the fact that most of the work involved in caring for and feeding children is performed by women connect our points here in meaningful ways to the arguments we make about reproductive labor in chapter 6.

As with other frontline workers, school cafeteria workers were hit especially hard by the COVID-19 pandemic, facing increased risk of contracting the virus as they continued to work in tight quarters and often with inadequate PPE. While some cafeteria workers were laid off as schools went remote, many continued to work on site in schools that were deemed too dangerous for students to attend.[47] In the K–12 context, these workers produced millions of meals for students qualifying for free and reduced breakfast and lunch who were now learning from home.

According to a report by the Economic Policy Institute, the staffing shortages that followed the onset of the pandemic were linked both to the higher average age of school cafeteria workers and the abysmal wages they receive. More than half (50.4%) of school service workers are over the age of fifty, compared to less than a third of all US workers. The fact that school cafeteria workers are on average older than other workers means that they were at higher risk of becoming seriously ill, encouraging many to leave this sector. Between 2014 and 2019, school cafeteria workers earned a median weekly wage of $331, compared to the overall US median of $790.[48] This median wage is also lower than that received by teaching assistants and school bus drivers, who also earn far below the median wage.

Local and state policies and guidance on school meals have proven to be an important leverage point for improving pay and working conditions, and these efforts often connect to broader calls for improving school food. In a recent report by the Center for Cities and Schools at the University of California, Berkeley, the authors note that the broader movement for more "scratch cooking" in place of heat-and-serve meals has the potential to shape labor patterns in school cafeterias, creating more full-time jobs with benefits and, potentially, greater job satisfaction.[49] In Colorado, HB22-1414, "Healthy Meals for All Public School Students," which was passed by public ballot in November 2022, included funding for increased wages for cafeteria workers in schools providing universal meals.[50] At the federal level, new guidance for best practices was issued in 2023 that encouraged schools to contract with management companies that offered benefits consistent with other school employees and "family sustaining wages."[51] These changes, while incremental, signal a growing recognition of the importance of school meals and those who prepare them. As a recent report by Healthy School Meals for All Wisconsin argues, there is tremendous potential for combining state policy and federal action and guidance to make school food work good work.[52]

The campaigns that are working to improve working conditions and wages in the food service sector engage a wide array of strategies and have different goals and objectives in mind. Here we focus on three important movements and strategies that have called for better pay and working conditions for food service workers: the Fight for $15, the #MeToo movement, and unionization efforts among both restaurant and school food workers.

Fight for $15

The Fight for $15 calls for the federal minimum wage to be raised to $15 per hour, a significant increase from the current rate of $7.25 set in 2009 and still in place as of 2024. What is particularly inspiring about the Fight for $15 is the fact that it has drawn together not only fast-food workers but also home care workers, airport workers, and even contingent university faculty.[53] Although the Fight for $15 is not limited to food service workers, the movement has gained the most traction among fast-food workers, who especially feel the impact of the absence of a living wage and barriers to worker organizing. While the Fight for $15 is currently the most visible and active movement seeking to improve the economic realities of food service workers, it has a longer history and draws on decades of organizing efforts among low-wage workers. In *"We Are All Fast-food Workers Now,"* the historian Annelise Orleck links the current movement of low-wage workers to a long history of African American protest: "From its beginnings, the low-wage workers' struggle in the US was rooted in the long history of African American protest: against exploitation of black labor, black bodies, and attempts to break the spirit of black workers."[54]

The Fight for $15 has attracted workers of all backgrounds and began in earnest in November 2012 when hundreds of fast-food workers walked off the job in New York City. Despite the relatively small number of workers who walked out (estimates range between one hundred and more than two hundred), at the time this was the largest strike of fast-food employees in US history. A second strike, held on the forty-fifth anniversary of the assassination of Martin Luther King Jr. and the Memphis sanitation strike, was organized in New York City on April 4, 2013. Subsequent strikes were organized in the following months in Chicago, St. Louis, Detroit, Seattle, and Milwaukee. On July 29, 2013, an estimated 2,200 workers went on strike in these cities, as well as Flint, Michigan, and Kansas City, Missouri.

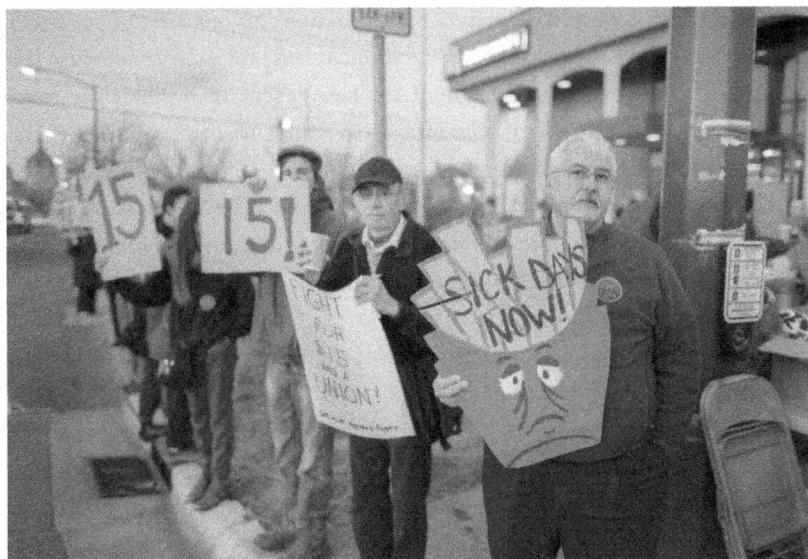

FIGURE 16. Fast-Food Workers on Strike, St. Paul, Minnesota, 2016. Fibonacci Blue, photographer. Creative Commons.

In 2014 and 2015, the Fight for $15 organized strikes and sit-ins in hundreds of US cities, bringing together thousands of fast-food workers with those laboring as home healthcare and childcare workers, convenience store clerks, airport service providers, adjunct professors, and Walmart employees. Internationally, protests over wages at fast-food restaurants were also organized in the United Kingdom, Japan, India, and Brazil. The US protests during this period were often held in conjunction with Black Lives Matter protests over the murders of Michael Brown and Eric Garner in 2014, revealing important solidarities around issues of race, class, and labor. The largest strike during this time happened on April 15, 2015, when thousands of workers walked off their jobs in more than two hundred US cities. The movement has seen growing support from the Democratic Party over time, particularly from Senator Bernie Sanders, who centered the call for a minimum wage of $15 in his 2016 bid for president.

In 2019, the US House of Representatives passed the Raise the Wage Act, which would gradually bring the federal minimum wage up to $15 per hour, yet it was not taken up by the US Senate. Two years later, during the COVID-19 pandemic, the bill (HR603) was reintroduced in both the House and the Senate by Democrats and was then referred to the House Committee on

Education and Labor. Ultimately, the bill was not successful. Another attempt was made by Senator Sanders to include a provision to increase the minimum wage to $15 through the American Rescue Plan pandemic relief package that was passed in February 2021, but it was removed from the Senate version of the legislation.

Although the movement has not yet realized a national increase in the minimum wage, it has motivated significant gains at the municipal and state levels. Numerous states, including California, Massachusetts, Maryland, New Jersey, Illinois, Connecticut, and Florida, have passed legislation that requires a gradual increase to $15 per hour, and the cities of Seattle, San Francisco, and New York have done so as well. In a 2021 report on the impacts of the Fight for $15, the Economic Policy Institute presents findings that the movement has increased the wages of 26 million workers, who have earned an additional $150 billion of income.[55] Of these workers, an estimated 12 million are workers of color and 18 million are women. The report unfortunately does not provide a breakdown of how many of these workers are in food service.

In 2023, Governor Gavin Newsom of California went even further and raised the state minimum wage to $20 an hour. This increase affected over half a million workers across sectors and includes an annual wage adjustment set to the cost of living or 3.5%, whichever is lower. For food service workers, this increase was especially impactful given the disparities in wages across sectors. When signing the bill, Newsom specifically addressed the notion that fast-food work is populated by teenagers just entering the workforce. "That's a romanticized version of a world that doesn't exist," Newsom said. "We have the opportunity to reward that contribution, reward that sacrifice and stabilize an industry." Another separate new law was passed in California the same year to fund a dormant labor-management council, the Industrial Welfare Commission (IWC), a division of the state Department of Industrial Relations, which has the power to set wage levels and standards across industries, as well collaborate with the Department of Labor to monitor and enforce labor violations. Organizers noted these moves to increase wages and enforce oversight of existing laws were directly in response to the mobilizations of the Fight for $15 movement, which had held 450 strikes across the state over the previous two years.[56]

The Fight for $15 campaign makes demands that go beyond wages to include working conditions. One of its biggest demands is the end of just-in-time and erratic scheduling practices for restaurant workers, particularly those in fast food. As Orleck explains, when schedules are planned by a computer algorithm, workers are unable to plan for childcare or have any security that they can pay their bills.[57] An important success of the Fight for $15 occurred in 2017, when the New York City Council passed legislation requiring that fast-food workers receive their work schedules fourteen days in advance and banning back-to-back shifts.

Critics of the Fight for $15 movement argue that menu prices must increase to account for increased labor costs or that workers will receive fewer hours at the increased rate of pay. When looking at chain restaurants in particular, these arguments are merely distractions from the immense corporate profits these chains earn. For example, in 2022 alone, the net profit for McDonald's was $6.17 billion, and for Starbucks it was $3.28 billion. Some believe that the turn to automated order kiosks, like those found at McDonald's and other fast-food restaurants, has accelerated because of calls for higher pay. Indeed, automation has certainly been a strategy for cost cutting in the fast-food industry for decades, and a fast-food hamburger made by human hands might soon be a thing of the past as robots like Flippy 2 become more commonplace. Yet we remain skeptical that robots will simply or quickly replace the human labor required to make and serve food, and as we have seen in the retail sector, automation and the related divorce of the food system from human labor is not moving at the pace predicted and hoped for by industry executives. We are hopeful that campaigns such as the Fight for $15 will continue to improve the pay and working conditions of those workers who cannot be replaced.

#Me Too

Originally coined by the activist Tarana Burke in 2006, the term "Me Too" (which later morphed into the hashtag #MeToo) has been a loud rallying cry against sexual assault, rape culture, and sexual abuse. Spreading virally through social media nearly ten years after Burke first used this phrase, the #MeToo movement has highlighted the rampant and widespread persistence of sexual abuse, calling for solidarity among those who have been victimized by it. Amid the broader #MeToo reckoning, celebrity chefs like Mario Batali and John Besh were brought into the limelight for the sexual violence that they both perpetrated and condoned within their food empires. While both Batali and Besh stepped away from their businesses as a result of their behavior being exposed, the insidiousness of what Anthony Bourdain deemed "meathead culture" still persists, with differential impacts on women in the restaurant industry.[58] Grassroots groups like Women in Hospitality United have formed to challenge sexism in the restaurant industry and to provide more resources and support for women in this line of work.[59] The One Fair Wage campaign, which we highlighted earlier in this chapter, has also called for an end to what they refer to as a "subminimum" wage and to tipping culture given the disproportionate impacts it has on women workers. While the broader #MeToo movement has always been a diffuse and widespread call for gender equity and the abolition of gendered violence, its particular relevance to the food service industry is profound.

Unionizing Food Service Workers

Although campaigns like the Fight for $15 and the #MeToo movement have seen important wins, traditional union organizing has not historically been as effective in organizing food service workers. While unions like the Service Employees International Union (SEIU) have backed the Fight for $15, fast-food and restaurant workers remain largely nonunionized. Indeed, the proportion of unionized workers in food service, 1.3%, is the lowest of all sectors of paid food systems work. In a piece titled, "Why Don't Restaurant Workers Unionize?," Sam Bloch claims that the expansion of fast food has watered down union concentration in dining, in part because unionization in the franchise model and in jobs with high turnover is extremely challenging.[60] At the same time, he argues, in fine dining the possibility of front of the house workers earning enough to achieve a comfortable standard of living (even with no benefits) often leads these workers to believe that unions would not offer much in the way of better compensation or working conditions. Of course, as we discussed above, workers in the back of the house often have very different earning potential.

Perhaps the most visible and successful growth of unions in food service has recently taken place at Starbucks, with workers voting to unionize in more than 385 locations across the United States at the time of writing.[61] This exponential growth of unionized locations is particularly impressive as the first store to unionize, located in Buffalo, New York, did so in December 2021. This is reported to be the fastest rate of union growth for any company in the past twenty years. This growth has been so rapid in part because Starbucks is not currently franchised, so all stores are owned by the same central company. This facilitates unionization as worker grievances do not

FIGURE 17. Starbucks Employees React to Union Election, Buffalo, New York, 2021. Joshua Bessex, photographer. Courtesy of Associated Press.

have to go through individual franchise owners but rather are aimed directly at the corporation. Workers United, the union organizing this campaign, is affiliated with the SEIU and has been in existence since 1900. Originally representing garment workers, Workers United now has more than 85,000 members across various industries.[62] In addition to Starbucks employees, SEIU represents food service workers in public schools and hospitals, and it also established the National Fast-Food Workers Union to carry out the union's support for the Fight for $15.

As expected, the success of this union campaign has not gone unnoticed by the Starbucks corporate offices, with widespread union busting intensifying over 2022 and 2023. These union busting tactics included intimidating employees in "captive audience meetings," denying benefits to union members, firing employees, and closing stores that had voted to unionize. In March 2023, after being accused of union busting, CEO Howard Schultz stepped down from his position and was later asked to testify before the US Senate's Health, Education, Labor and Pensions Committee. Though Schultz denied that the company was engaged in preventing unionization, on March 2, 2023, the NLRB issued a ruling that consolidated thirty-five unfair labor practices at twenty-one stores. In the order, NLRB administrative law judge

Rosas noted that the corporation's "egregious and widespread misconduct demonstrat[es] a general disregard for the employees' fundamental rights."[63]

Despite some of the challenges in organizing restaurant workers, it is important to acknowledge that unionization among food service workers has been more successful in institutional food spaces. These successes may be because many of these institutional workers are longer-term employees and more centralized, with more employees at a single location than a typical restaurant. UNITE HERE, affiliated with the AFL-CIO and a member of the Food Chain Workers Alliance, has been organizing food service workers since 1891, when it received its first charter as the Hotel and Restaurant Employees International Alliance. The union has expanded from hospitality workers to now include over one hundred thousand food service workers in stadium and airport concessions, casinos, university food service, amusement parks, and government cafeterias, including workers at companies like Sodexo, Aramark, and Compass. UNITE HERE is also responsible for unionizing workers in Google cafeterias; it is reported that 90% of food service workers at the company are now unionized.[64]

Given the low wages and often poor working conditions of public school cafeteria workers, unionization and collective bargaining have also been important strategies for bringing about improvements for this group of laborers. As Gaddis notes, UNITE HERE "has organized some of the most visible worker-led campaigns in Chicago (Local 1), New Haven (Local 217), and Philadelphia (Local 634)."[65] However, maintaining the momentum in a local union after contract negotiation or the resolution of a crisis can be a challenge for cafeteria workers, who often must work two or more jobs to make ends meet. In response to the shortage of cafeteria workers, the Biden administration's Task Force on Worker Organizing and Empowerment released a report in early 2022 calling for school food service workers to be employed full-time and for increased union density in this area of the food system. The report makes the case that more full-time and highly unionized school food employees are more likely to ensure consistent school food service for children, which is in the public interest of securing the national needs of the nation's children and recommends that the secretary of agriculture and USDA ensure this reality.[66] As of this writing, the results of this directive are yet to be seen, but it represents an important acknowledgment of the needs of cafeteria workers and the significant role they play in ensuring children are fed. Given the strength of these national groups and the growing public support for labor organizing, we are optimistic that the union model will be vital to improving the pay and working conditions of restaurant workers for years to come.

CONCLUSION: THE GREAT RESIGNATION?

In the aftermath of the pandemic, it is now commonplace to see fast-food outlets advertising starting wages of $15 an hour and other benefits like healthcare, paid time off, and guaranteed opportunities for advancement. Employment postings for restaurants fill the online classifieds ads, and nearly every kind of dining establishment is currently looking for more workers. Wait times for tables have increased, and reservations for dinner are harder to come by. As we have noted elsewhere in this book, viewing these changes as merely a response to a labor shortage obscures the more fundamental issues in food service work. Rather than a worker shortage, we see that fewer workers are willing to tolerate the low pay and poor working conditions that have persisted in food service for too long. Based on our research, we know that attributing labor issues to supposed worker shortages (rather than substandard pay) happened well before the pandemic and will continue to occur if food work is underpaid and undervalued.

While the impacts of the pandemic on the food system are immense, the food service industry was hit particularly hard. Droves of workers in restaurants, school cafeterias, and catering operations were left without work amid closures and stay-at-home orders in 2020. With the onset of the COVID-19 pandemic in 2020, the number of food service workers plunged to just under 9.9 million, leaving more than 2 million in this sector alone unemployed or forced to find employment in other sectors.[67] An estimated 6 million people lost work temporarily or permanently because of the pandemic, but millions more kept working, often at considerable risk to their health. High-end restaurants pivoted to offering take-out, and using delivery options like Uber Eats and Grubhub became the norm for many US households. In institutional food spaces, cafeteria workers continued to produce packaged meals for children to eat at home while attending school remotely, helping ensure that hungry children still had access to nutritious food. Like farmworkers and grocery workers, food service workers were deemed essential, but ultimately their health and well-being were determined to be secondary to their role in feeding others.

These pressures have led thousands of workers to leave the food service industry altogether, finding work in other sectors that offer better pay and better working conditions. In a collaborative report, One Fair Wage and the UC Berkeley Food Labor Research Center examine how and why the pandemic caused workers, particularly women, to leave the restaurant industry.[68] Based on a survey of 2,800 food service workers in late 2020 and early 2021, researchers found that more than half were considering leaving their job because of the pandemic and that more than three-quarters were leaving due to the low wages and tips they received. Perhaps even more importantly, the vast majority reported that they would consider staying at their jobs if they received a full, stable, and living wage, and many reported that having paid sick leave and health coverage would also be important factors.

But the fact remains that people will continue to dine out, stop at the drive-through on their way home from work, and send their children to school where they will receive lunch and sometimes even breakfast. Restaurants will continue to be central sites in our food landscapes, and as a world experiencing late-stage capitalism, we are increasingly consuming meals crafted by someone else's hands. As we have discussed throughout this chapter, food service work is disproportionately performed by workers who experience intersectional oppressions linked to race, class, gender, and citizenship, among other factors. These intersectional forms of oppression have been a central target for food service organizers and campaigns like the Fight for $15 and an important reminder that food system workers already possess the ability to analyze what power means and what is necessary to build a more just food system.

SIX

Reproductive Labor, Gender, and Food Work in the Home

For me the home profoundly affects personal expression. Artistically, it's not just about maintaining and keeping it nice, it's about it being an expression of myself as an art form. . . . As soon as we started planning a wedding and getting married, I knew that I didn't want anybody else raising my kids. Homeschooling had begun to become accepted more widely, but you still had to get permission, and it was not common. I had always thought, well, maybe we'll homeschool because we can do a better job than schools. We were in Virginia then and we were also big into a food coop, so with a lot of our food, we ordered with other people from this place called Mountain Warehouse. There were very few health food stores and natural food stores, so we would all order together and then the order would come every month, so we cut it all up and break it down and it was a huge part of our lives. We had no success as gardeners because by then we lived in the rocky lands of the hills of Ithaca, in a forest. . . . I got to the point where I was kind of done gardening, but I love putting food up. I love it. It's an art form. It's a delight. It's super satisfying. It's a lot of fun. I had four young kids in the house for many, many years, and anytime a meal was prepared, no matter how beautiful it was, no matter how hard you worked on it, the minute you set that on the table, it was devoured as my family would rush to eat . . . in contrast with when we preserved and processed food, it was both consumable and storable, and I'd have a chance to admire all the work in shiny bottles and jars on our storage shelves.

THERESA, *mother of four, homeschooler, canner, former gardener*

IT WILL LIKELY COME as no surprise to other working parents that writing this chapter began on a day that Laura-Anne's daughter was home from school with a bad cold. Between efforts to theorize about the links between food systems and reproductive labor, she warmed leftover macaroni and cheese, doled out apple slices and granola bars, and wiped a runny nose at least three dozen times. She also chopped vegetables for dinner, wiped crumbs off the table, and felt some good old-fashioned motherhood guilt as she streamed another round of cartoons on the iPad so that some precious time could be spent writing on a Friday morning. Laura-Anne's experiences are simultaneously worlds apart and have much in common with Theresa's, whose narrative opens this chapter. For both women, there is deep love of family and recognition of the artistry involved in managing a home. There is a shared respect of mothering and shared frustrations with growing some of one's own food. However, the work involved with raising (and schooling) four children for Theresa requires a different set of negotiations than Laura-Anne has raising two children, worrying about an aging parent, and maintaining a career outside of the home. For the latter, the ever present pressure to balance career and family obligations often leaves room for little else, and many of the writing sessions for this book were interspersed with the coauthors discussing the current needs of our children and the exhaustion that we often feel because of so many competing demands on our time. It is necessary to note that we have supportive partners, flexible jobs with excellent health benefits, access to high-quality childcare and schooling for our children, and consistent food security—all factors that make our balancing act much less arduous than that of so many parents without these privileges.

Despite the many wins of feminist movements, women still perform the majority of care work in the home. In each of the preceding chapters, we provided BLS data on each sector, and it is telling that these data are not available for home-based food work given that it is unpaid. However, according to a 2019 poll by the Pew Research Center, 80% of women with children reported being the primary grocery shopper and meal preparer, and for childless couples, the numbers are 75% and 68%, respectively.[1] Further, 2021 averages from BLS data show that women spend more than double the amount of time each day preparing food and cleaning up than men do (.86 hour vs. .42 hour) and nearly double the amount of time caring for children.[2] This kind of work, which is essential to society's functioning, remains chronically undervalued and taken for granted, not only in the United States, but in most cultures and societies around the world. The arguments that feminist thinkers have long made about the "double day" or "second shift" remain relevant to unpacking these disparities and value systems. It has become increasingly difficult for families to support themselves financially with the work of one parent, and the social reproductive work that has been required to maintain families has seen important shifts, not only in who is doing this work to feed the family, but also in what kind of food is being consumed.

The labor that happens in the home is usually not categorized with other food work, as it is done in a private setting and is part of the reproductive labor, or unpaid work, performed to quite literally reproduce members of society. This is in contrast to work considered productive labor, that is, wage work performed in the public economic sphere to produce the material goods and services for societies. Whether it is called care work, affective labor, or domestic work, the planning, shopping, cooking, and serving that goes into feeding families, households, and communities is rarely given a platform equal to that of other sectors, even in the more expansive and comprehensive scholarship on food systems. In this chapter, we argue that reproductive labor is food work, and like all forms of food work, it is essential to the food system. We believe that bringing greater dignity to the work of feeding families is key to the broader movements for labor justice, in the food system and beyond.

From the time the idea for this book was born, we have been devoted to ensuring that the work of sustaining families and households is considered with the same care and attention given to labor in the other sectors of the food chain. As we engage with questions of gendered work in this chapter, we echo the points made in the introduction that our approach to gender throughout this book is not meant to reify binary definitions of gender but rather to underscore how binary and heteronormative expectations are both damaging for all people and not reflective of the diversity of lived experiences. As we point to the food-related expectations of those identifying as women, we take care to note that there are exceptions to every rule of gendered work and that feminism is a complex and often contradictory set of movements. Indeed, queer visions and practices related to family offer generative possibilities for egalitarianism, chosen rather than prescribed roles, and progressive arrangements of labor in the home.[3] And yet while enormous shifts have taken place with respect to gendered expectations in the domestic sphere, career opportunities, and expanding and diversifying understandings of family and love, the responsibility for feeding the family still falls disproportionately on those who identify as women.

Given the differences between food work that takes place in the home and paid food work, this chapter is organized differently from the preceding chapters and weaves theory, history, and resistance throughout. It begins by outlining the concept of reproductive labor and demonstrating how this framework is instrumental for understanding the links between the food work performed within the household and broader social, political, and economic structures. Given the scope of these questions, we then discuss three specific historical moments in the United States when major political and social changes have transformed reproductive labor inside the home and its relationship to work outside the home. First, we examine the dominant patterns of reproductive labor under slavery and the shifts that occurred with emancipation for both Black and white women. Second, we examine the emergence of second wave feminism in the United States, which began in the 1960s and continued to shape gender relationships and political organizing over the next several decades. Third, we turn to the impacts of the COVID-19 pandemic on reproductive labor, showing how women have borne the brunt of the burden of the stay-at-home orders, school closures, and unemployment and were the primary participants in *mutual aid*, or the voluntary collaborative exchange of organizing goods and resources that cared for and fed so many others. We conclude this chapter by considering how food work fits into a broader crisis of care and what is needed to ensure that this labor is taken seriously by both food systems and labor advocates.

REPRODUCTIVE LABOR AND THE WORK OF FEEDING OTHERS

The unequal burden that women face in the home and the often-damaging ways that care work is gendered have long interested feminist thinkers and activists. The delineation between productive and reproductive labor serves as a necessary anchor for feminists offering important critiques of the value and power systems that are linked to these different kinds of work. However, as we emphasize in this chapter, the very terms "productive labor" and "reproductive labor" are laden with connotations that reflect value systems in which wage labor is considered more important than the work that must happen to keep families fed and cared for. Without reproductive labor, society would not be able to sustain itself. As the sociologist Marjorie DeVault observes in

FIGURE 18. Woman Preparing Food in Kitchen, 1910–1930. Photographer unknown. University of Washington Libraries, Special Collections, UW11456.

Feeding the Family, caring labor sustains both life and community and is simultaneously a source of pride, satisfaction, and the "suppression of other capacities and desires."[4] Not only does reproductive labor keep families functioning; it is essential to maintaining the processes of production and consumption in our profit-driven food system.

In reaction to the mostly gender-blind analyses of political economic systems that focus on theorizing work outside the home, feminist Marxists have taken it upon themselves to explore how the sexual division of labor can either support or undermine the social power of women. As the feminist scholar and activist Silvia Federici argues, capitalism benefits from the exploitation of women and their work.[5] In her discussion of the Wages for Housework campaign, a global movement she cofounded in the 1970s that dared to demand that women be paid wages for their home labor, Federici underscores that the extraction of labor from the "workday of millions of unwaged house-workers as well as many other unpaid and un-free labourers" is a key ingredient in the profit-making processes of capitalism.[6] We build on this critique to show how this extraction of largely female labor is specifically foundational to value creation in the food system.

The feminist sociologists Patricia Allen and Carolyn Sachs have consistently made persuasive and grounded arguments about inequities in the food system.[7] In their work, they connect representations of care work with women's lack of access to power, decision making, and material resources in relation to food. They observe that amid the dynamism and global change that was transforming the food system from a subsistence to an industrial one during the early twenty-first century, rigid constructs connected to gendered work persisted, with women maintaining responsibility for care-related food labor. They aptly point out that while women bear the primary burden of feeding others, they often struggle with sufficiently feeding themselves. Allen and Sachs categorize the relationships between women and the food system in three interconnected and overlapping domains, the material, the sociocultural, and the corporeal, and note the damaging irony that women are more likely to experience disordered eating even as they feed others.

The work to access, prepare, and serve food to others (often at the expense of feeding themselves) has been analyzed in depth by Megan Carney as a daily struggle, "la lucha diaria," in the case of migrant women in the United States and by Hanna Garth as "la lucha" for women in contemporary Cuba.[8] As anthropologists, Garth and Carney trace the daily lives of women as they navigate the daily challenges and constraints of feeding their families and loved ones. Similarly, in their 2019 book, *Pressure Cooker*, the sociologists Sarah Bowen, Joslyn Brenton, and Sinikka Elliott look at the pressure on women across boundaries of class and race in the United States to cook from scratch for their families and meet increasingly complex societal expectations for children's diets.[9] They argue that this pressure increases women's labor and stress without regard for the systemic constraints to simultaneously labor outside the home, at times in precarious and food-related jobs. Importantly, this body of ethnographic scholarship brings together an analysis of the lived experience of doing food work with an analysis of broader political economic structures that constrain the agency of socially marginalized groups of women.

While alternative food movements have raised our collective consciousness about our food system, even these movements are often propped up by women working a "third shift." This third shift encompasses the labor done on top of household labor and paid work, typically care or volunteer work connected to participating in alternative food networks. As noted by Theresa, the homeschooling mother quoted in the chapter's epigraph, this labor can be satisfying but also draining as it adds to caregivers' daily chores and to-do lists. This additional work can include tasks such as sourcing food from multiple outlets in search of the most local and sustainable products; meeting and building rapport with local farmers and producers; gardening, composting, canning, and preserving foods; and even taking part in local food policy councils and other food-based community organizations.[10]

As we look at issues of gender equity and food work, we wish to emphasize that feeding others is not merely a process of blindly subscribing to gender conventions and strict divisions of labor. It is possible, even common, for care work connected to food to be simultaneously enjoyable and an obligation. The multiple dimensions of cooking for others have been well illuminated by many feminist authors, underscoring how feeding others can be a source of pride, strengthening family relationships and creating domains of power within the home, particularly for women without much social power outside the home.[11] As two women who often take joy in feeding others (including our children, who in their younger years could be picky and demanding), we have experienced these contradictions and believe that this work can be creative, cathartic, and even fun. We also feel the pressures of "intense food moralization," described by the anthropologist Jennifer Patico, as we weigh our concerns for the health of our children against the limitations of our time.[12]

Moreover, in some communities, the work of feeding others and engaging in care work has been framed as potentially liberatory or as a means of resistance. As noted in the previous chapter, this approach was central to the philosophy of the Black Panther Party, for which care work and feeding others were seen as the backbone of radical activism connected to the Black Panthers' antihunger politics, which also served to create spaces for women's leadership.[13] Newer work by the geographer Priscilla McCutcheon on Black women working in church kitchens (many of whom are doing so as volunteers) underscores that feeding one's own community can be a form of activism. She argues that the ability to take care of one's home and prioritize this kind of work is "radical," particularly for Black women for whom that ability was taken away for much of US history.[14] Below we expand on these arguments in discussing the changes in care work that happened after emancipation.

FROM FORCED LABOR TO EMANCIPATION

As Black feminists like bell hooks, Angela Davis, Patricia Hill Collins, Psyche Williams-Forson, and Audre Lorde have long argued, the devastating forms of violence that Black women have experienced before and long after emancipation demand that we consider more carefully questions of race, work, and family and the gains as well as the limits of mainstream feminism. For Black women, working outside the home was not necessarily a feminist gain or a tool to empowerment but was brutally forced on them both during slavery and after emancipation. In her groundbreaking book, *Women, Race, and Class*, Angela Davis writes, "Proportionately, more Black women have always worked outside their homes than have their white sisters. The enormous space that work occupies in Black women's lives today follows a pattern established during the very earliest days of slavery. As slaves, compulsory labor overshadowed every other aspect of women's existence."[15] Davis challenges the notion that most women worked as house servants, a falsehood that damaging and racist "Black Mammy" stereotypes would lead us to believe.

Instead, the majority of enslaved women in the Deep South were field workers, as were men. With international pressures around abolition starting to mount, enslaved women faced intensified demands, and the associated threats and realities of violence, to reproduce. As Davis notes, enslaved women were seen and valued as "breeders," not as mothers, and the children they birthed (including those who resulted from rape) were more often than not sold as chattel; some states, such as South Carolina, codified into law that female slaves had no legal rights to their children. This intentional and cruel severing of Black families and the sexual violence perpetrated against Black women, along with the denial of reproductive justice, would persist long after emancipation to the present day. This has manifested in the horrific numbers of forced sterilizations of Black women, the high rates of Black mother and infant mortality, and the broader perinatal health disparities in the Black community.[16]

Even if most enslaved Black people were agricultural workers, it is crucial to examine the role of those who worked in the homes of slave owners and the reproductive labor they performed to feed and care for white families. This labor often started at the time of birth—but the birth of white children. It has been documented that enslaved Black women in the antebellum South and other sites of the transatlantic slave trade were used as wet nurses for the children of slave owners—an extension of the sexual violence just mentioned and a source of incalculable trauma.[17] Wet nursing, or breastfeeding another person's child, has ancient roots and has been practiced in many cultural settings around the world. However, as the historians Emily West and R.J. Knight note, wet nursing typically involves women in very different social positions, with the woman providing the milk being of a lower class or status than the mother of the child receiving the milk.[18]

While some scholars claim that wet nursing during and after slavery was an example of transgressing racial divides, West and Knight take the opposite view, arguing that using enslaved women as wet nurses was not transgression but rather a specific form of abuse, exploitation, and manipulation, typically at the hands of white women. They also note that often milk was provided to white children at the expense of continued breastfeeding of the children of the enslaved women: "Forcing their female slaves to wet-nurse hence illustrates how slaveholders denigrated black women's mothering of their own children as innately inferior and paid scant regard to the very real difficulties faced by black mothers attempting to raise their children under a system of bondage."[19] For this reason, and many others, the ability of Black women to care for their own children—or engage in reproductive labor for the benefit of their own families—holds deep meaning, a point we return to in considering the concept "homeplace" below.

Enslaved women were forced to both breastfeed white children and cook for older white children, slave owners, and visitors to the home. The historian and archaeologist Kelly Fanto Deetz notes the difficulty of fully understanding the histories and contributions of these cooks given that they left few accounts of their own (as enslaved people were typically not allowed the right of literacy) and were often erased from most historical accounts. Deetz writes that while enslaved cooks typically lived in the kitchen and were expected to feed any free person around the clock, they wielded "great power," even if they were constantly under the white gaze.[20] Indeed, it was the quality and abundance of the food prepared that reflected on the reputation and social power of the slave owners. Their skills, craft, and knowledge formed the core of Southern cuisine, which included ingredients with African origins like peanuts, okra, and rice, yet they were rarely given credit for their development of these crops and dishes.[21]

With emancipation in 1865 came a formalized end to the institution of slavery in the United States but certainly not an end to racialized violence, servitude, or the exploitation of Black workers. The transition from the plantation economy to the sharecropping system has been referred to by the journalist Douglas Blackmon as "slavery by another name," a point we discussed in chapter 1. For many Black women, the only employment option was domestic work, sometimes for the very same families that had enslaved them; their continued exploitation as domestic workers persisted for decades. Five years after emancipation, census data showed that 52% of employed women worked in "domestic and personal service." Until 1940, domestic work remained the largest category of women's paid labor overall.[22]

Given that most formerly enslaved Black women had little money or formal education, setting up their own homes and finding work was a challenge, but it represented an important form of agency and sovereignty. The historian Vanessa May observes that while many white employers sought to extend the exploitation of Black workers after emancipation by requiring them to live in their homes and work without contestation, refusal on the part of Black women was paramount. The ability to set boundaries over what work would be performed, the hours that would be worked, and where they would live represented a true sense of liberation for Black women.[23]

During Reconstruction and beyond, white families also experienced shifts in the domestic labor structures inside their homes, as many white women took on household managerial duties that were different from those under slavery. The relationships between Black cooks and their employers reflected broader societal patterns of segregation and racialized hierarchies. After emancipation, degrading relationships were often forcefully maintained by white women who were now tasked with managing the freewomen who worked in their homes for pay. In *Cooking in Other Women's Kitchens*, the historian Rebecca Sharpless devotes attention to the changes that came after emancipation and continued into the mid-twentieth century, specifically for those who cooked for a living.[24] Cooking was a skill in demand, as white women were often more willing to take on cleaning and childcare duties than cooking. In the antebellum United States, gendered expectations and relationships between Black and white women, employee and manager, were intimate sites of struggle. As the direct supervisors of domestic workers, white women yielded most of the direct power. The historian Thaviola Glymph discusses the transitions in these roles in *Out of the House of Bondage*, disputing the myth that white women did little to uphold the brutal realities of slavery before emancipation and racial hierarchies following it.[25] Rather, Glymph argues that it was more common for mistresses to physically abuse enslaved people than for masters to do so.

While popular representations of domestic workers, such as the film *The Help*, make light of the racialized dynamics present in homes with African American domestic workers, domestic workers often confronted real violence, ranging from physical abuse to sexual harassment and assault to physical segregation and the forced wearing of uniforms for the performance of

FIGURE 19. Domestic Servant, Atlanta, Georgia, 1939. Marion Post Wolcott, photographer. Library of Congress, Prints & Photographs Division, FSA/OWI Collection, LC-USF34-T01-051738-D.

the employers' class status. Black women were vulnerable not only to exploitation and violence but also to the pressure to endure it for their own families, who depended on them financially. Moreover, the imagined love between African American domestic workers and the white families they worked for is merely an illusion in service of white supremacy. Sharpless makes this clear, noting, "Although many white women chose to believe that the relationships between them and their employees remained affective, African American women knew that the arrangements were in fact material. To be sure, many worked out of love. But the love was not for their employees but for their own families.[26]

Societal racism limited Black women's employment opportunities, and low-paid cooking jobs offered by even the poorest white families reinforced their social positioning as low-waged workers.[27] This vulnerability was reinforced by the exclusion of domestic work from the labor protections embedded in the New Deal of the 1930s, which provided basic work standards such as a minimum wage and a standard workweek. Like the exclusion of agricultural labor, the exclusion of domestic workers from these labor protections was meant to specifically target Black workers and as such is a forceful example of structural racism.[28]

This is not to say that they had no agency in these arrangements. Cooks struggled to limit their working hours, demand fair compensation, and, over time, started to leave their jobs with greater frequency as better employment options became available[29]. In her foundational book, *Building Houses Out of Chicken Legs*, Psyche Williams-Forson writes about Black women's foodways after emancipation, describing how they resisted stereotypes, specifically, the "mammy" imagery of deferential Black women in domestic service roles.[30] Focusing on the contributions of Black women's knowledge in the kitchen and culinary spaces, as well as their resistance by developing their own culinary businesses, she tells a different story of Black women's domestic labor.

The love for one's own family and the sacrifice involved in working for another family is centered in bell hooks's essay, "Homeplace: A Site of Resistance."[31] As a social critic and author, hooks is widely known for her important contributions to intersectional feminist theory and unpacking what she termed "white supremacist capitalist patriarchy." hooks traces the difficult work of Black women in creating create spaces for their families to shelter, heal, and affirm one another amid white supremacy and violence, what she calls making "homeplace." In this piece, hooks simultaneously celebrates the work of Black women and their efforts to create homeplace and critiques the sexist and patriarchal forces that determine service is a woman's natural role. She remembers the reproductive labor and care work of women like her mother and grandmother: "Their lives were not easy. Their lives were hard. They were black women who for the most part worked outside the home serving white folks, cleaning their houses, washing their clothes, tending their children—black women who worked in the fields or in the streets, whatever they could do to make ends meet, whatever was necessary. Then they returned to their homes to make life happen there."[32] This balance, between caring for white families as well as caring for their own, often resulted in exhaustion and stress for Black women, but the choice to prioritize their own families also represented a "racially subversive political gesture" that gave dignity and humanity to Black families in the homeplace.[33] In this homeplace, the special domain of women, "all that truly mattered in life took place—the warmth and comfort of shelter, the feeding of our bodies, the nurturing of our souls."[34] As we discuss in more depth below, these different meanings of productive and reproductive labor reflect women's different and intersectional positions in racialized and economic hierarchies.

The history of US feminism is typically divided into waves, with each being unique for its demands, its leadership, and the means of protest and activism. Food and the work that it takes to feed a family figures prominently in each of the waves. Over the past two centuries, enormous changes have occurred with respect to work expectations inside and outside the home, career and educational opportunities for women, and political and civil rights. However, women have not experienced or benefited from these changes equally, as just discussed. The first wave of US feminism, which occurred from the mid- to late 1800s to the early 1900s, was centered on suffrage and increasing political rights for women. Propelled by the Seneca Falls Convention of 1848, this phase was mostly led by middle-class white women who were sometimes opposed to expanding civil rights for Black Americans, even as Black activists like Sojourner Truth and Frances Ellen Watkins Harber linked the calls for the abolition of slavery and women's rights.

The second wave, connected to the broader social upheaval of the 1960s and 1970s, was centered on calls for reproductive rights and economic rights and saw the (still unpassed) Equal Rights Amendment as a beacon for political change. This wave is also linked to the common term "Women's Lib," which, depending on who is uttering it, is sometimes said with celebration or with disdain. While seeing more leadership from women of color, this wave was still dominated by cisgender white women and their priorities, and because of this it has been rightly criticized for largely ignoring the experiences and priorities of women of color and the LGBTQ+ community, particularly concerning questions of work.[35] This section focuses on this second wave and the important sociopolitical changes it galvanized but did not entirely materialize, in terms of reproductive labor and how these changes were linked to broader political economic patterns.

While there were many organizing efforts within the second wave of the feminist movement, one of the most active groups was the National Organization for Women (NOW). Still in existence, NOW was inspired in part by Betty Friedan's best-selling 1963 book, *The Feminine Mystique*.[36] Other influences on second wave feminism included political efforts such as President John F. Kennedy's creation of the President's Commission on the Status of Women in 1961 and, under President Lyndon B. Johnson, passage of the Civil Rights Act of 1964, in particular, Title VII, which protects employees and job applicants from discrimination based on race, color, religion, sex, and national origin. As the first president of NOW, Friedan was influenced in her writing by her training in psychology and drew on her interviews with fellow alumni from Smith College and other college-educated middle-class (usually white) women. In *The Feminine Mystique*, Friedan challenged the commonly held assumption that women should be completely fulfilled in their role as housewives rather than seek opportunities outside the home in higher education, political participation, or other careers. For her, (fairly paid) labor in the public sphere, rather than the private sphere, was the key to women's emancipation. Looking back, scholars have noted that by rejecting women's expected role of homemaker, Friedan and other second wave feminists devalued kitchen work by defining feminists as those who did not identify with labor in the home.[37] Here we see a clear illustration of how second wave feminist views on reproductive work did not reflect the diversity of women's experiences and the complex meanings and histories of reproductive labor discussed in the previous section.

Alongside the growth of second wave feminism, the Wages for Housework movement originated in the early to mid-1970s in tandem with the National Women's Liberation Conference in Manchester, England, and the Power of Women Collective.[38] The campaign then spread throughout England, Italy, Canada, and the United States, becoming the International Wages for Housework Campaign (IFHAC). Taking a different approach from feminists like Friedan, this campaign has sought to revalue housework as paid work rather than see paid work outside the home as the most fulfilling option. We return to this campaign in the conclusion to this chapter when we consider how it might guide a more comprehensive and intersectional feminist future.

While Friedan and other second wave feminists have been blamed by public figures like Michael Pollan for killing home cooking (see the introduction to his book *Cooked: A Natural History of Transformation* for this jab), in fact the relationship between women's labor inside and outside the home is much more complex. In a rather poetic essay published by the *New York Times* in 1977, Friedan reflected on her own evolving relationship with food and cooking, noting that she had "lost her zest" for creatively cooking for herself and those she loved alongside her political mobilizing. Later in her life, she came to embrace cooking on her own terms.

> I think now that I will cook when I feel like it, when I want to or need to, and even maybe mostly enjoy it. I will cook for people I love or even for myself, maybe, with a minimum of fuss, or with a lot of relaxed, communal fuss, if the occasion arises. No big deal. But why deprive myself of the joys of chicken

soup, of any part of my basic roots as a woman, or even the refined sophistication of cooking as an art, which my men friends are free to enjoy. We women had to liberate ourselves from the slavish necessities, the excessive drudgery and guilt related to cooking in order to be able to now liberate ourselves from an excessive need to react against it. As for me, I've come out the other end of women's liberation—to make my own soup.[39]

As the journalist Emily Matchar explains in relation to women's domestic labor and cooking today, "The mid-century transition from scratch-cooking to using prepared foods had nothing to do with Betty Friedan and everything to do with industrialization."[40] To see this as an either/or question, in our perspective, is limited. Instead, we see both feminism and increased industrialization as linked to broader political economic changes in the United States, where reconfigurations of family and work were necessary to meet new economic challenges and opportunities. Indeed, the parallel effects of second wave feminism and the increasing industrialization of our food supply are both linked to changing political economic realities where more (white, middle-class) women were entering college, seeking work outside the home, and rethinking what it meant to be a wife and a mother. The ability of middle-class white women to enter the workforce has been linked to, or indeed was only possible by, transferring reproductive labor onto other women who are marginalized by virtue of their race/ethnicity, class position, or immigration status. When domestic labor is transferred from a family member to a paid staff member or employee there is an inherent power relation, which historically and still today tends to be between white women and women of color.[41]

Critiques of the industrialized food system are often linked to critiques of easy to prepare convenience foods, which are seen as having a negative impact on our health and environment. More subtly, though, these critiques, and related societal pressures on women, reinforce expectations that home cooks should and will be available to prepare food from scratch as part of resisting convenience foods.[42] As discussed in chapter 2, deskilling, or the shift from complex multistep tasks to an assembly line model of production, where workers are assigned one repetitive task with the goal of increasing efficiency, is prevalent in commercial food processing. The rural sociologist Philip Howard provides us with an expanded meaning of food systems deskilling, wherein "capitalists reshape socio-cultural practices to increase purchases, moving us away from self-provisioning to become mere 'consumers.'"[43] Howard argues that this form of deskilling has resulted in the explosion of a "pseudovariety" of packaged food and beverages that has made immense profits for food conglomerates. These foods include items like bagged salads, ready-to-heat meals, canned soup, prewashed and pre-sliced produce, and meal replacement bars, all items we have relied on in our own efforts to feed ourselves and our families.

Yet the availability of convenience food, and the supposed and related deskilling of home labor, is a mixed bag for working women. The deskilling of food preparation processes and the increasing reliance on convenience foods are both linked to changing patterns of social reproductive labor and broader constraints on worker power. Given that women working outside the home have less time to cook, convenience foods come in handy, even as they often profit large agrifood companies that often rely on the labor of low-income women working in less than ideal conditions. These foods are usually more expensive, which stretches the already thin food budgets of low-income women.[44] Moreover, as Amy Trubek argues, we are not necessarily cooking less as a society, but the sites of cooking have shifted as new pressures are placed on those who engage in reproductive labor. As she notes, "The expanding number of opportunities to obtain food cooked outside the home and the increased possibility of relying on others to cook is both a result of and a response to a long-term shift in the link between food, domestic life and gender."[45] This underscores the importance of connecting an analysis of food work within the home to the work that happens across the food system and to the broader social, political, and economic contexts.

PEELING BACK THE APRON: THE PANDEMIC AND COOKING AT HOME

The years since the COVID-19 pandemic have once again revealed the complexities of the connections between food work in the home and the unequal social worlds in which we live. In early 2020, as the virus was rapidly spreading and creating havoc in the food system and in family life, the reproductive labor that it takes to sustain a family took on new meanings and, more importantly, often entailed life or death decision making. Throughout this book, we have drawn attention to how the assaults on the well-being of essential food workers that occurred during the pandemic exacerbated preexisting structural inequalities linked to race, class, gender, and citizenship. These inequalities extended from the public sphere of paid work to the private

FIGURE 20. Heather Hernandez Caring for Children during COVID Pandemic, Denver, Colorado, 2021. Hart Van Denberg, photographer. Courtesy of Colorado Public Radio.

sphere of unpaid work, prompting renewed attention to the disproportionate load carried by women with respect to reproductive labor and how these disparities are linked to their participation in the labor force and earning potential. As we show in this section, this is more than just a question of gender but an extension of the intersectional histories and inequities linked to reproductive labor already discussed.

Essential workers of all genders were disproportionately affected by COVID-19 and faced the impossible dilemma of exposing themselves and their families to the virus or leaving their jobs. This dilemma was layered on top of the need to feed and care for children who were no longer able to attend daycare or school, often while supporting remote learning as well. Those who had the flexibility and privilege to work from home continued to earn a paycheck but also had to balance paid work with additional and often unpredictable reproductive labor in the home. The early phases of the pandemic were marked by great uncertainty—about how dangerous the virus was, when life might return to normal, and the long-term impacts of stay-at-home orders on our collective well-being. Based on an analysis of the Current Population Survey during the early months of the pandemic (February–April 2020), the sociologist Liana Landivar and colleagues found that mothers with young children left the labor force at higher rates than did fathers (3.2% for mothers with children under 6 and 4.3% for mothers with children ages 6–12, with exit rates 1% to 2% lower for fathers). In just these three months, nearly 250,000 more mothers than fathers left their jobs.[46] These numbers increased over the next two years.

Throughout the pandemic, mothers faced a "triple whammy": (1) as frontline workers at risk for contracting COVID; (2) as workers in industries experiencing greater economic distress, including the other sectors of food work we discuss; and (3) as caregivers shouldering increased domestic work due to school and daycare closures.[47] As the pandemic stretched on, this triple whammy deepened and will continue to have long-lasting negative consequences for women. To build on the intersectional analysis we offer throughout this book, we must look at how these gendered consequences also have been shaped by inequalities related to race and class. While many of the impacts of COVID are immeasurable and are still unfolding, women of color in particular have borne the brunt of the negative consequences, in terms of paid employment but also in terms of increased demands on their reproductive labor.

Jocelyn Frye, president of the National Partnership for Women and Families, shows that the pandemic had cascading effects on women of color, women who were typically left out of the policy debates concerning what was needed to repair the economy and the well-being of families. As she described, women of color are more likely to work as frontline workers providing care and critical services, including work in the food system. Their work is also key to the economic stability of their families, and "any erosion of their earnings would be disastrous, worsening instability and robbing families of essential resources," particularly given that women of color often earn the same as or more than their partners and are often the sole earners for their families.[48] Drawing on an analysis of 2018 data, Frye writes that "67.5 percent of Black mothers and 41.4 percent of Latina mothers were the primary or sole breadwinners for their families, compared with 37 percent of white mothers." Data from 2014 show that "67.1 percent of Native American mothers and 44.2 percent of Asian and Pacific Islander mothers provide at least 40 percent of their family's income."[49] As Frye emphasizes, the impacts of COVID-19 on women of color exacerbates the long-standing inequalities that have negatively impacted their economic standing.

The disparate impacts of the pandemic on women of color, in terms of both productive and reproductive labor, have many causes, and it is impossible to quantify what are deeply unquantifiable realities. However, we underscore that the demands, opportunities, and challenges linked to both productive and reproductive labor are intersectional in nature and are deeply and often violently rooted in the historical movements discussed previously in this chapter. A particularly compelling piece by the journalists Jahdziah St. Julien and Emily Hallgren argues, "With brute force, COVID took a sledgehammer to white feminism's illusions of progress to expose a harrowing reality: despite decades of feminist organizing, women are still sinking under the weight of inequality at work and at home."[50] Moreover, they argue that times of crisis like the pandemic bring into sharp relief the failures of white feminism to push for broader work-family policy supports that would level the playing field for women of color, such as universal paid family and medical leave and a robust infrastructure for childcare. We add to this that essential to this movement for feminist inclusivity at the family level, food work must be understood as central.

CONCLUSION: A CRISIS OF CARE

At the time of writing, we find ourselves in a national and personal crisis of care, from the care of our children to the care of our aging parents. As two working mothers balancing both productive and reproductive labor, we experience this crisis of care every day and see this in our local communities and beyond. Food prices are high, caregivers are struggling, and most reproductive labor still falls primarily on women. Both schools and daycares across the United States are struggling to fill positions, and it seems like every day we hear of centers closing because of staffing issues, adding to the burden and stress of families everywhere. While food-related labor is just one part of reproductive labor, it remains both essential and rendered invisible. These points underscore that food work is all too often women's work, in both the productive and reproductive realms. If we are to build a truly sustainable and just food system, food policies must be considered in tandem with broad efforts to support healthy, thriving families of all kinds.

In this chapter, we focused on three main social transformations when there have been major shifts in who is doing reproductive labor and why. Across US history, we have seen reproductive labor shift from work that was forced on Black women against their will to work that was rejected by white women engaged in feminist social activism to duties that became essential during a global crisis. These shifts will continue to happen, and as we have

seen over time, when some women receive more opportunities for meaningful work outside the home, the work that it takes to keep their households
running often falls to the most socially marginalized women. This outsourcing of work now falls disproportionately on immigrant women and other
women of color, and it is imperative that those who benefit from these
arrangements do not become complicit with this exploitation. Further,
women cannot be the only bearers of this systemic and gendered problem.
Bringing greater dignity to reproductive labor is dependent on systemic
change in labor and gender equity.

It is a tremendous and difficult task to organize those who engage in
reproductive labor to make demands for change as the work is so dispersed,
nuanced, and intertwined with affective politics and human relationships.
The Wages for Housework movement might provide a template for comprehensive actions and efforts given that its platform has evolved from focusing
solely on compensating care work to calling for strikes in association with the
Global Women Strike and working on issues as diverse as pay equity, sex
workers' rights, and violence against women. In the United States specifically, proposals for childcare subsidies and better parental leave policies that
were included in the Green New Deal and the calls for public pre-K and
universal school meals have the potential to take some of the burden off
women's household labor in more systematic ways. Whether this work is
performed by family members or paid caregivers, revaluing reproductive
labor is intertwined with ensuring that all workers can support their families
in dignified ways. Thus we must take a broader view to support the work of
all people through comprehensive policies and social movements that support work both inside and outside the home. For these efforts to succeed,
political will and nothing short of a refusal of patriarchy are necessary.

SEVEN

Value, Work, and Food Waste
at the End of the Line

If you've worked at a farm that's producing food for sale, if you've
worked at a bakery, if you've worked in a supermarket, if you've
worked at any restaurant, you know that there's a lot of food
produced that's edible but you aren't going to sell. Because it's
misshapen, because you messed up the ingredients in the order,
because you made too many that day, because the next shipment
is coming in, because it doesn't make sense to pay workers to go
out and harvest that row of peppers and then ship them to the
customer. That food is always going to exist. There's no technical
fix to that. People who have enough money to buy food can integrate more of that food into their diets, that free food, and that
makes it dignified! Then it's not surplus food for surplus people,
then it's a civic duty to eat this food that would otherwise rot. If
we're all eating some of that excess, then somewhere out there,
there's less acreage being deforested for agriculture. So I see it
as our civic duty to eat some free food and the fact that well-off
people are doing it in a highly unequal society, in theory softens
the stigma around it.

SAM, *Food Not Cops organizer and food researcher*

IT IS A DEEP CONTRADICTION of the US food system that so much food
is wasted while millions of people remain food insecure. Food waste is a
particularly large issue in institutional dining spaces, such as those in schools
and hospitals. Even at a university that prides itself on its sustainability
efforts, food waste is a persistent problem. On one spring day, heaping plat-
ters of food were left over after a lunch for the food systems graduate program
that Teresa coordinates at the University of Vermont—a group for whom
avoiding food waste is assumed to be a top priority.

After most of the students departed the lunch (most with a plate loaded
with extra food to take home), Teresa started packing up containers of feta
cheese, baba ghanoush, cucumber and tomato salad, and grilled chicken,

preferring to take food home or share it with colleagues than see it dumped in the compost or trash stream. This voluntary task of packaging and storing excess food before it is wasted is part of the unpaid labor performed in this sector. As Sam describes in the epigraph, these efforts were engaged as a civic duty; a personal crusade against food waste, as well an effort to avoid cooking dinner after a long day of work. Just as she was putting the top on the last container and taking a cookie to go, the Sodexo catering staff arrived to clean up whatever remained, casting a disapproving look at the containers of leftovers. One staff member announced, "You are not supposed to take food with you. That's it, I am just supposed to tell you that," becoming in that instant an enforcer of corporate and university policy set by administrators and upper-level management. This condemnation quickly turned into a conversation about the amount of food that is wasted after catered events and the fact that this policy stemmed from concerns over food safety more anything else. After assurances that the smuggled food was headed straight to the refrigerator, the remaining half-filled chafing dishes and bowls were loaded onto carts and made their way back to the central catering kitchen.

Building on the pioneering work of the FCWA, whose important advocacy for food workers is discussed throughout this book, we add waste and recycling workers in our collective vision to shift to labor in the food system. Our inclusion of food waste workers in this book reflects the social movements to create a more ecologically sustainable food system, which puts great emphasis on food waste reduction and recovery.

Food waste is perhaps the most underexamined area of food systems labor and includes the work involved in disposing of, rescuing, and recycling food that isn't consumed. Globally, a third of all food produced goes to waste. Food waste accounts for about 15% of the total solid waste in the United States.[1] In 2019, the Environmental Protection Agency (EPA) found that 66.2 million tons of wasted food were generated in the food retail, food service, and residential sectors. Of this, 40% was from households, 40% was from food service providers, and 20% was from food retailers. Almost 60% of this food ended up in a landfill. An additional 40.1 million tons of wasted food were generated by the food manufacturing and processing sector.[2] Food waste in the United States has increased 50% per capita since 1974, accounting for more than one-quarter of the total freshwater consumption and about 300 million barrels of oil per year.[3] Americans waste $218 billion of food a year, while at the same time, 44 million people are food insecure.[4] This food waste translates into untold hours of wasted labor.

This chapter discusses both waged and unwaged work, including the volunteer labor necessary to manage this waste. In the realm of paid food waste labor, workers are employed in trash collection, composting facilities, school programs, and *emergency food* networks and institutions that serve people experiencing hunger, such as food banks and pantries. In unpaid work, volunteers and activists perform tasks in places like food banks and pantries, as well as in *food recovery* organizations, where they collect edible food that would otherwise go to waste and distribute it to those in need. There are also people volunteering in more decentralized organizations such as Food Not Bombs and informal spaces such as community mutual aid networks that organize the collective sharing of goods and services.

Like the previous chapter on reproductive labor, the official data on food waste workers is not clear-cut. While there are numerous paid jobs in this sector, untold tons of redistributed food and compost are handled by unpaid workers each year. Later in this chapter we discuss this unpaid work, but for the purposes of comparison with other sectors, we include here the data on paid workers. According to our analysis of BLS data, there were 473,479 workers in the waste collection industry in 2023 (including recycling and compost workers), which is 2.8% of all food system workers. They made an annual median salary of $46,680 and an hourly median wage of $22.05.[5] The best-paid 25% of these workers made $51,530 that year, while the lowest-paid 25% made as little as $30,180.[6] Of those workers, 10.7% were covered by a union contract. In some cases, waste workers do both trash and recycling pickups. These workers, while not solely collecting food waste, do the labor of hauling, sorting, and managing the immense amount of waste that households and institutions create throughout the United States. They receive higher wages than many other food systems workers but do perhaps some of the least appreciated jobs.

Especially in the Global North, food waste is a mounting concern and reflects social standards about what is and isn't acceptable to eat. Throughout this chapter we explore how food waste is defined and the different ways it gets handled to understand the workers who do this labor. We frame this chapter with questions regarding *exchange value* versus *use value* of food labor, building on critical work in the field of political economy that unpacks the commodification of goods and extending it to examinations of labor. Exchange value is the price a person can be charged for something, or its quantitative value when bought or sold as a commodity. In contrast, an item's use value is what it is used for or its qualitative value. Food waste, by

FRONTLINE WORKERS IN FOOD WASTE MANAGEMENT, 2023

Total Employment:

473,479 workers

Union Density:

10.7% coverage, 10.3% membership

Mean Hourly Wage:

$22.05

Mean Annual Wage:

$45,862.11

Data Source: Occupational Employment and Wage Survey (OEWS), US Bureau of Labor Statistics

definition, has a low exchange value, as it is a product that has been deemed unacceptable for sale, often based on relatively arbitrary measures. We argue that the low exchange value of food waste is then reflected in the treatment and valuation (wages) of the workers who handle this food, such as general sanitation workers. This chapter covers how food that is perceived as waste, including edible unused or unsold food, gets put into a waste stream, a compost stream, or an emergency food stream and who does the labor to manage this end of the food chain.

Typically, we think of labor in food waste at the end of the food chain, and the organization of this book reflects this thinking. Yet, as we note here, there is labor required to address food waste across the food chain, from the farm to the kitchen. Given the difficulty of following waste through the chain due to a lack of transparency and the complexity of the system, we have organized this chapter by attending to the value of the different forms of labor required to manage the tremendous amount of food that goes unconsumed and redirected through the food system.

We begin with an overview of exchange and use value, forging a connection between how we value food waste and how we value those who handle food waste. Next we examine the different kinds of work that are entailed in dealing with food waste, beginning with waste prevention and regulation. We then turn to the paid labor in the food waste sector, starting with trash collection (including recycling) and moving through commercial composting and off-market food sales. We follow with sections on unpaid work in the home, broader community-level volunteerism, and informal mutual aid work, all of which help direct food away from the waste stream. In addition to municipal, private, and institutional food waste streams, we take an in-depth look at food recovery activities, which includes gleaning and dumpster diving for food from farms, grocery stores, dining facilities, and restaurants, as well as using or donating the food to emergency food programs, highlighting the work of those who see wasted food as a resource. We conclude by making the case that food waste work must be included in any efforts to build a just and sustainable food system.

THE VALUE OF FOOD WASTE AND FOOD LABOR

The terms "use value" and "exchange value" come from classic Marxist theorization of political economy and capitalism and have been used to assess the value of commodities in the market. As Marx argues, neither exchange nor use value is fixed, with exchange value defined by a social agreement (which may or may not correlate with the price of a good) and use value varying from person to person. Like any commodity, the exchange value of food may not correlate with its use value. However, the disposal of food sets it apart from other commodities. For example, food is usually disposed of once it is close to or past the "best if used by" or "sell by" dates. These dates are inconsistent across food groups and create confusion for consumers trying to understand the difference between food safety and food quality, further adding to the food waste problem.[7] Food may still be edible after these dates, even once it is past its prime. A spot on an apple, for example, might mean it is hard to sell, but it can still be safely consumed once the spot is cut off. Day-old bread may be unmarketable but can be consumed for many days after it is baked, and it is even desirable for certain dishes such as bread pudding or panzanella salad. Similarly, a brown banana with no exchange value may have a use value if one makes it into banana bread or blends it into a smoothie.

There is a central difference between this sector and the other food sectors discussed in this book: food waste is not typically valued by a profit-driven society. Food waste, by definition, is food that is seen as a by-product, as unprofitable, or as lacking in exchange value. In this way, this sector stands out as the product being handled does not have value from an economic perspective. Yet, as many scholars have noted, waste is purposefully built into our transnational and corporate food system.[8] On this point, the geographer Jon Cloke argues that "global food production systems not only create waste; these are systems characterized by forms of creating waste that have become mechanisms for increasing profit."[9] This purposeful and subsidized overproduction occurs while people across the globe simultaneously suffer from chronic malnutrition and diet-related diseases. Tragically, the global food system reinforces both widespread environmental degradation and structural food insecurity through this planned obsolescence.

The anthropologist David Giles frames this value system as "abject capital, those once-commodities that are still useful but that are more profitable to throw away than to sell."[10] Giles's work builds on Marx's discussion of overproduction as "a fundamental contradiction of developed capitalism" and explores the question of how "labor *devalues* commodities, and things become trash merely by being thrown away[;] . . . *sometimes the value of things is determined not by what we keep, but what we throw away.*"[11] We develop this notion of assigning value, arguing that the devaluation of such food waste functions to devalue the labor necessary to handle it.

Despite the lack of exchange value, food waste must still be dealt with from a public service and public health perspective; a society filled with trash or a society that does not responsibly deal with this waste is seen as underdeveloped or dirty. Waste work on a global scale is often taken care of via an informal network of pickers and resellers of discarded goods. In industrialized countries, this sector is typically more formally organized, managed by either the private or the public sector.[12] No matter how waste work is managed, it is inherently the work of dealing with discarded goods or goods perceived as unworthy of social and/or economic value.

There is, however, a growing awareness of and debate over the potential profitability of food waste and "ugly" food if it is diverted from the waste stream. There have been efforts to reclaim the exchange value of food waste by diverting it from landfills in the form of off-market or "second" food products, along the lines of US-based companies like Misfits Market, Hungry Harvest, and Imperfect Foods.[13] These new industries also bring new opportunities for employment in this sector. However, it is too soon to know if these new forms of food waste labor will be meaningful and well compensated and thereby contribute to a truly good food movement or if they will be merely another opportunity for food system profiteers to squeeze their employees. Certainly, the most effective way to decrease food waste, if that is truly the goal, is to decrease the overproduction and maldistribution of food. However, given current agricultural policies and the values underlying our food system, that is unfortunately not as profitable a venture.

Alongside these intricate devaluations and revaluations of food we must consider how we value the work that it takes to handle food waste. Paid work in this sector is stigmatized; dealing with the waste of the food system as a trash collector or food compost manager is quite literally some of the dirtiest work in the food chain. Doing work that is perceived as dirty and undesirable serves to justify poor wages and mistreatment. In the unpaid realm of volunteer and mutual aid labor, many doing this work are trying to address the problem of overproduction of food directly, through food rescue and recovery programs and activities like dumpster diving. Both kinds of efforts seek to transform a broken food system where so many are hungry while food goes to waste. Other volunteers are attempting to address the environmental effects of food waste going into the trash stream by creating household and community composting programs. The problem with much of this work at the tail end of the food system is that such volunteerism often relies on the unpaid, and thereby unvalued, labor of people who are themselves marginalized.

PREVENTING AND REGULATING FOOD WASTE

Reducing food waste starts with effective and systematic prevention so there is less waste to manage at the end of the cycle. The goal of an efficient and sustainable food system is of course to prevent food waste from being created at all points, from production to consumption, which involves work on the farm and in food processing, transportation, retail, service work, and household labor. Further, to make changes in these sectors, it is necessary to change food system governance and regulation so that practices become regularized and institutionalized.[14] Once food waste has been created, the labor to manage and redistribute excess food, or food that will no longer be sold for profit, enters the food redistribution and recovery and waste management streams. Where it goes is based on the type and condition of the food and who or what might consume it.

As outlined by the EPA (figure 21), the most ecologically sustainable approach to food waste is to prevent its creation in the first place (source reduction), then redirect it to feed hungry people, to feed animals, to industrial use such as fuel production and energy recovery, composting to create soil amendments, and finally, into landfills.[15]

According to USDA, one-third of food waste occurs at the household level, and managing it is a common struggle for families. Studies of the causes

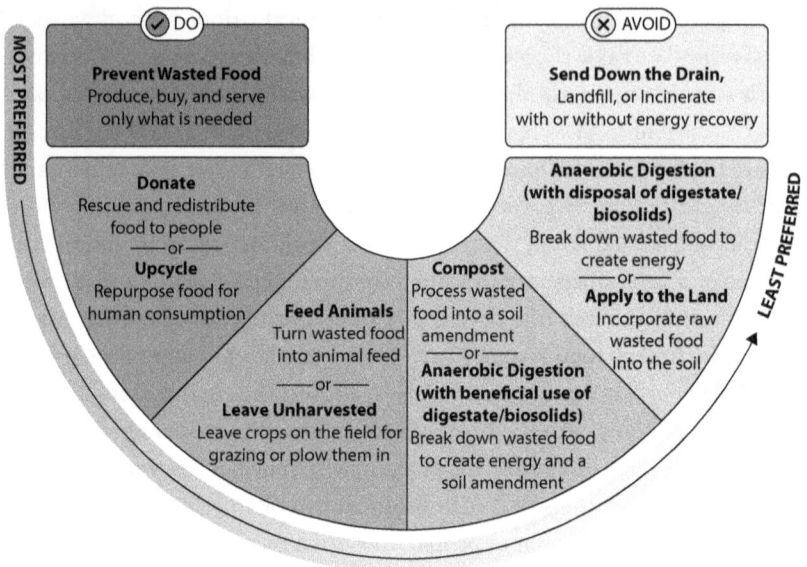

✓ DO

Prevent Wasted Food
Produce, buy, and serve
only what is needed

✗ AVOID

Send Down the Drain,
Landfill, or Incinerate
with or without energy recovery

Donate
Rescue and redistribute
food to people
—— or ——
Upcycle
Repurpose food for
human consumption

Feed Animals
Turn wasted food
into animal feed
—— or ——
Leave Unharvested
Leave crops on the field for
grazing or plow them in

Compost
Process wasted
food into a soil
amendment
—— or ——
**Anaerobic Digestion
(with beneficial use of
digestate/biosolids)**
Break down wasted food
to create energy and a
soil amendment

**Anaerobic Digestion
(with disposal of digestate/
biosolids)**
Break down wasted food to
create energy
—— or ——
Apply to the Land
Incorporate raw
wasted food
into the soil

FIGURE 21. Wasted Food Scale: How to Reduce the Environmental Impacts of Wasted Food, 2023. US Environmental Protection Agency.

of household food waste report various factors affecting levels of household waste, including increases in bulk food purchasing and larger packaging sizes, aggressive food marketing and pricing, changing messages about food safety and expiration dates, disparate knowledge regarding food storage, and shifting social values around waste and environmental consciousness. Despite these shifting causes and differences among individual households, a major factor in preventing waste is the time available for meal planning, prepping, and cooking, particularly the labor-intensive work to forecast the exact amount of food to purchase and prepare while planning weekly meals.[16] Scholars have critiqued the policy and media focus on individual or household food waste as a consumer responsibility or problem to solve, given that causes of waste are ultimately rooted in the production of excess or surplus food and its marketing by retailers. Further, the focus on consumers disregards the structural limitations individuals face when attempting to limit and redirect food deemed as waste, which for many consumers is related to excess labor to cook, compost, and/or regift such food. As we made clear in the previous chapter, this work commonly falls to women.[17]

Outside of the home, workers throughout the food chain face the issue of food waste prevention, yet not surprisingly, they are rarely consulted or given decision-making powers about how to address the problem. Another third of food waste in the United States comes from grocery and retail food stores. A study by the public health scholar Caitlin Ceryes and colleagues looked at retail employees' experiences with food waste.[18] Workers consistently reported that in-store policies related to food waste were either nonexistent or inconsistent, which led to inefficiency in discarding waste. Workers also generally felt that management was unreceptive to their suggestions for improvement. Ceryes and colleagues did not find that there was a lack of food waste awareness in employees but rather that employees did not have the power necessary to implement practices to reduce this waste. Similarly, another study found that the key to reducing food waste in the hospitality industry was to look to the workers.[19] Food is expensive to transport and loses quality and sellability quickly. Food that does not successfully make it to the buyer in time must be disposed of, placing much of the responsibility for avoiding food waste in the hands of truck drivers and others working in warehousing and logistics.[20] Research shows that if food companies wish to reduce wasted food for environmental or financial reasons, they must look to workers, who are key to understanding its challenges and opportunities.

Reducing food waste has been identified as a key goal for addressing climate change and the overuse of natural resources such as water, land, and oil.[21] In the United States, food waste is responsible for creating twice the greenhouse gas emissions as commercial aviation, leading experts and policy makers to look at food waste reduction as essential to preventing climate disaster.[22] That said, policies vary on global and local levels, and labor is not at the center of this discussion.

While there is no federal or comprehensive law in the United States to address food waste directly, there is a long history of redirecting agricultural surpluses to food donations through government and nonprofit channels. Since the passage of the Agricultural Adjustment Act of 1933, the USDA has purchased surplus commodity crops to redistribute through hunger relief programs. This act was the precursor to the creation of the federal food stamp program, now called SNAP. More recently, the Good Samaritan Act of 1996 ensures that if a person or institution donates food or grocery products through a nonprofit or gleaning organization, they are released from liability if that food were to make someone ill. This law was created to address the fears of restaurant, grocery, and farm owners that they could be accountable for donating second quality foods (often called seconds) to organizations. A wealth of research has shown how legislation functions to further institutionalize food

FIGURE 22. Huerta del Valle Employee Nicolas Reza Picks Up Organic Waste for Composting, Ontario, California, 2018. Photographer unknown. US Department of Agriculture.

donations as part of a relationship between corporate agrifood industries and the federal government through providing tax incentives, unfortunately undercutting long-term strategies to address poverty and hunger.[23]

Despite such efforts, most food waste does not end up donated and instead enters the general waste stream. Regarding waste more generally, there have been two major legislative developments relating to solid waste in the United States. The first was the Solid Waste Disposal Act in 1965, and the second was the Resource Conservation and Recovery Act (RCRA) of 1976. While neither act specifically regulated food waste and largely focused on hazardous waste materials, both drew attention to waste as a public health and environmental hazard when not properly attended to. By setting minimum safety standards regarding waste and landfill management, these laws helped support the creation of local infrastructure to deal with waste, in effect creating the need for waste management jobs in the public and private sectors.[24]

In the RCRA, the federal government provides minimum waste management guidelines to the states. Under this legislation, it is still up to local municipalities to determine how to manage recycling and trash collection, which are often outsourced to private companies. A small number of states and cities have instituted new laws to regulate food waste, including streamlining or getting rid of date label requirements (California and New York City), extending liability protections for food donations (New Jersey and Oregon), instituting tax incentives for donations at the state level (California and West Virginia), and creating food waste disposal bans, requiring businesses to divert food waste from other waste streams (California and Vermont).[25] While some states and cities are making progress in centralizing food scrap diversion through these regulations, nothing is centralized on a national level.[26] With the lack of consistent laws and regulation to address food waste comes an inconsistent and often incoherent discussion about who handles food waste and what this work entails.

In contrast, in 2023, the European Union (EU) set progressive goals to reduce food waste, including legally binding targets for food reduction across the EU to be achieved by 2030 and the establishment of EU-wide guidelines for monitoring food waste levels. Goals will be met by systematic monitoring and assessment of waste creation and plans to address unavoidable waste, such as comprehensive plans for food composting.[27] Given the impact of food waste on climate change, it can be expected that other regions of the world will follow suit, and there will be increased demand for more coordinated food waste prevention and sustainable management. Those of us who care about creating a just and sustainable food system must pay close attention to who will be tasked with this work and how current workers in the food system will be called on to change current practices. In addition, we must stay critical of how such changes will affect food system workers across the food chain and advocate for their inclusion in decision making. This global move to address food waste points to the importance of better understanding this sector from a labor perspective if it is indeed a growing industry.

TAKING OUT THE TRASH (AND COMPOST): WAGED LABOR IN FOOD WASTE

Paid work in the food waste steam is generally undercompensated, dangerous, and unappreciated. Early mornings, heavy lifting, and exposure to toxic substances characterize these jobs, from the traditional sanitation workers employed by big private companies and city governments to small-scale composting operations attempting to divert wasted food to soil creation. What all these workers have in common is that they are generally invisible to food and labor advocates and activists, as their work is not commonly included in accounts of food system labor. Despite this invisibility, without their labor, the food system as we know it would collapse. In the United States in particular, food waste is an insidious problem, largely addressed by people throwing uneaten food in with the rest of their household trash. Therefore, we start with sanitation workers, who collect the majority of discarded food, along with other items deemed without value.

Trash Collection

Despite efforts to prevent and redirect unconsumed food, most food waste ends up in the trash collection stream that ends at landfills. In traditional trash collection work at the nonindustrial scale, consumers usually think of those who do the groundwork, the drivers and "ground men" who pick up the garbage bins and empty them into the truck. These workers are called sanitation workers, solid waste workers, or garbage collectors. Depending on the route and location, this work can be done in teams of two or three or just one person doing the groundwork and truck driving. These jobs are physically demanding, and workers labor outdoors, in extreme heat, rain, and snow.

Today the waste industry is split between public and private employment, with workers in the public sector typically faring much better, with higher wages, more comprehensive benefits, shorter workdays, and union contracts. According to journalistic work done by Kiera Feldman in New York City, most of these workers are male and white. Privately employed sanitation workers, in contrast, can work ten- to fourteen-hour days, are often paid per shift at or below the minimum wage, and do not have access to publicly provided pensions, health benefits, retirement plans, or paid time off. They are often not hired as full-time workers, are much less likely to be unionized, and are more likely to be immigrants and people of color. Private trash collection companies are also more likely to fall behind on vehicle upkeep and regulation, which can lead to dangerous workplaces and increased worker (and bystander) injuries. Feldman's 2018 report also found that some workers hired by private waste companies were paid as little as $80 a shift, no matter the hours, with a third of workers making less than $35,000 a year, as compared to publicly hired sanitation workers who made a median base pay of $69,000 a year plus benefits. Further, the private trash collection industry is rife with corruption at the organizational level, with a history of Mafia affiliations.[28]

Given that trash collection requires no formal education and carries a stigma, in addition to early-morning hours and hard physical labor, it is not perceived as a desired occupation in society, and therefore workers may feel devalued. As an industry, turnover is high and morale is low. Garbage collectors are not easily replaced, and newer workers usually do not remain for long because the work is so strenuous.[29] Research has shown that at times garbage collectors endure verbal abuse in their regular interaction with the public in a service position that is perceived as not worthy of respect. This context is exacerbated in the United States, where waste removal, despite being proven a public good, is seen as an individual choice and responsibility.[30]

Being a garbage collector is one of the top five most dangerous jobs in the United States; workers are at high risk of suffering from illness and work-related injuries.[31] Those who work in the private sector are more likely to have injuries resulting in worker compensation claims. Private sector workers' injuries involve more breaks and automobile injuries, while public sector workers suffer more strains, pulls, and lacerations.[32] Further, workers in waste management, including garbage collectors and sorters, are at higher risk of respiratory health complications, presumably due to their exposure to toxins in the waste stream, as they usually do not wear protective respiratory equipment while handling waste.[33] The waste industry averages about one worker fatality a week, a higher rate than police officers, construction workers, or miners.[34] Most of these deaths (82%) occur in the private waste collection sector.[35]

The COVID-19 pandemic put additional stress on residential garbage collectors. During the height of the pandemic, when people were asked to stay home, residential waste increased to the point of overfilling cans, and in some areas, work was increased from four to five days a week. Some workers feared touching trash that may have been contaminated with the coronavirus. These workers explained that their work often goes unnoticed, but if the trash wasn't picked up, it would cover the streets and attract unwanted pests.[36] This is especially a problem with food waste if not properly managed.[37]

In 2023, 10% of sanitation workers were members of a union.[38] Most of these sanitation workers are organized by the Teamsters Union in its Solid Waste and Recycling Division, which negotiates contracts for tens of thousands of workers across both large and small companies.[39] At the same time, private trash collection is currently struggling with suspected independent workers' "unions," which work more closely with the owners than the workers and draw on the industry's sullied past.[40] There is additional advocacy work done on behalf of waste workers today through groups such as the Solid Waste Association of North America and the National Waste and Recycling Association that lobby for increased safety standards and organize industry-wide worker trainings. Unfortunately, these groups are largely supportive of industry and ownership and are not lobbying for worker-led initiatives such as increased wages or benefits.

There is a strong labor organizing history among Black sanitation workers. A famous strike by these workers in 1968 gained the support of Dr. Martin Luther King Jr., who gave his final speech in a Memphis church when he traveled to support the strikers' efforts. The Memphis city council voted to approve the union two weeks after Dr. King's assassination; and the union's success was seen as an inspiration for the following decades of organizing and strikes by workers of color. Sanitation workers in Memphis are still organized by the Teamsters today, and Black workers are in a better position than they were fifty years ago as they can hold higher-level jobs like drivers, which were unavailable due to the racial hierarchies between drivers and collectors in the 1960s. Yet even unionized workers today are struggling to make ends meet, taking on second jobs and leaving for better-paid work outside the industry.[41] There is still much work to be done to incorporate sanitation and other waste workers into a socially just food system.

Composting

While most uneaten food enters the trash-to-landfill stream managed by the workers described above, about 5% of US food waste is diverted to composting. Composting is a more ecologically sustainable approach to food waste and is being encouraged through policies described at the beginning of this chapter. Composting is the practice of controlled decomposition of organic matter and can take place at the household scale in a backyard compost pile, on a farm rotated by tractors, or in commercial facilities with various forms of technology and tools. While composting as an agricultural practice has been around for thousands of years, it was not until the twentieth century that large-scale composting developed as a commercial enterprise as a result of research showing the benefits of compost for amending soil and therefore proving it is an economically valuable resource.[42]

Commercial or industrial-scale composting is designed to handle a large volume of compostable material and is done in a facility that collects organic matter from restaurants, grocery stores, schools, and other institutions that handle food in large quantities. Some compost facilities also accept household materials, both food and yard waste, either through a city-organized pickup or personal drop-off system. Farms and landscaping companies may drop off compostable materials as well. The compost created is then sold to farms, nurseries, landscaping companies, or individuals and, when publicly managed, sometimes offered for free. Some of these facilities are run alongside municipal recycling and solid waste management, while others are private companies. Commercial composting has been growing in scale as landfills become less available and more expensive to use and regulations regarding land use and waste management encourage more ecologically sustainable practices.[43]

Depending on the type of composting, workers must manage the process daily, turning or rotating it, adding amendments, and checking the temperature to ensure the large quantities of food and other organic waste is composting effectively and safely. They also use temperature sensors and probes to draw bacteria samples from inside the compost.[44] Compost management can happen indoors or outdoors, depending on the facility and type of waste. Two studies of compost workers at commercial facilities, one conducted in Belgium and another in France, found high levels of respiratory and gastrointestinal issues and irritation of the skin, eyes, nose, and throat due to exposure to organic dust particles created in the composting process. Both studies found that health concerns were higher among workers in indoor composting plants than outdoor facilities.[45] An additional study in Germany found an increased risk of chronic bronchitis among compost workers from bioaerosol exposure.[46] These studies all note the need for further research to assess the health of compost worker facilities and increased access to PPE such as respirator masks. Especially as global demand for commercial composting grows, these precautions will be essential to protecting this growing workforce.[47]

One of the sources for commercial composting is educational institutions. Schools ranging from K–12 to the university level, are leading the charge to compost at the institutional scale. At K–12 schools, composting has been used as a teaching tool, to educate students on the life cycle and issues of environmental sustainability. Composting in schools often involves class projects, managed by teachers and community volunteers like master gardeners, who may come into classrooms for supplementary lessons. However, initiating food composting at the schoolwide level can be costly and require student activism as well as available funds to enlist commercial compost pickup services. On-site composting of food scraps, a more affordable option, depends on extra work by teachers, custodial and facilities maintenance staff, and community volunteers.[48] It is often difficult for schools and school districts to take on the issue of food waste, even if it is educationally and environmentally beneficial, as there is usually no dedicated staff to work on food waste reduction and management. A review of the literature tells us that successful food waste programs in K–12 institutions rely on student and community volunteers and activists. When paid positions relating to food system sustainability do exist in schools, they are usually on private and temporary finance streams and not equally distributed across school systems.[49] As we discuss below, much food waste and recovery work is done by volunteers, which presents a barrier to creating a sustainable and stable food waste system in schools and beyond.

Within higher education, active composting programs are often connected to university responses to the environmental values of students, environmental research conducted on campus, and environmental ranking and challenges related to food, sustainability, and campus waste. In addition to addressing student interests and faculty research initiatives, universities are rewarded for sustainability metrics by evaluation systems like the Sustainability Tracking, Assessment & Rating System (STARS) and the Real Food Challenge, both of which address food waste reduction. At some schools, students are involved in the national Food Recovery Network, where they collect uneaten food at the end of the day to redistribute to food banks and pantries. Yet these volunteer programs are not consistent across campuses, and the availability of labor is reported to be a major limiting factor to successful waste diversion on university campuses.[50] As in K–12 schools, improvements in reducing food waste and incorporating composting in institutional food service are usually dependent on volunteer organizing and activism, as well as additional labor by dining hall and maintenance facilities staff.[51]

Another group of employees working in composting and the food waste sector is part of the cooperative extension system across US land grant universities. The extension system is a federally funded program to support rural agricultural development and other resource issues and traditionally connected farmers with university-based agricultural research. Today university extension agencies employ thirty-two thousand state and local professionals and have over one million volunteers through programs like 4-H clubs to make research related to environmental resources more accessible to the US population at large.[52] Cooperative extension offices provide resources on how to reduce food waste and discuss composting and donation. Some extension offices and their employees offer educational workshops and classes on how to compost.

Looking at commercially available composting at the household level, a 2017 national survey of residential food waste collection found 148 curbside collection programs, including sidewalk green bins, and 67 drop-off programs for people to opt in and have their home food waste commercially composted.[53] This includes 362 communities that have instituted some form of residential food scrap collection program, covering over 2.7 million US households, or 2.1% of the total US households.[54]

Of course, since there is money to be made in the composting business, there are a variety of start-ups, from large-scale national companies to microenterprise and small nonprofits, that will pick up household food waste for a cost. Similarly, there is growing interest among for-profit companies looking to get in on the food waste problem, however it is defined. Companies like Too Good to Go have developed web-based apps to connect food that would be purportedly wasted with consumers. These companies have been criticized for creating a profit-driven scheme from a system where still-consumable food is usually diverted for food donations and animal feed, as they are not interested in picking up food that has gone bad or is at the compost stage.[55] As these are relatively new business models, there is currently no labor data on them, but it deserves mention as a growing food labor sector.

UNWAGED LABOR IN FOOD WASTE

There is a diversity of unpaid homemakers, volunteers, activists, and community organizers who are working to reclaim and make use of the surplus in our capitalist food system. In doing so, they are going against the grain of a production- and profit-driven society and aiming to salvage the use value of food, whether to amend gardens with nutrient-rich compost or to support community food security. All these people are working without wages to make up for the ills of a structurally wasteful system, although not necessarily with the same motivations.

At the household level, there is an emphasis on composting to divert food and scraps from landfills, as described above. Composting at the domestic and community level has the environmental and social benefits of reducing transportation costs and energy as well as the labor costs at the public and private facilities necessary to process compostable materials. With simple technologies such as plastic bins and newer indoor heating and grinding mechanisms, home composting can divert food scraps from the waste stream and benefit a home or community garden project. For many communities where a centralized pickup or drop-off system is not available, cities and other municipalities offer free or subsidized backyard compost bins and encourage households to compost on their own.[56] To do so, home composters and master gardeners create personal and/or community-based systems to process food waste in their community and create soil amendments that can be used in local gardens, obviating the need to send it to a municipal or for-profit composting service or program.

Studies of home composting from an environmental standpoint emphasize that home composting "saves the labor" of an industrial composting system.[57] Yet it is important to note that without an industrial composting system, the need for labor does not simply disappear. Instead, this work is transferred to the home, where it is not reflected in labor statistics or economic accounting. While household composting may not be the most labor-intensive food task we discuss in this book, it does entail waste separation in the kitchen, as well as compost handling, which can be messy and requires necessary space and planning to manage. Moreover, this often lacks the efficiency of a more centrally coordinated municipal system.[58] The work to deal with food waste adds to the other labor required to prepare and serve food in the home, as we discussed in relation to reproductive labor in the previous chapter. Aside from the challenge of additional work, backyard composting necessitates physical space and relative household stability as it is harder to create and maintain a compost pile in an apartment or rental. At the community level, composting means additional coordination and location of land by community volunteers, who must then spend time managing the compost system. While this work is admirable from a community care and sustainability standpoint, it raises the important question of who has the free time to do this volunteer labor and how the work is valued.

THE EMERGENCY FOOD SYSTEM: RECAPTURING
FOOD THROUGH VOLUNTEER LABOR

In addition to composting food scraps, strategic meal planning to reduce waste, and other methods to avoid food being carted to landfills, many working in the unpaid labor economy of food waste are redirecting food waste streams for humanitarian purposes. Many food recovery volunteers are motivated by the wish to feed hungry or underfed people in their community and often have experienced or are experiencing food insecurity themselves.[59] Some people approach food rescue from a charity perspective, a way to help the poor in an immediate sense, while others do this work with a larger structural and political critique in mind—as a way to subvert the capitalist food system and the commodification of food more broadly.

The emergency food system has been heavily criticized for its dependence on the overproduction of food, particularly commodity crops, which are more beholden to a political system of agricultural subsidies and surpluses than the needs of an underpaid and underfed population. In her foundational work on the shortcomings of a volunteer-driven emergency food system, the sociologist Janet Poppendieck points to the ways that it has created a nonprofit system that supports the business of hunger alleviation instead of addressing the roots of food insecurity.[60] This system allows the government to be absolved of responsibility for structural inequality and ensuring its citizens are fed by providing ample social supports. Scholarly work that has followed Poppendieck's contributions has critiqued the neoliberal foundations of this system. There are multiple issues connected to these foundations, including the low-paid and unpaid labor required for food banks and pantries to function, the poor quality of food and treatment of clients, the propping up of agroindustry, and the dependence on grants and faith-based charity donations.[61]

As can be expected, most research on emergency food looks at the recipients of this care work rather than the workers that keep these networks functioning. What goes undiscussed in the realm of emergency food and food recovery is the gendered and undervalued nature of this unpaid labor from the perspective of community care work. The reality is that women are typically the ones meeting these needs with what is assumed to be free time and free labor. How we value or undervalue this kind of work says a lot about our societal priorities, as many communities now depend on emergency food to offset structural inequalities, low wages, and a shaky social safety net. Pressure on volunteers to meet the deep needs of emergency food recipients is high, including the emotional weight of supplying food and performing the labor to provide networks of care and resources for economic and social security.[62]

In addition to community care networks, recovery work occurs at the production level where nonprofit and volunteer organizations attempt to capture unharvested produce before it leaves the farm. Following an age-old tradition of allowing poor travelers and hungry people to take unharvested food from agricultural lands, volunteer groups and people use the practice of gleaning on farms to collect food from the site of production. With the growth in global awareness of food waste and farm-level food loss, new organizations are forming to create a more systemic and organized gleaning system.[63] As gleaned food is traditionally donated, the system is based on a not-for-profit system, which requires in-kind support (in the form of gleaned produce) and monetary donations to operate. While it may be an ecologically wise solution to the issue of on-farm food waste, it is typically not a sustainable livelihood for those engaged in the work.

For institutions that are willing to address food waste at the source of service, such as schools and universities, the absence of extra time and labor in the cafeterias and food service operations limits the ability to prioritize food donations. Food recovery work is dependent on the use value of the food as well as moral economies to make sure good food does not go to waste. In this context, food service providers must work within a budget that includes labor. If food donations occur, they are usually dependent on student volunteers. As one study of waste practices in university food services explains, "Although donation was widespread in our sample, a main barrier was reported to be a lack of labor. Donation requires staff capacity to package and store food and manage recipient organizations. Enlisting help from student or community volunteer groups could minimize the need for extra labor."[64] The nationwide Food Recovery Network (FRN) was founded in 2011 by students at the University of Maryland who wanted to address food waste on their campus and redirect that food to people in need.[65] While there are plenty of interested students on college campuses who volunteer through FRN chapters in almost every state, gaining resume-building leadership skills, this is not the case in other kinds of institutions. On our own campuses, we have seen the success of this organization rise and fall with the level of student engagement while community partners addressing hunger in the community are stuck hoping that a new crop of eager students will enter each year. The expectation and dependence on volunteer labor filling a gap in the paid and regular workforce to address unsustainable food waste is a theme throughout such discussions. This is especially true in food recovery work, where there must be a moral rather than profit-driven motivation for the labor to be performed.

The broader landscape of emergency food has proliferated since the 1980s as a response to the simultaneous trend of stagnant wages and reduction of the welfare state. Some emergency food organizations do offer paid but low-wage work to people who may struggle to gain employment, including formerly incarcerated people and those with a history of substance abuse. Some of these organizations also offer culinary and other workplace training to these vulnerable groups. Yet many of these volunteers and low-wage workers are food insecure or formerly food insecure themselves, a problematic condition where those who work to combat food insecurity are used for their free labor.[66] As the anthropologist Maggie Dickinson aptly explains:

> Emergency food providers have become a competitive survival niche for hungry people who provide much of the labor on which soup kitchens and food pantries depend. By mobilizing large numbers of poor, hungry people as volunteers to distribute surplus food, emergency food providers transform both wasted food and people who are typically considered "burdens" on the state into an important new form of "free labor for a struggling economy" in ways that exacerbate entrenched social inequalities.[67]

These volunteers and poorly paid workers are largely elderly, unemployed, or marginally employed women, many of whom literally work in exchange for food to feed their families. This dependence on marginalized, female, and volunteer labor has huge economic consequences, subsidizing the emergency food system at an obscene level. As Dickinson reports:

> Sixty-eight percent of food pantries and 42 percent of soup kitchens in Feeding America's national network report relying entirely on volunteers and have no paid staff. Approximately two million Feeding America network volunteers provided more than 8.4 million hours of service each month in 2012. If these volunteers were paid at the prevailing federal minimum wage of $7.25 per hour, their work would cost more than $60 million in additional monthly wages.[68]

She argues that these volunteer armies institutionalize the labor of people marginalized by other societal structures, taking the place of collective action that might result in transformative change. The motivations of volunteers in emergency food range from religious commitments to personal callings to simply wanting to help people and make the world a better place. Yet critiques of such projects are important reminders that emergency food as an approach to addressing community food insecurity may take away from efforts and time devoted to addressing the structural and economic sources of food insecurity in the first place, efforts that also require labor and time.[69]

ANTICAPITALIST APPROACHES TO
FOOD WASTE AND RECOVERY:
MUTUAL AID, FREEGANS, AND FOOD NOT BOMBS

There are myriad grassroots social movements dedicated to explicitly anti-capitalist and subversive approaches to repurposing so-called food waste to feed hungry people, including broad mutual aid networks, freegans, dumpster divers, and activists involved with Food Not Bombs. Mutual aid, as defined by the activist David Spade, is the "collective coordination to meet each other's needs, usually from an awareness that the systems we have in place are not going to meet them."[70] During the COVID-19 pandemic, communities of color were hit particularly hard in terms of food insecurity and hunger. Institutional emergency food systems, including food pantries, soup kitchens, and food banks, were ill equipped to handle the sudden need. Across the country, grassroots volunteers, drawing on existing social networks, rose to the challenge and built on their relationships and local food systems to reduce waste and provide food to those who needed it. The spread of mutual aid associations and organizations grew among a larger diversity of communities to address the immediate need created by closed institutions, shifts in supply chains, and unemployment. In one example based in Los Angeles, community fridges, managed by volunteer individuals, businesses, and organizations, filled with donated food popped up across the city. Organizers insist that this movement is different from charity, that as a mutual aid project the food comes directly from the community they live in, not from outsiders, lowering the level of stigma associated with food aid.[71] For some, this strengthening and broadening of social networks, which were able to quickly shift as needed to address the needs of neighbors and community members, was a hopeful silver lining of the pandemic.[72]

The underlying argument for mutual aid networks is that they create connections in a radical tradition of community resilience to fill gaps in state-led systems with an explicit antiauthoritarian and nonhierarchical vision. Reciprocity is key as mutual aid is not a system of one-way charity; people are taking part in providing for others to also engage with their own community from the inside.[73] Mutual aid is not a new concept. The definition of mutual aid was coined by Peter Kropotkin, a Russian anarchist philosopher who published a collection of essays titled, *Mutual Aid: A Factor of Evolution*.[74] This seminal work has inspired generations of activists and scholars who argue that his scholarship provides an alternative to a competitive capitalist worldview, one where love, cooperation, and human solidarity are at the root of human nature.[75]

While we do not wish to be overly cynical in light of the large mutual aid networks that grew during the pandemic, from the perspective of labor, it cannot be denied that mutual aid networks rely on the free time and volunteerism of those involved in these struggles. There is an explicit objection to this work being paid as it reinforces capitalist and hierarchical structures. As explained by Spade, "We bring our learned practices of hierarchy with us even with no paycheck or punishment enforces our participation, so even in volunteer groups we often find ourselves in conflicts stemming from learning dominance behaviors."[76] While aspiring to a vision where community members meet each other's basic needs powered by a deep communal commitment to resistance and care is a laudable goal, as women and mothers studying food labor, we are skeptical as such networks can (and do) unfortunately also reinforce gendered norms in food and other care work. In our own communities, during the height of the pandemic, we observed mutual aid networks forming and found it jarring that it was mostly women, and largely mothers, who were volunteering to bring others food, take trips to the store, and find needed resources. While we respect the underlying vision of mutual aid as an approach to build egalitarian social movements and challenge capitalist formations, we also wish to bring an awareness to the problem of volunteerism as a way to address food inequalities and community needs in a broader capitalist context.

Similarly, freegans, a social movement of people who salvage unconsumed food from dumpsters and other trash receptacles, also termed "dumpster divers," are explicitly anticapitalist. Alex Barnard writes in *Freegans: Diving into the Wealth of Food Waste in America*:

> To hear freegans talk about ex-commodities call[s] into question some of the canonical tenets of mainstream economics. Free markets *do not* efficiently distribute goods. Supply often *does not* equal demand. And modern capitalist economies are as much about creating scarcity out of excess as they are mechanisms for providing abundance.[77]

He argues that "instead of placing their faith in the market, through recovering ex-commodities, freegans took tentative steps into experimenting with a new system outside it."[78] Yet, as Barnard notes, the majority of freegans he interviewed were from middle-class backgrounds, and most are were single college graduates without children. In another study of dumpster divers in

FIGURE 23. Rose Thackeray Rescues Food from Supermarket Compost Bins, Burlington, Vermont, 2017. Matthew Thorsen, photographer. Courtesy of Seven Days.

Montreal, Canada, Russell Vinegar and colleagues found that while some people who dumpster dive do so out of need and to avoid the social stigma associated with more structured social assistance programs (more readily available in Canada than the United States, we would note), most are college-educated young white men who do so as part of a social network with shared values regarding the redistribution of commodified goods and resources.[79] We emphasize these demographic details not to argue with the underlying motivations and justification of the freegan movement but to point to the somewhat privileged notion that unpaid labor will solve the excesses of the capitalist food system and the waste that is created by it.

In his portrayal of close community networks developed through subverting food waste, Giles looks at the global grassroots movement behind Food Not Bombs, understanding food recovery and the practice of dumpster diving as an explicit anticapitalist social movement. He argues that the revaluing and redefining of food as a social good and human right and the prioritization of the use value, as compared to the exchange value, of food underlies this underground food rescue movement. Giles explains that while there is an explicit commitment to social activism and community building, most FNB activists see the group as a way of self-sustaining and as a response to a lack of personal economic stability: "[It is] [a] modest sort of grassroots safety net for local activists, many of whom as precariously employed and (contrary to popular stereotypes), don't have middle class families to fall back on."[80] He describes these activists as a nonhomogeneous group of people who have been forced to the margins, through economic insecurity, cultural dislocation, racialized discrimination, and/or lack of job market stability. Their shared commitment to food recovery also offers them food security, albeit along with community and philosophical camaraderie via undermining capitalist social norms. The connections between our current neoliberal state and the need and desire for creating an alternative noncapitalist food system are inescapable. The labor to do this work is filled by those who see and feel the need, often because of their own economic displacement.

While the community building that happens in mutual aid networks is important, the question of labor remains. Although we are not critical of these approaches philosophically, we wish to problematize them from a labor perspective, where the efforts to redistribute structurally produced waste is being handled by an unpaid volunteer workforce, often composed of socially marginalized people. How we value the work of dealing with food waste is reflective of broader value systems that must be transformed to build more just food futures.

CONCLUSION:
TAKING FOOD WASTE LABOR SERIOUSLY

There is a growing movement of people seeking to reduce and recover food waste for environmental, social, and even economic purposes, and this will likely be a growing sector of the economy over time. Yet the paid workers who currently handle food waste, from traditional trash collection to line cooks and farmworkers, are not treated as knowledgeable actors in solving the food waste problem. As noted at the beginning of the chapter, across the food chain workers are more typically tasked with protecting companies and organizations from liability regarding excess food and food waste than as actors in preventing or repurposing it.

One of the barriers to creating a more efficient and sustainable food system, where less food goes to waste, is that such a system typically requires more labor. Whether on the farm or in the commercial kitchen, taking additional time to sort, process, and repurpose food waste in an ecologically and socially sustainable way usually means additional labor and, for business owners, additional costs. While this is generally the case, Robb White, former culinary dean of the Culinary Institute of Michigan and self-proclaimed "food waste prevention catalyst," argues that this cost is actually more complex. By paying closer attention to preventing food waste on the preparation end, restaurants can save money not only in ingredient costs (less is wasted and therefore less is purchased) but also in shifting labor to more efficient and sustainable tasks, such as a focus on food quality instead of preparing food that will be wasted.[81] In this way, by adding financial value to the food chain, repurposing food waste can be part of economic development and job creation.[82]

If society wants to address the environmental and social ills of wasted food and redistribute food that has been wasted or disposed of, a shift to focus on its use value (providing sustenance to hungry people) opens up the opportunity to consider whose responsibility it is to take care of the wasted food. The movement to redistribute food waste raises important questions of whether our current food system is sustainable from a labor standpoint. These questions include the following: If food waste is a growing concern from environmental and humanitarian perspectives, who does the work to address this food labor sector? How do we better recognize and value this labor? And, given that most people working to tackle excess food and waste are currently volunteers and unpaid activists, how do we make food waste reduction and redirection a sustainable job for them?

In this chapter, we sought to shed light on these questions, discussing the ways that labor perspectives sideline food waste from food chain analyses. Currently, most consumers are not educated in the work that it takes to deal with wasted food, and therefore even organizations advocating for food chain laborers have overlooked this sector in their mobilizing. Given the devaluation of waste as a purposeful by-product of a wholly commodified food system, food waste, and therefore food labor, is an afterthought, only taken seriously by those looking to subvert this system. As this is a new line of inquiry for food systems and labor scholars, we leave this chapter with more questions than answers. Yet one thing is clear: food chain and labor researchers and advocates must think seriously about waste as a food labor sector and consider how incorporating these workers might strengthen their efforts to reimagine food system justice.

Conclusion

WORKING TOWARD A JUST FOOD FUTURE

IN THIS BOOK WE MAKE the argument that improving labor standards and creating opportunities for solidarity among frontline workers across sectors are necessary for building a more just food system. As former food workers, we experienced the best and worst of laboring in the food system. We made lifelong friendships and learned transferable skills but also witnessed (and endured) insidious examples of abuse and harassment. We dealt with aching feet and cracked hands from washing dishes but also the joys of saving heirloom seeds and seeing customers take pleasure in a meal we helped prepare and serve. More recently, as mothers, we have struggled to balance our careers and make sure our children are nourished with food produced through fair and dignified means. These lived insights have guided the systemic and structural analysis that we advance here.

In bringing together the historical and current conditions of food system workers we make the case that these workers are all connected through a political and economic system mediated by an increasingly globalized, consolidated, and deregulated version of corporate capitalism. This political and economic system reproduces intersectional exploitation of workers, with immigrants, workers of color, and those who identify as women and nonbinary more vulnerable to abuse and stagnant work conditions. As we show, unchecked capitalism, including corporate consolidation, deregulation of labor and environmental protections, and the fissuring of the workforce, exacerbates this exploitation. Throughout this book we engage a political economic framing and highlight key concepts to illuminate the connections between sectors of the food system and show how all workers are linked in larger struggle within a global capitalist system.

Food chain workers are seemingly a disparate group of laborers, working in spaces as varied as industrial-scale poultry processing to meal preparation in private homes. While these workers may not often be in the same physical places or come from the same racial, ethnic, or economic backgrounds, they all take part in the constant and global endeavor to feed us all. This indispensable labor crosses all cultures, political systems, and time frames and is a critical point for possible solidarities. By bringing food chain workers together under one conceptual umbrella, we draw on and hold up the organizing and advocacy work being undertaken by activists and advocates, especially those connected to the Food Chain Workers Alliance, whose approaches and successes open this book. Activists and workers have created bridges across the food chain to uncover points of financial leverage, such as in Worker-Driven Social Responsibility models like the Coalition of Immokalee Workers' Fair Food Program and Migrant Justice's Milk with Dignity campaign. Such movements have also coalesced points of solidarity, such as in the Fight for $15 movement, where fast-food workers have gained the support of retail worker unions and their minimum wage demands were taken up by those selling food at retailers such as Walmart.[1] We celebrate this work and argue that an even more encompassing set of solidarities is necessary.

. . .

The development of these innovative approaches reflects what we argue throughout the book—that food system workers are stronger when they come together as one labor movement. The building of this movement requires a deeper analysis of why food workers are systemically paid low wages, with few benefits and opportunities for advancement, as well as the conditions that allow for the persistence of unenforced or nonexistent workplace regulations. Although the food supply chain may be purposefully opaque in terms of labor, workers are realizing the power of drawing connections between the various links across the food system. While any one labor sector may struggle to gain consumer recognition, when workers and activists band together across the food chain, they start to see change on the ground. This systems-based perspective mirrors the task of this book. In recognizing their commonalities throughout the food chain, food workers bring new potential and strength to movement building in the public and private spaces of food system and beyond.

As we conclude this book, we are in the midst of a global revival of worker organizing that has not been seen for many decades. Workers are organizing through traditional unions, public campaigns, and worker centers. This revival is happening unevenly across the sectors of food systems work, and different kinds of organizing methods are useful for certain groups of workers. As we show, recent organizing work has resulted in concrete gains, and that makes us cautiously optimistic. While this book focuses on frontline workers in the United States, we have seen how such movements gain international traction. We highlight some of these examples in chapter 2 with international fishing collectives and chapter 6 with the Wages for Housework Movement. Further, the Fight for $15 movement, started by two hundred workers protesting in New York City, has extended to other places across the globe, such as Japan, where workers have organized under the group, AEQUITAS, meaning "justice" in Latin. Inspired by the US-born campaign for $15 an hour for all fast-food workers, they have fought nationwide to raise the minimum wage to 1,500 yen, roughly $15.[2] Similarly, the CIW's Worker-Driven Social Responsibility model has expanded from tomatoes in Florida to fisheries in the United Kingdom and tulips in Chile and South Africa.

In the 1960s, one in three workers in the United States were unionized, while in the 1980s, that number had been reduced to one in five. By 2023, only one in ten workers were currently in a union.[3] However, public perception in favor of unions is now at the highest level since 1965, and we hope this will translate into reversing, or at least slowing, the downward trend in unionization.[4] In their State of the Unions 2022 report, on recent unionization shifts in New York City, Ruth Milkman and Joseph Van der Naald note that the recent wins for the union model in cases like Starbucks demonstrates that overall union success is a question of scale. Given the smaller relative number of Starbucks employees, it will take bigger wins in larger-scale companies to fully reverse the downward trend.[5] It is also a question of place, as states like New York have higher rates of unionization than national averages, and New York City has even higher averages than other left-leaning cities like Seattle, Boston, and San Francisco. As the authors note, when we see declines in employment in sectors that previously had high rates of unionization, such as manufacturing, the numbers of unionized workers nationally falls as well. Given that nearly 23 million people perform paid work in the food system, there is a great possibility for unions to grow and make sweeping changes in pay and working conditions, especially if food system workers start to see their struggles as interconnected.

As we emphasize, the union model is not the only, and not always the most effective, form of worker organizing. In our current political moment, unionization is difficult (if not legally impossible) for farmworkers, domestic workers, and gig workers specifically and undocumented workers throughout the food system more broadly. This is where other kinds of worker institutions have a significant role to play. We find inspiration in the current and potential successes of worker centers across sectors like Restaurant Opportunities Center United and organizations following a WSR model like the Coalition of Immokalee Workers and Migrant Justice, which represent farmworkers, and Venceremos, which represents poultry processors. While it is certainly the case that the workers covered by WSR agreements are worlds apart in how they live and labor, the model is powerful in that it recognizes the common forces that endanger and exploit workers across different supply chains.

Worker organizations have advocated for more just labor standards, including living wages, paid medical leave and healthcare benefits, and worker training for increasing job mobility and promotions, among other workplace improvements. These standards have been institutionalized by programs such as the Good Food Purchasing Policy (GFPP), developed by the Los Angeles Food Policy Council, along with representatives from the Food Chain Workers Alliance, the Natural Resources Defense Council, Compassion Over Killing, and the Los Angeles County Department of Public Health, as well as farmers, processors, distributors, chefs, institutional buyers, school food advocates, and faith-based leaders. This policy, which has been used as a model by other food policy councils, city and regional governments, school systems, and sustainable procurement advocates, establishes values-based purchasing guidelines that highlight a "valued workforce." It creates a tiered system for institutional purchasers to be assured that their suppliers follow standards such as protecting the right to collective bargaining, paying living wages, increasing health and safety standards, creating employee advancement and worker retention programs, and ensuring freedom from all forms of forced labor, child labor, and discrimination in employment.[6]

In a recent report from the FCWA and the Heal Food Alliance that analyzes the success of public sector values-based procurement, ten US cities are highlighted that have adopted these procurement policies. In these cities, food suppliers and contractors to city governments, schools, and other public institutions have been held accountable to these standards, accounting for $540 million in public spending.[7] Similar to WSR models, the GFPP creates checks and balances for transparency and third-party monitoring and provides examples for smaller-scale businesses to take the high road as employers and build a food system that feeds their own community rather than extract from it.[8]

In addition to opt-in programs like the GFPP and the Fair Food Program, reinforcing and creating regulations and laws for protecting food workers' rights are crucial to institutionalizing worker justice. Throughout this book we focus on progress in the policy realm, from increases in farm labor overtime and heat protections to abolishing the tipped wage structure. On May 31, 2023, the US Senate Committee on the Judiciary held a hearing titled, "From Farm to Table: Immigrant Workers Get the Job Done." It included testimonies from farmers and farm managers, an immigration law expert, and a farmworker union representative.[9] While comprehensive solutions to the deeply embedded food labor injustices are yet to be accomplished, federal hearings and state-level policy are an important indication of progress.

One of the key mechanisms for policy reform in the United States food chain is the farm bill, an enormous package of federal legislation that touches on nearly every food and farming system. This legislation represents one of the biggest points of power in our contemporary food system and as such should be a central focus for organizing around improvements to pay and working conditions. The farm bill was drafted primarily by members of Congress who sit on the Senate Committee on Agriculture, Nutrition and Forestry and the House Committee on Agriculture. Unfortunately, some of the policies that are most needed to improve the rights and protections for food and farmworkers fall under the mandate of other committees.[10] This is telling of the reality that labor issues are typically separated from food and agriculture issues in most federal policy circles. Given this, it is imperative that advocacy work concerning the farm bill push for the involvement of a broader and more encompassing body of policy makers in drafting this legislation.

We are starting to see food justice and labor organizations such as the HEAL (Health, Environment, Agriculture and Labor) Food Alliance and the United Food and Commercial Workers mobilize around labor equity in the farm bill. They focus on the needs of food workers and farmworkers, arguing for expanding and equalizing labor laws and improving oversight of federal funding. These improvements include providing for better safety oversight and training in workplaces, protection from harmful working conditions (e.g., smoke, pesticides, and dangerous viruses), enacting mandatory line speed limits in food processing, and fully enacting the Protecting

America's Meatpacking Workers Act.[11] The UFCW makes the case for a "worker friendly farm bill," including fair labor standards in food procurement, providing funding for the Farm and Food Worker Relief Grant Program, the protected right of farmworkers to form unions, and reforms to the H-2A seasonal guest worker program.[12] In collaboration with the HEAL Alliance, the UFCW calls for the farm bill to include protections around processing line speeds and to limit preparatory corporate power. For change to succeed, policy makers must not only be responsive to worker organizations; they must also center their knowledge and experiences to formulate legislation that is grounded in the realities of labor in the food system. Following the guidance of organizations like the HEAL Alliance and the UFCW would be an important first step.

As scholars, we would be remiss if we didn't mention the need for more cross-cutting research on the systemic and intertwined inequities and possibilities confronting food workers. For this scholarship to be most effective, it should engage a systems framework to further interrogate the connections between workers' rights and ecological sustainability as a starting point for study and action. This work needs to "study up" to uncover the mechanisms of corporate consolidation and financialization that lead to worker oppression, as well as study across the food chain, highlighting voices and stories to foreground the needs of workers themselves and center their knowledge and worldviews as a foundation for making systemic change. Further, the connection between productive wage labor and reproductive labor, including private caregiving and food waste recovery, is crucial to a comprehensive analysis of food system inequality. This work will require researchers from across disciplines and methods, as well as those connected to organizers and activists who can apply new research to make a vision of change possible.

Many readers will want to know what they can do to support this kind of structural change, especially in the face of such overwhelming and entrenched challenges to food worker justice. As we teach our students, individual actions such as "voting with your fork" need to be tied to broader social movements. This can include supporting worker strikes and boycotts by showing up in person, volunteering one's time on worker-driven campaigns, writing letters to representatives and business owners, raising one's voice at cooperative board meetings, and finding out what organizations need financially and in terms of everyday support. Start by finding worker-led groups locally, nationally, or globally and see how you can get involved with what resources you have to give, whether money, skills, or time. One way to begin is to follow groups we mention throughout this book on social media to see what campaigns they are working on and where there are opportunities to sign on to letters and show up at rallies. Becoming educated on these issues is an important step toward raising the political awareness necessary to move a vision of food worker justice forward.

NOT ONLY POSSIBLE, . . . BUT ESSENTIAL

When we started writing this book in 2020, we were in the early days of the COVID-19 pandemic. As we concluded writing nearly four years later, the height of the pandemic was over, yet the lingering economic and social impacts remain. Writing this book together during countless Zoom sessions has been one of the most engaging projects of our academic careers, and it has also coincided with a period of erratic swings of the worker justice pendulum. At times, it has felt like anything is possible in terms of tangible wins for worker organizing, and at other times, we are reminded of the persistence of structural violence and inequality in our food system. Despite a growing awareness of essential workers, we are far from a comprehensive retooling of the inherently unequal capitalist system of food production. While the barriers to sustained and structural change feel overwhelming, there is no option but to believe that a more just food system is not only possible, but essential.

Fortunately, awareness of the issues confronting food workers is growing in our broader society. *Civil Eats*, an award-winning daily news source on food systems issues, had published more than sixteen hundred articles on food labor issues as of July 2024, with a shift toward more labor-focused articles since the beginning of the pandemic. In addition, since 2014, the founders of Good Food Jobs, a well-known job search tool specific to the good food field, "designed to link people looking for meaningful food work with the businesses that need their energy, enthusiasm, and intellect," have been making explicit and somewhat controversial decisions to shift their website toward equitable and socially sustainable employment practices. In a public announcement in 2020, they stated that they would no longer post jobs that paid less than the minimum wage (excluding jobs advertising the agricultural minimum wage) or the tipped minimum wage, which are below federal or state minimums. This included their previous policy against internships that are volunteer or pay below minimum wage. In 2022, they raised the bar to exclude jobs offering below $15 an hour. This growing public awareness is another reason for optimism.

We acknowledge that while we have focused on spaces of hope in this conclusion, in the realm of reproductive labor, we cannot identify a similar structural change or active campaign to improve the conditions of and disparities within domestic food work. While the pandemic highlighted the fragility of care work systems in the public sphere, it also increased women's labor in the home. Studies show that while some men took a more active role in household labor during and after the lockdown phase of the pandemic, women's labor increased at a higher rate than their male partners'. At the same time, their employment opportunities and wage earning potential were impeded significantly, and reproductive labor inequity was thus intensified.[13] We are likely to see the impacts of these economic constraints for decades to come. That said, history shows us that gender equality is progressing, although incrementally and unevenly, and today many people who identify as women are in a position to share the burden of care and feeding work as cultural norms around work shift over time. Moreover, as discussed in chapter 6, the queering of family life and work expectations offers important openings for reenvisioning what domestic life can and might look like.

Further, investment in increased mechanization for the explicit purpose of replacing human labor is a growing threat to worker organizing, as noted throughout the book. This vulnerability became even more apparent during the pandemic, as employers became increasingly aware of human vulnerabilities due to the spread of the virus. Yet, as we have seen throughout food sectors, food work is also care work, and we believe that at a fundamental level food work requires human touch and care. While certain sectors and tasks are more prone to mechanization, and certainly public health emergencies and politicized immigration policy further motivate employers to seek non-human solutions to their labor struggles, we have also seen resistance to this pattern as consumers reject highly processed foods that are disconnected from farm-level production, self-checkouts in grocery stores, and QR codes at restaurants. We do not buy the argument that food labor will be wholly replaced with machines anytime soon.

For the frontline workers performing day-to-day tasks like laying down drip irrigation, trimming fat on a conveyor belt, and scraping food off our plates, we must continue to work toward better jobs in the food system— ones with living wages, cooperative decision making, and opportunities for advancement and ownership. Given that everyone must eat, all people must participate in making this change. What we do know is that these goals will meet much resistance, and there is much profit being made off the backs of workers in our current capitalist economy. Yet there is also light coming through the cracks, and by arguing for the potential and necessity of food system organizing across sectors, we hope to be part of growing that light. To build a truly sustainable and just food system, we must recognize, compensate, and celebrate the work that happens at all stages of the food chain and those who are doing this work. We hope that this book not only sheds light on the problems but also highlights the path toward a better future.

ACKNOWLEDGMENTS

This book was inspired by the food chain workers, activists, and organizers who keep the food chain running. We hope this book honors the time, skill, and knowledge they devote to the work it takes to keep us all fed.

Thank you to the programs and institutions that have provided financial and in-kind support for this project, including the University of California Press First Generation Program, Syracuse University's SOURCE Grant Program, and the University of Vermont Humanities Center.

We are very grateful for the support of all our student research assistants. At the University of Vermont, Quinn DiFalco and Michelle Nikfarjam were instrumental in collecting and analyzing data and organizing scholarly sources. We were fortunate to have the support of Esi Boidzey Oppong, Megan Cooper, Dea Closson, Sarah Rosenthal, and Alexandra Brooks at Syracuse University, as well as Isabel M. Valentín at SUNY College of Environmental Science and Forestry, in everything from data collection to website development.

We are appreciative of the anonymous reviewers who pushed us to realize this book's full potential. To Alison Alkon, we owe a debt of deep gratitude to you and your keen editorial eye. To Kate Marshall at the University of California Press, we are honored you saw the need for this project and supported us from start to finish. Thank you also to Chad Attenborough for all of your help with the final details in moving this book into production.

We are thankful to the students who took our food labor courses over the years, at UVM in Teresa's Anthropology of Food and Labor course and at Syracuse in Laura-Anne's Will Work for Food course, as well as graduate students in Laura-Anne's Food Studies and Systems course who read early versions of the manuscript and provided feedback. These students, as we note in the introductory chapter, provided space for us to reflect on how young people view labor in the food system, and many of these conversations became the contextual backdrop for how we present the issues in this book. Laura-Anne is also grateful to former graduate students,

April Lopez and Michelle Tynan, as the insightful readings they chose for their independent reading group helped shape her thinking regarding bordering and immigration, as well as Katherine Mott, for sharing scholarly insights on food retail and transportation work in her PhD studies.

This book was workshopped at various conferences and symposiums throughout the years we were drafting our manuscript. We are grateful for the generous and critical feedback from colleagues we received at the Hamilton College "Food Justice, Aesthetics, and Morality" symposium, the joint conference of the Agriculture Food and Human Values Society and the Society for Food and Society in Boston, the annual meeting of the American Association of Geographers (AAG) in Denver, and the "Good Work for Good Food Conference" at Cardiff University. We would also like to credit Cassidy Tawse-Garcia for highlighting the Good Food Jobs discussion on equitable job posting after our first book presentation at AGG in Denver. We appreciate permission from the journal *Agriculture and Human Values* to reprint sections of our 2024 coauthored article, "The Essential Work of Feeding Others: Connecting Food Labor in Public and Private Spaces."

Laura-Anne: I am grateful for the ongoing love and support of my family and friends, especially Jonah, whose patience and confidence in me keeps me grounded. To my daughters, Aviva and Mira, thank you for providing laughter and a healthy perspective during my hours of Zoom writing calls and early-morning brainstorms while I worked on this book. I have ongoing gratitude for my father, Larry, who proudly celebrates my accomplishments; my brother, Richard, who always asks hard questions; and my mother, Rosemary, who is no longer with us but always present in the ways I think and who I am. This book would have been much harder to write without the care work of Kathy McRae, our extended family in Syracuse. Thank you to Rick Welsh and Tom Perreault, who have served as steady mentors, supporting me in maintaining my focus and feeling assured in my work, especially over the past several years. And finally, I feel so lucky to have worked on this project with Teresa, a coauthor with whom I have enjoyed more hours laughing and brainstorming on Zoom than I could have imagined possible. She has become a confidante on issues great and small and makes me think this academic thing is much better done with good friends.

Teresa: As with any big project, I am thankful to my colleagues, friends, and family who provided countless hours of support and good humor during the years it took to write this book. To Henry and Evie, thank you for being my favorite dining companions and for being enthusiastic about another night of take-out when I'm exhausted by the demands of productive and reproductive labor. For teaching me the value of labor and workers, I owe so much to my parents, Dave and Joyce, who raised four kids while moving around the country and trying their hand at running a food franchise. The broader food systems community at UVM has been a productive space to consider the politics of food, and I am fortunate to be surrounded by faculty and student colleagues who are pushing the field forward. To Laura-Anne, thank you for being my Zoom buddy for so many hours, talking about food and labor and all of the other parts of our personal and professional lives. It has been a joy to work on this book with you, and I look forward to many more years of collaboration.

APPENDIX

DATA ANALYSIS METHODS: EMPLOYMENT DATA BY SECTOR

This study is an extraction of data on the food chain sectors, Production, Processing, Distribution, Retail, Services, and Waste, from the US Bureau of Labor Statistics on Occupational Employment and Wage Survey (OEWS) based on the North American Industry Classification System (NAICS), National Industry-Specific Occupational Employment and Wage Estimates.

OEWS defines *wage* as including the base rate of pay, cost of living allowances, guaranteed pay, hazardous duty pay, incentive pay such as commissions and production bonuses, and tips. Back pay, jury duty pay, overtime pay, severance pay, shift differentials, nonproduction bonuses, and employer costs for supplementary benefits and tuition reimbursement were excluded.

Data selections were made for the various sectors using the following steps (table A.1).

1. Go to Occupational Employment and Wage Statistics (bls.gov)
2. Select your search type by clicking on multiple occupations for one industry
3. Select one industry sector
4. Select one industry (see list below)
5. Select All Occupations, click on next
6. Select Employment; Employment percent relative standard error; hourly mean wages, Annual Mean wage, and Wage percent relative standard error; click on next
7. Select May 2023 and set output to "Excel"

TABLE A.1 Industries and Sectors Included in Employment Data

Industries	Sectors
Forestry and Logging	
Support Activities for Agriculture	Support Activities for Crop Production
	Support Activities for Animal Production
Food Manufacturing	Animal Food Manufacturing
	Grain and Oilseed Milling
	Sugar and Confectionery
	Fruit and Vegetable Preserving and Specialty Food Manufacturing
	Dairy Product Manufacturing
	Animal Slaughter and Processing
	Seafood Product Preparation and Packaging
	Bakeries and Tortilla Manufacturing
	Other Food Manufacturing
Merchant Wholesalers, Nondurable Goods (4244 and 4248 Only)	Grocery and Related Product Merchant Wholesalers
	Beer, Wine, and Distilled Alcoholic Beverage Merchant Wholesalers
Warehousing and Storage	
Truck Transportation	
Food and Beverage Retailers	Food and Beverage Retailers (Food and Beverage Retailers; Beer, Wine and Liquor Retailers)
Food Services and Drinking Places	Special Food Services
	Drinking Places (Alcoholic Beverages)
	Restaurants (Full-Service) and Other Eating Places
Farm Product Raw Material Merchant Wholesaler	
Beverage Manufacturing	Beverage Manufacturing Only (Not Tobacco)
Waste Management and Remediation Services	Waste Collection
	Waste Treatment and Disposal
	Remediation and Other Waste Management Services

Once the data were entered into an Excel sheet, the research team went through each industry and included only occupations that they considered frontline workers (excluding supervisory positions) and people who would directly touch food based on their presumed role, informed by the context of the industry and sector relevant to the selection. Then each occupation was sorted by its relevant place on the food chain for analysis (e.g., Food Processing workers were put into the "Processing" category, which corresponds to the book chapters). Tables A.2–A.7 provide details on how occupations from each industry were sorted into their place along the food chain. Once the occupations were chosen, we totaled the number of employees in those occupations and created averages of the workers' average annual salary and average hourly rate.

TABLE A.2 Frontline Workers in Production

Industries Included	Sectors Included in Search	Occupation Names Included	SOC Code
Forestry and Logging	Support Activities for Crop Production	Agricultural Workers	452000
Support Activities for Agriculture and Forestry	Support Activities for Animal Production	Building Cleaning and Pest Control Workers	372000
		Grounds Maintenance Workers	373010
		Animal Care and Service Workers	392000
		Agricultural Workers	452000
		Other Production Occupations	519000
Food Manufacturing	Animal Food Manufacturing	Animal Care and Service Workers	392000
	Grain and Oilseed Milling		
	Sugar and Confectionery	Agricultural Workers	452000
	Fruit and Vegetable Preserving and Specialty Food Manufacturing		
	Dairy Product Manufacturing	Other Production Occupations	519000
	Animal Slaughter and Processing		
	Seafood Product Preparation and Packaging		
	Bakeries and Tortilla Manufacturing		
	Other Food Manufacturing		
Merchant Wholesalers, Nondurable Goods (4244 and 4248 Only)	Grocery and Related Product Merchant Wholesalers	Agricultural Workers	452000
	Beer, Wine, and Distilled Alcoholic Beverage Merchant Wholesaler	Other Production Occupations	519000
Warehousing and Storage		Agricultural Workers	452000
		Other Production Occupations	519000
Truck Transportation		Agricultural Workers	452000

(continued)

TABLE A.2 *(continued)*

Industries Included	Sectors Included in Search	Occupation Names Included	SOC Code
Food and Beverage Retailers	Food and Beverage Retailers (Food and Beverage Retailers; Beer, Wine and Liquor Retailers)	Grounds Maintenance Workers	373010
		Agricultural Workers	452000
Food Services and Drinking Places	Special Food Services	Grounds Maintenance Workers	373010
	Drinking Places (Alcoholic Beverages)	Agricultural Workers	452000
	Restaurants (Full-Service) and Other Eating Places		
Farm Product Raw Material Merchant Wholesaler		Agricultural Workers	452000
Beverage Manufacturing	Beverage Manufacturing Only (Not Tobacco)	Grounds Maintenance Workers	373010
		Agricultural Workers	452000
		Other Production Occupations	519000

TABLE A.3 Frontline Workers in Processing

Industries Included	Sectors Included in Search	Occupation Names Included	SOC Code
Support Activities for Agriculture	Support Activities for Crop Production Support Activities for Animal Production	Food Processing Workers	513000
Food Manufacturing	Animal Food Manufacturing Grain and Oilseed Milling	Assemblers and Fabricators	512000
	Sugar and Confectionery	Food Processing Workers	513000
	Fruit and Vegetable Preserving and Specialty Food Manufacturing	Miscellaneous Production Workers	519190
	Dairy Product Manufacturing Animal Slaughter and Processing		
	Seafood Product Preparation and Packaging Bakeries and Tortilla Manufacturing Other Food Manufacturing	Building Cleaning and Pest Control Workers	372000
Merchant Wholesalers, Nondurable Goods (4244 and 4248 Only)	Grocery and Related Product Merchant Wholesalers	Cooks and Food Preparation Workers	352000
	Beer, Wine, and Distilled Alcoholic Beverage Merchant Wholesaler	Food Processing Workers	513000
Warehousing and Storage		Food Processing Workers	513000
Food and Beverage Retailers	Food and Beverage Retailers (Food and Beverage Retailers; Beer, Wine and Liquor Retailers)	Food Processing Workers	513000

(continued)

TABLE A.3 *(continued)*

Industries Included	Sectors Included in Search	Occupation Names Included	SOC Code
Food Services and Drinking Places	Special Food Services	Food Processing Workers	513000
	Drinking Places (Alcoholic Beverages)	Chemical Processing Machine Setters, Operators and Tenders	519010
	Restaurants (Full-Service) and Other Eating Places		
Farm Product Raw Material Merchant Wholesaler		Food Processing Workers	513000
Beverage Manufacturing	Beverage Manufacturing Only (Not Tobacco)	Assemblers and Fabricators	512000
		Food Processing Workers	513000
		Building Cleaning and Pest Control Workers	372000

TABLE A.4 Frontline Workers in Distribution

Industries Included	Sectors Included in Search	Occupation Names Included	SOC Code
Warehousing and Storage		Motor Vehicle Operators	533000
		Other Transportation Workers	536000
		Material Moving Workers	537000
		Building Cleaning and Pest Control Workers	372000
Truck Transportation		Motor Vehicle Operators	533000
		Rail Transportation Workers	534000
		Material Moving Workers	537000
		Grounds Maintenance Workers	373010
		Building Cleaning and Pest Control Workers	372000
Food and Beverage Retailers	Food and Beverage Retailers (Food and Beverage Retailers; Beer, Wine and Liquor Retailers)	Motor Vehicle Operators	533000
		Material Moving Workers	537000
Food Services and Drinking Places	Special Food Services	Motor Vehicle Operators	533000
	Drinking Places (Alcoholic Beverages)		
	Restaurants (Full-Service) and Other Eating Places	Material Moving Workers	537000
Farm Product Raw Material Merchant Wholesalers	Grocery and Related Product Merchant Wholesalers	Building Cleaning and Pest Control Workers	372000
Merchant Wholesalers, Nondurable Goods (4244 and 4248 Only)	Beer, Wine, and Distilled Alcoholic Beverage Merchant Wholesaler	Building Cleaning and Pest Control Workers	372000

TABLE A.5 Frontline Workers in Retail

Industries Included	Sectors Included in Search	Occupation Names Included	SOC Code
Support Activities for Agriculture	Support Activities for Crop Production	Retail Sales Workers	412000
	Support Activities for Animal Production		
Food and Beverage Retailers	Food and Beverage Retailers (Food and Beverage Retailers; Beer, Wine and Liquor Retailers)	Retail Sales Workers	412000
		Cooks and Food Preparation Workers	352000
		Building Cleaning and Pest Control Workers	372000
Food Services and Drinking Places	Special Food Services	Retail Sales Workers	412000
	Drinking Places (Alcoholic Beverages)		
	Restaurants (Full-Service) and Other Eating Places		
Merchant Wholesalers, Nondurable Goods (4244 and 4248 Only)	Grocery and Related Product Merchant Wholesalers	Cooks and Food Preparation Workers	352000
	Beer, Wine, and Distilled Alcoholic Beverage Merchant Wholesaler		

TABLE A.6 Frontline Workers in Service

Industries Included	Sectors Included in Search	Occupation Names Included	SOC Code
Food Manufacturing	Animal Food Manufacturing Grain and Oilseed Milling	Food and Beverage Serving Workers	353000
	Sugar and Confectionery Fruit and Vegetable Preserving and Specialty Food Manufacturing Dairy Product Manufacturing Animal Slaughter and Processing	Other Food Preparation and Serving Related Workers	359000
	Seafood Product Preparation and Packaging Bakeries and Tortilla Manufacturing Other Food Manufacturing	Cooks and Food Preparation Workers	352000
Support Activities for Agriculture	Support Activities for Crop Production Support Activities for Animal Production	Food Preparation and Serving Related Occupations	350000
Merchant Wholesalers, Nondurable Goods (4244 and 4248 Only)	Grocery and Related Product Merchant Wholesalers	Food and Beverage Serving Workers	353000
	Beer, Wine, and Distilled Alcoholic Beverage Merchant Wholesaler	Other Food Preparation and Serving Related Workers	359000
Warehousing and Storage Truck Transportation		Food Preparation and Serving Related Occupations Food Preparation and Serving Related Occupations	350000 350000
Food Services and Drinking Places	Special Food Services Drinking Places (Alcoholic Beverages) Restaurants (Full-Service) and Other Eating Places	Food and Beverage Serving Workers Other Food Preparation and Serving Related Workers Cooks and Food Preparation Workers Building Cleaning and Pest Control Workers	353000 359000 352000 372000
Farm Product Raw Material Merchant Wholesaler		Food Preparation and Serving Related Occupations	350000
Beverage Manufacturing		Food and Beverage Serving Workers Other Food Preparation and Serving Related Workers Cooks and Food Preparation Workers	353000 359000 352000

TABLE A.7 Frontline Workers in Waste

Industries Included	Sectors Included in Search	Occupation Names Included	SOC Code
Waste Management and Remediation Services	Waste Collection	Building Cleaning and Pest Control Workers	372000
	Waste Treatment and Disposal	Building Cleaning Workers	372010
	Remediation and Other Waste Management Services	Janitors and Cleaners, Except Maids and Housekeeping Cleaners	372011
		Building Cleaning Workers, All Others	372019
		Grounds Maintenance Workers	373010
		Landscaping and Groundskeeping Workers	373011
		Grounds Maintenance Workers, All Others	373019
		Construction Trades Workers	472000
		Operating Engineers and Other Construction Equipment Operators	472073
		Hazardous Materials Removal Workers	474041
		Crushing, Grinding, Polishing, Mixing, and Blending Workers	519020
		Cutting Workers	519030
		Inspectors, Testers, Sorters, Samplers, and Weighers	519061
		Motor Vehicle Operators	530000
		Heavy and Tractor-Trailor Truck Drivers	533032
		Light Truck Drivers	533033
		Material Moving Workers	537000
		Refuse and Recyclable Material Collectors	537081
		Material Moving Workers, All Others	537199

TABLE A.3 Industries and Sectors Analyzed for Unionization Data

Part of Food Chain	Industries Included	Sectors Included
Production	Agriculture, Forestry, Fishing, and Hunting	Crop production Animal production Fishing, hunting, and trapping Support activities for agriculture
Processing	Nondurable Goods	Animal food, grain, and oilseed milling Sugar and confectionery products Fruit and vegetable preserving and specialty food manufacturing Dairy product manufacturing Animal slaughtering and processing Retail bakeries Bakeries and tortilla manufacturing, except retail Seafood and other miscellaneous foods Not specified food industries Beverage manufacturing
Distribution	Wholesale Trade	Groceries and related products, merchant wholesalers Farm product raw materials, merchant wholesalers Alcoholic beverages, merchant wholesalers
	Transportation and Warehousing	Truck transportation Warehousing and storage
Retail	Retail Trade	Supermarkets and other grocery (except convenience) stores Convenience stores Specialty food stores Beer, wine, and liquor stores
Service	Accommodation and Food Services	Restaurant and other food services Drinking places, alcoholic beverages
Waste	Management and Related Services	Waste management and remediation services

For data on unionization in each industry, we utilized the Union Membership and Coverage Database from the Current Population Survey. To get the data, we went to the tab "By Industry: 1983–2023." The industries and sectors included in the analysis are shown in table A.8.

The union data available from CPS were represented by members in the 1000s. To find out the average coverage and membership of each part of the food chain, we multiplied the number of employees in each sector by the % membership in unions given in this set. This gave us a more accurate number of the employees who are members of a union. We then totaled the number of members and divided that by the total number of employees. This gave us an average percentage of membership for each step of the chain. This process was repeated for union coverage.

RACE AND SEX DATA

For data on race presented in this book, we utilized the US Census Bureau's Microdata App feature. Within the microdata app, we used the American Community Survey (ACS) 1-Year Estimates Public Use Microdata Sample from 2022. We used the variables RAC1P (Recoded detailed race code) and HHLDRHISP (Recoded Detailed Hispanic origin of the householder) for race and NAICS as the Industry variables. To capture data related specifically to food, we used the industries and sectors in table A.9 in the analysis. In some figures, data from the RAC1P and HHLDRHISP variables are shown because the RAC1P does not include anyone of Latino or Hispanic descent; these are denoted with an "*." In these figures, it is likely that many individuals are counted twice. In the graph showing "White Only" and "BIPOC," the HHLDRHISP variable was not included, and all individuals who did not check the "White Only" box were totaled under BIPOC. In its use in this table, "BIPOC" (Black, Indigenous, and People of Color) includes the following US Census racial categories: Black or African American Alone; American Indian Alone; Alaska Native Alone; American Indian and Alaska Native tribes specified or American Indian or Alaska Native, not specified and no other races; Asian Alone; Native Hawaiian and Other Pacific Islander Alone; Some other race alone; Two or More Races. The 2022 US Census did not have a variable for Gender. Despite this limitation, we used the variables NAICS and SEX.

TABLE A.9 Percentage of Total Employment in Food Chain Sectors,
BIPOC Workers and Female Workers, 2022

Sector	BIPOC % of Workforce	Female % of Workforce
Production	35.7	27.4
Processing	45.7	39.5
Distribution	48	23.2
Retail	38.8	49.2
Service	45.6	53.5
Waste	41	18.2

DATA SOURCE: American Community Survey, US Census Bureau

GLOSSARY OF TERMS

CORPORATE CONSOLIDATION the merger of smaller companies into a larger one, increasing scales of operation

DEREGULATION the removal of legal regulations or restrictions

DESKILLING primarily defines the process by which employers reduce the necessary skilled or technical work within an industry. This term is also used to characterize the change in home-based food labor toward the use of convenience foods.

DISPOSSESSION the process of taking away property or rights through legal or illegal means

DRAYAGE the transportation of goods over short distances, such as from a shipping port to a warehouse, and trucking includes hauling containers on trailer chassis by diesel-powered truck cabs, usually for long distances

ECONOMIES OF SCALE the ability of businesses to outcompete smaller firms due to cost savings throughout the production chain

EMERGENCY FOOD networks and institutions that serve people experiencing hunger, such as food banks and pantries

ESSENTIAL WORKER workers whose jobs are necessarily in person and crucial to the functioning of businesses and services

EXCHANGE VALUE the price a person can be charged for something, or its quantitative value when bought or sold as a commodity

FISSURING the process of employers shedding direct responsibility for their employees, which has been enabled by corporate deregulation and the weakening of protective labor laws in the United States over time

FOOD CHAIN sequential steps through which food is produced, processed, transported, sold, served, consumed, and put to waste or recycled

FOOD RECOVERY activities where volunteers collect edible food that would otherwise go to waste and distribute it to those in need

FOOD SYSTEM complex web of institutions, resources, and processes that bring food from the farm to the table and into the waste stream

FORDISM the manufacturing technology of the assembly line model and an ideology motivating advanced capitalism and the drive toward efficiency and standardization

FRANCHISE a business arrangement where the lead corporation provides permission for a local owner to use the company's name, brand image, and products

GIG ECONOMY a sector of the labor economy where workers are employed through online platforms for short-term contracts

GLOBALIZATION the increasing interdependence of global political economies and cultures resulting from the expansion of trade, technology, and transnational investment

GUEST WORKER PROGRAM government programs giving foreign workers permission to work in another country, influencing the current landscape for worker mobilizations

INDEPENDENT CONTRACTOR employee who works on a per assignment contract or freelance basis

INDUSTRIALIZATION the process of transition from a primarily agriculturally based economy to one focused on manufacturing

INTERSECTIONALITY sociological and theoretical framework that considers how political and social identities intersect to impact individuals' experiences of oppression and/or privilege

JUST-IN-TIME labor employment approach where workers are hired only as needed for a particular order, task, or job

LIVING WAGE wage required for a full-time worker to meet their basic needs and the needs of their family where they live

LOGISTICS general management of product flow from the point of production to the point of consumption

MCDONALDIZATION the process by which the mode of business operation exemplified by fast-food restaurants has served as a model for business and society

MINIMUM WAGE lowest amount that can legally be paid by an employer according to federal or state law

MUTUAL AID voluntary collaborative exchange of organizing goods and resources, especially in times of crisis

NEOLIBERALISM a philosophy that promotes a market-led approach to social relations and deregulation of business, which has had profound impacts on international food supply chains

OUTSOURCING hiring a worker from outside a company to perform a specific job, task, or project; can be done locally by hiring a contract worker or moving a job to a region or country with lower wages or labor regulations

PIECE RATE payment to a worker per unit that they produce or tasks they complete

POLITICAL ECONOMY an interdisciplinary academic field that incorporates a critical and comprehensive analysis of economic systems and their relationship to society, including the influence of political and social institutions, morality, and ideology

POVERTY WAGE income that is not enough for a worker to meet the standards of living in their own community

PRECARITY a state of persistent economic insecurity

PRODUCTIVE LABOR work that contributes to the capitalist or exchange-driven economy largely in the public sphere

RACIAL CAPITALISM the notion that capitalist processes are historically rooted in the extraction of wealth and labor from racialized populations

RACIALIZATION the social processes that designate racial identities and meaning in the context of hierarchical power relations

RACIALIZED DISPOSSESSION specific patterns and impacts that people of color have experienced as they have lost rights and property due to their racialized identities

REPRODUCTIVE LABOR work performed for the reproduction of society, usually done in the private space of the home

SETTLER COLONIALISM the systematic genocide of Indigenous communities by people who established a settled community in their place

SUBCONTRACTING when a person or firm is contracted outside of the lead company

TAYLORISM theory and practice of scientific labor management, based on Frederick Taylor's methods of studying workplace efficiency

TEMPORARY HIRING AGENCY business that connects workers to employers for temporary positions

TEMPORARY WORKERS employees who are paid for a specific period of time or a time-limited task; includes workers who are independently employed and/or hired through a third-party labor contractor

THIRD-PARTY CERTIFICATION a process where an independent organization certifies the stated quality and standards of a product

TIPPED WAGE a base wage paid to a worker who receives a substantial portion of their wage in customer tips; this may be lower than the legal minimum wage

UNION a group of workers formed to make decisions and protect their rights and interests in the workplace

USE VALUE what an item is used for, or its qualitative value

VERTICAL INTEGRATION the process by which companies attempt to streamline the production process by purchasing various stages of production

WAGE THEFT not being paid a legal minimum wage or the wage one is contracted for

WORKER CENTER nonprofit and community-based organizations that provide support and advocacy for low-wage workers who are not part of a formal union

WORKER-DRIVEN SOCIAL RESPONSIBILITY (WSR) MODEL a worker-led approach to monitoring labor standards and looking for labor abuses, which can include a mechanism of handling complaints as well as worker trainings

NOTES

INTRODUCTION

1. Agyeman, Bullard, and Evans, *Just Sustainabilities*; Allen and Sachs, "The Social Side of Sustainability"; Lo and Jacobson, "Human Rights from Field to Fork"; Lo and Koenig, "Food Workers and Consumers Organizing Together for Food Justice."

2. Agyeman and Alkon, *Cultivating Food Justice*; Alkon, *Black, White, and Green*; Alkon and McCullen, "Whiteness and Farmers Markets"; Allen, *Together at the Table*; Chang et al., "Food Justice and Food Sovereignty"; Gottlieb and Joshi, *Food Justice*; Pilgeram, "Social Sustainability and the White, Nuclear Family"; Sbicca, *Food Justice Now!*; Slocum, "Thinking Race through Corporeal Feminist Theory."

3. Alkon and Guthman, *The New Food Activism*; Lo, "Social Justice for Food Workers in a Foodie World."

4. Rodman et al., "Agricultural Exceptionalism at the State Level"; Stuesse, *Scratching Out a Living*; McClure et al., "Racial Capitalism within Public Health"; Sbicca, "Resetting the 'Good Food' Table."

5. McNicholas and Poydock, "Who Are Essential Workers?"

6. Crenshaw, "Demarginalizing the Intersection of Race and Sex."

7. Besky, *The Darjeeling Distinction*; Besky and Brown, "Looking for Work"; Gaddis, *The Labor of Lunch*; Gray, *Labor and the Locavore*; Harrison, "Lessons Learned from Pesticide Drift"; Jacobson and Lo, "Human Rights from Field to Fork"; Jayaraman, *Behind the Kitchen Door*; Kurtz et al., "Community Food Assistance, Informal Social Networks, and the Labor of Care"; Levine and Striffler, "From Field to Table in Labor History"; Levkoe et al., "Forging Links between Food Chain Labor Activists and Academics"; Lo and Koenig, "Food Workers and Consumers Organizing Together for Food Justice"; Minkoff-Zern, "The Case for Taking Account of Labor in Sustainable Food Systems in the United States"; Sbicca, "Food Labor, Economic Inequality, and the Imperfect Politics of Process in the Alternative Food Movement"; Shreck, Getz, and Feenstra, "Social Sustainability, Farm Labor, and Organic Agriculture"; Wald, "Visible Farmers/Invisible Workers."

8. Adams, "Individualism, Efficiency, and Domesticity"; Sachs and Allen, "Women and Food Chains"; Bowen, Brenton, and Eliott, *Pressure Cooker*; Carney, *The Unending Hunger*; Cairns, Johnston, and MacKendrick, "Feeding the 'Organic Child'"; Cairns, Johnston, and Baumann, "Caring about Food"; Mares, "Navigating Gendered Labor and Local Food."

9. Sackrey, Schneider, and Knoedler, *Introduction to Political Economy, Eighth Edition*.

10. Holt-Giménez, *A Foodie's Guide to Capitalism*; Howard, *Power and Concentration in the Food System*; Patel and Moore, *A History of the World in Seven Cheap Things: A Guide to Capitalism, Nature, and the Future of the Planet*

11. Robinson, *Black Marxism*.

12. Bonanno et al., *From Columbus to ConAgra*; McMichael, "Global Development and the Corporate Food Regime"; McMichael, *The Global Restructuring of Agro-Food Systems*; Friedmann, "The Political Economy of Food"; Friedmann, "Feeding the Empire."

13. Lo, "Social Justice for Food Workers in a Foodie World."

14. Gray, *Labor and the Locavore*.

15. Sinclair, "What Life Means to Me," 594.

16. McNicholas and Poydock, "Who Are Essential Workers?"

17. McCallum, *Essential*.

18. Morrill, Santo, and Bassarab, "Shining a Light on Labor."

19. Food Chain Workers Alliance and Solidarity Research Cooperative, "The Hands That Feed Us"; Liu and Apollon, "The Color of Food."

20. Guthman, "Teaching the Politics of Obesity"; Guthman, *Weighing In*; Hursh, Henderson, and Greenwood, "Environmental Education in a Neoliberal Climate"; Schindel, "Supporting Youth to Develop Environmental Citizenship within/against a Neoliberal Context."

21. Clapp, *Food*; Freidberg, *French Beans and Food Scares*; Howard, *Power and Concentration in the Food System*; Patel, *Stuffed and Starved*; Mintz, *Sweetness and Power*; Welsh, *The Industrial Reorganization of U.S. Agriculture*.

22. These surveys use the North American Industry Classification System (NAICS) and National Industry-Specific Occupational Employment and Wage Estimates (OEWS). OEWS defines *wage* to include the base rate of pay, cost of living allowances, guaranteed pay, hazardous duty pay, incentive pay such as commissions and production bonuses, and tips. Back pay, jury duty pay, overtime pay, severance pay, shift differentials, nonproduction bonuses, employer costs for supplementary benefits and tuition reimbursement were excluded. Annual wages have been calculated by multiplying the hourly mean wage by a "year-round, full-time" hours figure of 2,080 hours; for those occupations where there is not an hourly mean wage published, the annual wage has been calculated directly from the reported survey data.

23. BLS, "2022 Occupational Employment and Wage Statistics."

24. In our courses, we encourage students to look at the Living Wage Calculator project hosted by the Massachusetts Institute of Technology to explore the differ-

ence between a poverty wage, a minimum wage, and a living wage in different regions of the United States. See https://livingwage.mit.edu/.

CHAPTER 1

1. Asbed and Hitov, "Preventing Forced Labor in Corporate Supply Chains"; CIW, "Fair Food Program Report"; Minkoff-Zern, "Farmworker-Led Food Movements Then and Now."

2. BLS, "2022 Occupational Employment and Wage Statistics."

3. BLS, "2022 Occupational Employment and Wage Statistics"; Mares, *Life on the Other Border*; Minkoff-Zern, *The New American Farmer*.

4. Hirsch, Macpherson, and Even, "Union Membership, Coverage, and Earnings from the Current Population Survey."

5. USDA ERS, "USDA ERS—Farm Labor."

6. Bowers and Chand, "An Examination of Wage and Income Inequality within the American Farmworker Community."

7. Bacon, "Living with Climate Change in Farmworker Communities"; Greenaway, "Climate Change–Fueled Valley Fever Is Hitting Farmworkers Hard"; Moran, "As the Climate Emergency Grows, Farmworkers Lack Protection from Deadly Heat."

8. Ferguson, "Farmworkers at Risk."

9. Covert, "As Average Temperatures Rise, Workers Will Finally Get Protection from Extreme Heat."

10. Holmes, *Fresh Fruit, Broken Bodies*.

11. Gordon et al., "Integrating Indigenous Traditional Ecological Knowledge of Land"; Greer, "Commons and Enclosure in the Colonization of North America."

12. Fisher, "'Why Shall Wee Have Peace to Bee Made Slaves.'"

13. Buck, *Worked to the Bone*.

14. Hacker, "From '20. and Odd' to 10 Million."

15. Sears, "Indentured Servants in Colonial America."

16. Wright, *Slavery and American Economic Development*.

17. Carney, *Black Rice*.

18. Mintz, *Sweetness and Power*.

19. Carney, *Black Rice*; Twitty, *The Cooking Gene*.

20. Mintz, *Sweetness and Power*.

21. Sousa and Raizada, "Contributions of African Crops to American Culture and Beyond"; Twitty, *The Cooking Gene*.

22. Johnson, *Warriors into Workers*; Lause, *Free Labor*.

23. Chandra, "The Black/White Wealth Gap"; Copeland, "In the Beginning"; Schweninger, "A Vanishing Breed."

24. Daniel, *Dispossession*; Minkoff-Zern, *The New American Farmer*; Penniman, *Farming While Black*.

25. Daniel, *Dispossession*.

26. Gray, *Labor and the Locavore*.

27. Carlisle, "Critical Agrarianism"; Guthman, *Agrarian Dreams*; Thompson and Wiggins, *The Human Cost of Food*.

28. Mitchell, *Lie of the Land*.

29. Walker, *The Conquest of Bread*.

30. Chan, *This Bittersweet Soil*; Lee, *At America's Gates*; Lew-Williams, *The Chinese Must Go*.

31. Almaguer, *Racial Fault Lines*.

32. Minkoff-Zern et al., "Race and Regulation."

33. Tsu, "Immigration in a Rural Context."

34. We discuss the relationship between domestic work exceptions and food-based labor in home spaces in chapter 6.

35. Thompson and Wiggins, *The Human Cost of Food*; Rodman et al., "Agricultural Exceptionalism at the State Level."

36. Perea, "The Echoes of Slavery."

37. Loza, *Defiant Braceros*.

38. Mitchell, *They Saved the Crops*.

39. Loza, *Defiant Braceros*.

40. Calavita, *Inside the State*; Mitchell, *They Saved the Crops*; Weiler, Sexsmith, and Minkoff-Zern, "Parallel Precarity."

41. Minkoff-Zern et al., "Protracted Dependence and Unstable Relations."

42. Thompson and Wiggins, *The Human Cost of Food*.

43. García-Colón, *Colonial Migrants at the Heart of Empire*.

44. Barndt, *Tangled Routes*.

45. US Department of Labor, "The Migrant & Seasonal Agricultural Worker Protection Act."

46. Gray, *Labor and the Locavore*.

47. Martin, "Good Intentions Gone Awry."

48. De León, *The Land of Open Graves*.

49. De Genova, "The Legal Production of Mexican/Migrant 'Illegality'"; Durand, Massey, and Charvet, "The Changing Geography of Mexican Immigration to the United States."

50. US Department of Labor, "State Child Labor Laws Applicable to Agricultural Employment."

51. Beattie and Taylor, *The Economics of Production*.

52. Hahamovitch, *The Fruits of Their Labor*; Mitchell, *They Saved the Crops*.

53. Taylor, Charlton, and Yúnez-Naude, "The End of Farm Labor Abundance."

54. Dobis et al., "Rural America at a Glance"; Johnson and Lichter, "Rural Depopulation"; Stephan and Debert, "Rural Population Decline in the 1980s."

55. Associated Press, "Rural Population Losses Add to Farm and Ranch Labor Shortage"; Henderson, "Shrinking Rural America Faces State Power Struggle."

56. Minkoff-Zern et al., "Protracted Dependence and Unstable Relations."

57. Mares, *Life on the Other Border*; Minkoff-Zern et al., "Protracted Dependence and Unstable Relations."

58. Bowers and Chand, "An Examination of Wage and Income Inequality within the American Farmworker Community."

59. Entralgo, "Forum."

60. Lopez et al., "Risk Factors for Intimate Partner Violence in a Migrant Farmworker Community in Baja California, Mexico"; Murphy et al., "'They Talk Like That, but We Keep Working.'"

61. Southern Poverty Law Center, "Injustice on Our Plates."

62. Waugh, "Examining the Sexual Harassment Experiences of Mexican Immigrant Farmworking Women."

63. Arcury et al., "Work Safety Culture of Latinx Child Farmworkers in North Carolina"; Volz, "It Is Time for the U.S. to Overhaul Its Agricultural Child Labor Laws."

64. Quandt et al., "The Health of Women Farmworkers and Women in Farmworker Families in the Eastern United States."

65. U.S. Department of Labor, "State Child Labor Laws Applicable to Agricultural Employment."

66. Coleman and Kocher, "Detention, Deportation, Devolution and Immigrant Incapacitation in the US, Post 9/11."

67. Walia, *Border and Rule*.

68. Costa, "How Many Farmworkers Are Employed in the United States?"

69. The H-2 program was originally established by the Immigration and Nationality Act of 1952 to allow US businesses to employ non-US citizens under a temporary work status. This program was split into the H-2A and H-2B programs under the Immigration Reform and Control Act of 1986, which separated workers into two categories, seasonal agricultural workers (H-2A) and seasonal nonagricultural employment (H-2B).

70. Martin, "The Role of the H-2A Program in California Agriculture."

71. Martin, "Farm Labor Shortages"; Rickard, "On the Political Economy of Guest Worker Programs in Agriculture.".

72. Gray, *Labor and the Locavore*; Sbicca, Minkoff-Zern, and Coopwood, "'Because They Are Connected'"; Weiler, Sexsmith, and Minkoff-Zern, "Parallel Precarity."

73. Mazzenga, "Global Lockdowns and Economic Downturns due to COVID-19 Increased Risk of Human Trafficking for Vulnerable Populations"; Ockerman, "Farm Workers Were Trafficked and Threatened With a Gun in South Carolina, Feds Say"; Spacek, "Idaho Farm Gave Workers a Choice"; Business Journal Staff, "Investigation Finds Labor Violations on Turlock Farm."

74. Minkoff-Zern et al., "Protracted Dependence and Unstable Relations."

75. Zoodsma, Dudley, and Minkoff-Zern, "National Food Security, Immigration Reform, and the Importance of Worker Engagement in Agricultural Guestworker Debates."

76. Baur and Iles, "Inserting Machines, Displacing People," 136.

77. Salfer et al., "Finances and Returns for Robotic Dairies."

78. Friedland, Barton, and Thomas, *Manufacturing Green Gold*; Guthman, *Agrarian Dreams*.

79. Costa and Martin, "How Much Would It Cost Consumers to Give Farmworkers a Significant Raise?"; Ganz, *Why David Sometimes Wins*; Minkoff-Zern, "Farmworker-Led Food Movements Then and Now."

80. Garcia, *From the Jaws of Victory*; Paiz, *The Strikers of Coachella*; Shaw, *Beyond the Fields*.

81. Martin, "Promise Unfulfilled."

82. Garcia, *From the Jaws of Victory*.

83. Barger, *The Farm Labor Movement in the Midwest*; Rosenbaum, "Farm Labor Organizing Committee (FLOC)"; Sifuentez, *Of Forests and Fields*; Weinger and Lyons, "Problem-Solving in the Fields."

84. Nieves, "Newsom Reverses Course and Signs Farmworker Bill Backed by Biden."

85. Bethel and Harger, "Heat-Related Illness among Oregon Farmworkers"; Tseng et al., "Risk of Chronic Kidney Disease in Patients with Heat Injury."

86. Tanglis and Devine, "Extreme Heat and Unprotected Workers."

87. Cal/OSHA, "Heat Illness Prevention in Outdoor Places of Employment"; Covert, "As Average Temperatures Rise, Workers Will Finally Get Protection From Extreme Heat"; Olmos, "When Hard Jobs Turn Hazardous"; OSHA, "Heat—Standards"; Oregon OSHA, "Oregon OSHA Adopting 2 Emergency Rules Protecting Workers against Wildfire Smoke and Occupants of Employer-Provided Housing against Heat Dangers."

88. Held, "Congress Killed a Bill to Give Farmworkers a Path to Citizenship"; Zoodsma, Dudley, and Minkoff-Zern, "National Food Security, Immigration Reform, and the Importance of Worker Engagement in Agricultural Guestworker Debates."

89. Zoodsma, Dudley, and Minkoff-Zern, "National Food Security, Immigration Reform, and the Importance of Worker Engagement in Agricultural Guestworker Debates."

90. Darrow, "SB 5438 Unanimously Passes in WA House Bringing Hope for H2A Farmworker Protections"; Sbicca, Minkoff-Zern, and Coopwood, "'Because They Are Connected.'"

91. Fairness for Farmworkers Coalition, "Fairness for Farmworkers Act."

92. Farmworker Justice, "The Fairness for Farm Workers Act."

93. Bardacke, "The UFW and the Undocumented"; Garcia, *From the Jaws of Victory*.

94. Liptak, "Supreme Court Rules against Union Recruiting on California Farms."

95. Chang, "After #MeToo, This Group Has Nearly Erased Sexual Harassment in Farm Fields."

96. Coalition of Immokalee Workers, "The Fair Food Program—Consumer Powered, Worker Certified."

97. CIW, "Fair Food Program Report."

98. Brown and Getz, "Privatizing Farm Worker Justice," 1184.

99. Minkoff-Zern, "Farmworker-Led Food Movements Then and Now."

100. Walker, *The Conquest of Bread*.

CHAPTER 2

1. Tyson, "Feeding the Nation and Keeping Our Team Members Healthy."
2. Reardon and Swinnen, "COVID-19 and Resilience Innovations in Food Supply Chains."
3. Howard, *Power and Concentration in the Food System*, 53.
4. BLS, "2022 Occupational Employment and Wage Statistics."
5. BLS, "2022 Occupational Employment and Wage Statistics."
6. Howard, *Power and Concentration in the Food System*, 56.
7. Taylor, *Scientific Management*.
8. Peña, *The Terror of the Machine*, 24.
9. Horowitz, *Putting Meat on the American Table*; Hounshell, *From the American System to Mass Production, 1800–1932*; Nye, *America's Assembly Line*; Ruiz, *Cannery Women, Cannery Lives*; Striffler, *Chicken*.
10. Ritzer, *The McDonaldization of Society*.
11. Nilsson, "Why Did Henry Ford Double His Minimum Wage?"
12. Zetka, "Work Organization and Wildcat Strikes in the U.S. Automobile Industry, 1946 to 1963."
13. Attewell, "What Is Skill?," 441.
14. Paxson, *The Life of Cheese*.
15. Weiler, "Seeing the Workers for the Trees."
16. Pachirat, *Every Twelve Seconds*.
17. Somers and Soldatic, "Productive Bodies."
18. BLS, "Incidence Rates of Nonfatal Occupational Injuries and Illnesses by Industry and Case Types."
19. Cartwright et al., "The Prevalence of Carpal Tunnel Syndrome in Latino Poultry Processing Workers and Other Latino Manual Workers."
20. Syron et al., "Injury and Illness among Onshore Workers in Alaska's Seafood Processing Industry."
21. Sparkman, "EEOC Cracks Down on Pre-Employment Physical Testing."
22. Driver, "Tyson Says Its Nurses Help Workers."
23. Schulte et al., "Potential Scenarios and Hazards in the Work of the Future"
24. Slade and Alleyne, "The Psychological Impact of Slaughterhouse Employment."
25. Schlosser, *Fast Food Nation*.
26. Hendrix and Dollar, "American Slaughterhouses and the Need for Speed," 145.
27. Huber, "How Did Europe Avoid the COVID-19 Catastrophe Ravaging US Meatpacking Plants?"; McCallum, *Essential*.
28. US Congress, Senate, Select Subcommittee on the Coronavirus Crisis, Hybrid Hearing on "How the Meatpacking Industry Failed the Workers Who Feed America."
29. Chadde, "COVID-19 Cases, Deaths in Meatpacking Industry Were Much Higher Than Previously Known, Congressional Investigation Shows."

30. Kauffman, "Lawsuit: Tyson Managers Bet Money on How Many Workers Would Contract COVID-19."

31. Grabell, "The Plot to Keep Meatpacking Plants Open during COVID-19."

32. FCWA, "We Are Not Disposable."

33. United Food and Commercial Workers International Union, "UFCW: Biden USDA Puts Meatpacking Worker Safety First in Move to Comply with Court Ruling on Pork Line Speeds."

34. Taylor, Boulos, and Almond, "Livestock Plants and COVID-19 Transmission"; Yearby, "Meatpacking Plants Have Been Deadly COVID-19 Hot Spots."

35. Ramos et al., "Invisible No More."

36. Dreier and Luce, "Alone and Exploited, Migrant Children Work Brutal Jobs across the U.S."

37. Dreier and Kohut, "The Kids on the Night Shift."

38. Mast, "Child Labor Remains a Key State Legislative Issue in 2024."

39. Stuesse, *Scratching Out a Living*.

40. Stuesse, *Scratching Out a Living*, 61.

41. Striffler, *Chicken*, 124.

42. Stuesse, "The Poultry Industry Recruited Them."

43. Nabhan-Warren, *Meatpacking America*.

44. Stuesse, "The Poultry Industry Recruited Them."

45. Freshour, "Cheap Meat and Cheap Work in the US Poultry Industry."

46. Stuesse and Dollar, "Who Are America's Meat and Poultry Workers?"

47. Stuesse and Dollar, "Who Are America's Meat and Poultry Workers?"

48. Driver, "Tyson Says Its Nurses Help Workers."

49. Global Ag Media, "Women Underrepresented in Meat Industry Workforce—New Report."

50. Ruiz, *Cannery Women, Cannery Lives*.

51. Driver, "Tyson Says Its Nurses Help Workers."; Schweizer, "Magaly Licolli on Organizing Poultry Workers."

52. Brandworkers, "Manhattan Cafe Tisserie Agrees to Drop Tom Cat Bakery Products"; Community Development Project at the Urban Justice Center and Brandworkers, "Feeding New York."

53. Cheney et al., "Worker Cooperatives as an Organizational Alternative"; Clement, "Canada's Coastal Fisheries"; Foley and McCay, "Certifying the Commons."

54. Marschke and Vandergeest, "Slavery Scandals"; McDonald et al., "Satellites Can Reveal Global Extent of Forced Labor in the World's Fishing Fleet"; Nakamura et al., "Seeing Slavery in Seafood Supply Chains."

CHAPTER 3

1. Jaffee and Bensman, "Draying and Picking."

2. BLS, "2022 Occupational Employment and Wage Statistics."

3. Weil, *The Fissured Workplace.*

4. Herod, "Neoliberalism and Working Precariously"; Peck and Tickell, "Neoliberalizing Space."

5. Jaffee and Bensman, "Draying and Picking."

6. Peck and Tickell, "Neoliberalizing Space."

7. Herod, "Neoliberalism and Working Precariously"; Weil, *The Fissured Workplace.*

8. Lopez, *Reorganizing the Rust Belt.*

9. Warehouse Workers for Justice, "The Shell Game."

10. Clapp, *Food.*

11. Hirsh, "How Trader Joe's, Whole Foods, and Kroger Make Their Store-Brand Products."

12. De Lara, Reese, and Struna, "Organizing Temporary, Subcontracted, and Immigrant Workers."

13. Alimahomed-Wilson and Reese, "Surveilling Amazon's Warehouse Workers"; Nguyen, "The Constant Boss."

14. Jaffee and Bensman, "Draying and Picking."

15. Johnson and Mathis, "Inland Empire 2021–2024 Regional Workforce Development Plan."

16. Warehouse Workers for Justice and UIC Center for Urban Economic Development, "Bad Jobs in Goods Movement."

17. For the purposes of this book, in this chapter we are discussing online grocery shopping in the context of when consumers make a food purchase on a website or app and the food is transported and delivered directly from the warehouse. This is in contrast to the example of a gig worker shopping for the consumer via a delivery app, which we discuss in chapter 5. We differentiate between shoppers working for Instacart and workers at a warehouse picking for Amazon, for example, as one still works directly with the consumer (retail) and one does not (warehouse, transportation, and logistics).

18. Gutelius and Theodore, "The Future of Warehouse Work."

19. East, "Online Grocery Sales after the Pandemic"; Tyrväinen and Karjaluoto, "Online Grocery Shopping before and during the COVID-19 Pandemic."

20. Heuzeroth, "Amazon Fresh"; Lingyu, Lauren, and Zhijie, "Strategic Development of Fresh E-Commerce with Respect to New Retail"; Ruddick, "Amazon to Start Selling Fresh and Frozen Morrisons Food."

21. Strategic Organizing Center, "The Injury Machine."

22. Alimahomed-Wilson and Reese, "Surveilling Amazon's Warehouse Workers."

23. Salles, "Immediacy and Its Hidden Infrastructure"; Vallas, Johnston, and Mommadova, "Prime Suspect."

24. Kantor, Weise, and Ashford, "The Amazon That Customers Don't See"; Sainato, "'They Want Us to Be Robots.'"

25. Sainato, "'They Want Us to Be Robots.'"

26. Hanley and Hubbard, "Eyes Everywhere."

27. Jaffee and Bensman, "Draying and Picking."

28. Hait and Day, "Number of Truckers at All-Time High"; Scott and Davis-Sramek, *Driving in a Man's World*.

29. Hait and Day, "Number of Truckers at All-Time High."

30. Hait and Day. "Number of Truckers at All-Time High."

31. Scott and Davis-Sramek, *Driving in a Man's World*.

32. Hait and Day, "Number of Truckers at All-Time High."

33. Viscelli, *The Big Rig*.

34. Belzer, *Sweatshops on Wheels*.

35. Jaffee and Bensman, "Draying and Picking"; Viscelli, *The Big Rig*.

36. Hamilton, *Trucking Country*.

37. Hamilton, *Trucking Country*, 2.

38. Hamilton, *Trucking Country*.

39. Hamilton, *Trucking Country*, 2.

40. Viscelli, *The Big Rig*.

41. Viscelli, *The Big Rig*.

42. Belman and Monaco, "The Effects of Deregulation, De-Unionization, Technology, and Human Capital on the Work and Work Lives of Truck Drivers"; Belzer, *Sweatshops on Wheels*.

43. Hamilton, *Trucking Country*.

44. Belman and Monaco, "The Effects of Deregulation, De-Unionization, Technology, and Human Capital on the Work and Work Lives of Truck Drivers"; Viscelli, *The Big Rig*.

45. Hamilton, *Trucking Country*, 3.

46. Belman and Monaco, "The Effects of Deregulation, De-Unionization, Technology, and Human Capital on the Work and Work Lives of Truck Drivers."

47. Belzer, *Sweatshops on Wheels*; Viscelli, *The Big Rig*.

48. It has been argued this corruption was inflamed in the media and political spheres by employers to their benefit; see Witwer, *Corruption and Reform in the Teamsters Union*.

49. Barndt, *Tangled Routes*.

50. Barndt, *Tangled Routes*.

51. Lorr, *The Secret Life of Groceries*.

52. Eavis, "Women Could Fill Truck Driver Jobs. Companies Won't Let Them"; Fisher, "Stevens Transport Faces EEOC Sexual Discrimination Charge."

53. Taete, "Arcades, Churches and Laundromats."

54. Waschik et al., "Macroeconomic Impacts of Automated Driving Systems in Long-Haul Trucking."

55. Gittleman and Monaco, "Truck-Driving Jobs."

56. Figueroa et al., "Essential but Unprotected"; van Doorn and Vijay, "Gig Work as Migrant Work."

57. Figueroa et al., "Essential but Unprotected"; van Doorn and Vijay, "Gig Work as Migrant Work."

58. Anderson et al., "The State of Gig Work in 2021."

59. Newlands, "Algorithmic Surveillance in the Gig Economy."

60. Vallas, "Platform Capitalism."

61. Figueroa et al., "Essential but Unprotected."

62. Figueroa et al. "Essential but Unprotected."

63. New York City Department of Consumer and Worker Protection, "A Minimum Pay Rate for App-Based Restaurant Delivery Workers in NYC."

64. Mayorquin, "Food Delivery Workers, Overlooked in Life, Are Honored in Death."

65. De Lara, Reese, and Struna, "Organizing Temporary, Subcontracted, and Immigrant Workers."

66. De Lara, Reese, and Struna "Organizing Temporary, Subcontracted, and Immigrant Workers"; Reese and Bielitz, "The Warehouse Workers Resource Center in Southern California"; Warehouse Worker Resource Center, "About Us Warehouse Worker Resource Center"

67. Warehouse Workers for Justice, "The Shell Game."

68. Reese and Bielitz, "The Warehouse Workers Resource Center in Southern California."

69. De Lara, Reese, and Struna, "Organizing Temporary, Subcontracted, and Immigrant Workers"; Warehouse Workers for Justice, "The Shell Game."

70. Milkman, "The Amazon Labor Union's Historic Breakthrough."

71. Hadero, "Divided Amazon Labor Union Lurches toward a Leadership Election."

72. International Brotherhood of Teamsters, "Front Page."

73. McNicholas and Margaret, "How California's AB5 Protects Workers from Misclassification."

74. California Legislature, "Worker Status: Employees and Independent Contractors"; Kelloway, "Op-Ed: California Sets a Dangerous Precedent for Food Delivery Workers Nationwide."

75. Gedye, "Court Upholds California Prop. 22 in Big Win for Gig Firms like Lyft and Uber"; Melley, "Judge: California Ride-Hailing Law Is Unconstitutional"; Tan, "In Win for Uber and Lyft, California Court Upholds Gig-Worker Proposition."

76. Held, "The Next Frontier of Labor Organizing."

77. Figueroa et al., "Essential but Unprotected."

78. Rana, "DoorDash's 2021 Revenue Tops Pandemic Record."

79. For more information on delivery app worker organizing, see https://losdeliveristasunidos.org/, http://www.workersjustice.org/, https://weareiadw.org/, and https://justiceforappworkers.org/.

80. Fischels, "Why DoorDash Drivers Are on Strike."

81. Held, "The Next Frontier of Labor Organizing"; Lootens and Acosta, "Mayor Adams, Department of Consumer and Worker Protection Announce New Protections for Food Delivery Workers."

82. Chen, "New York City Sets New Minimum Wage for Food Delivery Workers"; Hu, "Inside the Fight to Pay Food Delivery Workers $23 an Hour."

83. Browning, "Massachusetts Court Throws Out Gig Worker Ballot Measure."

84. Wiessner, "US Labor Board Ruling Could Spur Unionizing by Gig Workers, Others."

CHAPTER 4

1. BLS, "2022 Occupational Employment and Wage Statistics."

2. These statistics only include retail establishments categorized as "food and beverage stores." Supercenters and general goods stores such as Walmart, Target, and Costco, as well as dollar store chains, are not included in these numbers, as they are considered "general merchandise stores" by the US Census Bureau, "North American Industry Classification System (NAICS) U.S. Census Bureau," 2022, https://www.census.gov/naics/?input=45&year=2022&details=45521.

3. Flaming et al., "Hungry at the Table."

4. Hirsch, Macpherson, and Even, "Union Membership, Coverage, and Earnings from the Current Population Survey"

5. Milkman, "Grocery Unions under the Gun in New York City and the Nation."

6. Howard, *Power and Concentration in the Food System*.

7. Mott, "Precarity beyond Food."

8. Howard, *Power and Concentration in the Food System*.

9. Howard, *Power and Concentration in the Food System*.

10. Wall Street Journal, "Walmart Inc. Annual Income Statement."

11. Kroger, "History—The Kroger Co."

12. USDA ERS, "Composition of Top U.S. Food Retailers Shifted in 2016."

13. USDA ERS, "Retail Trends."

14. Meyersohn, "Two of the Largest Supermarkets in America Are Merging."

15. Singh, "Proposed Kroger, Albertsons Merger Will Take More Time to Close."

16. Hamilton, *Supermarket USA*.

17. DiFelice, "The Real Root of High Food Prices."

18. Ellickson, "The Evolution of the Supermarket Industry."

19. Glover, "Gender, Power and Succession in Family Farm Business."

20. Levinson, *The Great A&P and the Struggle for Small Business in America*.

21. Lorr, *The Secret Life of Groceries*.

22. Levinson, *The Great A&P and the Struggle for Small Business in America*.

23. Levinson, *The Great A&P and the Struggle for Small Business in America*.

24. Patel, *Stuffed and Starved*.

25. Patel, *Stuffed and Starved*.

26. Deutsch, *Building a Housewife's Paradise*; Reese, *Black Food Geographies*.

27. Lorr, *The Secret Life of Groceries*.

28. Patel, *Stuffed and Starved*, 237.

29. Anderson, *A & P*; Walsh, *The Rise and Decline of the Great Atlantic & Pacific Tea Company*.

30. Levinson, *The Great A&P and the Struggle for Small Business in America*.

31. Ellickson, "The Evolution of the Supermarket Industry."

32. Levinson, *The Great A&P and the Struggle for Small Business in America*.

33. Levinson, *The Great A&P and the Struggle for Small Business in America*.

34. Lorr, *The Secret Life of Groceries*.

35. Lorr, *The Secret Life of Groceries*.

36. Stiegert and Hovhannisyan, "Food Retailing in the United States"

37. Lorr, *The Secret Life of Groceries*.

38. Anderson, "Walmart Was a More Essential Retailer Than Target in Q2"; Inklebarger, "Walmart, Kroger, Costco Make Top Three Grocery Retailers List"; Meyersohn, "America's Largest Private Employer Just Hiked Wages."

39. Muñoz, Kenny, and Stecher, *Walmart in the Global South*.

40. Patel, *Stuffed and Starved*.

41. Bahn, "How a Large Employer's Low-Road Practices Harm Local Labor Markets"; Wiltshire, "Walmart Is a Monopsonist That Depresses Earnings and Employment beyond Its Own Walls, but U.S. Policymakers Can Do Something about It."

42. Good Jobs First, "Walmart | Violation Tracker."

43. Ungar, "Walmart Store Holding Thanksgiving Charity Food Drive—for Its Own Employees."

44. Thanos and Corser, "Trapped In Part-Time."

45. Milkman, "Grocery Unions under the Gun in New York City and the Nation."

46. Meyersohn, "The Self-Checkout Reversal Is Growing."

47. Milkman, "Grocery Unions under the Gun in New York City and the Nation."

48. Vidal and Kusnet, *Organizing Prosperity*.

49. Ellickson and Grieco, "Wal-Mart and the Geography of Grocery Retailing."

50. Artz and Stone, "Analyzing the Impact of Wal-Mart Supercenters on Local Food Store Sales"; Neumark, Zhang, and Ciccarella, "The Effects of Wal-Mart on Local Labor Markets"; Myers and Sbicca, "Bridging Good Food and Good Jobs."

51. Milkman, "Grocery Unions under the Gun in New York City and the Nation."

52. Fan-Yun Lan et al., "Association between SARS-CoV-2 Infection, Exposure Risk and Mental Health among a Cohort of Essential Retail Workers in the USA"; Miranda, "Grocery Workers Died Feeding the Nation."

53. Mayer et al., "Essential but Ill-Prepared."

54. Ceryes et al., "Exploring U.S. Food System Workers' Intentions to Work While Ill during the Early COVID-19 Pandemic"; Corser, "Walmart's Failure to Prioritize Employee and Public Health."

55. Ceryes et al., "Frequency of Workplace Controls and Associations with Safety Perceptions among a National Sample of US Food Retail Workers during the COVID-19 Pandemic."

56. Crowell et al., "Union Efforts to Reduce COVID-19 Infections among Grocery Store Workers."

57. Hernandez, "Grocery Store Shortages Are Back"; Moran, "FMI: 80% of Food Retailers Say Hiring Issues Are Hurting Business."

58. MarketWatch, "KR | Kroger Co. Annual Income Statement."

59. Flaming et al., "Hungry at the Table."

60. Melin, "Kroger, Blasted for Ending Hazard Pay, Gave CEO $22 Million."

61. Melin "Kroger, Blasted for Ending Hazard Pay, Gave CEO $22 Million"; Schweizer, "Why Kroger's Store Closures and Hazard Pay Reaction Are So Unsettling."

62. Wall Street Journal, "ACI | Albertsons Cos. Inc. Annual Income Statement."

63. Lorr, *The Secret Life of Groceries*.

64. Gebauer and Laska, "Convenience Stores Surrounding Urban Schools"; Sharkey, Dean, and Nalty, "Convenience Stores and the Marketing of Foods and Beverages through Product Assortment."

65. Entrepreneur, "Franchise 500 Ranking Franchises"; Hunt et al., *7-Eleven Inc.*

66. Hunt et al., *7-Eleven Inc.*

67. Meisenzahl, "7-Eleven Franchisees Say a 'Dire' Labor Shortage Is Threatening Their Ability to Keep Stores Open Overnight."

68. Hunt et al., *7-Eleven Inc.*

69. Pen, "Justice for Temporary Migrant Workers."

70. Smith, "Dollar Store Restrictions." Despite this growth in store locations, Walmart remains the largest seller of groceries per market share (Fitzpatrick and Davis, "The Most Popular Grocery Stores in the U.S.").

71. Mitchell and Donahue, "Dollar Stores Are Targeting Struggling Urban Neighborhoods and Small Towns."

72. Meyersohn, "The Self-Checkout Reversal Is Growing."

73. Vargas, "Consumer Redlining and the Reproduction of Inequality at Dollar General."

74. Allen, *Together at the Table*; Gray, *Labor and the Locavore*.

75. Agyeman and Alkon, *Cultivating Food Justice*; Alkon, *Black, White, and Green*; Alkon and McCullen, "Whiteness and Farmers Markets"; Allen, *Together at the Table*; Pilgeram, "Social Sustainability and the White, Nuclear Family"; Slocum, "Thinking Race through Corporeal Feminist Theory."

76. Gray, *Labor and the Locavore*.

77. Minkoff-Zern, *The New American Farmer*; Pilgeram, "Social Sustainability and the White, Nuclear Family."

78. Ekers et al., "Will Work for Food."

79. Galassi, "Policy Clarification on OSHA's Enforcement Authority at Small Farms."

80. Reuge and Mares, "Workplace Democracy and Civic Engagement in Vermont Food Cooperatives."

81. Upright, *Grocery Activism*.

82. Reuge and Mares, "Workplace Democracy and Civic Engagement in Vermont Food Cooperatives."

83. Hale and Carolan, "Cooperative or Uncooperative Cooperatives?"

84. Zoller, "Re-Imagining Localism and Food Justice."

85. Reese, *Black Food Geographies*.

86. Ceryes, Flamm, and Fitzgerald, "Investigating the Occupational Challenges of Corner Store Workers Operating in Baltimore City Food Deserts."

87. Milkman, "Grocery Unions under the Gun in New York City and the Nation."

88. Levinson, *The Great A&P and the Struggle for Small Business in America*.

89. Milkman, "Grocery Unions under the Gun in New York City and the Nation."

90. Howard, *Power and Concentration in the Food System*.

91. Howard, *Power and Concentration in the Food System*; Jayaraman, "Shelved."

92. DiNatale and West, "Union Representation Petitions Are Up 57 Percent, but That's Not All!"

93. Milkman, "Grocery Unions under the Gun in New York City and the Nation."

94. Myers and Sbicca, "Bridging Good Food and Good Jobs."

95. Bisaha, "Dollar Store Workers in the South Have a Labor Movement"; Kerzinski, "Dollar Store Workers Organize in New Orleans."

96. Mitchell and Donahue, "Dollar Stores Are Targeting Struggling Urban Neighborhoods and Small Towns."

97. Milkman, "Grocery Unions under the Gun in New York City and the Nation."

98. Jamieson, "Trader Joe's Accused Of Doing Something Totally Illegal To Retaliate Against Workers"; Sainato, "Trader Joe's Broke Labor Laws in Effort to Stop Stores Unionizing, Workers Say."

99. Ikeler, *Hard Sell*.

100. Corkery, "Amid Attacks and Thefts, Some Retail Workers Want to Fight Back"; Jamieson, "Trader Joe's Union Effort Gains Steam as More Workers Seek Elections."

101. DiNatale and West, "Union Representation Petitions Are up 57 Percent, but That's Not All!"

102. Miao, "Walmart and McDonald's Are among Top Employers of Medicaid and Food Stamp Beneficiaries, Report Says."

103. Thanos and Corser, "Trapped In Part-Time."

104. Flaming et al., "Hungry at the Table."

105. Taillie, Ng, and Popkin, "Global Growth of 'Big Box' Stores and the Potential Impact on Human Health and Nutrition."

CHAPTER 5

1. BLS, "2022 Occupational Employment and Wage Statistics."

2. BLS, "2022 Occupational Employment and Wage Statistics."

3. BLS, "2022 Occupational Employment and Wage Statistics."

4. Billings, Donovan, and Bryan, "The School Foodservice Workforce"; One Fair Wage and UC Berkeley Food Labor Research Center, "It's a Wage Shortage, not a Worker Shortage."

5. McCarthy, "U.S. Approval of Labor Unions at Highest Point since 1965."

6. Crenshaw, "Demarginalizing the Intersection of Race and Sex."

7. Williams-Forson and Wilkerson, "Intersectionality and Food Studies," 10.

8. Mojab and Carpenter, "Marxism, Feminism, and 'Intersectionality,'" 278.

9. Jayaraman, *Behind the Kitchen Door*.

10. Chatterjee, "For People with Developmental Disabilities, Food Work Means More Self Reliance"; National Restaurant Association, "Inclusive Hiring."

11. Trubek, *Making Modern Meals*.

12. USDA, "2021 U.S. Food-Away-from-Home Spending 10 Percent Higher than Pre-Pandemic Levels."

13. USDA ERS, "Summary Findings."

14. Johnston, Rodney, and Chong, "Making Change in the Kitchen?"

15. Ritzer, *The McDonaldization of Society*.

16. Schlosser, *Fast Food Nation*.

17. Schmitt and Jones, "Slow Progress for Fast-Food Workers."

18. Jayaraman, *One Fair Wage*.

19. Albala, "Fast Food."

20. Leidner, *Fast Food, Fast Talk*.

21. BLS, "Fast Food and Counter Workers."

22. Maze, "McDonald's CEO Chris Kempczinski Got a Big Raise Last Year."

23. Brown, "The Food Industry's Food Stamps Problem."

24. Justie et al., "Fast-Food Frontline."

25. US Department of Labor, "Minimum Wages for Tipped Employees."

26. Selvam, "The Battle over Chicago's Tipped Minimum Wage Is Over."

27. Allegretto and Cooper, "Twenty-Three Years and Still Waiting for Change."

28. Alexander, "Tipping Is a Legacy of Slavery"; Dempsey, "Racialized and Gendered Constructions of the 'Ideal Server'"; Jayaraman and Sebastian, "Dining Out."

29. Alexander, "Tipping Is a Legacy of Slavery."

30. Martyris, "When Tipping Was Considered Deeply Un-American."

31. One Fair Wage and UC Berkeley Food Labor Research Center, "It's a Wage Shortage, not a Worker Shortage."

32. Allegretto and Cooper, "Twenty-Three Years and Still Waiting for Change."

33. Johnson and Madera, "Sexual Harassment Is Pervasive in the Restaurant Industry."

34. Johnson and Madera, "Sexual Harassment Is Pervasive in the Restaurant Industry."

35. Jayaraman, *One Fair Wage*.

36. Strong, "Do You Know Where Your Tip Money Is Going?"

37. Wilson, *Front of the House, Back of the House*.

38. Jayaraman, *Behind the Kitchen Door.*

39. Herrera et al., "Worker Ownership, COVID-19, and the Future of the Gig Economy."

40. Sedacca and Yaffe-Bellany, "Cooking Eggs in the Morning and Shucking Oysters at Night, Thanks to an App."

41. McCarron, "Blue Hill at Stone Barns Tells a Beautiful Story."

42. Mintz, "The World's 50 Best Restaurants Get by with a Lot of Unpaid Labor."

43. Heynen, "Bending the Bars of Empire from Every Ghetto for Survival."

44. USDA ERS, "National School Lunch Program."

45. Gaddis, *The Labor of Lunch.*

46. Billings, Donovan, and Bryan, "The School Foodservice Workforce."

47. Heyward, "The Silent Suffering of Cafeteria Workers."

48. Cooper and Hickey, "Raising Pay in Public K–12 Schools Is Critical to Solving Staffing Shortages."

49. Vincent et al., "Are California Public Schools Scratch-Cooking Ready?"

50. Colorado General Assembly, "Healthy Meals for All Public School Students."

51. Saracino, "Best Practices for Contracting with Food Service Management Companies."

52. Healthy School Meals for All Wisconsin, "Hungry for Good Jobs."

53. Orleck, *"We Are All Fast-Food Workers Now."*

54. Orleck, *"We Are All Fast-Food Workers Now,"* 34.

55. Lathrop, Lester, and Wilson, "Quantifying the Impact of the Fight for $15."

56. Beam, "New California Law Raises Minimum Wage for Fast Food Workers to $20 per Hour, among Nation's Highest"; Meyerson, "Half a Million California Workers Get a Raise—and a Seat at the Table."

57. Orleck, *"We Are All Fast-Food Workers Now."*

58. Chotiner, "Anthony Bourdain on Weinstein, John Besh, and Meathead Restaurant Culture."

59. Schoenfein, "Women Are Uniting to Fight Sexual Harassment in the Restaurant Industry."

60. Bloch, "Why Don't Restaurant Workers Unionize?"

61. Starbucks Workers United, "Starbucks Workers United."

62. Workers United Labor Union, "Workers United Labor Union."

63. Rochester Regional Joint Board, Workers United, "Starbucks Corporation."

64. De Vynck and Gurley, "4,000 Google Cafeteria Workers Quietly Unionized during the Pandemic."

65. Gaddis, *The Labor of Lunch*, 225–26.

66. The White House, "White House Task Force on Worker Organizing and Empowerment Report."

67. BLS, "Occupational Employment and Wage Statistics."

68. One Fair Wage and UC Berkeley Food Labor Research Center, "It's a Wage Shortage, not a Worker Shortage."

CHAPTER 6

1. Schaeffer, "Among U.S. Couples, Women Do More Cooking and Grocery Shopping Than Men."
2. US Department of Labor, "American Time Use Survey."
3. Goldberg, "'Doing' and 'Undoing' Gender"; Kelly and Hauck, "Doing Housework, Redoing Gender."
4. Devault, *Feeding the Family*, 1.
5. Federici, "Social Reproduction Theory."
6. Federici, "Social Reproduction Theory," 55.
7. Sachs and Allen, "Women and Food Chains."
8. Carney, *The Unending Hunger*; Garth, *Food in Cuba*.
9. Bowen, Brenton, and Eliott, *Pressure Cooker*.
10. Som Castellano, "Alternative Food Networks and the Labor of Food Provisioning."
11. Abarca, *Voices in the Kitchen*; Williams, "Why Migrant Women Make Their Husbands Tamales."
12. Patico, *The Trouble with Snack Time*.
13. Heynen, "Bending the Bars of Empire from Every Ghetto for Survival."
14. McCutcheon, "Geography and the Environment Colloquium Series."
15. Davis, *Women, Race & Class*.
16. Brightman, Lenning, and McElrath, "State-Directed Sterilizations in North Carolina"; Brown et al., "Black Women Health Inequity"; Campbell, "Medical Violence, Obstetric Racism, and the Limits of Informed Consent for Black Women"; Crockett, "Quietly under Control"; Roberts, *Killing the Black Body*.
17. Wood, "Introduction."
18. West and Knight, "Mothers' Milk."
19. West and Knight, "Mothers' Milk, 49.
20. Fanto Deetz, "How Enslaved Chefs Helped Shape American Cuisine."
21. Carney, *Black Rice*; Twitty, *The Cooking Gene*.
22. Blackmon, *Slavery by Another Name*.
23. May, "Domestic Workers in U.S. History."
24. Sharpless, *Cooking in Other Women's Kitchens*.
25. Glymph, *Out of the House of Bondage*.
26. Sharpless, *Cooking in Other Women's Kitchens*, xiv.
27. Sharpless, *Cooking in Other Women's Kitchens*.
28. Perea, "The Echoes of Slavery."
29. Sharpless, *Cooking in Other Women's Kitchens*.
30. Williams-Forson, *Building Houses out of Chicken Legs*.
31. hooks, *Yearning*.
32. hooks, *Yearning*, 42.
33. Hooks, *Yearning*, 43.
34. hooks, *Yearning*, 41.

35. Beck, *White Feminism*; Collins, *Black Feminist Thought*; Zakaria, *Against White Feminism*.

36. Friedan, *The Feminine Mystique*.

37. Stovall, Baker-Sperry, and Dallinger, "A New Discourse on the Kitchen"

38. Federici, "Social Reproduction Theory."

39. Friedan, "Cooking with Betty Friedan . . . Yes, Betty Friedan," n.p.

40. Matchar, "Is Michael Pollan a Sexist Pig?"

41. Duffy, "Reproducing Labor Inequalities"; Romero, "Nanny Diaries and Other Stories"; Tronto, "The 'Nanny' Question in Feminism"; Wu, "More Than a Paycheck."

42. Bowen, Brenton, and Eliott, *Pressure Cooker*.

43. Howard, *Power and Concentration in the Food System*.

44. Sachs and Allen, "Women and Food Chains."

45. Trubek, *Making Modern Meals*, 4.

46. Landivar et al., "Early Signs Indicate That COVID-19 Is Exacerbating Gender Inequality in the Labor Force."

47. Landivar et al., "Early Signs Indicate That COVID-19 Is Exacerbating Gender Inequality in the Labor Force," 2.

48. Frye, "On the Frontlines at Work and at Home," n.p.

49. Frye, "On the Frontlines at Work and at Home," n.p.

50. St. Julien and Hallgren, "The Gaps of White Feminism and the Women of Color Who Fall Through."

CHAPTER 7

1. EPA, "Advancing Sustainable Materials Management."

2. EPA, "Food."

3. Hall et al., "The Progressive Increase of Food Waste in America and Its Environmental Impact."

4. Feeding America, "Food Waste in America."

5. BLS, "2022 Occupational Employment and Wage Statistics."

6. U.S. News, "How Much Can a Garbage Collector Expect to Get Paid?"

7. Wilson et al., "Food Waste."

8. Cloke, "Empires of Waste and the Food Security Meme"; McMichael, "Global Development and the Corporate Food Regime"; McMichael, "A Food Regime Genealogy."

9. Cloke, "Empires of Waste and the Food Security Meme," 629.

10. Giles, *A Mass Conspiracy to Feed People*.

11. Giles, *A Mass Conspiracy to Feed People*, 32–33; original emphasis.

12. Castilloberthier, "Garbage, Work and Society."

13. Pedtke and Pedtke, "Food Waste, Wasted Food"; Yoder, "Food Waste Is Heating up the Planet."

14. Mourad, "Recycling, Recovering and Preventing 'Food Waste.'"

15. EPA, "Food Recovery Hierarchy."

16. Landry and Smith, "Demand for Household Food Waste"; Schanes, Dobernig, and Gözet, "Food Waste Matters"; Visschers, Wickli, and Siegrist, "Sorting out Food Waste Behaviour"; Williams et al., "Reasons for Household Food Waste with Special Attention to Packaging."

17. Evans, Campbell, and Murcott, *Waste Matters*; Welch, Swaffield, and Evans, "Who's Responsible for Food Waste?"

18. Ceryes et al., "'Maybe It's Still Good?'"

19. Filimonau and. De Coteau, "Food Waste Management in Hospitality Operations."

20. Chrobog, "Wasted."

21. Hawken, *Drawdown*.

22. ReFED, "Food Waste Monitor."

23. Henderson, "'Free' Food, the Local Production of Worth, and the Circuit of Decommodification"; Lindenbaum, "Countermovement, Neoliberal Platoon, or Re-Gifting Depot?"; Lohnes, "Regulating Surplus"; Poppendieck, *Sweet Charity?*; Tarasuk and Eakin, "Food Assistance through 'Surplus' Food."

24. Kovacs and Klucsik, "The New Federal Role in Solid Waste Management," 205; Louis, "A Historical Context of Municipal Solid Waste Management in the United States"; Silyok, *Environmental Laws*.

25. ReFED, "U.S. Waste Policy Finder."

26. Chrobog, "Wasted."

27. European Commission, "Food Waste Reduction Targets—European Commission."

28. Feldman, "Why Private Waste Management Is One of the Nation's Most Hazardous Jobs."

29. Horsley, "'Hard, Dirty Job.'"

30. Rich, "The Moral Choices of Garbage Collectors."

31. Lam, "The Dangerous Life of a Trash Collector."

32. Bunn, Slavova, and Tang, "Injuries among Solid Waste Collectors in the Private versus Public Sectors."

33. Vimercati et al., "Respiratory Health in Waste Collection and Disposal Workers."

34. Lam, "The Dangerous Life of a Trash Collector."

35. Feldman, "Why Private Waste Management Is One of the Nation's Most Hazardous Jobs."

36. Horsley, "'Hard, Dirty Job.'"

37. EPA, "Advancing Sustainable Materials Management."

38. BLS, "Union Members—2023."

39. Cypress, "Solid Waste and Recycling Division."

40. Feldman, "A Trash Industry Union Thrives, and Employees Say They Are Left Holding the Bag."

41. Lee, "How the Memphis Sanitation Workers' Strike Changed the Labor Movement."

42. Cooperband, "Composting"; Fitzpatrick, Worden, and Vendrame, "Historical Development of Composting Technology during the 20th Century."

43. Fitzpatrick, Worden, and Vendrame, "Historical Development of Composting Technology during the 20th Century"; Hambach et al., "Work-Related Health Symptoms among Compost Facility Workers."

44. Olivia, "What Is Commercial Composting?"

45. Demange et al., "Effects of Plant Features on Symptoms and Airway Inflammation in Compost Workers Followed over 18 Months"; Hambach et al., "Work-Related Health Symptoms among Compost Facility Workers."

46. Schantora et al., "Prevalence of Work-Related Rhino-Conjunctivitis and Respiratory Symptoms among Domestic Waste Collectors."

47. Domingo and Nadal, "Domestic Waste Composting Facilities."

48. Feeney, "Tackling Food Waste in Iowa's K–12 Schools"; Schwarz Bonhotal, "School Composting—Let's Get Growing."

49. Allen and Guthman, "From 'Old School' to 'Farm-to-School.'"

50. Musicus et al., "Food Waste Management Practices and Barriers to Progress in U.S. University Foodservice."

51. Dang, "Recover, Redistribute, and Reduce"; Galvan, Hanson, and George, "Repurposing Waste Streams"; Murakami et al., "Student Leadership and Sustainability."

52. Association of Public and Land-Grant Universities, "ECOP Handout."

53. Streeter and Platt, "Residential Food Waste Collection Access In The U.S."

54. Pai, Ai, and Zheng, "Decentralized Community Composting Feasibility Analysis for Residential Food Waste."

55. Yoder, "Food Waste Is Heating up the Planet."

56. Pai, Ai, and Zheng, "Decentralized Community Composting Feasibility Analysis for Residential Food Waste."

57. Zhou et al., "Rapid In-Situ Composting of Household Food Waste."

58. Adhikari et al., "Home and Community Composting for On-Site Treatment of Urban Organic Waste"; Zhou et al., "Rapid In-Situ Composting of Household Food Waste."

59. Dickinson, *Feeding the Crisis.*

60. Poppendieck, *Sweet Charity?*

61. Dickinson, *Feeding the Crisis*; Kurtz et al., "Community Food Assistance, Informal Social Networks, and the Labor of Care"; Lohnes, "Regulating Surplus"; Warshawsky, "New Power Relations Served Here."

62. Kurtz et al., "Community Food Assistance, Informal Social Networks, and the Labor of Care."

63. Peart, "How Gleaning Could Reshape the Farm Economy."

64. Musicus et al., "Food Waste Management Practices and Barriers to Progress in U.S. University Foodservice," 6.

65. Food Recovery Network, "Our Story."

66. Chrobog, "Wasted"; Dickinson, *Feeding the Crisis*.

67. Dickinson, *Feeding the Crisis*, 1–2.

68. Dickinson *Feeding the Crisis*, 10, citing Mabli et al., "Hunger in America."

69. Dickinson, *Feeding the Crisis*; Poppendieck, *Sweet Charity?*

70. Spade, *Mutual Aid*, 7.

71. James, "Community Fridges Show up in L.A. Neighborhoods to Feed Those in Need."

72. Bell, "Amplified Injustices and Mutual Aid in the COVID-19 Pandemic"; Lofton et al., "Mutual Aid Organisations and Their Role in Reducing Food Insecurity in Chicago's Urban Communities during COVID-19"; Travlou, "Kropotkin-19."

73. Spade, *Mutual Aid*.

74. Kropotkin, *Mutual Aid*.

75. Kropotkin et al., *Mutual Aid*.

76. Spade, *Mutual Aid*, 17.

77. Barnard, *Freegans*, 18; original emphasis.

78. Barnard, *Freegans*, 23.

79. Vinegar, Parker, and McCourt, "More Than a Response to Food Insecurity."

80. Giles, *A Mass Conspiracy to Feed People*, 36.

81. White, "Food Waste Prevention Means More Efficient Labor."

82. Chrobog, "Wasted."

CHAPTER 8

1. Resnikoff, "Fight for $15 Goes Global."

2. McCarthy, "The US Fight for $15 Minimum Wage Has Spread to Japan."

3. BLS, "Union Members Summary—2023 A01 Results."

4. McCarthy, "U.S. Approval of Labor Unions at Highest Point since 1965."

5. Milkman and Van Der Naald, "The State of Unions 2023."

6. Lo and Delwiche, "The Good Food Purchasing Policy."

7. Food Chain Workers Alliance and HEAL Food Alliance, "Procuring Food Justice."

8. Lo and Delwiche, "The Good Food Purchasing Policy."

9. U.S. Senate, Committee on the Judiciary, "From Farm to Table."

10. National Sustainable Agriculture Coalition, "What Is the Farm Bill?"

11. HEAL Food Alliance, "Securing Dignity and Fairness for Food Chain Workers and Their Families."

12. United Food and Commercial Workers International Union, "Worker Friendly Farm Bill."

13. Garcia, "Exploring the Domestic Division of Labor When Both Parents Are Involuntarily Working from Home"; Hutchinson, Khan, and Matfess, "Childcare, Work, and Household Labor during a Pandemic"; van Tienoven et al., "Locking Down Gender Roles?"

BIBLIOGRAPHY

Abarca, Meredith E. *Voices in the Kitchen: Views of Food and the World from Working-Class Mexican and Mexican American Women*. College Station: Texas A&M University Press, 2006.

Adams, Jane. "Individualism, Efficiency, and Domesticity: Ideological Aspects of the Exploitation of Farm Families and Farm Women." *Agriculture and Human Values* 12, no. 4 (1995): 2–17. https://doi.org/10.1007/BF02218564.

Adhikari, Bijaya K., Anne Trémier, José Martinez, and Suzelle Barrington. "Home and Community Composting for On-Site Treatment of Urban Organic Waste: Perspective for Europe and Canada." *Waste Management & Research* 28, no. 11 (2010): 1039–53. https://doi.org/10.1177/0734242X10373801.

Agyeman, Julian, and Alison Alkon, eds. *Cultivating Food Justice: Race, Class, and Sustainability*. Cambridge, MA: MIT Press, 2011.

Agyeman, Julian, Robert Doyle Bullard, and Bob Evans. *Just Sustainabilities: Development in an Unequal World*. Cambridge, MA: MIT Press, 2003.

Albala, Ken. "Fast Food." In *The SAGE Encyclopedia of Food Issues*, edited by Ken Albala. Los Angeles: SAGE Publications, 2015. https://doi.org/10.4135/9781483346304.

Alexander, Michelle, "Opinion: Tipping Is a Legacy of Slavery." *New York Times*, February 5, 2021. https://www.nytimes.com/2021/02/05/opinion/minimum-wage-racism.html.

Alimahomed-Wilson, Jake, and Ellen Reese. "Surveilling Amazon's Warehouse Workers: Racism, Retaliation, and Worker Resistance amid the Pandemic." *Work in the Global Economy* 1, no. 1–2 (2021): 55–73. https://doi.org/10.1332/273241721X16295348549014.

Alkon, Alison Hope. *Black, White, and Green: Farmers Markets, Race, and the Green Economy*. Athens: University of Georgia Press, 2012.

Alkon, Alison Hope, and Julie Guthman, eds. *The New Food Activism: Opposition, Cooperation, and Collective Action*. Berkeley: University of California Press, 2017.

Alkon, Alison Hope, and Christie Grace McCullen. "Whiteness and Farmers Markets: Performances, Perpetuations . . . Contestations?" *Antipode* 43, no. 4 (2011): 937–59. https://doi.org/10.1111/j.1467-8330.2010.00818.x.

Allegretto, Sylvia, and David Cooper. "Twenty-Three Years and Still Waiting for Change: Why It's Time to Give Tipped Workers the Regular Minimum Wage." BriefingPaper379,2014.https://www.epi.org/publication/waiting-for-change-tipped-minimum-wage/.

Allen, Patricia. *Together at the Table: Sustainability and Sustenance in the American Agrifood System*. University Park: Pennsylvania State University Press, 2004.

Allen, Patricia, and Julie Guthman. "From 'Old School' to 'Farm-to-School': Neoliberalization from the Ground Up." *Agriculture and Human Values* 23, no. 4: (2006): 401–15. https://doi.org/10.1007/s10460-006-9019-z.

Allen, Patricia L., and Carolyn E. Sachs. "The Social Side of Sustainability: Class, Gender and Race." *Science as Culture* 2, no. 4 (1991): 569–90. https://doi.org/10.1080/09505439109526328.

Almaguer, Tomas. *Racial Fault Lines: The Historical Origins of White Supremacy in California*. Berkeley: University of California Press, 2008.

Anderson, Avis H. *A & P: The Story of the Great Atlantic and Pacific Tea Company*. Mount Pleasant, SC: Arcadia Publishing, 2002.

Anderson, George. "Walmart Was a More Essential Retailer Than Target in Q2." *Forbes*, August 21, 2023. https://www.forbes.com/sites/georgeanderson/2023/08/21/walmart-was-a-more-essential-retailer-than-target-in-q2/.

Anderson, Monica, Colleen Mcclain, Michelle Faverio, and Risa Gelles-Watnick. "The State of Gig Work in 2021." Pew Research Center: Internet, Science & Tech, December 8, 2021. https://www.pewresearch.org/internet/2021/12/08/the-state-of-gig-work-in-2021/.

Arcury, Thomas A., Sara A. Quandt, Taylor J. Arnold, Haiying Chen, Joanne C. Sandberg, Gregory D. Kearney, and Stephanie S. Daniel. "Work Safety Culture of Latinx Child Farmworkers in North Carolina." *American Journal of Industrial Medicine* 63, no. 10 (2020): 917–27. https://doi.org/10.1002/ajim.23161.

Artz, Georgeanne M., and Kenneth E. Stone. "Analyzing the Impact of Wal-Mart Supercenters on Local Food Store Sales." *American Journal of Agricultural Economics* 88, no. 5 (2006): 1296–1303. https://doi.org/10.1111/j.1467-8276.2006.00948.x.

Asbed, Greg, and Steve Hitov. "Preventing Forced Labor in Corporate Supply Chains: The Fair Food Program and Worker-Driven Social Responsibility." *Wake Forest Law Review* 52 (2017): 497–531.

Association of Public and Land-Grant Universities. "ECOP Handout." 2022. https://www.aplu.org/members/commissions/food-environment-and-renewable-resources/CFERR_Library/ecop-handout/file.

Attewell, Paul. "What Is Skill?" *Work and Occupations* 17, no. 4 (1990): 422–48. https://doi.org/10.1177/0730888490017004003.

Bacon, David. "Living with Climate Change in Farmworker Communities." *Reality Check*, August 3, 2021. https://davidbaconrealitycheck.blogspot.com/2021/08/living-with-climate-change-in.htm.

Bahn, Kate. "How a Large Employer's Low-Road Practices Harm Local Labor Markets: The Impact of Walmart Supercenters." Equitable Growth, January 28, 2022. https://equitablegrowth.org/how-a-large-employers-low-road-practices-harm-local -labor-markets-the-impact-of-walmart-supercenters/.

Bank Muñoz, Carolina, Bridget Kenny, and Antonio Stecher. *Walmart in the Global South: Workplace Culture, Labor Politics, and Supply Chains.* Austin: University of Texas Press, 2018.

Bardacke, Frank. "The UFW and the Undocumented." *International Labor and Working Class History* 83, no 83 (2013): 162–69. https://doi.org/10.1017 /S0147547913000045.

Barger, W. K. *The Farm Labor Movement in the Midwest: Social Change and Adaptation among Migrant Farmworkers.* Austin: University of Texas Press, 1994.

Barnard, Alex V. *Freegans: Diving into the Wealth of Food Waste in America.* Minneapolis: University of Minnesota Press, 2016.

Barndt, Deborah. *Tangled Routes: Women, Work, and Globalization on the Tomato Trail.* Lanham, MD: Rowman & Littlefield, 2007.

Baur, Patrick, and Alastair Iles. "Replacing Humans with Machines: A Historical Look at Technology Politics in California Agriculture." *Agriculture and Human Values* 40, no. 1 (2023): 113–40. https://doi.org/10.1007/s10460-022-10341-2.

Beam, Adam. "New California Law Raises Minimum Wage for Fast Food Workers to $20 per Hour, among Nation's Highest." *KTLA News*, September 28, 2023. https://ktla.com/news/ap-us-news/ap-california-gov-gavin-newsom-signs-law -to-raise-minimum-wage-for-fast-food-workers-to-20-per-hour/.

Beattie, Bruce R., and C Robert Taylor. *The Economics of Production.* New York: Wiley, 1985.

Beck, Koa. *White Feminism: From the Suffragettes to Influencers and Who They Leave Behind.* New York: Atria Books, 2021.

Bell, Finn McLafferty. "Amplified Injustices and Mutual Aid in the COVID-19 Pandemic." *Qualitative Social Work* 20, no. 1–2 (2021): 410–15. https://doi .org/10.1177/1473325020973326.

Belman, Dale L., and Kristen A. Monaco. "The Effects of Deregulation, De-Unionization, Technology, and Human Capital on the Work and Work Lives of Truck Drivers." *ILR Review* 54, no. 2A (2001): 502–24. https://doi.org/10.1177 /001979390105400227.

Belzer, Michael H. *Sweatshops on Wheels: Winners and Losers in Trucking Deregulation.* Oxford: Oxford University Press, 2000.

Besky, Sarah. *The Darjeeling Distinction: Labor and Justice on Fair-Trade Tea Plantations in India.* Berkeley; University of California Press, 2013.

Besky, Sarah, and Sandy Brown. "Looking for Work: Placing Labor in Food Studies." *Labor Studies in Working-Class History of the Americas* 12, no. 1–2 (2015): 19–43. https://doi.org/10.1215/15476715-2837484.

Bethel, Jeffrey W., and Renee Harger. "Heat-Related Illness among Oregon Farmworkers." *International Journal of Environmental Research and Public Health* 11, no. 9 (2014): 9273–85. https://doi.org/10.3390/ijerph110909273.

Billings, Kara Clifford, Sarah A. Donovan, and Sylvia L. Bryan. "The School Food-service Workforce: Characteristics and Labor Market Outcomes." Congressional Research Service. CRS Report, R47199. 2022. https://eric.ed.gov/?id=ED622443.

Bisaha, Stephan. "Dollar Store Workers in the South Have a Labor Movement. Just Don't Call It a Union." NPR, September 3, 2022. https://www.npr.org/2022/09/03/1120473763/dollar-stores-labor-unions-workers-wages-organizing.

Blackmon, Douglas A. Slavery by Another Name: The Re-Enslavement of Black Americans from the Civil War to World War II. New York: Penguin Random House, 2008.

Bloch. "Why Don't Restaurant Workers Unionize?" The Counter, April 29, 2019. https://thecounter.org/restaurants-unionize-seiu-aoc-warren/.

Bonanno, Alessandro, Lawrence Busch, William Friedland, Lourdes Gouveia, and Enzo Mingione, eds. From Columbus to ConAgra: The Globalization of Agriculture and Food. Lawrence: University Press of Kansas, 1994.

Bowen, Sarah, Joslyn Brenton, and Sinikka Eliott. Pressure Cooker: Why Home Cooking Won't Solve Our Problems and What We Can Do about It. Oxford: Oxford University Press, 2019.

Bowers, Marianne, and Daniel E Chand. "An Examination of Wage and Income Inequality within the American Farmworker Community." Journal on Migration and Human Security 6, no. 3 (2018): 182–91.

Brandworkers. "Manhattan Cafe Tisserie Agrees to Drop Tom Cat Bakery Products." April 24, 2018. https://brandworkers.org/manhattan-cafe-tisserie-agrees-to-drop-tom-cat-bakery-products/.

Brightman, Sarah, Emily Lenning, and Karen McElrath. "State-Directed Sterilizations in North Carolina: Victim-Centredness and Reparations." British Journal of Criminology 55, no. 3 (2015): 474–93. http://www.jstor.org/stable/43819293.

Brown, Haywood L., Maria J. Small, Camille A. Clare, and Washington C. Hill. "Black Women Health Inequity: The Origin of Perinatal Health Disparity." Journal of the National Medical Association 113, no. 1 (2021): 105–13. https://doi.org/10.1016/j.jnma.2020.11.008.

Brown, Sandy, and Christy Getz. "Privatizing Farm Worker Justice: Regulating Labor through Voluntary Certification and Labeling." Geoforum 39, no. 3 (2008): 1184. https://doi.org/10.1016/j.geoforum.2007.01.002.

Browning, Kellen. "Massachusetts Court Throws out Gig Worker Ballot Measure." New York Times, June 14, 2022. https://www.nytimes.com/2022/06/14/technology/massachusetts-gig-workers.html.

Buck, P. D. Worked to the Bone: Race, Class, Power, and Privilege in Kentucky. New York: NYU Press, 2001.

Bunn, Terry L., Svetla Slavova, and Minao Tang. "Injuries among Solid Waste Collectors in the Private versus Public Sectors." Waste Management & Research: The Journal of the International Solid Wastes and Public Cleansing Association (ISWA) 29, no. 10 (2011): 1043–52. https://doi.org/10.1177/0734242X11410115.

Business Journal Staff. "Investigation Finds Labor Violations on Turlock Farm." Business Journal, 2022. https://thebusinessjournal.com/investigation-finds-labor-violations-on-turlock-farm/.

Cairns, Kate, Joseé Johnston, and Shyon Baumann. "Caring about Food: Doing Gender in the Foodie Kitchen." *Gender and Society* 24, no. 5 (2010): 591–615. https://doi.org/10.1177/0891243210383419.

Cairns, Kate, Joseé Johnston, and Norah MacKendrick. "Feeding the 'Organic Child': Mothering through Ethical Consumption." *Journal of Consumer Culture,* 13, no. 2 (2013): 97–118. https://doi.org/10.1177/1469540513480162.

Calavita, Kitty. *Inside the State: The Bracero Program, Immigration, and the INS.* New Orleans, LA: Quid Pro Books, 2010.

California Legislature. "Worker Status: Employees and Independent Contractors." California Assembly Bill No. 5, Chapter 296, 2019. https://leginfo.legislature .ca.gov/faces/billTextClient.xhtml?bill_id=201920200AB5.

Cal/OSHA. "Heat Illness Prevention in Outdoor Places of Employment." *California Code of Regulations.* 2013. https://www.dir.ca.gov/title8/3395.html.

Campbell, Colleen. "Medical Violence, Obstetric Racism, and the Limits of Informed Consent for Black Women." *Michigan Journal of Race & Law* 26 (2021): 47–75. https://doi.org/10.36643/mjrl.26.sp.medical.

Carlisle, Liz. "Critical Agrarianism." *Renewable Agriculture and Food Systems* 29, no. 2 (2014): 135–45. https://doi.org/10.1017/S1742170512000427.

Carney, Judith Ann. *Black Rice.* Cambridge, MA: Harvard University Press, 2001.

Carney, Megan A. *The Unending Hunger: Tracing Women and Food Insecurity across Borders.* Berkeley: University of California Press, 2015.

Cartwright, Michael S., Francis O. Walker, Jill N. Blocker, Mark R. Schulz, Thomas A. Arcury, Joseph G. Grzywacz, Dana Mora, Haiying Chen, Antonio J. Marín, and Sara A. Quandt. "The Prevalence of Carpal Tunnel Syndrome in Latino Poultry Processing Workers and Other Latino Manual Workers." *Journal of Occupational and Environmental Medicine* 54, no. 2 (2012): 198–201. https://doi .org/10.1097/JOM.0b013e31823fdf53.

Castilloberthier, H. "Garbage, Work and Society." *Resources, Conservation and Recycling* 39, no. 3 (2003): 193–210. https://doi.org/10.1016/S0921-3449(03)00027-2.

Ceryes, Caitlin A., Jacqueline Agnew, Andrea L. Wirtz, Daniel J. Barnett, and Roni A. Neff. "Exploring U.S. Food System Workers' Intentions to Work While Ill during the Early COVID-19 Pandemic: A National Survey." *International Journal of Environmental Research and Public Health* 20, no. 2 (2023): 1638. https:// doi.org/10.3390/ijerph20021638.

Ceryes, Caitlin A., Cerra C. Antonacci, Steven A. Harvey, Marie L. Spiker, Anna Bickers, and Roni A. Neff. "'Maybe It's Still Good?' A Qualitative Study of Factors Influencing Food Waste and Application of the E.P.A. Food Recovery Hierarchy in U.S. Supermarkets." *Appetite* 161 (2021): 105111. https://doi.org/10.1016 /j.appet.2021.105111.

Ceryes, Caitlin A., Laura Flamm, and Sheila Fitzgerald. "Investigating the Occupational Challenges of Corner Store Workers Operating in Baltimore City Food Deserts." *Workplace Health & Safety* 65, no. 2 (2017): 92–92.

Ceryes, Caitlin, Joelle Robinson, Erin Biehl, Andrea L. Wirtz, Daniel J. Barnett, and Roni Neff. "Frequency of Workplace Controls and Associations with Safety

Perceptions among a National Sample of US Food Retail Workers during the COVID-19 Pandemic." *Journal of Occupational and Environmental Medicine* 63, no. 7 (2021): 557–64. https://doi.org/10.1097/JOM.0000000000002218.

Chadde, Sky. "COVID-19 Cases, Deaths in Meatpacking Industry Were Much Higher Than Previously Known, Congressional Investigation Shows." Investigate Midwest, October 28, 2021. https://investigatemidwest.org/2021/10/28/covid-19-cases-deaths-in-meatpacking-industry-were-much-higher-than-previously-known-congressional-investigation-shows/.

Chan, Sucheng. *This Bittersweet Soil: The Chinese in California Agriculture, 1860–1910.* Berkeley: University of California Press, 1989.

Chandra, Michelle Veena. "The Black/White Wealth Gap : The Transgenerational Effects of Post-Reconstruction Sharecropping and Racial Systems on African Americans Today." MA thesis, University of British Columbia. 2011. https://doi.org/10.14288/1.0072197.

Chang, Vera. "After #MeToo, This Group Has Nearly Erased Sexual Harassment in Farm Fields." *Civil Eats*, March 9, 2020. https://civileats.com/2020/03/09/after-metoo-this-group-has-nearly-erased-sexual-harassment-in-farm-fields/.

Chatterjee, Rhitu. "For People with Developmental Disabilities, Food Work Means More Self Reliance." *NPR*, January 14, 2017. https://www.npr.org/sections/thesalt/2017/01/14/508602730/for-people-with-developmental-disabilities-food-work-means-more-self-reliance.

Chen, Stefanos. "New York City Sets New Minimum Wage for Food Delivery Workers." *New York Times*, June 12, 2023. https://www.nytimes.com/2023/06/12/nyregion/nyc-delivery-workers-minimum-wage.html.

Cheney, George, Inaki Santa Cruz, Ana Maria Peredo, and Elias Nazareno. "Worker Cooperatives as an Organizational Alternative: Challenges, Achievements and Promise in Business Governance and Ownership." *Organization* 21, no. 5 (2014): 591–603. https://doi.org/10.1177/1350508414539784.

Chotiner, Isaac. "Anthony Bourdain on Weinstein, John Besh, and Meathead Restaurant Culture." *Slate*, October 24, 2017. https://slate.com/news-and-politics/2017/10/anthony-bourdain-on-weinstein-john-besh-and-meathead-restaurant-culture.html.

Chrobog, Christian Karim. "Wasted: Understanding the Economic and Social Impact of Food Waste." Master's thesis, Escola Brasileira de Administração Pública e de Empresas (Brazilian School of Public and Business Administration), 2014. http://bibliotecadigital.fgv.br:80/dspace/handle/10438/13325.

Clair Brown, H. "The Food Industry's Food Stamps Problem." The Counter, April 19, 2018. https://thecounter.org/food-industry-food-stamps-problem/.

Clapp, Jennifer. *Food.* Bristol: Policy Press, 2020.

Clement, Wallace. "Canada's Coastal Fisheries: Formation of Unions, Cooperatives, and Associations." *Journal of Canadian Studies* 19, no. 1 (1984): 5–33. https://doi.org/10.3138/jcs.19.1.5.

Cloke, Jon. "Empires of Waste and the Food Security Meme." *Geography Compass* 7, no. 9 (2013): 622–36. https://doi.org/10.1111/gec3.12068.

Coalition of Immokalee Workers (CIW). "The Fair Food Program—Consumer Powered, Worker Certified." 2024. https://fairfoodprogram.org/.

———. "Fair Food Program Report." 2021. https://ciw-online.org/blog/2021/09/released-2021-fair-food-program-report/.

Coleman, Matthew, and Austin Kocher. "Detention, Deportation, Devolution and Immigrant Incapacitation in the US, Post 9/11." *Geographical Journal* 177, no. 3 (2011): 228–37.

Collins, Patricia Hill. *Black Feminist Thought: Knowledge, Consciousness, and the Politics of Empowerment*. London: Routledge, 2008.

Colorado General Assembly. "Healthy Meals for All Public School Students." 2022. https://www.leg.colorado.gov/bills/hb22-1414.

Community Development Project at the Urban Justice Center and Brandworkers. "Feeding New York: Challenges and Opportunities for Workers in New York City's Food Manufacturing Industry." 2014. https://search.issuelab.org/resource/feeding-new-york-challenges-and-opportunities-for-workers-in-new-york-city-s-food-manufacturing-industry.html.

Cooper, David, and Sebastian Martinez Hickey. "Raising Pay in Public K–12 Schools Is Critical to Solving Staffing Shortages." Economic Policy Institute, 2022. https://www.epi.org/publication/solving-k-12-staffing-shortages/.

Cooperband, Leslie R. "Composting: Art and Science of Organic Waste Conversion to a Valuable Soil Resource." *Laboratory Medicine* 3, no. 5 (2000): 283–90. https://doi.org/10.1309/W286-LQF1-R2M2-1WNT.

Copeland, Roy W. "In the Beginning: Origins of African American Real Property Ownership in the United States." *Journal of Black Studies* 44, no. 6 (2013): 646–64. https://doi.org/10.1177/0021934713506010.

Corkery, Michael. "Amid Attacks and Thefts, Some Retail Workers Want to Fight Back." *New York Times*, June 28, 2022. https://www.nytimes.com/2022/06/28/business/retail-workers-assaults.html.

Corser, Maggie. "Walmart's Failure to Prioritize Employee and Public Health: A Timeline of Dangerous Delays and Critical Missteps in Walmart's COVID-19 Response and What Can Be Done Today to Save Lives at Walmart." Center for Popular Democracy, 2020. https://www.populardemocracy.org/news/publications/walmarts-failure-prioritize-employee-and-public-health-timeline-dangerous-delays.

Costa, Daniel. "How Many Farmworkers Are Employed in the United States?" *Economic Policy Institute Working Economics Blog*, 2023. https://www.epi.org/blog/how-many-farmworkers-are-employed-in-the-united-states/#:~:text=If%20we%20use%20a%20low,crop%20employment%20on%20U.S.%20farms.

Costa, Daniel, and Philip Martin. "How Much Would It Cost Consumers to Give Farmworkers a Significant Raise? A 40% Increase in Pay Would Cost Just $25 per Household." Economic Policy Institute, October 15, 2020. https://www.epi.org/blog/how-much-would-it-cost-consumers-to-give-farmworkers-a-significant-raise-a-40-increase-in-pay-would-cost-just-25-per-household/.

Covert, Bryce. "As Average Temperatures Rise, Workers Will Finally Get Protection from Extreme Heat." *The Nation*, November 10, 2021. https://www .thenation.com/article/economy/osha-heat-workers/.

Crenshaw, Kimberle. "Demarginalizing the Intersection of Race and Sex: A Black Feminist Critique of Antidiscrimination Doctrine, Feminist Theory and Anti-racist Politics." *University of Chicago Legal Forum* 1, no. 8 (1989): 139–67. http:// chicagounbound.uchicago.edu/uclf/vol1989/iss1/8.

Crockett, Amanda. "Quietly under Control: A History of Forced Sterilization in the African-American Community." *New Views on Gender* 14 (2013): 70–79. https://scholarworks.iu.edu/journals/index.php/iusbgender/article/view/13661.

Crowell, Nancy A., Alan Hanson, Louisa Boudreau, Robyn Robbins, and Rosemary K. Sokas. "Union Efforts to Reduce COVID-19 Infections among Grocery Store Workers." *NEW SOLUTIONS: A Journal of Environmental and Occupational Health Policy* 31, no. 2 (2021): 170–77. https://doi.org/10.1177/10482911211015676.

Cypress, K. C. "Solid Waste and Recycling Division." International Brotherhood of Teamsters, December 13, 2019. https://teamster.org/divisions/soild-waste-and-recycling-division/.

Dang, Kelsey L. "Recover, Redistribute, and Reduce: Food Waste in the Stanford Community." *Intersect: The Stanford Journal of Science, Technology, and Society* 7, no. 1 (2014). https://ojs.stanford.edu/ojs/index.php/intersect/article/view/547.

Daniel, Pete. *Dispossession: Discrimination against African American Farmers in the Age of Civil Rights*. Chapel Hill: University of North Carolina Press, 2013.

Darrow, Liz. "SB 5438 Unanimously Passes in WA House Bringing Hope for H2A Farmworker Protections." Community to Community, April 12, 2019. https:// www.foodjustice.org/blog/2019/4/12/sb-5438-unanimously-passes-in-wa-house-bringing-hope-for-h2a-farmworker-protections.

Davis, Angela Y. *Women, Race and Class*. New York: Random House, 1981.

De Genova, Nicholas. "The Legal Production of Mexican/Migrant 'Illegality.'" *Latino Studies* 2, no. 2 (2004): 160–85. https://doi.org/10.1057/palgrave.lst.8600085.

De Lara, Juan D., Ellen R. Reese, and Jason Struna. "Organizing Temporary, Sub-contracted, and Immigrant Workers: Lessons from Change to Win's Warehouse Workers United Campaign." *Labor Studies Journal* 41, no. 4 (2016): 309–32. https://doi.org/10.1177/0160449X16664415.

De León, Jason. *The Land of Open Graves: Living and Dying on the Migrant Trail*. Berkeley: University of California Press, 2015.

Demange, Valérie, Coralie Barrera, Audrey Laboissière, Philippe Duquenne, Xavier Simon, Laurence Millon, Gabriel Reboux, and Michel Grzebyk. "Effects of Plant Features on Symptoms and Airway Inflammation in Compost Workers Followed over 18 Months." *Archives of Environmental & Occupational Health* 75, no. 4 (2020): 191–200. https://doi.org/10.1080/19338244.2019.1584086.

Dempsey, Sarah E. "Racialized and Gendered Constructions of the 'Ideal Server': Contesting Historical Occupational Discourses of Restaurant Service." *Frontiers in Sustainable Food Systems* 5 (2021): 1–12. https://www.frontiersin.org /articles/10.3389/fsufs.2021.727473.

Deutsch, Tracey. *Building a Housewife's Paradise: Gender, Politics, and American Grocery Stores in the Twentieth Century.* Chapel Hill: University of North Carolina Press, 2010.

Devault, Marjorie L. *Feeding the Family: The Social Organization of Caring as Gendered Work.* Chicago: University of Chicago Press, 1994.

Dickinson, Maggie. *Feeding the Crisis: Care and Abandonment in America's Food Safety Net.* Berkeley: University of California Press, 2019.

———. "Free to Serve? Emergency Food and Volunteer Labor in the Urban U.S." *Gastronomica* 17, no. 2 (2017): 16–25. https://doi.org/10.1525/gfc.2017.17.2.16.

DiFelice, Mia. "The Real Root of High Food Prices: Corporate Greed and Consolidation." Food & Water Watch, March 26, 2024. https://www.foodandwaterwatch.org/2024/03/26/high-food-prices-consolidation/.

Dimick Schindel, Alexandra. "Supporting Youth to Develop Environmental Citizenship within/against a Neoliberal Context." *Environmental Education Research* 21, no. 3 (2015): 390–402. https://doi.org/10.1080/13504622.2014.994164.

DiNatale, Natale, and Kayla West. "Union Representation Petitions Are up 57 Percent, but That's Not All!" *National Law Review*, May 16, 2022. https://www.natlawreview.com/article/union-representation-petitions-are-57-percent-s-not-all.

Dobis, Elizabeth A., Thomas Krumel, Jr., John Cromartie, Kelsey Conley, Austin Sanders, and Ruben Ortiz. "Rural America at a Glance: 2021 Edition." USDA Economic Research Service, *Economic Information Bulletin*, no. (EIB-230), 2021. https://www.ers.usda.gov/publications/pub-details?pubid=102575.

Domingo, José L., and Martí Nadal. "Domestic Waste Composting Facilities: A Review of Human Health Risks." *Environment International* 35, no. 2 (2009): 382–89. https://doi.org/10.1016/j.envint.2008.07.004.

Dreier, Hannah, and Meridith Kohut. "The Kids on the Night Shift." *New York Times*, September 19, 2023. https://www.nytimes.com/2023/09/18/magazine/child-labor-dangerous-jobs.html.

Dreier, Hannah, and Kirsten Luce. "Alone and Exploited, Migrant Children Work Brutal Jobs across the U.S." *New York Times*, February 25, 2023. https://www.nytimes.com/2023/02/25/us/unaccompanied-migrant-child-workers-exploitation.html.

Driver, Alice. "Tyson Says Its Nurses Help Workers. Critics Charge They Stymie OSHA." *Civil Eats*, November 17, 2022. https://civileats.com/2022/11/17/injured-and-invisible-worker-safety-chicken-hospital-healthcare-osha-injury/.

Duffy, Mignon. "Reproducing Labor Inequalities: Challenges for Feminists Conceptualizing Care at the Intersections of Gender, Race, and Class." *Gender and Society* 19, no. 1 (2005): 66–82. https://doi.org/10.1177/08912432042694.

Durand, Jorge, Douglas S. Massey, and Fernando Charvet. "The Changing Geography of Mexican Immigration to the United States: 1910–1996." *Social Science Quarterly* 81, no. 1 (2000): 1–15. https://www.jstor.org/stable/42864364.

East, Robert. "Online Grocery Sales after the Pandemic." *International Journal of Market Research* 64, no. 1 (2022): 13–18. https://doi.org/10.1177/14707853211055047.

Eavis, Peter. "Women Could Fill Truck Driver Jobs. Companies Won't Let Them." *New York Times*, October 5, 2023. https://www.nytimes.com/2023/10/05/business/economy/women-truck-drivers.html.

Ekers, Michael, Charles Z. Levkoe, Samuel Walker, and Bryan Dale. "Will Work for Food: Agricultural Interns, Apprentices, Volunteers, and the Agrarian Question." *Agriculture and Human Values* 33, no. 3 (2016): 705–20. https://doi.org/10.1007/s10460-015-9660-5.

Ellickson, Paul B. "The Evolution of the Supermarket Industry: From A & P to Walmart." In *Handbook on the Economics of Retailing and Distribution*, edited by Emek Basker, 368–91. Cheltenham: Edward Elgar, 2016.

Ellickson, Paul B., and Paul L. E. Grieco. "Wal-Mart and the Geography of Grocery Retailing." *Journal of Urban Economics* 75 (2013): 1–14. https://doi.org/10.1016/j.jue.2012.09.005.

Entralgo, Rebekah. "Forum: Migrant Women Farmworkers Are Invisible Essential Labor Force." *Caller Times*, May 7, 2021. https://www.caller.com/story/opinion/forums/2021/05/07/forum-migrant-women-farmworkers-invisible-essential-labor-force/4980108001/.

Entrepreneur. "Franchise 500 Ranking Franchises." 2023. https://www.entrepreneur.com/franchise500.

European Commission. "Food Waste Reduction Targets." 2024. https://food.ec.europa.eu/safety/food-waste/eu-actions-against-food-waste/food-waste-reduction-targets_en.

Evans, David, Hugh Campbell, and Anne Murcott, eds. *Waste Matters: New Perspectives of Food and Society*. Hoboken, NJ: Wiley-Blackwell, 2013.

Fairness for Farmworkers Coalition. "Fairness for Farmworkers Act." Mass Legal Services, 2021. https://www.masslegalservices.org/content/fairness-farmworkers-act

Fanto Deetz, Kelley. "How Enslaved Chefs Helped Shape American Cuisine." *Smithsonian Magazine*, July 20, 2018. https://www.smithsonianmag.com/history/how-enslaved-chefs-helped-shape-american-cuisine-180969697/.

Farmworker Justice. "The Fairness for Farm Workers Act: It's Time to End Discrimination against Farmworkers." 2023. https://www.farmworkerjustice.org/wp-content/uploads/2023/07/Fairness-for-Farm-Workers-Act-2023-Fact-Sheet.pdf.

Federici, Silvia. "Social Reproduction Theory: History, Issues and Present Challenges." *Radical Philosophy*, 2, no. 4 (2019): 55–57.

Feeding America. "Food Waste in America." 2022. https://www.feedingamerica.org/our-work/reduce-food-waste.

Feeney, Mallory. "Tackling Food Waste in Iowa's K-12 Schools." *BioCycle* 58, no. 3 (2017): 44–45. https://scholarworks.uni.edu/facpub/905.

Feldman, Kiera. "A Trash Industry Union Thrives, and Employees Say They Are Left Holding the Bag." *ProPublica*, November 2, 2018. https://www.propublica.org/article/a-trash-industry-union-thrives-and-employees-say-they-are-left-holding-the-bag.

———. "Why Private Waste Management Is One of the Nation's Most Hazardous Jobs." *PBS NewsHour*, January 4, 2018. https://www.pbs.org/newshour/nation/why-private-waste-management-is-one-of-the-nations-most-hazardous-jobs.

Ferguson, Rafter, Kristina Dahl and Marcia DeLonge. "Farmworkers at Risk: The Growing Dangers of Pesticides and Heat." Union of Concerned Scientists, 2019. https://www.ucsusa.org/resources/farmworkers-at-risk.

Figueroa, Maria, L. Guallpa, A. Wolf, G. Tsitouras, and H. C. Hernandez. "Essential but Unprotected: App-Based Food Couriers in New York City." Cornell University, ILR School, Workers Institute, 2023. https://hdl.handle.net/1813/113534.

Filimonau, Viachaslau, and Delysia A. De Coteau. "Food Waste Management in Hospitality Operations: A Critical Review." *Tourism Management* 7 (2019): 234–45. https://doi.org/10.1016/j.tourman.2018.10.009.

Fischels, Josie. "Why DoorDash Drivers Are on Strike." National Public Radio, July 31, 2021. https://wamu.org/story/21/07/31/why-doordash-drivers-are-on-strike/.

Fisher, Linford D. "'Why Shall Wee Have Peace to Bee Made Slaves': Indian Surrenderers during and after King Philip's War." *Ethnohistory* 64, no. 1 (2017): 91–114. https://doi.org/10.1215/00141801-3688391.

Fisher, Tyson. "Stevens Transport Faces EEOC Sexual Discrimination Charge." Land Line, October 10, 2023. https://landline.media/stevens-transport-faces-eeoc-sexual-discrimination-charge/.

Fitzpatrick, Alex, and Erin Davis. "The Most Popular Grocery Stores in the U.S." Axios, April 20, 2023. https://www.axios.com/2023/04/20/most-popular-grocery-stores.

Fitzpatrick, George E., Eva C. Worden, and Wagner A. Vendrame. "Historical Development of Composting Technology during the 20th Century." *HortTechnology* 15, no. 1 (2005): 48–51. https://doi.org/10.21273/HORTTECH.15.1.0048.

Flaming, Daniel, Peter Dreier, Patrick Burns, and Aaron Danielson. "Hungry at the Table: White Paper on Grocery Workers at the Kroger Company." SSRN Scholarly Paper, 2022. https://doi.org/10.2139/ssrn.4013906.

Foley, Paul, and Bonnie McCay. "Certifying the Commons: Eco-Certification, Privatization, and Collective Action." *Ecology and Society* 19, no. 2 (2014): 28. https://doi.org/10.5751/ES-06459-190228.

Food Chain Workers Alliance (FCWA). "We Are Not Disposable: Food Workers Organizing on the Frontlines." February 23, 2021. https://foodchainworkers.org/2021/02/new-report-we-are-not-disposable-food-workers-organizing-on-the-covid-frontlines/.

Food Chain Workers Alliance and HEAL Food Alliance. "Procuring Food Justice: Grassroots Solutions for Reclaiming Our Public Supply Chains." 2023. https://procuringfoodjustice.org/.

Food Chain Workers Alliance and Solidarity Research Cooperative. "The Hands That Feed Us: Challenges and Opportunities Along the Food Chain." June 6, 2012. https://foodchainworkers.org/2012/06/the-hands-that-feed-us/.

Food Recovery Network. "Our Story." 2021. https://www.foodrecoverynetwork .org/what-we-do.

Freidberg, Sussane. *French Beans and Food Scares: Culture and Commerce in an Anxious Age.* Oxford: Oxford University Press, 2004.

Freshour, Carrie. "Cheap Meat and Cheap Work in the US Poultry Industry: Race, Gender, and Immigration in Corporate Strategies to Shape Labor." In *Global Meat: Social and Environmental Consequences of the Expanding Meat Industry,* edited by Bill Winders and Elizabeth Ransom, 1221–40. Cambridge, MA: MIT Press, 2019.

Friedan, Betty. "Cooking with Betty Friedan ... Yes, Betty Friedan." *New York Times,* January 5, 1977. https://archive.nytimes.com/www.nytimes.com /books/99/05/09/specials/friedan-cooking.html.

———. *The Feminine Mystique.* New York: Norton, 1963.

Friedland, William H., Amy E. Barton, and Robert J. Thomas. *Manufacturing Green Gold: Capital, Labor, and Technology in the Lettuce Industry.* Cambridge: Cambridge University Press, 1981.

Friedmann, Harriet. "Feeding the Empire: The Pathologies of Globalized Agriculture." *Socialist Register* 41 (2005): 124–23.

———. "The Political Economy of Food: A Global Crisis." *New Left Review* 197 (1993): 29–57.

Frye, Jocelyn. "On the Frontlines at Work and at Home: The Disproportionate Economic Effects of the Coronavirus Pandemic on Women of Color." Center for American Progress, April 23, 2020. https://www.americanprogress.org/article /frontlines-work-home/.

Gaddis, Jennifer E. *The Labor of Lunch: Why We Need Real Food and Real Jobs in American Public Schools.* Berkeley: University of California Press, 2019.

Galassi, Thomas. "Policy Clarification on OSHA's Enforcement Authority at Small Farms." US Occupational Safety and Health Administration, 2014. https:// www.osha.gov/memos/2014-07-29/policy-clarification-oshas-enforcement- authority-small-farms.

Galvan, Adri M., Ryan Hanson, and Daniel R. George. "Repurposing Waste Streams: Lessons on Integrating Hospital Food Waste into a Community Garden." *Journal of Community Health* 43, no. 5 (2018): 944–46. https://doi .org/10.1007/s10900-018-0509-x.

Ganz, Marshall. *Why David Sometimes Wins: Leadership, Organization, and Strategy in the California Farm Worker Movement.* New York: Oxford University Press, 2009.

Garcia, Matt. *From the Jaws of Victory: The Triumph and Tragedy of Cesar Chavez and the Farm Worker Movement.* Berkeley: University of California Press, 2012.

Garcia, Reece. "Exploring the Domestic Division of Labor When Both Parents Are Involuntarily Working from Home: The Effects of the UK COVID Pandemic." *Gender, Work & Organization* 29, no. 4 (2022): 1065–81. https://doi.org/10.1111 /gwao.12796.

García-Colón, Ismael. *Colonial Migrants at the Heart of Empire: Puerto Rican Workers on U.S. Farms*. Oakland: University of California Press, 2020.

Garth, Hanna. *Food in Cuba: The Pursuit of a Decent Meal*. Stanford: Stanford University Press, 2020.

Gedye, Grace. "Court Upholds California Prop. 22 in Big Win for Gig Firms Like Lyft and Uber." CalMatters, March 14, 2023. http://calmatters.org/economy/2023/03/prop-22-appeal/.

Giles, David Boarder. *A Mass Conspiracy to Feed People: Food Not Bombs and the World-Class Waste of Global Cities*. Durham, NC: Duke University Press, 2021.

Gittleman, Maury, and Kristen Monaco. "Truck-Driving Jobs: Are They Headed for Rapid Elimination?" *ILR Review* 73, no. 1 (2020): 3–24. https://doi.org/10.1177/0019793919858079.

Global Ag Media. "Women Underrepresented in Meat Industry Workforce." The Pig Site, 2020. https://www.thepigsite.com/news/2020/10/women-underrepresented-in-meat-industry-workforce-new-report.

Glover, Jane L. "Gender, Power and Succession in Family Farm Business." *International Journal of Gender and Entrepreneurship* 6, no. 3 (2014): 276–95. https://doi.org/10.1108/IJGE-01-2012-0006.

Glymph, Thavolia. *Out of the House of Bondage: The Transformation of the Plantation Household*. Cambridge: Cambridge University Press, 2008.

Goldberg, Abbie E. "'Doing' and 'Undoing' Gender: The Meaning and Division of Housework in Same-Sex Couples." *Journal of Family Theory & Review* 5, no. 2 (2013): 85–104. https://doi.org/10.1111/jftr.12009.

Good Jobs First. "Walmart." Violation Tracker Current Parent Company Summary, 2022. https://violationtracker.goodjobsfirst.org/parent/walmart.

Gordon, Heather, Sauyaq Jean, J. Ashleigh Ross, Cheryl Bauer-Armstrong, Maria Moreno, Rachel Byington, and Nicole Bowman. "Integrating Indigenous Traditional Ecological Knowledge of Land into Land Management through Indigenous-Academic Partnerships." *Land Use Policy* 125 (2023): 106469. https://doi.org/10.1016/j.landusepol.2022.106469.

Grabell, Michael. "The Plot to Keep Meatpacking Plants Open during COVID-19." ProPublica, 2020. https://www.propublica.org/article/documents-covid-meatpacking-tyson-smithfield-trump.

Gray, Margaret. *Labor and the Locavore: The Making of a Comprehensive Food Ethic*. Berkeley: University of California Press, 2014.

Greenaway, Twilight. "Climate Change–Fueled Valley Fever Is Hitting Farmworkers Hard." *Civil Eats*, June 17, 2019. https://civileats.com/2019/06/17/climate-change-fueled-valley-fever-is-hitting-farmworkers-hard/?fbclid=IwAR1cpFtHu9R3_gdyf7gMHJ-pfSumToQJlms11KEUt5Vs-cjVER1IsVoYMuA.

Greer, Allan. "Commons and Enclosure in the Colonization of North America." *American Historical Review* 117, no. 2 (2012): 365–86. https://doi.org/10.1086/ahr.117.2.365.

Guthman, Julie. *Agrarian Dreams: The Paradox of Organic Farming in California*. Berkeley: University of California Press, 2004.

———. "Teaching the Politics of Obesity: Insights into Neoliberal Embodiment and Contemporary Biopolitics." *Antipode* 45, no. 5 (2009): 1110–3. https://doi .org/10.1111/j.1467-8330.2009.00707.x.

———. *Weighing In: Obesity, Food Justice, and the Limits of Capitalism.* Berkeley: University of California Press, 2011.

Hacker, J. David. "From '20. and Odd' to 10 Million: The Growth of the Slave Population in the United States." *Slavery & Abolition* 41, no. 4 (2020): 840–55. https:// doi.org/10.1080/0144039X.2020.1755502.

Hadero. Haleluya. "Divided Amazon Labor Union Lurches toward a Leadership Election." Associated Press. April 8, 2024. https://apnews.com/article/amazon -labor-union-election-35b63f38aa1c7f82bc86c21936e02a78.

Hait, Andrew, and Jennifer Cheeseman Day. "Number of Truckers at All-Time High." June, 2019. https://www.census.gov/library/stories/2019/06/america -keeps-on-trucking.html.

Hale, James, and Michael Carolan. "Cooperative or Uncooperative Cooperatives? Digging into the Process of Cooperation in Food and Agriculture Cooperatives." *Journal of Agriculture, Food Systems, and Community Development* 8, no. 1 (2018): 113–32. https://doi.org/10.5304/jafscd.2018.081.011.

Hall, Kevin D., Juen Guo, Michael Dore, and Carson C. Chow. "The Progressive Increase of Food Waste in America and Its Environmental Impact." *PLOS ONE* 4, no. 11 (2009): e7940. https://doi.org/10.1371/journal.pone.0007940.

Hambach, Ramona, Jos Droste, Guido François, Joost Weyler, Ulrik Van Soom, Antoon De Schryver, Jan Vanoeteren, and Marc van Sprundel. "Work-Related Health Symptoms among Compost Facility Workers: A Cross-Sectional Study." *Archives of Public Health* 70, no 13 (2012). https://doi.org/10.1186/0778-7367 -70-13.

Hamilton, Shane. *Supermarket USA: Food and Power in the Cold War Farms Race.* New Haven, CT: Yale University Press, 2018.

———. *Trucking Country: The Road to America's Wal-Mart Economy.* Princeton: Princeton University Press, 2014.

Hanley, Daniel, and Sally Hubbard. "Eyes Everywhere: Amazon's Surveillance Infrastructure and Revitalizing Worker Power." SSRN Scholarly Paper. 2020. https://doi.org/10.2139/ssrn.4089862.

Hawken, Paul, ed. *Drawdown: The Most Comprehensive Plan Ever Proposed to Reverse Global Warming.* London: Penguin Books, 2017.

HEAL Food Alliance. "Securing Dignity and Fairness for Food Chain Workers and Their Families." 2023. https://healfoodalliance.org/wp-content/uploads/2023 /02/Farm-Bill-One-Pagers-Labor.

Healthy School Meals for All Wisconsin. "Hungry for Good Jobs: The State of the School Nutrition Workforce in Wisconsin." 2023. https://www .healthyschoolmealsforallwi.org/.

Held, Lisa. "Congress Killed a Bill to Give Farmworkers a Path to Citizenship. What Comes Next?" *Civil Eats,* February 22, 2023. https://civileats.com/2023/02/22 /congress-killed-a-bill-to-give-farmworkers-a-path-to-citizenship-what-comes-next/.

———. "The Next Frontier of Labor Organizing: Food-Delivery Workers." *Civil Eats*, May 4, 2022. https://civileats.com/2022/05/04/the-next-frontier-of-labor-organizing-food-delivery-workers/.

Henderson, George L. "'Free' Food, the Local Production of Worth, and the Circuit of Decommodification: A Value Theory of the Surplus." *Environment and Planning D: Society and Space* 22, no. 4 (2004): 485–512. https://doi.org/10.1068/d379.

Henderson, Tim. "Shrinking Rural America Faces State Power Struggle." Stateline, August 10, 2021. https://stateline.org/2021/08/10/shrinking-rural-america-faces-state-power-struggle/.

Hendrix, Joshua A., and Cindy Brooks Dollar. "American Slaughterhouses and the Need for Speed: An Examination of the Meatpacking-Methamphetamine Hypothesis." *Organization & Environment* 31, no. 2 (2018): 133–51. https://doi.org/10.1177/1086026617697038.

Hernandez, Joe. "Grocery Store Shortages Are Back. Here Are Some of the Reasons Why." *NPR*, January 12, 2022. https://www.npr.org/2022/01/12/1072462477/grocery-shortage-shelves-reasons.

Herod, Andrew. *Labor.* Cambridge: Polity Press, 2017.

Herrera, Lucero, Brian Justie, Tia Koonse, and Saba Waheed. "Worker Ownership, COVID-19, and the Future of the Gig Economy." University of California Labor Center, 2020. https://escholarship.org/uc/item/3h60d754.

Heuzeroth, Thomas. "Amazon Fresh: Lebensmittelversand Startet in Deutschland." *Die Welt*, May 4, 2017. https://www.welt.de/wirtschaft/article164232416/Amazon-Fresh-bietet-Kunden-ein-unfassbares-Sortiment.html.

Heynen, Nik. "Bending the Bars of Empire from Every Ghetto for Survival: The Black Panther Party's Radical Antihunger Politics of Social Reproduction and Scale." *Annals of the Association of American Geographers* 99, no. 2 (2009): 406–22. https://doi.org/10.1080/00045600802683767.

Heyward, Giulia. "The Silent Suffering of Cafeteria Workers." *The Atlantic*, September 7, 2020. https://www.theatlantic.com/politics/archive/2020/09/school-cafeteria-workers-coronavirus-covid/616036/.

Hirsch, Barry, David Macpherson, and William Even. "Union Membership, Coverage, and Earnings from the Current Population Survey." 2022. http://unionstats.com/.

Hirsh, Sophie. "How Trader Joe's, Whole Foods, and Kroger Make Their Store-Brand Products." Green Matters, January 4, 2022. https://www.greenmatters.com/p/who-makes-store-brand-products.

Holmes, Seth. *Fresh Fruit, Broken Bodies: Migrant Farmworkers in the United States.* Berkeley: University of California Press, 2013.

Holt-Giménez, Eric. 2017. *A Foodie's Guide to Capitalism.* New York: NYU Press.

hooks, bell. *Yearning: Race, Gender, and Cultural Politics.* Brooklyn, NY: South End Press, 1999.

Horowitz, Roger. *Putting Meat on the American Table: Taste, Technology, Transformation.* Baltimore: Johns Hopkins University Press, 2005.

Horsley, Scott. "'Hard, Dirty Job': Cities Struggle to Clear Garbage Glut in Stay-at-Home World." *NPR*, September 21, 2020. https://www.npr.org/2020/09/21

/914029452/hard-dirty-job-cities-struggle-to-clear-garbage-glut-in-stay-at-home-world.

Hounshell, David A. *From the American System to Mass Production, 1800–1932: The Development of Manufacturing Technology in the United States*. Baltimore: Johns Hopkins University Press, 1985.

Howard, Phillip. *Power and Concentration in the Food System: Who Controls What We Eat?* London: Bloomsbury Publishing, 2021.

Hu, Winnie. "Inside the Fight to Pay Food Delivery Workers $23 an Hour." *New York Times*, December 8, 2022. https://www.nytimes.com/2022/12/08/nyregion/nyc-food-delivery-workers-wage-increase.html.

Huber, Bridget. "How Did Europe Avoid the COVID-19 Catastrophe Ravaging US Meatpacking Plants?" *Mother Jones*, 2020. https://www.motherjones.com/food/2020/06/meatpacking-plants-covid-hotspots-europe-regulations-line-speed/.

Hunt, Terrell, Cindy Lee, Charlotte Pekoske, and James O'Rourke. *7-Eleven Inc.: The Fine Line Between Franchise Independence and Interdependence*. Sage Business Cases. London: SAGE Publications, 2019. https://doi.org/10.4135/9781526498168.

Hursh, David, Joseph Henderson, and David Greenwood. "Environmental Education in a Neoliberal Climate." *Environmental Education Research* 21, no. 3 (2015): 299–318. doi:10.1080/13504622.2015.1018141.

Hutchinson, Annabelle, Sarah Khan, and Hilary Matfess. "Childcare, Work, and Household Labor during a Pandemic: Evidence on Parents' Preferences in the United States." *Journal of Experimental Political Science* 10, no. 2 (Summer 2023): 1–19. https://doi.org/10.1017/XPS.2022.24.

Ikeler, Peter. *Hard Sell: Work and Resistance in Retail Chains*. Ithaca, NY: Cornell University Press, 2016.

Inklebarger, Timothy. "Walmart, Kroger, Costco Make Top Three Grocery Retailers List." *Supermarket News*, March 6, 2024. https://www.supermarketnews.com/news/walmart-kroger-costco-make-top-three-grocery-retailers-list.

International Brotherhood of Teamsters. "Front Page." July 25, 2024. https://teamster.org/.

Jacobson, Ariel, and Joann Lo. "Human Rights from Field to Fork: Improving Labor Conditions for Food-Sector Workers by Organizing across Boundaries." *Race/Ethnicity: Multidisciplinary Global Contexts* 5, no. 1 (2011): 61–82. https://doi-org.libezproxy2.syr.edu/10.2979/racethmulglocon.5.1.61.

Jaffee, David, and David Bensman. "Draying and Picking: Precarious Work and Labor Action in the Logistics Sector." *WorkingUSA* 19, no. 1 (2016): 57–79. https://doi.org/10.1163/17434580-01901006.

James, Julissa. "Community Fridges Show up in L.A. Neighborhoods to Feed Those in Need." *Los Angeles Times*, July 14, 2020. https://www.latimes.com/california/story/2020-07-14/in-l-a-neighborhoods-struggling-under-pandemic-well-stocked-fridges-turn-up-to-help.

Jamieson, Dave. "Trader Joe's Accused of Doing Something Totally Illegal to Retaliate against Workers." *Huffington Post*, January 18, 2024. https://www.huffpost.com /entry/trader-joes-closes-new-york-store-union_n_65a99bb0e4b041f1ce655616.

———. "Trader Joe's Union Effort Gains Steam as More Workers Seek Elections." *Huffington Post*, August 10, 2022. https://www.huffpost.com/entry/trader-joes -union-organizing_n_62f2b209e4b0db71d8cce607.

Jayaraman, Saru. *Behind the Kitchen Door*. Ithaca, NY: Cornell University Press, 2013.

———. *One Fair Wage: Ending Subminimum Pay in America*. New York: New Press, 2021.

———. "Shelved: How Wages and Working Conditions for California's Food Retail Workers Have Declined as the Industry Has Thrived." UC Berkeley Labor Center, 2014. https://laborcenter.berkeley.edu/shelved-how-wages-and-working-conditions-for-californias-food-retail-workers-have-declined-as-the-industry -has-thrived/

Jayaraman, Saru, and Julia Sebastian. "Dining Out: The True Cost of Poor Wages." In *True Cost Accounting for Food: Balancing the Scale*, edited by Barbara Gemmill-Herren, Lauren E. Baker, and Paula A. Daniels, 244–50. London: Routledge, 2021.

Johnson, Kenneth, and Daniel Lichter. "Rural Depopulation: Growth and Decline Processes over the Past Century." *Rural Sociology* 84, no. 1 (2019). https:// onlinelibrary.wiley.com/doi/full/10.1111/ruso.12266.

Johnson, Mariann, and Tammy Mathis. "Inland Empire 2021–2024 Regional Workforce Development Plan." Inland Empire Regional Planning Unit, 2021. https://wp.sbcounty.gov/workforce/wp-content/uploads/sites/5/2021/08 /IE-Regional-Plan-FINAL.pdf?ref=frontline-observer.com.

Johnson, Russell. *Warriors into Workers: The Civil War and the Formation of the Urban-Industrial Society in a Northern City*. New York: Fordham University Press, 2003.

Johnson, Stefanie K., and Juan M. Madera. "Sexual Harassment Is Pervasive in the Restaurant Industry. Here's What Needs to Change." *Harvard Business Review* 18 (2018).

Johnston, Josée, Alexandra Rodney, and Phillipa Chong. "Making Change in the Kitchen? A Study of Celebrity Cookbooks, Culinary Personas, and Inequality." *Poetics* 47 (2014): 1–22. https://doi.org/10.1016/j.poetic.2014.10.001.

Justie, Brian, Tia Koonse, Monica Macias, Jennifer Ray, and Saba Waheed. "Fast-Food Frontline: COVID-19 and Working Conditions in Los Angeles." UCLA Labor Center, 2022. https://www.labor.ucla.edu/publication/fast-food-frontline-covid-19-and-working-conditions-in-los-angeles/.

Kantor, Jodi, Karen Weise, and Grace Ashford. "The Amazon That Customers Don't See." *New York Times*, June 15, 2021. https://www.nytimes.com /interactive/2021/06/15/us/amazon-workers.html.

Kauffman, Clark. "Lawsuit: Tyson Managers Bet Money on How Many Workers Would Contract COVID-19." *Iowa Capital Dispatch*, November 18, 2020. https:// iowacapitaldispatch.com/2020/11/18/lawsuit-tyson-managers-bet-money-on-how-many-workers-would-contract-covid-19/.

Kelloway, Claire. "Op-Ed: California Sets a Dangerous Precedent for Food Delivery Workers Nationwide." *Civil Eats*, November 12, 2020. https://civileats .com/2020/11/12/op-ed-california-sets-a-dangerous-precedent-for-food-delivery-workers-nationwide/.

Kelly, Maura, and Elizabeth Hauck. "Doing Housework, Redoing Gender: Queer Couples Negotiate the Household Division of Labor." *Journal of GLBT Family Studies* 11, no. 5 (2015): 438–64. https://doi.org/10.1080/1550428X.2015.1006750.

Kerzinski, Jason. "Dollar Store Workers Organize in New Orleans." *Facing South: A Voice for a Changing South*, January 11, 2023. https://www.facingsouth .org/2023/01/dollar-store-workers-organize-new-orleans.

Kovacs, William L., and John F. Klucsik. "The New Federal Role in Solid Waste Management: The Resource Conservation and Recovery Act of 1976." *Columbia Journal of Environmental Law* 3 (1976): 205.

Kroger. "The History of Kroger." 2024. https://www.thekrogerco.com/about-kroger /history/.

Kropotkin, Petr Alekseevich. *Mutual Aid: A Factor of Evolution*. New York: McClure, Philips & Co., 1902.

Kropotkine, Petr Alekseïevitch. *Mutual Aid: An Illuminated Factor of Evolution*. Binghamton, NY: PM Press, 2021.

Kurtz, Hilda, Abigail Borron, Jerry Shannon, and Alexis Weaver. "Community Food Assistance, Informal Social Networks, and the Labor of Care." *Agriculture and Human Values* 36, no. 3 (2019): 495–505. https://doi.org/10.1007 /s10460-019-09943-0.

Lam, Bourree. "The Dangerous Life of a Trash Collector." *The Atlantic*, September 1, 2016. https://www.theatlantic.com/business/archive/2016/09/trash-collector /498233/.

Lan, Fan-Yun, Christian Suharlim, Stefanos N. Kales, and Justin Yang. "Association between SARS-CoV-2 Infection, Exposure Risk and Mental Health among a Cohort of Essential Retail Workers in the USA." *Occupational and Environmental Medicine* 78, no. 4 (2021): 237–43. https://doi.org/10.1136/oemed-2020-106774.

Landivar, Liana Christin, Leah Ruppanner, William J. Scarborough, and Caitlyn Collins. "Early Signs Indicate That COVID-19 Is Exacerbating Gender Inequality in the Labor Force." *Socius* 6 (2020):2378023120947997. https:// doi.org/10.1177/2378023120947997.

Landry, Craig E., and Travis A. Smith. "Demand for Household Food Waste." *Applied Economic Perspectives and Policy* 41, no 1 (2019): 20–36. https://doi .org/10.1093/aepp/ppy037.

Lathrop, Yannet, T. William Lester, and Matthew Wilson. "Quantifying the Impact of the Fight for $15: $150 Billion in Raises for 26 Million Workers, with $76 Billion Going to Workers of Color." National Employment Law Project: Policy and Data Brief, 2021. https://www.nelp.org/publication/quantifying-the-impact-of-the-fight-for-15-150-billion-in-raises-for-26-million-workers-with -76-billion-going-to-workers-of-color/.

Lause, Mark A. *Free Labor: The Civil War and the Making of an American Working Class*. The Working Class in American History. Urbana: University of Illinois Press, 2015.

Lee, Erika. *At America's Gates: Chinese Immigration during the Exclusion Era, 1882–1943*. Chapel Hill: University of North Carolina Press, 2003.

Lee, Kurtis. "How the Memphis Sanitation Workers' Strike Changed the Labor Movement." *New York Times*, November 23, 2023. https://www.nytimes.com /2023/11/23/business/memphis-sanitation-strike-labor.html.

Leidner, Robin. *Fast Food, Fast Talk: Service Work and the Routinization of Everyday Life*. Berkeley: University of California Press, 1993.

Levinson, Marc. *The Great A&P and the Struggle for Small Business in America*. New York: Farrar, Straus and Giroux, 2019.

Levkoe, Charles, Nathan McClintock, Laura-Anne Minkoff-Zern, Amy Coplen, Jeniffer Gaddis, Joann Lo, Felipe Tendick-Matesanz, and Anelyse Weiler. "Forging Links between Food Chain Labor Activists and Academics." *Journal of Agriculture, Food Systems, and Community Development* 6, no. 2 (2016): 129–42. https://doi.org/10.5304/jafscd.2016.062.009.

Lew-Williams, Beth. *The Chinese Must Go: Violence, Exclusion, and the Making of the Alien in America*. Cambridge, MA: Harvard University Press, 2018.

Lindenbaum, John. "Countermovement, Neoliberal Platoon, or Re-Gifting Depot? Understanding Decommodification in US Food Banks." *Antipode* 48, no. 2 (2016): 375–92. https://doi.org/10.1111/anti.12192.

Lingyu, Meng, Christenson Lauren, and Dong Zhijie. "Strategic Development of Fresh E-Commerce with Respect to New Retail." In *2019 IEEE 16th International Conference on Networking, Sensing and Control (ICNSC)* (2019): 373–78. https://doi.org/10.1109/ICNSC.2019.8743243.

Liptak, Adam. "Supreme Court Rules against Union Recruiting on California Farms." *New York Times*, June 23, 2021. https://www.nytimes.com/2021/06/23 /us/supreme-court-unions-farms-california.html?campaign_id=60&emc=edit _na_20210623&instance_id=0&nl=breaking-news&ref=headline&regi _id=58224103&segment_id=61480&user_id=3e7035424b96fa84ae4dea48e4f9 e6fd.

Liu, Yvonne, and Dominique Apollon. "The Color of Food." Applied Research Center, 2011. https://papers.ssrn.com/sol3/papers.cfm?abstract_id=2594415.

Lo, Joann. "Social Justice for Food Workers in a Foodie World." *Journal of Critical Thought & Praxis* 13, no. 1 (2014). https://doi.org/10.31274/jctp-180810-29.

Lo, Joann, and Alexa Delwiche. "The Good Food Purchasing Policy: A Tool to Intertwine Worker Justice with a Sustainable Food System." *Journal of Agriculture, Food Systems, and Community Development* 6, no. 2 (2016): 185–94. https:// doi.org/10.5304/jafscd.2016.062.016.

Lo, Joann, and Ariel Jacobson. "Human Rights from Field to Fork: Improving Labor Conditions for Food-Sector Workers by Organizing across Boundaries." *Race/Ethnicity: Multidisciplinary Global Contexts* 5, no. 1 (2011): 61–82. https:// doi.org/10.2979/racethmulglocon.5.1.61.

Lo, Joann, and Biko Koenig. "Food Workers and Consumers Organizing Together for Food Justice." In *The New Food Activism: Opposition, Cooperation, and Collective Action*, edited by Alison Alkon and Julie Guthman, 133–56. Berkeley: University of California Press, 2017.

Lofton, Saria, Marjorie Kersten, Shannon D. Simonovich, and Akilah Martin. "Mutual Aid Organisations and Their Role in Reducing Food Insecurity in Chicago's Urban Communities during COVID-19." *Public Health Nutrition* 25, no. 1 (2022): 119–22. https://doi.org/10.1017/S1368980021003736.

Lohnes, Joshua. "Regulating Surplus: Charity and the Legal Geographies of Food Waste Enclosure." *Agriculture and Human Values* 38, no. 2 (2021): 351–63. https://doi.org/10.1007/s10460-020-10150-5.

Lohnes, Joshua, and Bradley Wilson. "Bailing out the Food Banks? Hunger Relief, Food Waste, and Crisis in Central Appalachia." *Environment and Planning A: Economy and Space* 50, no. 2 (2018): 350–69. https://doi.org/10.1177/0308518X17742154.

Lootens, Abigail, and Jade Acosta. "Mayor Adams, Department of Consumer and Worker Protection Announce New Protections for Food Delivery Workers." NYC Consumer and Worker Protection, April 21, 2022. https://www.nyc.gov/site/dca/news/018-22/mayor-adams-department-consumer-worker-protection-new-protections-food.

Lopez, Marcella, Rachel A. Mintle, Sylvia Smith, Alicia Garcia, Vanessa Torres, Allie Keough, and Hugo Salgado. "Risk Factors for Intimate Partner Violence in a Migrant Farmworker Community in Baja California, Mexico." *Journal of Immigrant and Minority Health* 17, no. 6 (2015): 1819–25.

Lopez, Steven Henry. *Reorganizing the Rust Belt: An Inside Study of the American Labor Movement.* Berkeley: University of California Press, 2004.

Lorr, Benjamin. *The Secret Life of Groceries: The Dark Miracle of the American Supermarket.* London: Penguin Random House, 2020.

Louis, Garrick E. "A Historical Context of Municipal Solid Waste Management in the United States." *Waste Management & Research: The Journal of the International Solid Wastes and Public Cleansing Association (ISWA)* 22, no. 4 (2004): 306–22. https://doi.org/10.1177/0734242X04045425.

Loza, Mireya. *Defiant Braceros: How Migrant Workers Fought for Racial, Sexual, and Political Freedom.* Chapel Hill: University of North Carolina Press, 2016.

Mabli, James, Rhoda Cohen, Frank Potter, and Zhanyun Zhao. "Hunger in America 2010 National Report Prepared for Feeding America." Mathematica Policy Research, 2010. https://www.mathematica.org/publications/hunger-in-america-2010-national-report-prepared-for-feeding-america#:~:text=Recipients%20represented%20a%20broad%20cross,Ten%20percent%20were%20homeless.

Mares, Teresa M. *Life on the Other Border: Farmworkers and Food Justice in Vermont.* Berkeley: University of California Press, 2019.

———. "Navigating Gendered Labor and Local Food: A Tale of Working Mothers in Vermont." *Food and Foodways* 25, no. 3 (2017): 177–92. https://doi.org/10.1080/07409710.2017.1343064.

MarketWatch. "KR | Kroger Co. Annual Income Statement." 2023. https://www
.marketwatch.com/investing/stock/kr/financials?mod=mw_quote_tab.

Marschke, Melissa, and Peter Vandergeest. "Slavery Scandals: Unpacking Labour Challenges and Policy Responses within the off-Shore Fisheries Sector." *Marine Policy* 68 (2016): 39–46. https://doi.org/10.1016/j.marpol.2016.02.009.

Martin, Philip. "Good Intentions Gone Awry: IRCA and U.S. Agriculture." *Annals of the American Academy of Political and Social Science* 534 (1994): 44–57.

———. *Promise Unfulfilled: Unions, Immigration, and the Farm Workers.* Ithaca, NY: Cornell University Press, 2003.

———. "The Role of the H-2A Program in California Agriculture." *Choices* 34, no. 1 (2019): 1–8. https://ageconsearch.umn.edu/record/287144/?v=pdf.

Martyris, Nina. "When Tipping Was Considered Deeply Un-American." *The Salt: NPR*, November 30, 2015. https://www.npr.org/sections/thesalt/2015/11/30 /457125740/when-tipping-was-considered-deeply-un-american.

Mast, Nina. "Child Labor Remains a Key State Legislative Issue in 2024: State Lawmakers Must Seize Opportunities to Strengthen Standards, Resist Ongoing Attacks on Child Labor Laws." Economic Policy Institute, February 7, 2024. https://www.epi.org/blog/child-labor-remains-a-key-state-legislative-issue-in-2024-state-lawmakers-must-seize-opportunities-to-strengthen-standards-resist -ongoing-attacks-on-child-labor-laws/.

Matchar, Emily. "Is Michael Pollan a Sexist Pig?" *Salon*, April 28, 2013. https:// www.salon.com/2013/04/28/is_michael_pollan_a_sexist_pig/.

May, Vanessa. "Domestic Workers in U.S. History." In *Oxford Research Encyclopedia of American History*, edited by Jon Butler. Oxford: Oxford University Press, 2017. https://doi.org/10.1093/acrefore/9780199329175.013.431.

Mayer, Brian, Mona Arora, Sabrina Helm, and Melissa Barnett. "Essential but Ill-Prepared: How the COVID-19 Pandemic Affects the Mental Health of the Grocery Store Workforce." *Public Health Reports* 137, no. 1 (2022): 120–27. https://doi.org/10.1177/00333549211045817.

Mayorquin, Orlando. "Food Delivery Workers, Overlooked in Life, Are Honored in Death." *New York Times*, January 11, 2024. https://www.nytimes.com/2024 /01/11/nyregion/food-delivery-worker-memorials-nyc.html.

Maze, Jonathan. "McDonald's CEO Chris Kempczinski Got a Big Raise Last Year." *Restaurant Business*, March 28, 2022. https://restaurantbusinessonline.com /financing/mcdonalds-ceo-chris-kempczinski-got-big-raise-last-year.

Mazzenga, David. "Global Lockdowns and Economic Downturns Due to COVID-19 Increased Risk of Human Trafficking for Vulnerable Populations." *Pocono Record*, February 3, 2022. https://www.poconorecord.com/story/news/2022 /02/03/covid-19-pandemic-increased-human-trafficking-risk/6607356001/.

McCallum, Jamie K. *Essential: How the Pandemic Transformed the Long Fight for Worker Justice.* New York: Basic Books, 2022.

McCarron, Meghan. "Blue Hill at Stone Barns Tells a Beautiful Story. Former Employees Say It's Too Good to Be True." *Eater*, July 6, 2022. https://www.eater

.com/22996588/blue-hill-stone-barns-dan-barber-restaurant-work-environment-ingredients.

McCarthy, Joe. "The US Fight for $15 Minimum Wage Has Spread to Japan." *Global Citizen*, June 12, 2017. https://www.globalcitizen.org/en/content/the-us-fight-for-15-inspired-a-movement-5000-miles/.

McCarthy, Justin. "U.S. Approval of Labor Unions at Highest Point Since 1965." Gallup, August 30, 2022. https://news.gallup.com/poll/398303/approval-labor-unions-highest-point-1965.aspx.

McClure, Elizabeth S., Pavithra Vasudevan, Zinzi Bailey, Snehal Patel, and Whitney R. Robinson. "Racial Capitalism within Public Health—How Occupational Settings Drive COVID-19 Disparities." *American Journal of Epidemiology* 189, no. 11 (2020): 1244–53. https://doi.org/10.1093/aje/kwaa126.

McCutcheon, Priscilla. "Rooted in Faith: Black Women and Black Religious Geographies of the U.S. South." Geography and the Environment Colloquium Series, Syracuse University. March 31, 2023.

McDonald, Gavin G., Christopher Costello, Jennifer Bone, Reniel B. Cabral, Valerie Farabee, Timothy Hochberg, David Kroodsma, Tracey Mangin, Kyle C. Meng, and Oliver Zahn. "Satellites Can Reveal Global Extent of Forced Labor in the World's Fishing Fleet." *Proceedings of the National Academy of Sciences—PNAS* 118, no 3 (2021). https://doi.org/10.1073/pnas.2016238117.

McMichael, Philip. "A Food Regime Genealogy." *Journal of Peasant Studies* 36, no. 1 (2009): 139–69. https://doi.org/10.1080/03066150902820354.

———. "Global Development and the Corporate Food Regime." *New Directions in the Sociology of Global Development*. 1 (2005): 265–99. https://doi.org/10.1016/S1057-1922(05)11010-5.

———, ed. *The Global Restructuring of Agro-Food Systems*. Ithaca, NY: Cornell University Press, 1994.

McNicholas, Celine, and Margaret Poydock. "How California's AB5 Protects Workers from Misclassification." Economic Policy Institute, November 2019. https://www.epi.org/publication/how-californias-ab5-protects-workers-from-misclassification/.

———. "Who Are Essential Workers? A Comprehensive Look at Their Wages, Demographics, and Unionization Rates." *Working Economics Blog*, May 19, 2020. https://www.epi.org/blog/who-are-essential-workers-a-comprehensive-look-at-their-wages-demographics-and-unionization-rates/.

Meisenzahl, Mary. "7-Eleven Franchisees Say a 'Dire' Labor Shortage Is Threatening Their Ability to Keep Stores Open Overnight." *Business Insider*, May 3, 2021. https://www.businessinsider.com/7-eleven-24-hour-opening-not-possible-labor-shortage-franchisees-2021-5.

Melin, Anders. "Kroger, Blasted for Ending Hazard Pay, Gave CEO $22 Million." *Bloomberg*, May 13, 2021. https://www.bloomberg.com/news/articles/2021-05-13/kroger-blasted-for-ending-hazard-pay-gave-its-ceo-22-million.

Melley, Brian. "Judge: California Ride-Hailing Law Is Unconstitutional." AP News, August 21, 2021. https://apnews.com/article/technology-business-california-d9cd497c25e0fc6420aa4f00e020c67d.

Meyersohn, Nathaniel. "America's Largest Private Employer Just Hiked Wages." *CNN Business*, January 24, 2023. https://www.cnn.com/2023/01/24/business /walmart-raising-wages/index.html.

———. "The Self-Checkout Reversal Is Growing." CNN, December 8, 2023. https://www.cnn.com/2023/12/08/business/self-checkout-dollar-general-retail /index.html.

Meyerson, Harold. "Half a Million California Workers Get a Raise—and a Seat at the Table." *American Prospect*, September 13, 2023. https://prospect.org /labor/2023-09-13-half-million-california-workers-get-raise/.

Miao, Hannah. "Walmart and McDonald's Are among Top Employers of Medicaid and Food Stamp Beneficiaries, Report Says." CNBC, November 19, 2020. https:// www.cnbc.com/2020/11/19/walmart-and-mcdonalds-among-top-employers-of -medicaid-and-food-stamp-beneficiaries.html.

Milkman, Ruth. "The Amazon Labor Union's Historic Breakthrough." *Dissent Magazine*, 2022. https://www.dissentmagazine.org/online_articles/the-amazon -labor-unions-historic-breakthrough.

———. "Grocery Unions under the Gun in New York City and the Nation." *New Labor Forum* 31, no. 2 (2022): 17–26. https://doi.org/10.1177 /10957960221091482.

Milkman, Ruth, and Joseph Van der Naald. "The State of Unions 2023: A Profile of Organized Labor in New York City, New York State, and the United States." CUNY School of Labor and Urban Studies, 2023. https://slu.cuny.edu/wp -content/uploads/2023/08/Union-Density-2023.pdf.

Minkoff-Zern, Laura Anne. "The Case for Taking Account of Labor in Sustainable Food Systems in the United States." *Renewable Agriculture and Food Systems* 32, no. 5 (2017): 576–78. https://doi.org/10.1017/S1742170517000060.

———. "Farmworker-Led Food Movements Then and Now: United Farm Workers, the Coalition of Immokalee Workers, and the Potential for Farm Labor Justice." In *The New Food Activism: Opposition, Cooperation, and Collective Action*, edited by Alison Alkon and Julie Guthman, 157–80. Berkeley: University of California Press, 2017.

———. *The New American Farmer: Immigration, Race, and the Struggle for Sustainability*. Cambridge, MA: MIT Press, 2019.

———. "Pushing the Boundaries of Indigeneity and Agricultural Knowledge: Oaxacan Immigrant Gardening in California." *Agriculture and Human Values* 29, no. 3 (2012): 381–92. https://doi.org/10.1007/s10460-011-9348-4.

Minkoff-Zern, Laura Anne, Mary Jo Dudley, Anna Zoodsma, Bhavneet Walia, and Rick Welsh. "Protracted Dependence and Unstable Relations: Agrarian Questions in the H-2A Visa Program." *Journal of Rural Studies* 93 (2022): 43–54. https://doi.org/10.1016/j.jrurstud.2022.05.006.

Minkoff-Zern, Laura-Anne, Nancy Peluso, Jennifer Sowerwine, and Christy Getz. "Race and Regulation: Asian Immigrants in California Agriculture." In *Cultivating Food Justice: Race, Class and Sustainability*, edited by Alison Hope Alkon and Julian Agyeman, 65–86. Cambridge, MA: MIT Press, 2011.

Mintz, Corey. "The World's 50 Best Restaurants Get by with a Lot of Unpaid Labor." *Eater*, April 13, 2017. https://www.eater.com/2017/4/13/15265868 /restaurant-intern-staging-worlds-50-best.

Mintz, Sidney Wilfred. *Sweetness and Power: The Place of Sugar in Modern History.* London: Penguin Books, 1985.

Miranda, Leticia. "Grocery Workers Died Feeding the Nation. Now, Their Families Are Left to Pick up the Pieces." *NBC News*, April 13, 2021. https://www.nbcnews .com/business/business-news/grocery-workers-died-feeding-nation-now-their- families-are-left-n1263693.

Mitchell, Don. *Lie of the Land: Migrant Workers and the California Landscape.* Minneapolis: University of Minnesota Press, 1996.

———. *They Saved the Crops: Labor, Landscape, and the Struggle over Industrial Farming in Bracero-Era California.* Athens: University of Georgia Press, 2012.

Mitchell, Stacy, and Marie Donahue. "Dollar Stores Are Targeting Struggling Urban Neighborhoods and Small Towns. One Community Is Showing How to Fight Back." Institute for Local Self-Reliance, December 6, 2018. https://ilsr.org /dollar-stores-target-cities-towns-one-fights-back/.

Mojab, Shahrzad, and Sara Carpenter. "Marxism, Feminism, and 'Intersectional- ity.'" *Journal of Labor and Society* 22, no. 2 (2019): 275–82. https://doi.org/10.1111 /wusa.12409.

Morales Waugh, Irma. "Examining the Sexual Harassment Experiences of Mexican Immigrant Farmworking Women." *Violence Against Women* 16, no. 3 (2010): 237–61. https://doi.org/10.1177/1077801209360857.

Moran, Catherine Douglas. "FMI: 80% of Food Retailers Say Hiring Issues Are Hurting Business." *Grocery Dive*, September 16, 2021. https://www.grocerydive .com/news/fmi-80-of-food-retailers-say-hiring-issues-are-hurting-business /606695/.

Moran, Greta. "As the Climate Emergency Grows, Farmworkers Lack Protection from Deadly Heat." *Civil Eats*, June 14, 2021. https://civileats.com/2021/06/14 /as-the-climate-emergency-grows-farmworkers-lack-protection-from-deadly -heat/.

Morrill, Valerie, Raychel Santo, and Karen Bassarab. "Shining a Light on Labor: How Food Policy Councils Can Support Food Chain Workers." Johns Hopkins Center for a Livable Future, 2018. https://doi.org/10.13140/RG.2.2.27848.78084.

Mott, Katherine Louisa Ravene. "Precarity beyond Food: How the Closure of an Independent Grocery Store Shed Light on the Limitations of Food Access Efforts in Syracuse, New York." MS thesis, Syracuse University, 2019. https://surface.syr .edu/thesis/379/.

Mourad, Marie. "Recycling, Recovering and Preventing 'Food Waste': Competing Solutions for Food Systems Sustainability in the United States and France." *Jour- nal of Cleaner Production* 126 (2016): 461–77. https://doi.org/10.1016 /j.jclepro.2016.03.084.

Murakami, Christopher D., Lori Boegershausen, James Karl Till, Tia Rowe, Tyler Offerman, Erica Lynn Klopf, Arlo Bradley Simonds, Kelly Ann Walsh, and

Deion Jones. "Student Leadership and Sustainability: The Florida Gulf Coast University Food Forest and the Real Food Challenge Pledge." In *Making the Sustainable University: Trials and Tribulations*, edited by Katie Leone, Simeon Komisar, and Edwin M. Everham III, 185–204. New York: Springer Nature, 2021. https://doi.org/10.1007/978-981-33-4477-8_12.

Murphy, Jeanne, Julie Samples, Mavel Morales, and Nargess Shadbeh. "'They Talk Like That, but We Keep Working': Sexual Harassment and Sexual Assault Experiences among Mexican Indigenous Farmworker Women in Oregon." *Journal of Immigrant and Minority Health* 17, no. 6 (2015): 1834–39. https://doi.org/10.1007/s10903-014-9992-z.

Musicus, Aviva A., Ghislaine C. Amsler Challamel, Robert McKenzie, Eric B. Rimm, and Stacy A. Blondin. "Food Waste Management Practices and Barriers to Progress in U.S. University Foodservice." *International Journal of Environmental Research and Public Health* 19, no. 11 (2022): 6512. https://doi.org/10.3390/ijerph19116512.

Myers, Justin Sean, and Joshua Sbicca. "Bridging Good Food and Good Jobs: From Secession to Confrontation within Alternative Food Movement Politics." *Geoforum* 61 (2015): 17–26. https://doi.org/10.1016/j.geoforum.2015.02.003.

Nabhan-Warren, Kristy. *Meatpacking America: How Migration, Work, and Faith Unite and Divide the Heartland*. Chapel Hill: University of North Carolina Press, 2021.

Nakamura, Katrina, Lori Bishop, Trevor Ward, Ganapathiraju Pramod, Dominic Chakra Thomson, Patima Tungpuchayakul, and Sompong Srakaew. "Seeing Slavery in Seafood Supply Chains." *Science Advances* 4, no. 7 (2018): e1701833. https://doi.org/10.1126/sciadv.1701833.

National Restaurant Association. "Inclusive Hiring: Welcoming Workers with Disabilities." March 7, 2022. https://restaurant.org/education-and-resources/resource-library/inclusive-hiring-welcoming-workers-with-disabilities/.

National Sustainable Agriculture Coalition. "What Is the Farm Bill?" National Sustainable Agriculture Coalition, 2023. https://sustainableagriculture.net/our-work/campaigns/fbcampaign/what-is-the-farm-bill/.

Neumark, David, Junfu Zhang, and Stephen Ciccarella. "The Effects of Wal-Mart on Local Labor Markets." *Journal of Urban Economics* 63, no. 2 (2008): 405–30. https://doi.org/10.1016/j.jue.2007.07.004.

New York City Department of Consumer and Worker Protection. "A Minimum Pay Rate for App-Based Restaurant Delivery Workers in NYC." 2022. https://www.nyc.gov/assets/dca/downloads/pdf/workers/Delivery-Worker-Study-November-2022.pdf.

Newlands, Gemma. "Algorithmic Surveillance in the Gig Economy: The Organization of Work through Lefebvrian Conceived Space." *Organization Studies* 42, no. 5 (2021): 719–37. https://doi.org/10.1177/0170840620937900.

Nguyen, Aiha. "The Constant Boss: Labor under Digital Surveillance." Data and Society, 2021. https://datasociety.net/library/the-constant-boss/.

Nieves, Alexander. "Newsom Reverses Course and Signs Farmworker Bill Backed by Biden." *Politico*, September 28, 2022. https://www.politico.com/news/2022/09/28/newsom-signs-biden-backed-union-bill-00056562.

Nilsson, Jeff. "Why Did Henry Ford Double His Minimum Wage?" *Saturday Evening Post*, January 2014. https://www.saturdayeveningpost.com/2014/01/ford-doubles-minimum-wage/.

Nye, David E. 2015. *America's Assembly Line*. Reprint edition. Cambridge, MA: MIT Press.

Ockerman, Emma. "Farm Workers Were Trafficked and Threatened with a Gun in South Carolina, Feds Say." *Vice*, January 21, 2022. https://www.vice.com/en/article/m7v38x/south-carolina-balcazar-human-trafficking-farm-workers.

Olivia, Lewis. "What Is Commercial Composting?" Medium, July 28, 2017. https://medium.com/@compostwindrow1/what-is-commercial-composting-2ec208348b30.

Olmos, Sergio. "When Hard Jobs Turn Hazardous." *New York Times*, September 4, 2021. https://www.nytimes.com/2021/09/04/business/economy/heat-wildfires-drought-farmworkers.html?referringSource=articleShare.

One Fair Wage and UC Berkeley Food Labor Research Center. "It's a Wage Shortage, Not a Worker Shortage: Why Restaurant Workers, Particularly Mothers, Are Leaving the Industry, and What Would Make Them Stay." One Fair Wage, May 2021. https://onefairwage.site/wp-content/uploads/2021/05/OFW_WageShortage_F.pdf

Orleck, Annelise. *"We Are All Fast-Food Workers Now": The Global Uprising against Poverty Wages*. Boston: Beacon Press, 2018.

Occupational Safety and Health Administration (OSHA). "Heat—Standards." 2022. https://www.osha.gov/heat-exposure/standards.

———. Oregon. "Oregon OSHA Adopting 2 Emergency Rules Protecting Workers against Wildfire Smoke and Occupants of Employer-Provided Housing against Heat Dangers." Oregon.Gov, August 2, 2021. https://osha.oregon.gov/news/2021/Pages/nr2021-33.aspx.

Pachirat, Timothy. *Every Twelve Seconds: Industrialized Slaughter and the Politics of Sight*. New Haven, CT: Yale University Press, 2013.

Pai, Shantanu, Ning Ai, and Junjun Zheng. "Decentralized Community Composting Feasibility Analysis for Residential Food Waste: A Chicago Case Study." *Sustainable Cities and Society* 50 (2019): 101683. https://doi.org/10.1016/j.scs.2019.101683.

Paiz, Christian O. *The Strikers of Coachella: A Rank-and-File History of the UFW Movement*. Justice, Power, and Politics. Chapel Hill: University of North Carolina Press, 2023.

Patel, Raj. *Stuffed and Starved: The Hidden Battle for the World Food System*. London: Penguin Random House, 2012.

Patel, Raj, and Jason W. Moore. *A History of the World in Seven Cheap Things: A Guide to Capitalism, Nature, and the Future of the Planet*. Berkeley: University of California Press, 2017.

Patico, Jennifer. *The Trouble with Snack Time: Children's Food and the Politics of Parenting*. New York: NYU Press, 2020.

Paxson, Heather. *The Life of Cheese: Crafting Food and Value in America*. Berkeley: University of California Press, 2012.

Peart, Natalie. "How Gleaning Could Reshape the Farm Economy." Civil Eats, July 9, 2021. https://civileats.com/2021/07/09/how-gleaning-could-reshape-the-farm-economy/.

Peck, Jamie, and Adam Tickell. "Neoliberalizing Space." *Antipode* 34, no. 3 (2002): 380–404. https://doi.org/10.1111/1467-8330.00247.

Pedtke, Cathy, and Thomas Pedtke. "Food Waste, Wasted Food: Reframing Waste and Edibility." Paper presented at Dublin Gastronomy Symposium, 2020. https://researchprofiles.tudublin.ie/en/publications/food-waste-wasted-food-reframing-waste-and-edibility.

Pen, Justin. "Justice for Temporary Migrant Workers: Lessons from the '7-Eleven Cases.'" *Alternative Law Journal* 43, no. 1 (2018): 24–29. https://doi.org/10.1177/1037969X17748209.

Peña, Devon. *The Terror of the Machine Technology, Work, Gender, and Ecology on the U.S.-Mexico Border*. Austin: University of Texas Press, 1997.

Perea, Juan F. "The Echoes of Slavery: Recognizing the Racist Origins of the Agricultural and Domestic Worker Exclusion from the National Labor Relations Act." *Ohio State Law Journal* 95 (2011). https://lawcommons.luc.edu/facpubs/151/.

Pilgeram, Ryanne. "Social Sustainability and the White, Nuclear Family: Constructions of Gender, Race, and Class at a Northwest Farmers' Market." *Race, Gender & Class* 19, no. 1–2 (2012): 37–60. https://www.jstor.org/stable/43496859.

Poppendieck, Janet. *Sweet Charity? Emergency Food and the End of Entitlement*. London: Penguin, 1999.

Quandt, Sara, Hannah Kinzer, Grisel Trejo, Dana Mora, and Joanne Sandberg. "The Health of Women Farmworkers and Women in Farmworker Families in the Eastern United States." In *Latinx Farmworkers in the Eastern United States*, edited by T. Arcury and S. Quandt, 133–61. Cham: Springer, 2020.

Ramos, Athena K., Abigail E. Lowe, Jocelyn J. Herstein, Shelly Schwedhelm, Kelly K. Dineen, and John J. Lowe. "Invisible No More: The Impact of COVID-19 on Essential Food Production Workers." *Journal of Agromedicine* 25, no. 4 (2020): 378–82. https://doi.org/10.1080/1059924X.2020.1814925.

Rana, Preetika. "DoorDash's 2021 Revenue Tops Pandemic Record." *Wall Street Journal*, February 16, 2022. https://www.wsj.com/articles/doordashs-2021-revenue-tops-pandemic-record-11645046230.

Reardon, Thomas, and Johan Swinnen. "COVID-19 and Resilience Innovations in Food Supply Chains." International Food Policy Research Institute, 2020. https://doi.org/10.2499/p15738coll2.133762_30.

Reese, Ashanté M. *Black Food Geographies: Race, Self-Reliance, and Food Access in Washington, D.C.* Chapel Hill: University of North Carolina Press, 2019.

Reese, Ellen, and Rudolph Bielitz. "The Warehouse Workers Resource Center in Southern California." In *Igniting Justice and Progressive Power: The Partnership for Working Families Cities*, edited by David B. Reynolds and Louise Simmons, 294–311. London: Routledge, 2021.

ReFED. "Food Waste Monitor." September 12, 2024. https://insights-engine.refed .org/food-waste-monitor?view=overview&year=2022.

———. "U.S. Waste Policy Finder." August 22, 2024. http://policyfinder.refed .com.

Resnikoff, Ned. "Fight for $15 Goes Global: Workers Set to Launch Worldwide Protest." *Al Jazeera America*, April 15, 2015. http://america.aljazeera.com /articles/2015/4/13/laborers-set-to-launch-worldwide-protest-for-a-living-wage .html.

Reuge, Cecile, and Teresa Mares. "Workplace Democracy and Civic Engagement in Vermont Food Cooperatives." *WorkingUSA* 19, no. 2 (2016): 207–27. https://doi .org/10.1163/17434580-01902006.

Rich, Wilbur C. "The Moral Choices of Garbage Collectors: Administrative Ethics from Below." *American Review of Public Administration* 26, no. 2 (1996): 201–12. https://doi.org/10.1177/027507409602600204.

Ritzer, George. 2013. *The McDonaldization of Society: 20th Anniversary Edition*. Thousand Oaks, CA: SAGE.

Roberts, Dorothy. *Killing the Black Body*. New York: Pantheon Books, 1997.

Robinson, Cedric J. *Black Marxism: The Making of the Black Radical Tradition*. Zed Third World Studies. London: Zed, 1983.

Rochester Regional Joint Board, Workers United. Starbucks Corporation | National Labor Relations Board, Region 03, Buffalo, New York. 2021. https://www.nlrb .gov/case/03-CB-306087.

Rodman, Sarah O., Colleen L. Barry, Megan L. Clayton, Shannon Frattaroli, Roni A. Neff, and Lainie Rutkow. "Agricultural Exceptionalism at the State Level: Characterization of Wage and Hour Laws for U.S. Farmworkers." *Journal of Agriculture, Food Systems, and Community Development* 6, no. 2 (2016): 89–110. https://doi.org/10.5304/jafscd.2016.062.013.

Romero, Mary. "Nanny Diaries and Other Stories: Immigrant Women's Labor in the Social Reproduction of American Families." *Revista de Estudios Sociales* 45 (2013): 186–97. https://doi.org/10.7440/res45.2013.15.

Rosenbaum, René Perez. "Farm Labor Organizing Committee (FLOC): Grassroots Organizing for the Empowerment of the Migrant Farm Worker Community." *Culture & Agriculture* 13, no. 47 (1993): 21–23. https://doi.org/10.1525/cuag.1993 .13.47.21.

Ruddick, Graham. "Amazon to Start Selling Fresh and Frozen Morrisons Food." *The Guardian*, February 29, 2016. https://www.theguardian.com/business/2016 /feb/29/amazon-is-to-start-selling-fresh-and-frozen-morrisons-food.

Ruiz, Vicki L. *Cannery Women, Cannery Lives: Mexican Women, Unionization, and the California Food Processing Industry, 1930–1950*. Albuquerque: University of New Mexico Press, 1987.

Sachs, Carolyn, and Patricia Allen. "Women and Food Chains: The Gendered Politics of Food." *International Journal of Sociology of Agriculture and Food* 15, no. 1 (2007): 23–40. https://doi.org/10.48416/ijsaf.v15i1.424.

Sackrey, C., G. Schneider, and J. Knoedler. *Introduction to Political Economy*. 8th ed. Boston: Economic Affairs Bureau, 2016.

Sainato, Michael. "'They Want Us to Be Robots': Whole Foods Workers Fear Amazon's Changes." *The Guardian*, October 1, 2018. https://www.theguardian.com /business/2018/oct/01/whole-foods-amazon-union-organization-grocery -chain.

———. "Trader Joe's Broke Labor Laws in Effort to Stop Stores Unionizing, Workers Say." *The Guardian*, September 4, 2022. https://www.theguardian.com /us-news/2022/sep/04/trader-joes-union-workers-labor-law.

Salfer, J. A., K. Minegishi, W. Lazarus, E. Berning, and M. I. Endres. "Finances and Returns for Robotic Dairies." *Journal of Dairy Science* 100, no. 9 (2017): 7739–49. https://doi.org/10.3168/jds.2016-11976.

Salles, Claire. "Immediacy and Its Hidden Infrastructure: When Amazon Extends Its Delivery Times during the Covid-19 Pandemic." *Img Journal*, no. 3 (2020): 380–95. https://doi.org/10.6092/issn.2724-2463/12265.

Saracino, Jessica. "Best Practices for Contracting with Food Service Management Companies." USDA Food and Nutrition Service, April 21, 2023. https://www .fns.usda.gov/resource/best-practices-contracting-food-service-management-companies.

Sbicca, Joshua. "Food Labor, Economic Inequality, and the Imperfect Politics of Process in the Alternative Food Movement." *Agriculture and Human Values* 32, no. 4 (2015): 675–87.

———. "Resetting the 'Good Food' Table: Labor and Food Justice Alliances in Los Angeles." In *The New Food Activism: Opposition, Cooperation, and Collective Action*, edited by Alison Alkon and Julie Guthman, 107–32. Berkeley: University of California Press, 2017.

Sbicca, Joshua, Laura-Anne Minkoff-Zern, and Shelby Coopwood. "'Because They Are Connected': Linking Structural Inequalities in Farmworker Organizing." *Human Geography* 13, no. 3 (2020): 263–76. https://doi.org/10.1177 /1942778620962045.

Schaeffer, Katherine. "Among U.S. Couples, Women Do More Cooking and Grocery Shopping Than Men." Pew Research Center, September 14, 2019. https:// www.pewresearch.org/fact-tank/2019/09/24/among-u-s-couples-women-do-more-cooking-and-grocery-shopping-than-men/.

Schanes, Karin, Karin Dobernig, and Burcu Gözet. "Food Waste Matters: A Systematic Review of Household Food Waste Practices and Their Policy Implications." *Journal of Cleaner Production* 182 (2018): 978–91. https://doi.org/10.1016/j. jclepro.2018.02.030.

Schantora, A. L., S. Casjens, A. Deckert, V. van Kampen, H.-D. Neumann, T. Brüning, M. Raulf, J. Bünger, and F. Hoffmeyer. "Prevalence of Work-Related Rhino-Conjunctivitis and Respiratory Symptoms among Domestic Waste Collectors."

Advances in Experimental Medicine and Biology 834 (2015): 53–61. https://doi .org/10.1007/5584_2014_71.

Schlosser, Eric. *Fast Food Nation: The Dark Side of the All-American Meal*. Boston: Mariner Books, 2012.

Schmitt, John, and Janelle Jones. "Slow Progress for Fast-Food Workers." Center for Economic Policy and Research, 2013. https://cepr.net/report/slow-progress-for-fast-food-workers-brief/.

Schoenfein, Liza. "Women Are Uniting to Fight Sexual Harassment in the Restaurant Industry." *Civil Eats*, October 29, 2018. https://civileats.com/2018/10/29 /women-are-uniting-to-fight-sexual-harassment-in-the-restaurant-industry/.

Schulte, Grant, and David Pitt. "Rural Population Losses Add to Farm and Ranch Labor Shortage." Associated Press, August 17, 2021. https://apnews.com/article /census-2020-farm-ranch-labor-business-83107b136c2c92b6c4b7830b12f5bd96.

Schulte, Paul A., Jessica M. K. Streit, Fatima Sheriff, George Delclos, Sarah A. Felknor, Sara L. Tamers, Sherry Fendinger, James Grosch, and Robert Sala. "Potential Scenarios and Hazards in the Work of the Future: A Systematic Review of the Peer-Reviewed and Gray Literatures." *Annals of Work Exposures and Health* 64, no. 8 (2020): 786–816. https://doi.org/10.1093/annweh/wxaa051.

Schwarz, Mary, and Jean Bonhotal. "School Composting—Let's Get Growing." Cornell University Library eCommons, 2017. https://ecommons.cornell.edu /items/2c52fd06-902a-4e2f-8366-abbe494b4744.

Schweizer, Errol. "Episode 100: Magaly Licolli on Organizing Poultry Workers." *The Checkout Podcast*, 2022. https://www.thecheckoutradio.com/podcast /magalay-licolli.

Schweninger, Loren. "A Vanishing Breed: Black Farm Owners in the South, 1651– 1982." *Agricultural History* 63, no. 3 (1989): 41–60.

Scott, Alex, and Beth Davis-Sramek. "Driving in a Man's World: Examining Gender Disparity in the Trucking Industry." *International Journal of Physical Distribution & Logistics Management* 53, no. 3 (2023): 330–53. DOI 10.1108 /IJPDLM-03-2022-0073.

Sears, William P. "Indentured Servants in Colonial America." *Dalhousie Review* 37. no. 2 (1957): 121–40.

Sedacca, Matthew, and David Yaffe-Bellany. "Cooking Eggs in the Morning and Shucking Oysters at Night, Thanks to an App." *New York Times*, September 1, 2019. https://www.nytimes.com/2019/09/01/business/restaurant-jobs-apps .html.

Selvam, Ashok. "The Battle over Chicago's Tipped Minimum Wage Is Over." *Eater Chicago*, September 19, 2023. https://chicago.eater.com/2023/9/19/23881229 /chicago-tipped-minimum-wage-ordinance-one-fair-wage-victory-restaurant -association-saru-jayaraman.

Sharpless, Rebecca. *Cooking in Other Women's Kitchens: Domestic Workers in the South, 1865–1960*. Chapel Hill: University of North Carolina Press, 2010.

Shaw, Randy. *Beyond the Fields: Cesar Chavez, the UFW, and the Struggle for Justice in the 21st Century*. Berkeley: University of California Press, 2008.

Sifuentez, Mario Jimenez. *Of Forests and Fields: Mexican Labor in the Pacific Northwest*. New Brunswick, NJ: Rutgers University Press, 2016.

Silyok, V. A. *Environmental Laws: Summaries of Statutes Administered by the Environmental Protection Agency*. Huntington, NY: Nova Science Publishers, 2001.

Sinclair, Upton. *The Jungle*. New York: Doubleday, Page and Co., 1906.

———. "What Life Means to Me." *Cosmopolitan* 41 (October 1906): 594.

Singh, Pia. "Proposed Kroger, Albertsons Merger Will Take More Time to Close." CNBC, January 15, 2024. https://www.cnbc.com/2024/01/15/proposed-kroger -albertsons-merger-will-take-more-time-to-close.html.

Slade, Jessica, and Emma Alleyne. "The Psychological Impact of Slaughterhouse Employment: A Systematic Literature Review." *Trauma, Violence, & Abuse* 24, no. 2 (2023): 429–40. doi:10.1177/15248380211030243.

Slocum, Rachel. "Thinking Race through Corporeal Feminist Theory: Divisions and Intimacies at the Minneapolis Farmers' Market." *Social & Cultural Geography* 9, no. 8 (2008): 849–69. https://doi.org/10.1080/14649360802441465.

Smith, Kennedy. "Dollar Store Restrictions." Institute for Local Self-Reliance, March 23, 2023. https://ilsr.org/dollar-store-restrictions/.

Som Castellano, Rebecca L. "Alternative Food Networks and the Labor of Food Provisioning: A Third Shift?" *Rural Sociology* 81, no. 3 (2016): 445–69. https:// doi.org/10.1111/ruso.12104.

Somers, Kelly, and Karen Soldatic. "Productive Bodies: How Neoliberalism Makes and Unmakes Disability in Human and Non-Human Animals." In *Disability and Animality: Crip Perspectives in Critical Animal Studies*, edited by Stephanie Jenkins, Kelly Struthers Montford, and Chloë Taylor, 35–56. Abingdon: Routledge, 2020.

Sousa, Emily C., and Manish N. Raizada. "Contributions of African Crops to American Culture and Beyond: The Slave Trade and Other Journeys of Resilient Peoples and Crops." *Frontiers in Sustainable Food Systems* 4 (2020). https://doi .org/10.3389/fsufs.2020.586340https://www.frontiersin.org/article/10.3389 /fsufs.2020.586340.

Southern Poverty Law Center (SPLC). "Injustice on Our Plates: Immigrant Women in the U.S. Food Industry." 2010. https://www.splcenter.org/sites/default/files /d6_legacy_files/downloads/publication/Injustice_on_Our_Plates.pdf.

Spacek, Rachel. "Idaho Farm Gave Workers a Choice: Illegal Low Wages or Deportation, Investigation Finds." *Spokesman-Review*, February 25, 2022. https://www .spokesman.com/stories/2022/feb/25/idaho-farm-gave-workers-a-choice-illegal-low- wages/.

Spade, Dean. *Mutual Aid: Building Solidarity during This Crisis*. London: Verso, 2020.

Sparkman, David. "EEOC Cracks Down on Pre-Employment Physical Testing." *EHS Today*, July 20, 2018. https://www.ehstoday.com/health/article/21919717 /eeoc-cracks-down-on-preemployment-physical-testing.

St. Julien, Jahdziah, and Emily Hallgren. "The Gaps of White Feminism and the Women of Color Who Fall Through." *New America*, July 20, 2021. http://

newamerica.org/the-thread/the-gaps-of-white-feminism-and-the-women-of-color-who-fall-through/.

Starbucks Workers United. "Starbucks Workers United." 2024. https://sbworkersunited.org.

Stephan, Goetz, and David Debertin. "Rural Population Decline in the 1980s: Impacts of Farm Structure and Federal Farm Programs." *American Journal of Agricultural Economics* 78, no. 3 (1996): 517–29. https://onlinelibrary.wiley.com/doi/abs/10.2307/1243270.

Stiegert, Kyle W., and Dong Hwan Kim. "Structural changes in Food Retailing: Six Country Case Studies." Food System Research Group, University of Wisconsin-Madison, 2009.

Stovall, Holly A., Lori Baker-Sperry, and Judith M. Dallinger. "A New Discourse on the Kitchen: Feminism and Environmental Education." *Australian Journal of Environmental Education* 31, no. 1 (2015): 110–31. http://dx.doi.org/10.1017/aee.2015.11.

Strategic Organizing Center. "The Injury Machine: How Amazon's Production System Hurts Workers." 2022. http://thesoc.org/what-we-do/the-injury-machine-how-amazons-production-system-hurts-workers/.

Streeter, Virginia, and Brenda Platt. "Residential Food Waste Collection Access in the U.S." BioCycle, 2017. https://www.biocycle.net/subscriber-exclusive-residential-food-waste-collection-access-u-s-complete-report/.

Striffler, Steve. *Chicken: The Dangerous Transformation of America's Favorite Food.* New Haven, CT: Yale University Press, 2007.

Strong, Andrea. "Do You Know Where Your Tip Money Is Going?" *Eater*, June 12, 2018. https://www.eater.com/2018/6/12/17439694/tipping-laws-tip-sharing-fair-labor-standards-act.

Stuesse, Angela. "The Poultry Industry Recruited Them. Now ICE Raids Are Devastating Their Communities." *Washington Post*, November 22, 2019. https://www.washingtonpost.com/outlook/2019/08/09/poultry-industry-recruited-them-now-ice-raids-are-devastating-their-communities/.

———. *Scratching Out a Living: Latinos, Race, and Work in the Deep South.* Berkeley: University of California Press, 2016.

Stuesse, Angela, and Nathan Dollar. "Who Are America's Meat and Poultry Workers?" *Economic Policy Institute Blog*, September 24, 2020. https://www.epi.org/blog/meat-and-poultry-worker-demographics/.

Syron, Laura N., Devin L. Lucas, Viktor E. Bovbjerg, and Laurel D. Kincl. "Injury and Illness among Onshore Workers in Alaska's Seafood Processing Industry: Analysis of Workers' Compensation Claims, 2014–2015." *American Journal of Industrial Medicine* 62, no. 3 (2019): 253–64. https://doi.org/10.1002/ajim.22953.

Taete, Jamie Lee. "Arcades, Churches and Laundromats: A Trucker's Haven on the Precipice of Change." *New York Times*, June 4, 2022. https://www.nytimes.com/2022/06/04/business/truck-driver-shortage-support.html.

Taillie, Lindsey Smith, Shu Wen Ng, and Barry M. Popkin. "Global Growth of 'Big Box' Stores and the Potential Impact on Human Health and Nutrition." *Nutrition Reviews* 74, no. 2 (2016): 83–97. https://doi.org/10.1093/nutrit/nuv062.

Tan, Eli. "In Win for Uber and Lyft, California Court Upholds Gig-Worker Proposition." *New York Times*, July 25, 2024. https://www.nytimes.com/2024/07/25/technology/california-gig-worker-court-decision.html.

Tanglis, Michael, and Shanna Devine. "Extreme Heat and Unprotected Workers: Public Citizen Petitions OSHA to Protect the Millions of Workers Who Labor in Dangerous Temperatures." Public Citizen, 2018. https://www.citizen.org/wp-content/uploads/extreme_heat_and_unprotected_workers.pdf.

Tarasuk, Valerie, and Joan M. Eakin. "Food Assistance through 'Surplus' Food: Insights from an Ethnographic Study of Food Bank Work." *Agriculture and Human Values* 22, no. 2 (2005): 177–86. https://doi.org/10.1007/s10460-004-8277-x.

Taylor, Charles A., Christopher Boulos, and Douglas Almond. "Livestock Plants and COVID-19 Transmission." *Proceedings of the National Academy of Sciences* 117, no. 50 (2020): 31706–15. https://doi.org/10.1073/pnas.2010115117.

Taylor, Frederick Winslow. *Scientific Management: Comprising Shop Management. The Principles of Scientific Management and Testimony before the Special House Committee.* New York: Harper, 1947.

Taylor, J. Edward, Diane Charlton, and Antonio Yúnez-Naude. "The End of Farm Labor Abundance." *Applied Economic Perspectives and Policy* 34, no. 4 (2012): 587–98. https://doi.org/10.1093/aepp/pps036.

Thanos, Nikki, and Maggie Corser. "Trapped in Part-Time: Walmart's Phantom Ladder of Opportunity." Center for Popular Democracy; Organization United for Respect; Fair Workweek Initiative, 2018. https://www.populardemocracy.org/news/publications/trapped-part-time-walmart-s-phantom-ladder-opportunity.

Thompson, Charles, and Melinda Wiggins. *The Human Cost of Food Farmworkers' Lives: Labor, and Advocacy.* Austin: University of Texas Press, 2002.

Tienoven, Theun Pieter van, Joeri Minnen, Anaïs Glorieux, Ilse Laurijssen, Petrus te Braak, and Ignace Glorieux. "Locking Down Gender Roles? A Time-Use Perspective on Gender Division of Household Labour during the COVID-19 Pandemic Lockdown in Belgium." *Journal of Family Issues* 44, no. 3 (2023): 654–80. https://doi.org/10.1177/0192513X211054463.

Travlou, Penny. "Kropotkin-19: A Mutual Aid Response to COVID-19 in Athens." *Design and Culture* 13, no. 1 (2021): 65–78. https://doi.org/10.1080/17547075.2020.1864119.

Tronto, Joan C. "The 'Nanny' Question in Feminism." *Hypatia* 17, no. 2 (2002): 34–51. https://doi.org/10.1111/j.1527-2001.2002.tb00764.x

Trubek, Amy B. *Making Modern Meals: How Americans Cook Today.* Berkeley: University of California Press, 2017.

Tseng, Min-Feng, Chu-Lin Chou, Chi-Hsiang Chung, Ying-Kai Chen, Wu-Chien Chien, Chia-Hsien Feng, and Pauling Chu. "Risk of Chronic Kidney Disease in Patients with Heat Injury: A Nationwide Longitudinal Cohort Study in Taiwan." *PLoS ONE* 15, no. 7 (2020): e0235607. https://doi.org/10.1371/journal.pone.0235607.

Tsu, Cecilia M. "Immigration in a Rural Context." In *The Routledge History of Rural America*, edited by Pamela Riney-Kehrberg, 215–29. London: Routledge, 2016.

Twitty, Michael. *The Cooking Gene: A Journey through African American Culinary History in the Old South*. New York: HarperCollins, 2017.

Tyrväinen, Olli, and Heikki Karjaluoto. "Online Grocery Shopping before and during the COVID-19 Pandemic: A Meta-Analytical Review." *Telematics and Informatics* 71 (2022): 101839. https://doi.org/10.1016/j.tele.2022.101839.

Tyson, John. "Feeding the Nation and Keeping Our Team Members Healthy." Tyson Foods, April 27, 2020. https://thefeed.blog/2020/04/26/feeding-the-nation-and-keeping-our-employees-healthy/.

Ungar, Rick. "Walmart Store Holding Thanksgiving Charity Food Drive—for Its Own Employees!" *Forbes*, November 13, 2013. https://www.forbes.com/sites/rickungar/2013/11/18/walmart-store-holding-thanksgiving-charity-food-drive-for-its-own-employees/.

United Food and Commercial Workers International Union (UFCW). "UFCW: Biden USDA Puts Meatpacking Worker Safety First in Move to Comply with Court Ruling on Pork Line Speeds." 2021. https://www.ufcw.org/press-releases/ufcw-biden-usda-puts-meatpacking-worker-safety-first-in-move-to-comply-with-court-ruling-on-pork-line-speeds/.

———. "Worker Friendly Farm Bill." 2023. https://www.ufcw.org/wp-content/blogs.dir/61/files/2023/02/Worker-Friendly-Farm-Bill-Fact-Sheet-January-2023.pdf.

US Bureau of Labor Statistics (BLS). "Fast Food and Counter Workers." Occupational Employment and Wage Statistics. 2022. https://www.bls.gov/oes/current/oes353023.htm.

———. "Incidence Rates of Nonfatal Occupational Injuries and Illnesses by Industry and Case Types." 2021. https://www.bls.gov/iif/nonfatal-injuries-and-illnesses-tables/table-1-injury-and-illness-rates-by-industry-2021-national.htm.

———. "Occupational Employment and Wage Statistics." 2022. www.bls.gov/oes/.

———. "Union Members Summary—2023 A01 Results." 2024. https://www.bls.gov/news.release/union2.nr0.htm.

———. "Union Members—2023." 2024. https://www.bls.gov/news.release/pdf/union2.pdf.

US Census Bureau. "North American Industry Classification System (NAICS) U.S. Census Bureau." 2022. https://www.census.gov/naics/?input=45&year=2022&details=45521.

US Congress. House of Representatives. Select Subcommittee on the Coronavirus Crisis. Hybrid Hearing on "How the Meatpacking Industry Failed the Workers Who Feed America." US House of Representatives Committee Repository, October 27, 2021. https://coronavirus.house.gov/subcommittee-activity/hearings/hybrid-hearing-how-meatpacking-industry-failed-workers-who-feed.

———. Senate. Committee on the Judiciary. "From Farm to Table: Immigrant Workers Get the Job Done." May 31, 2023. https://www.judiciary.senate.gov/from-farm-to-table-immigrant-workers-get-the-job-done.

US Department of Labor. "American Time Use Survey: Time Spent in Primary Activities and Percent of the Civilian Population Engaging in Each Activity, Averages per Day by Sex, 2021 Annual Averages—2021 A01 Results." 2022. https://www.bls.gov/news.release/atus.t01.htm.

———. "The Migrant & Seasonal Agricultural Worker Protection Act." 2022. https://www.dol.gov/agencies/whd/laws-and-regulations/laws/mspa.

———. "Minimum Wages for Tipped Employees." Wage and Hour Division. 2023. http://www.dol.gov/agencies/whd/state/minimum-wage/tipped.

———. "State Child Labor Laws Applicable to Agricultural Employment." 2022. https://www.dol.gov/agencies/whd/state/child-labor/agriculture.

US Environmental Protection Agency (EPA). "Advancing Sustainable Materials Management: Facts and Figures 2018." Report. 2020. https://digital.library.unt .edu/ark:/67531/metadc949098/.

———. "Food: Material-Specific Data." Overviews and Factsheets, April 4, 2023. https://www.epa.gov/facts-and-figures-about-materials-waste-and-recycling /food-material-specific-data.

———. "Food Recovery Hierarchy." Overviews and Factsheets, August 28, 2022. https://www.epa.gov/sustainable-management-food/food-recovery-hierarchy.

US Department of Agriculture (USDA). "2021 U.S. Food-Away-from-Home Spending 10 Percent Higher Than Pre-Pandemic Levels." Economic Research Service, Food Expenditure Series, 2022. http://www.ers.usda.gov/data-products /chart-gallery/gallery/chart-detail/?chartId=58364.

———. Economic Recovery Service (ERS). "Composition of Top U.S. Food Retailers Shifted in 2016." 2017. http://www.ers.usda.gov/data-products/chart-gallery /gallery/chart-detail/?chartId=86665.

———. "Retail Trends." Retailing and Wholesaling, December 22, 2021. https:// www.ers.usda.gov/topics/food-markets-prices/retailing-wholesaling/retail-trends.aspx#.UouybPldWSq.

———. "Summary Findings: Food Price Outlook, 2022 and 2023." 2022. https:// www.ers.usda.gov/data-products/food-price-outlook/summary-findings/.

———. "USDA ERS—Farm Labor." 2023. https://www.ers.usda.gov/topics/farm -economy/farm-labor/#demographic.

———. "USDA ERS—National School Lunch Program." 2024. https://www.ers .usda.gov/topics/food-nutrition-assistance/child-nutrition-programs/national-school-lunch-program/.

U.S. News. "How Much Can a Garbage Collector Expect to Get Paid?" 2022. https://money.usnews.com/careers/best-jobs/garbage-collector/salary.

Upright, Craig B. *Grocery Activism: The Radical History of Food Cooperatives in Minnesota*. Minneapolis: University of Minnesota Press, 2020.

Valinsky, Nathaniel, and Jordan Meyersohn. "Two of the Largest Supermarkets in America Are Merging." CNN, October 14, 2022. https://www.cnn.com/2022 /10/14/business/kroger-albertsons-merger/index.html.

Vallas, Steven P. "Platform Capitalism: What's at Stake for Workers?" *New Labor Forum* 28, no. 1 (2019): 48–59. https://doi.org/10.1177/1095796018817059.

Vallas, Steven P., Hannah Johnston, and Yana Mommadova. "Prime Suspect: Mechanisms of Labor Control at Amazon's Warehouses." *Work and Occupations*, June 2022. https://doi.org/10.1177/07308884221106922.

Vargas, Tracy L. "Consumer Redlining and the Reproduction of Inequality at Dollar General." *Qualitative Sociology* 44, no. 2 (2021): 205–29. https://doi.org/10.1007/s11133-020-09473-w.

van Doorn, N., and D. Vijay. Gig Work as Migrant Work: The Platformization of Migration Infrastructure." *Environment and Planning A: Economy and Space*, 56, no. 4 (2024): 1129–49. https://doi.org/10.1177/0308518X211065049.

Vidal, Matt, and David Kusnet. *Organizing Prosperity: Union Effects on Job Quality, Community Betterment and Industry Standards*. Economic Policy Institute, 2009. https://www.epi.org/publication/book_organizing_prosperity/#:~:text=The%20benefits%20that%20arise%20from,even%20businesses%20themselves%20in%20a.

Vimercati, Luigi, Antonio Baldassarre, Maria Franca Gatti, Luigi De Maria, Antonio Caputi, Angelica A. Dirodi, Francesco Cuccaro, and Raffaello Maria Bellino. "Respiratory Health in Waste Collection and Disposal Workers." *International Journal of Environmental Research and Public Health* 13, no. 7 (2016): 631. https://doi.org/10.3390/ijerph13070631.

Vincent, Jeffrey M., Ariana Gunderson, Debbie Friedman, Angela McKee Brown, Sadie Wilson, and Vanessa Gomez. "Are California Public Schools Scratch-Cooking Ready? A Survey of Food Service Directors on the State of School Kitchens." Center for Cities + Schools, University of California, Berkeley, 2020. https://citiesandschools.berkeley.edu/publications.

Vinegar, Russell, Pete Parker, and George McCourt. "More Than a Response to Food Insecurity: Demographics and Social Networks of Urban Dumpster Divers." *Local Environment* 21, no. 2 (2016): 241–53. https://doi.org/10.1080/13549839.2014.943708.

Viscelli, Steve. *The Big Rig: Trucking and the Decline of the American Dream*. Berkeley: University of California Press, 2016.

Visschers, Vivianne H. M., Nadine Wickli, and Michael Siegrist. "Sorting out Food Waste Behaviour: A Survey on the Motivators and Barriers of Self-Reported Amounts of Food Waste in Households." *Journal of Environmental Psychology* 45 (2016): 66–78. https://doi.org/10.1016/j.jenvp.2015.11.007.

Volz, Amy. "It Is Time for the U.S. to Overhaul Its Agricultural Child Labor Laws." *Immigration and Human Rights Law Review Blog*, October 25, 2022. https://lawblogs.uc.edu/ihrlr/2022/10/25/it-is-time-for-the-u-s-to-overhaul-its-agricultural-child-labor-laws/.

Vynck, Gerrit De, and Lauren Kaori Gurley. "4,000 Google Cafeteria Workers Quietly Unionized during the Pandemic." *Washington Post*, September 5, 2022. https://www.washingtonpost.com/technology/2022/09/05/google-union-pandemic/.

Wald, Sarah D. "Visible Farmers/Invisible Workers: Locating Immigrant Labor in Food Studies." *Food, Culture & Society* 14, no. 4 (2011): 567–86. https://doi.org/10.2752/175174411X13046092851479.

Walia, Harsha. *Border and Rule: Global Migration, Capitalism, and the Rise of Racist Nationalism*. Chicago: Haymarket Books, 2021.

Walker, Richard. *The Conquest of Bread: 150 Years of Agribusiness in California*. New York: New Press, 2004.

Wall Street Journal. "Albertsons Cos. Inc. Annual Income Statement." 2023. https://www.wsj.com/market-data/quotes/ACI/financials/annual/income-statement.

———. "Walmart Inc. Annual Income Statement." 2023. https://www.wsj.com/market-data/quotes/WMT/financials/annual/income-statement.

Walsh, William I. *The Rise and Decline of the Great Atlantic & Pacific Tea Company*. New York: Lyle Stuart, 1986.

Warehouse Worker Resource Center. "About Us Warehouse Worker Resource Center." 2024. https://warehouseworkers.org/about-us/.

Warehouse Workers for Justice. "The Shell Game: Corporations Routinely Outsource Responsibility for the Workers Who Move Their Products." 2022. https://www.ww4j.org/industry.html.

Warehouse Workers for Justice and UIC Center for Urban Economic Development. "Bad Jobs in Goods Movement: Warehouse Work in Will County, Illinois." Warehouse Worker Resource Library, 2009. https://workercenterlibrary.org/product/bad-jobs-in-goods-movement-warehouse-work-in-will-county-illinois/.

Warshawsky, Daniel Novik. "New Power Relations Served Here: The Growth of Food Banking in Chicago." *Geoforum* 41, no. 5 (2010): 763–75. https://doi.org/10.1016/j.geoforum.2010.04.008.

Waschik, Robert, Daniel Friedman, Catherine Taylor, Jasmine Boatner, and John A. Volpe. "Macroeconomic Impacts of Automated Driving Systems in Long-Haul Trucking." US Department of Transportation, 2021. https://rosap.ntl.bts.gov/view/dot/54596.

Weil, David. *The Fissured Workplace: Why Work Became So Bad for So Many and What Can Be Done to Improve It*. Cambridge, MA: Harvard University Press, 2014.

Weiler, Anelyse M. "Seeing the Workers for the Trees: Exalted and Devalued Manual Labour in the Pacific Northwest Craft Cider Industry." *Agriculture and Human Values* 39, no. 1 (2022): 65–78. https://doi.org/10.1007/s10460-021-10226-w.

Weiler, Anelyse M., Kathleen Sexsmith, and Laura Anne Minkoff-Zern. "Parallel Precarity: A Comparison of U.S. and Canadian Agricultural Guest Worker Programs." *International Journal of Sociology of Agriculture and Food* 26, no. 2 (2020): 143–63. https://doi.org/10.48416/IJSAF.V26I2.57.

Weinger, Merri, and Mark Lyons. "Problem-Solving in the Fields: An Action-Oriented Approach to Farmworker Education about Pesticides." *American Journal of Industrial Medicine* 22, no. 5 (1992): 677–90. https://doi.org/10.1002/ajim.4700220506.

Welch, Daniel, Joanne Swaffield, and David Evans. "Who's Responsible for Food Waste? Consumers, Retailers and the Food Waste Discourse Coalition in the

United Kingdom." *Journal of Consumer Culture* 21, no. 2 (2021): 236–56. https://doi.org/10.1177/1469540518773801.

Welsh, Rick. "The Industrial Reorganization of U.S. Agriculture: An Overview and Background Report." Henry A. Wallace Institute for Sustainable Agriculture, 1996. https://www.researchgate.net/publication/237325369_The_Industrial_Reorganization_of_US_Agriculture_An_Overview_Background_Report.

West, Emily, and R.J. Knight. "Mothers' Milk: Slavery, Wet-Nursing, and Black and White Women in the Antebellum South." *Journal of Southern History* 83, no 1 (2017): 37–68. https://doi.org/10.1353/soh.2017.0001.

White, Robb. "Food Waste Prevention Means More Efficient Labor. Here's What That Looks Like." March 15, 2019. https://blog.leanpath.com/labor-cost-of-food-waste.

White House. "White House Task Force on Worker Organizing and Empowerment Report." Report to the President, 2022. https://www.whitehouse.gov/briefing-room/statements-releases/2022/02/07/white-house-task-force-on-worker-organizing-and-empowerment-report/.

Wiessner, Daniel. "US Labor Board Ruling Could Spur Unionizing by Gig Workers, Others." Reuters, June 12, 2023. https://www.reuters.com/world/us/us-labor-board-ruling-could-spur-unionizing-by-gig-workers-others-2023-06-13/.

Williams, Brett. " Why Migrant Women Feed Their Husbands Tamales." In *Ethnic and Regional Foodways in the United States: The Performance of Group Identity*, edited by Linda Keller Brown and Kay Mussell, 113–26. Knoxville: University of Tennessee Press, 1984.

Williams, Helén, Fredrik Wikström, Tobias Otterbring, Martin Löfgren, and Anders Gustafsson. "Reasons for Household Food Waste with Special Attention to Packaging." *Journal of Cleaner Production* 24 (2012): 141–48. https://doi.org/10.1016/j.jclepro.2011.11.044.

Williams-Forson, Psyche A. *Building Houses out of Chicken Legs: Black Women, Food, and Power.* Chapel Hill: University of North Carolina Press, 2006.

Williams-Forson, Psyche, and Abby Wilkerson. "Intersectionality and Food Studies." *Food, Culture & Society* 14, no. 1 (2011): 7–28. https://doi.org/10.2752/175174411X12810842291119.

Wilson, Eli Revelle Yano. *Front of the House, Back of the House: Race and Inequality in the Lives of Restaurant Workers.* New York: New York University Press, 2020.

Wilson, Norbert L.W., Bradley J. Rickard, Rachel Saputo, and Shuay-Tsyr Ho. "Food Waste: The Role of Date Labels, Package Size, and Product Category." *Food Quality and Preference* 55 (2017): 35–44. https://doi.org/10.1016/j.foodqual.2016.08.004.

Wiltshire, Justin. "Walmart Is a Monopsonist That Depresses Earnings and Employment beyond Its Own Walls, but U.S. Policymakers Can Do Something about It." Equitable Growth, March 29, 2022. https://equitablegrowth.org/walmart-is-a-monopsonist-that-depresses-earnings-and-employment-beyond-its-own-walls-but-u-s-policymakers-can-do-something-about-it/.

Witwer, David Scott. *Corruption and Reform in the Teamsters Union*. Urbana: University of Illinois Press, 2003.

Wood, Marcus. *Black Milk: Imagining Slavery in the Visual Cultures of Brazil and America*. Oxford: Oxford University Press, 2013.

Workers United Labor Union. "Workers United Labor Union: An SEIU Affiliate." May 24, 2023. https://workersunited.org/.

Wright, Gavin. *Slavery and American Economic Development*. Baton Rouge: Louisiana State University Press, 2006.

Wu, Tina. "More Than a Paycheck: Nannies, Work, and Identity." *Citizenship Studies* 20, no. 3–4 (2016): 295–310. https://doi.org/10.1080/13621025.2016.1158358.

Yearby, Ruqaiijah. "Meatpacking Plants Have Been Deadly COVID-19 Hot Spots—but Policies That Encourage Workers to Show up Sick Are Legal." *The Conversation*, February 26, 2021. http://theconversation.com/meatpacking-plants-have-been-deadly-covid-19-hot-spots-but-policies-that-encourage-workers-to-show-up-sick-are-legal-152572.

Yoder, Katie. "Food Waste Is Heating up the Planet. Is Dumpster-Diving by App a Solution?" *Salon*, May 30, 2021. https://www.salon.com/2021/05/29/food-waste-is-heating-up-the-planet-is-dumpster-diving-by-app-a-solution_partner/.

Zakaria, Rafia. *Against White Feminism: Notes on Disruption*. New York: Norton, 2021.

Zetka, James R. "Work Organization and Wildcat Strikes in the U.S. Automobile Industry, 1946 to 1963." *American Sociological Review* 57, no. 2 (1992): 214–26. https://doi.org/10.2307/2096206.

Zhou, Xule, Jiaqian Yang, Shuning Xu, Jiade Wang, Qingqing Zhou, Yiren Li, and Xinyi Tong. "Rapid In-Situ Composting of Household Food Waste." *Process Safety and Environmental Protection* 141 (2020): 259–66. https://doi.org/10.1016/j.psep.2020.05.039.

Zoller, Heather M. "Re-Imagining Localism and Food Justice: Co-Op Cincy and the Union Cooperative Movement." *Frontiers in Communication* 6 (2021). https://doi.org/10.3389/fcomm.2021.686400.

Zoodsma, Anna, Mary Jo Dudley, and Laura-Anne Minkoff-Zern. "National Food Security, Immigration Reform, and the Importance of Worker Engagement in Agricultural Guestworker Debates." *Journal of Agriculture, Food Systems, and Community Development* 11, no. 4 (2022): 139–51. https://doi.org/10.5304/jafscd.2022.114.009.

INDEX

A&P (Atlantic and Pacific Tea Company), 106, 107, 122

ACS (American Community Survey), 4, 64, 65, 224, 225

AEQUITAS (Japan), 201

Affordable and Secure Food Act, 41

AFL-CIO (American Federation of Labor and Congress of Industrial Organizations), 38, 39, 45, 122, 150

Agricultural Adjustment Act of 1933, 181

agricultural exceptionalism: ending, 46–47; federal policy and, 27–33; industrial agriculture and, 23

Agricultural Justice Project, 46

Agricultural Workers Organizing Committee, 8, 38

AI (artificial intelligence), 23, 37, 38, 72, 75, 80

air quality issues, 1, 22–23, 41. *See also* climate change; forest fires

Albertsons, 100, 101, 114

Aldi, 123

Alien Laws of 1913–1927, 28–29

Amalgamated Meat Cutters Union, 121, 122

Amazon, 4, 70, 78–80, 89–90, 92, 96, 111, 112, 123, 125, 239n17

Amazon Fresh, 78–79, 111

Amazon Labor Union, 92

American Community Survey (ACS), 4, 64, 65, 224, 225

American Federation of Labor and Congress of Industrial Organizations (AFL-CIO), 38, 39, 45, 122, 150

American Rescue Plan, 146

antitrust laws, 17, 100

antiunionization, 4, 17, 66, 92, 112, 122, 123. *See also* unionization

app-based platforms, 17, 88–89, 93–95, 140

Applied Research Center (Race Forward), 9, 12

Aramark, 150

artificial intelligence (AI), 23, 37, 38, 72, 75, 80

assembly line model: deskilling and, 48; food processing and, 67–68; food processing workers and, 59; Ford and, 49, 53–55; Taylorism and, 52

Asunción Valdivia Heat Illness and Fatality Prevention Act, 40

automation, 17, 53, 58, 86–87, 105, 111–12, 135, 147

back pay, 213, 232n22

Ben and Jerry's, 46

Biden administration, 40, 60, 150

Black Codes, 27

Black Panther Party, 141, 159

BLS (US Bureau of Labor Statistics). *See* US Bureau of Labor Statistics (BLS)

Blue Hill at Stone Barns, 141

border politicization: IRCA (Immigration Reform and Control Act of 1986), 32, 235n69; limited skilled laborers and, 34; migrant labor and, 36; worker mobilizations and, 23, 30

Bourdain, Anthony, 147–148

boycotts: CIW and, 45; Delano Grape
Strike and Boycott, 8–9; supporting,
204; UFW grape boycotts, 38–39, 120;
workers' centers and, 66
Bracero Program, 30, 36
Burger King, 44, 135

café workers, 17, 128
California Agricultural Labor Relations
Act of 1975 (CALRA), 39, 42
California Assembly Bill 5 (AB5), 93
California Heat Illness Prevention Standard, 40–41
CALRA (California Agricultural Labor
Relations Act of 1975), 39, 42
Campaign for Fair Food, 43
Canada, 166; NAFTA and, 85
care work: Black women and, 159–165;
childcare work, 145; crisis in, 171–172;
domestic labor and, 18; emergency food
and, 191; Fight for $15 and, 144; as food
work, 18, 155, 159, 206; as gendered, 156,
195; home healthcare work, 145; pandemic and, 9, 206; Wages for Housework
movement, 172; women and, 154, 158
Carter, Jimmy, 84
cash crops, 24, 25, 26
CATA (El Comité de Apoyo a los Trabajadores Agrícolas / Farm Workers Support Committee), 39
catering, 10, 17, 128, 151, 174
Center for a Livable Future (John Hopkins
University), 9–10
chain retailers, corporate consolidation
and, 46, 118, 126
Chavez, Cesar, 8, 38–39, 42
child labor: in agriculture, 35; piece rate
work, 33; prohibition of, 29; in retail
sector, 103–104; undocumented workers, 34; in US food processing, 61
Chinese Exclusion Act of 1882, 28
Chipotle, 135
citizenship inequality, 67; ethnicity-citizenship hierarchy, 23; inequities linked
to citizenship, 9; vulnerabilities linked
to, 16
Civil Eats (digital news site), 45, 57–58, 65,
205

Civil Rights Act of 1964, 165
CIW (Coalition of Immokalee Workers).
See Coalition of Immokalee Workers
(CIW)
climate change: food system maintenance
and, 2; food waste and recovery, 181, 183;
risks from, 16, 22–23, 40–41
Coalition of Immokalee Workers (CIW),
4, 20–21, 43–45, 66, 200, 201, 202
collective bargaining, 22, 29, 42, 124–125
Colorado Farmworkers' Rights Coalition,
42
Colorado State Bill 21–087, 40
El Comité de Apoyo a los Trabajadores
Agrícolas/Farm Workers Support
Committee (CATA), 39
commissions, 213, 232n22
commodities: commodity crops, 181, 191;
exchange value of, 175, 177; meals as,
132; Taylorism and, 52; transnational
commodity chains, 6
Community to Community (C2C), 41, 42
composting, 18, 159, 174–176, 179, 180, 183,
186–189, 190, 196–189
ConAgra, 49, 76
consolidation: about, 97–100; consequences for retail workers, 109–114;
corporate consolidation in food retail,
6, 17, 99, 100–103, 227; national policies
and, 17, 74; in transportation sector, 81;
in warehouse sector, 81; of workers, 6.
See also mergers
contract work, 22, 70, 72, 74, 228. See also
independent contractor(s)
convenience stores: cost of, 115–117; retail
workers in, 98; wages at, 108
corner stores, 120–121
corporations: corporate consolidation in
food retail, 6, 17, 99, 100–103, 227;
deskilling and, 6; food shipping and,
70; leadership, 17. See also specific
corporations
corruption, 85, 184, 240n48
Costco, 101, 108, 110, 242n2
Council on Occupational Health and
Safety, 91
Current Population Survey (CPS), 12,
224

dairy workers, 22, 37–38, 41, 45
Davis, Angela, 159, 160
Delano Grape Strike and Boycott, 8–9, 38–39
delivery drivers, 11, 69, 89, 93; delivery apps, 239n17; as essential to food system, 96; gig economy and, 17; place in food chain, 70; precarity and, 87–89; surveillance of, 80
demographic shifts, 32, 62, 63, 68, 72, 81
deregulation: defined, 70, 227; impact on distribution sector, 95; impact on retail sector, 99–100, 108; impact on transportation sector, 69–73, 85, 95; neoliberalism and, 6; profiting from, 6; temporary hiring agencies and, 70; in warehouse sector, 69–73
deskilling: about, 49–52, 67; assembly line and, 48, 55–61; defined, 227; factory floor and, 48; multinational corporations and, 6. See also Fordism
"El Diario de Los Deliveryboys en La Gran Manzana" (The Journal of the Deliveryboys in the Big Apple), 89
disparity between profits and wages, 6, 43, 114
dispossession: defined, 23, 227; exceptionalism and, 32; impact on food sectors of, 15, 67–68; plantation agriculture and, 24–27
Dollar General, 116–117, 123, 125
dollar store chains, 98, 116–117, 123, 125
Dollar Tree, 116, 123
Domestic Fair Trade Working Group, 46
domestic labor: composting and, 189; data and, 5; disparities in, 206; gender and, 5, 18, 155, 161–163, 168, 206; history of, 18, 162; industrialization and, 167; labor laws and, 29; as paid labor, 161–162; pandemic and, 9, 170; race and, 18, 29, 32, 161–164; unionization and, 29, 202; as unpaid, 5, 6, 9, 15, 155. See also reproductive labor
domestic migration, 67
DoorDash, 72, 87, 93, 94
drayage, 81, 227
drive-throughs, 132–133

dumpster diving, 18, 177, 179, 196
Dust Bowl, 30

e-commerce: fissuring and, 80–81; takeover of retail by logistics and, 70; takeover of warehouse work by, 76–79. See also Amazon
Economic Policy Institute, 137, 146
Economic Research Service (ERS), 101
economies of scale, 102, 106, 111, 227
emancipation, 27, 138, 156, 159–164, 166
emergency food system, 18, 175, 176, 177, 190–193, 194, 227
environmental issues: air quality issues, 1, 22–23, 41; from climate change, 22–23; Dust Bowl, 30; forest fires, 1, 22, 41; temperature extremes, 1, 22–23; waste sector and, 18
Environmental Protection Agency (EPA), 174, 179
Equal Employment Opportunity Commission, 86
Equal Rights Amendment, 165
essential workers: defined, 9, 227; designation of, 68; exploitation of, 114; pandemic and, 4, 9, 49, 114
exchange value, 15, 18, 175–176, 177, 178, 193, 196, 227

factory farming, 83
Fair Food Program, 21, 44–45, 200, 203
Fair Labor Standards Act (FLSA), 29, 31, 82, 137, 139
Fairness for Farmworkers Act (Massachusetts), 42
Familias Unidas por la Justicia, 41
Family Dollar, 123
family-owned stores, 102, 103, 107, 120, 121. See also mom-and-pop markets
Farm and Food Worker Relief Grant Program, 204
farmers' markets, 2, 75, 98, 100, 118–19
Farm Labor Agreement of 1942 (Mexico), 30
Farm Laborers Fair Labor Practices Act of 2019 (New York), 39–40
Farm Labor Organizing Committee (FLOC), 39, 45

Farm Labor Program (FLP) (Puerto Rico), 30–31
Farm Workers Support Committee/*El Comité de Apoyo a los Trabajadores Agrícolas* (CATA), 39
Farm Workforce Modernization Act (FWMA), 41
fast-food chains, 133–136; fast-food workers, 17; workers' rights and, 7. See also *specific companies*
FCWA (Food Chain Workers Alliance). *See* Food Chain Workers Alliance (FCWA)
Federal Meat Inspection Act of 1906, 8
federal policy: agricultural exceptionalism and, 27–33, 46; state laws violating, 61; trucker drivers and, 83
Federal Trade Commission, 100, 101
The Feminine Mystique (Friedan), 165, 166
feminism: feminist Marxism, 130, 157; second wave, 165–168
Fight for $15 movement, 4, 123, 128, 130, 136, 144–147, 148, 149, 152, 200, 201
fine dining, 132–133
fissuring: defined, 227; e-commerce and, 80–81; impact on distribution sector, 74–75, 95; impact on transportation sector, 74–75, 95
FLOC (Farm Labor Organizing Committee), 39, 45
FLP (Farm Labor Program) (Puerto Rico), 30–31
FLSA (Fair Labor Standards Act), 29, 31, 82, 137, 139
FNB (Food Not Bombs), 175, 194–197
FNS (Food and Nutrition Service), 141–142
Food and Nutrition Service (FNS), 141, 141–142
Food Chain Workers Alliance (FCWA), 68; advocacy work of, 9, 174, 200; farm level, 41; food system perspective of, 1, 2, 3, 10, 12; labor violations and, 66; meat processing industry and, 60; procurement policy report, 202; UFCW and, 91; UNITE HERE and, 150
food cooperatives, 97, 98, 119–120

food distribution. *See* distribution sector of the food chain
food insecurity, 6, 98, 100, 116, 125–126, 173, 174, 178, 191, 193–194
food justice, 2, 125, 203
food miles, 75–76
Food Not Bombs (FNB), 175, 194–197
Food Policy Councils, data from, 9–10
Food Policy Network, data from, 9–10
food recovery: defined, 228; food chain and, 3; organizations, 175; programs for, 18
Food Recovery Network (FRN), 188, 192
Food Retail Expansion to Support Health (FRESH), 123
food supply chain. *See* distribution; logistics
forced labor, 159–164
Ford, Henry, 49, 53, 54–55
Fordism: defined, 228; deskilling and, 49, 50; in food processing, 16, 52–55; in retail sector, 105–106. See also deskilling
Ford Motor Company, 49, 55
forest fires, 1, 22, 41
franchises, 17, 115–116, 134, 148–149, 228
freegans, 194–197, 195–196
FRESH (Food Retail Expansion to Support Health), 123
Friedan, Betty, 165, 166–167
FRN (Food Recovery Network), 188, 192
FWMA (Farm Workforce Modernization Act), 41

gig economy: defined, 228; delivery drivers and, 17; diverse work of, 17; gig worker shopping, 239n17
gig workers: California Assembly Bill 5 (AB5), 93; COVID-19 pandemic and, 93; in food delivery sector, 70; minimum wage and, 17; in New York, 94–95; precarity and, 87–89; time off and, 17; unavailability of data for, 12. *See also* delivery drivers; temporary workers
Gig Workers Collective (GWC), 93
gleaning, 18
global issues: global neoliberal governance, 70; globalization, 6, 16, 228; increased competition, 7; urbanization, 34

Global North, 175
Global Women Strike, 172
good food movements, 2–3, 9
Good Food Purchasing Policy (GFPP), 202–203
Good Samaritan Act of 1996, 181–182
Gramsci, Antonio, 53, 54
grape boycott, 8–9, 38–39
Great Depression, 107, 141
Great Resignation, 130, 151–152
Green New Deal, 172
grocery giants, 108; consolidation and, 109–114; trade reclassification and, 100–101
grocery retailers: consolidation and, 99–100; mergers, 101–102, 108, 109, 112; trade reclassification and, 100–101. *See also* grocery retailers
grocery shopping: online, 239n17; traditional outlets, 98; Walmart and, 244n70
grocery store chains: consolidation of, 17, 98; economies of scale and, 107; management, 102–103; mergers, 101–102, 108, 109, 112; standardization of labor in, 106; trade reclassification and, 100–101
Grubhub, 87, 151
guest worker programs: as alternative, 36–37; Bracero Program, 30; defined, 228; expansion and regulation of, 41; FLP (Farm Labor Program) (Puerto Rico), 30–31; issue of, 16; West Indies Programs, 30; worker mobilizations and, 23
GWC (Gig Workers Collective), 93

H-2A program, 36–37, 41, 235n69. *See also* Immigration Reform and Control Act of 1986 (IRCA)
H-2B program, 235n69. *See also* Immigration Reform and Control Act of 1986 (IRCA)
H-2 program, 235n69. *See also* Immigration and Nationality Act of 1952
Hannaford, 45
Harvest of Shame (1960 documentary) (Murrow), 8

Hawaii: annexation of, 28; food imports, 69
hazardous duty pay, 113, 114, 232n22
HEAL (Health, Environment, Agriculture and Labor) Food Alliance, 202, 203, 204
health insurance, lack of, 50, 72, 77, 127, 184
health issues: climate change and, 22–23, 40–41; disregard for, 70, 96; farmworkers and, 22–23, 40–41; food workers vulnerability to, 68; in processing sector, 56–61; in retail sector, 99, 113; risks, 16, 22–23; stability of food system and, 70; workforce vulnerability to, 67. *See also* COVID-19 pandemic
Hello Fresh, 78
Hernandez, Crispin, 39
hero/hazard pay, 113, 114, 232n22
Hispanic Federation, 39
hooks, bell, 159, 164
horizontal integration, 6, 98
hospital food service workers, 17
hourly mean wages, 232n22
housing: agricultural workers and, 1, 8, 41; domestic workers and, 162
Huerta, Dolores, 8, 38–39
Hungry Harvest, 178

ICE (Immigration and Customs Enforcement), 63–64
IFHAC (International Wages for Housework Campaign), 166
Immigration Act of 1924, 28–29
Immigration and Customs Enforcement (ICE), 63–64
Immigration and Nationality Act of 1952, 235n69. *See also* H-2 program
Immigration Reform and Control Act of 1986 (IRCA), 32, 235n69. *See also* H-2A program; H-2B program
incentive pay, 232n22. *See also* commissions; tipped wage system
independent contractor(s): defined, 228; dependence on, 70, 71; gig economy and, 17, 72; unavailability of data for, 12
Indigenous peoples, 145, 170; in data, 224; settler colonialism and, 23; US food system and, 16

industrial agriculture: agricultural exceptionalism and, 23, 27–33, 46–47;
exploitative conditions, 46; exploitative
conditions and, 16, 23; urbanization
and, 34
industrialization: about, 20–23; defined,
228; labor shortage myth and, 33–36;
precarious labor conditions and, 83; in
US North, 25–26; worker vulnerability
and, 33–36
Industrial Revolution, 132
input costs, 7, 102
Instacart, 93, 239n17
International Alliance of Delivery Workers, 93
international labor standards, 96
international migration, 67
International Wages for Housework Campaign (IFHAC), 166
intersectionality, 17; about, 127–130; capitalism and, 17, 130–132; defined, 228;
inequalities in the restaurant industry,
131–133; labor in the food system and, 4,
17–18; service sector of the food chain
and, 17
IRCA (Immigration Reform and Control
Act of 1986). See Immigration Reform
and Control Act of 1986 (IRCA)
Itliong, Larry, 8, 38

Japanese Internment Act of 1942, 28, 28–29
Japanese workers, in agricultural work, 28,
29
Jayaraman, Saru, 140
Jim Crow laws, 29
Jobs with Justice, 123
The Jungle (Sinclair), 8
just food system: building of, 3, 152, 171,
199–207; COVID-19 pandemic and, 9;
food waste and, 186, 197; visions of, 3, 7.
See also sustainability
Justice for App Workers, 93
Justice for Migrant Women, 34
just-in-time approach, 76, 79, 88, 99, 109,
110, 228

Kmart, 100, 112
Kroger, 98–99, 101, 102, 114, 125

labor laws: agricultural exceptionalism,
27–28; agricultural workers and, 27–33;
collective bargaining, 22, 29, 42; exclusionary laws, 28–29, 46–47; farmworkers exclusion from, 29, 31; New Deal
reforms, 29; state level, 31, 39–42, 46
labor shortage myth, 9, 33–36
large-scale farms: agricultural exceptionalism and, 28; agricultural technology
and, 37–38; economics of, 6; H-2A
program and, 37; industrialization and,
21; trucker drivers and, 83
large-scale retailers: consolidation of, 96;
national policies and, 17. See also specific
retailers
living wage, 13–14, 228, 233n24
Living Wage Calculator project, 232n24
lobbying, 8, 30, 41, 42–43, 137, 186
Los Deliveristas Unidos, 93
Lyft, 93, 94

Marx, Karl, 52–53, 55, 177, 178
McDonaldization, 53, 134, 228
McDonald's, 44, 53, 116, 125, 133–136, 134,
135, 147
MD (Milk with Dignity), 45–46, 200
meat and poultry processing: child labor
and, 61; intersectional violence in,
52–55, 61–66, 67; labor patterns in US
South and, 68; pandemic and, 59–61;
safety issues in, 56–61. See also processing sector of the food chain
meatpacking industry: organizing and, 3;
pandemic and, 49; reforms in, 8
mechanization: as alternative, 36, 38;
increasing, 21; worker mobilizations
and, 23. See also assembly line model
megafarms, 7
megastores, 6, 103–108. See also specific
stores
membership-based stores, 108
mergers, 17, 74, 100–102, 108, 112. See also
consolidation
methodology, 10–14, 213–225
#MeToo movement, 45, 144, 147–148
Mexican Farm Labor Agreement of
1942, 30
Mexico: Bracero Program, 30; child labor

and, 61; FLOC and, 39; food system labor demands in, 34; H-2A program and, 36; immigrant farmworkers from, 10, 16; Mexican Farm Labor Agreement of 1942, 30; NAFTA and, 85; transportation workers in, 85–86; undocumented immigrants from, 63, 65; US-Mexico border issues, 32, 36

Migrant and Seasonal Agricultural Workers Protection Act (MSPA), 31

Migrant Justice, 41, 45, 200, 202

Milk with Dignity (MD), 45–46, 200

minimum age, 35–36

minimum wage, 233n24; below, 72, 88; defined, 14, 228; farmworkers and, 33; federal, 29, 33, 42; gig economy and, 17

mom-and-pop markets, 121; history of, 103–108; shift from, 17, 98. *See also* family-owned stores

monocropping systems, 24–25

Motor Carriers Act of 1935, 84

MSPA (Migrant and Seasonal Agricultural Workers Protection Act), 31

Murrow, Edward R., 8

mutual aid, 18, 194–197; defined, 228

Mutual Aid (Kropotkin), 194–195

National Agricultural Workers Survey (NAWS), 22, 34, 65

National Employment Law Project, 60

National Farm Workers Association (NFWA), 8, 38

National Fast-Food Workers Union, 149

National Industry-Specific Occupational Employment and Wage Estimates (OEWS), 232n22

National Labor Relations Act (NLRA), 29, 32, 66, 88, 122

National Labor Relations Board (NLRB), 95, 149–150

National Organization for Women (NOW), 165

National Partnership for Women and Families, 170

National Resources Defense Council, 202

National Restaurant Association, 131, 137

National School Lunch Act, 141

National School Lunch Program (NSLP), 141–142

National Women's Law Center, 86

NAWS (National Agricultural Workers Survey), 22, 34, 65

neoliberalism: defined, 6, 228; deregulation and, 100; global process of, 95–96; individual freedom violations and, 96; precarity and, 96; precarity in the logistics sector and, 70–76

New Deal reforms, 29, 83, 163

New Swine Inspection Service, 59

New York Civil Liberties Union, 39

New York Office of Consumer and Worker Protection, 89

New York State AFL-CIO, 39

NLRA (National Labor Relations Act), 29, 32, 66, 88, 122

NLRB (National Labor Relations Board), 95, 149–150

non-US citizen employees, 235n69. *See also* H-2A program; H-2B program; H-2 program

North American Free Trade Agreement (NAFTA), 85

North American Industry Classification System (NAICS), 232n22

Occupational Employment and Wage Survey (OEWS), 12–15, 22, 51, 71, 99, 129, 176, 213, 232n22

Occupational Safety and Health Administration (OSHA), 40, 58, 60, 65, 79, 91, 119

OEWS (Occupational Employment and Wage Survey). *See* Occupational Employment and Wage Survey (OEWS)

One Fair Wage Campaign, 127–128, 137, 148, 152

online procurement: intensity levels and, 79; large-scale companies and, 80–81; pandemic and, 78; push for, 17; shift to, 16. *See also* delivery drivers

OSHA (Occupational Safety and Health Administration). *See* Occupational Safety and Health Administration (OSHA)

outsourcing, 16, 74, 228
overtime pay, 29, 33, 42, 232n22

part-time employment, 16, 99, 112
PCUN (Pineros y Campesinos Unidos del
    Noroeste), 39
PepsiCo, 76
Perdue, 49, 61
personal protective equipment (PPE), 9, 66,
    143, 187
picker-packers, 77, 79
piece rate work: defined, 33, 229; minimum
    wage and, 33; vulnerability to violations
    in, 14
Piggly Wiggly, 104, 105
Pineros y Campesinos Unidos del Noroeste
    (PCUN), 39
Pizza Hut, 135
plantation agriculture, 16, 24–27, 29, 80,
    116, 161
Postmates, 93
poverty wage, 13, 67, 229, 233n24
Power of Women Collective, 166
PPE (personal protective equipment), 9, 66,
    143, 187
precarity: defined, 71, 229; gig economy and,
    87–89; globalization and, 16; logistics
    sector, 73–76; neoliberalism and, 70–71,
    96, 100; in transportation sector, 69–73,
    81–87; in warehouse sector, 69–73, 76–81;
    worker organizing and, 71, 125–126
Pre-Employment Physical Ability testing, 65
President's Commission on the Status of
    Women, 165
Proposition 22 (California), 93
Protecting America's Meatpacking Work-
    ers Act, 203–204
Public Citizen, 40, 59
public institution service workers, 17. *See
    also* hospital food service workers;
    school food service workers

QCEW (Quarterly Census of Employment
    and Wages, US Department of Labor),
    64, 65
Quarterly Census of Employment and
    Wages, US Department of Labor
    (QCEW), 64, 65

Race Forward (Applied Research Center),
    9, 12
racial capitalism, 5, 67, 229
racial inequality, 9, 15, 21, 27, 67
racialization: defined, 229; exceptionalism
    and, 32; of industrial farm labor force,
    36, 46–47; in service sector, 17; US food
    system and, 24–25
racialized dispossession: about, 20–23;
    defined, 23, 229; farm labor conditions
    and, 15–16
Raise the Wage Act, 145–146
RCIA (Retail Clerks International Asso-
    ciation), 122
RCRA (Resource Conservation and Recov-
    ery Act), 182
Real Food Challenge, 188
reclassification of trade, 17, 101, 108
Reconstruction era, 26
regional approaches: Food Policy Councils,
    9–10; small-scale businesses and, 7
reproductive labor: about, 153–156, 171–172;
    defined, 5, 229; feminization of school
    food service, 142; gender and, 18; organ-
    izing and, 3; unavailability of data for,
    12; work of feeding others and, 5,
    156–159
Resource Conservation and Recovery Act
    (RCRA), 182
Restaurant Opportunities Center United
    (ROC-United), 4, 127–128, 202
Retail, Wholesale and Department Store
    Union (RWDSU), 91, 122
Retail Clerks International Association
    (RCIA), 122
retirement, 8, 50, 127, 184
risks from climate change, 16, 22–23
ROC-United (Restaurant Opportunities
    Center United), 4, 127–128, 202
Rural Migrant Ministries, 39
RWDSU (Retail, Wholesale and Depart-
    ment Store Union), 91, 122

safety issues: in agricultural work, 35,
    40–41; delivery workers and, 89; denial
    of basic protections and rights, 7; disre-
    gard for, 70, 96; food workers vulner-
    ability to, 68; PPEs, 9, 66, 143, 187; in

processing sector, 56–61; protections for workers, 1; in retail sector, 99; stability of food system and, 70; in warehouse sector, 79–80; workforce vulnerability to, 67

Safeway, 76, 100, 101, 102, 109, 122

Sam's Club, 108

school food service workers, 17, 141–144

school lunches, 2, 141–141

scientific management: assembly line model, 53–55; expansion of, 67–68; Fordism, 16, 49, 52–55; processing sector and, 49; Taylorism, 52–53

seafood industry, 57, 67

seasonal agricultural workers (H-2A), 36–37, 41, 235n69

seasonal nonagricultural employment (H-2B), 235n69

second wave feminism, 165–168

self-serve grocers, 104

Seneca Falls Convention, 165

Service Employees International Union (SEIU), 148–149

settler colonialism, 23, 24, 229

7-Eleven, 108, 115–116

severance pay, 213, 232n22

sharecropping, 26–30, 68, 161

ShopRite, 123

sick days: lack of paid, 9, 50, 72, 77, 88, 184; pandemic and, 113; punitive measures and, 60; unionization and, 9

slavery, 16, 18, 23–27, 68, 138, 156, 160–163, 165

small-scale operations: agricultural exceptionalism and, 28; consolidation of, 83; labor law exemptions for, 28, 31; pandemic and, 48; reforms and, 7; in retail sector, 103, 118–119; in US North, 25; in waste sector, 183–184; workers' rights and, 7

SNAP (Supplemental Nutrition Assistance Program), 125, 135, 181

Sodexo, 44, 150, 174

solidarity: across industries, 1, 200; across sectors, 2, 47, 199; barriers to, 42, 74–75; CIW and, 43–46; data accessibility and, 10; with food workers, 11–12, 19; human nature and, 194–195;

labor organizers and, 3; logistics sector and, 73; #MeToo movement, 45, 144, 147–148; transportation sector and, 92; worker solidarity, 47, 124

Solid Waste Disposal Act in 1965, 182

Southern Poverty Law Center (SPLC), 35

Staffing Workers Alliance, 91

Standard Industry Codes, 100

standardization of labor, 106

Starbucks, 123, 133–136, 147, 148–149; unionization, 4

STARS (Sustainability Tracking Assessment & Rating System), 188

strikes: Delano Grape Strike and Boycott, 38; Fight for $15 movement, 144–145

structural inequalities, 3, 15, 21, 23, 38, 117, 125, 168–169, 191

subcontracting, 74; defined, 229; large-scale retailers and, 96; move to, 16; vulnerability to violations in, 14; in warehouse sector, 76–77

Subway, 44, 135

supercenters/superstores: antiunion stances of, 112; consolidation and, 17, 98, 108, 118; reclassification of, 17; retail workers in, 98; trade reclassification and, 100–101

Supplemental Nutrition Assistance Program (SNAP), 125, 135, 181

supply chain(s): consumers and, 70; horizontal integration, 6, 98; pandemic and, 49; vertical integration, 6, 81, 96, 98, 101–102, 106, 229

surveillance: in distribution sector, 77; effects of, 72–73; in warehouse sector, 77, 80; of workers, 75, 80, 96. See also artificial intelligence (AI)

sustainability: advocacy for, 7; economic, 2; good food movements and, 2. See also just food system

Sustainability Tracking Assessment & Rating System (STARS), 188

Taco Bell, 135

Target, 100, 112, 124

Task Force on Worker Organizing and Empowerment, 150

Taylorism: defined, 52, 229; legacy, 52–55

Teamsters Union: corruption in, 240n48; deregulation and, 85; organizing efforts, 92; retail sector and, 122; sanitation workers, 185–186; trucker drivers and, 84; warehouse workers and, 92

technological solutions: as alternative, 36, 37–38; in retail sector, 108; in service sector, 135; in transportation sector, 86–87; in warehouse sector, 79–80

temporary hiring agencies: defined, 70, 229; dependence on, 70

temporary workers: defined, 229; increase in, 16; in transportation sector, 72; West Indies Programs, 30. *See also* gig workers; H-2 program

third-party certification, 43–46, 46, 229

third-party employers: dependence on, 70; large-scale retailers and, 96; in logistics sector, 77; subcontracting by, 16; in transportation sector, 72

time and motion studies, Taylorism and, 52

time off: gig economy and, 17; lack of paid, 50, 77, 184; pandemic and, 9

tipped wage system, 128, 136, 136–141, 232n22; defined, 229; vulnerability to violations in, 14

Title VII, 165–166

Trader Joe's, 4, 76, 108, 109, 123–124

trash collection, 18, 184–186

truck drivers, 69, 70, 72, 73, 73*fig.*, 81–87, 92, 181, 222*tab*. *See also* Teamsters Union

Trucking Country (Hamilton), 82–83

Trump administration, 59, 95

Tyson Foods, 59, 65; pandemic and, 49

Uber, 93, 94

Uber Eats, 72, 87, 94–95, 151

UCLA Labor Occupational Safety and Health Program, 91

UFCW (United Food and Commercial Workers), 59, 90–91, 98, 112, 123, 124, 203–204

UFW (United Farm Workers). *See* United Farm Workers (UFW)

ultraprocessed foods, 51, 126

undocumented workers: alternatives to, 36–38; as farmworkers, 22, 34–35, 42; IRCA (Immigration Reform and Con-

trol Act of 1986), 32; low pay, 22; as under/miscounted, 12, 22; in warehouse sector, 76; women as, 34–35

unemployment insurance, 88

Unilever, 46

unionization: among Amazon workers, 96; in California, 40; collective bargaining, 22, 29, 42, 124–125; in distribution sector, 76; of food service workers, 148–151; in logistics sector, 89–95; pandemic and, 9; present status of, 16; in processing sector, 52; in retail sector, 4, 91, 97, 99, 112, 121–122; by service sector workers, 17; stagnant period of, 4, 6; trucker drivers and, 83; union model, 4, 229; in warehouse sector, 76, 96. *See also* antiunionization; Teamsters Union

United (union), 124

United Farm Workers (UFW), 38–39, 41, 42, 45, 120. *See also* Chavez, Cesar

United Farm Workers Organizing Committee, 38

United Food and Commercial Workers (UFCW), 59, 90–91, 98, 112, 123, 124, 203–204

UNITE HERE, 150untipped restaurant work, 133–136

unwaged labor: in food waste, 189–190. *See also* domestic labor

US Bureau of Labor Statistics (BLS): fast-food workers, 135, 136; food distribution workers, 71; food processing workers, 50–51, 56–57; food production workers, 21–22; food retail workers, 98–99; food service workers, 129; food waste workers, 175–176; frontline workers, 12–15; home-based food work, 154–155; methodology and, 213

US Census Bureau, 12

USDA (US Department of Agriculture), 27, 59, 60, 101, 131, 141, 150, 179, 181. *See also* Food and Nutrition Service (FNS)

US Department of Transportation, 87

use value, 15, 18, 175–176, 177, 189, 192, 196, 198, 229

value, 18, 173–177. *See also* exchange value

Venceremos, 66

vertical integration, 6, 81, 96, 98, 101–102, 106, 229

violence: agricultural exceptionalism and, 28–29, 47; against Black women, 159–164; dispossession and, 24; plantation agriculture and, 24–25; in service sector, 136, 137, 138; structural violence, 23; against women, 20, 21, 35, 86, 138

visa programs, 36–37

volunteer labor, 18, 175, 176, 179, 190–193

Wages for Housework campaign, 157, 166, 172, 201

Walmart, 44, 70, 75, 76, 80, 91, 100, 101, 102, 108, 109, 110, 112, 116, 117, 122, 123, 125, 126

Warehouse Workers for Justice (WWJ), 75, 77, 90

Warehouse Workers Resource Center (WWRC), 90

Warehouse Workers United (WWU), 90, 90–91

Washington State Bill 5172, 40

Whole Foods, 44, 79, 111

Wilkerson, Abby, 130

Women in Hospitality United, 148

worker centers, 230

worker compensation, 52, 88

Worker-Driven Social Responsibility (WSR), 21, 43–45, 66, 200, 201, 202, 230

Worker Institute (Cornell University), 88–89

Worker Justice Center of New York, 39

Workers' Center of Central New York, 39, 42

Workers Justice, 93

Workers' Justice Project, 88

Workers United, 149

WSR (Worker-Driven Social Responsibility), 21, 43–45, 66, 200, 201, 202

WWJ (Warehouse Workers for Justice), 75, 77, 90

WWRC (Warehouse Workers Resource Center), 90

WWU (Warehouse Workers United), 90

Founded in 1893,
UNIVERSITY OF CALIFORNIA PRESS
publishes bold, progressive books and journals
on topics in the arts, humanities, social sciences,
and natural sciences—with a focus on social
justice issues—that inspire thought and action
among readers worldwide.

The UC PRESS FOUNDATION
raises funds to uphold the press's vital role
as an independent, nonprofit publisher, and
receives philanthropic support from a wide
range of individuals and institutions—and from
committed readers like you. To learn more, visit
ucpress.edu/supportus.

www.ingramcontent.com/pod-product-compliance
Lightning Source LLC
Chambersburg PA
CBHW020826270326
41928CB00006B/455